CARLISLE INDIAN INDUSTRIAL SCHOOL

CARLISLE INDIAN INDUSTRIAL SCHOOL

Indigenous Histories, Memories, and Reclamations

Edited by Jacqueline Fear-Segal and Susan D. Rose

UNIVERSITY OF NEBRASKA PRESS

LINCOLN AND LONDON

© 2016 by the Board of Regents of the University of Nebraska

An earlier version of chapter 3 was previously published as "Photo-graph: Carlisle Indian School (1879–1918)" in *Studies in American Indian Literatures*, 2nd ser., 4, no. 2 (Winter 1992).

An earlier version of chapter 15 was previously published as "Dickin-son College Builds Carlisle Indian Industrial School Resource Center" in *Native American and Indigenous Studies* 1, no. 2 (Fall 2014). © 2014 by the Native American and Indigenous Studies Association. Used with permission of the University of Minnesota Press.

Library of Congress Cataloging-in-Publication Data
Names: Fear-Segal, Jacqueline, editor of compilation. | Rose, Susan D., 1955– editor of compilation.
Title: Carlisle Indian Industrial School: indigenous histories, memories, and reclamations / edited by Jacqueline Fear-Segal and Susan D. Rose.
Description: Lincoln: University of Nebraska Press, [2016] | Series: Indigenous education | Includes bibliographical references and index.
Identifiers: LCCN 2016013673
ISBN 9780803278912 (cloth: alk. paper)
ISBN 9781496207692 (paper: alk. paper)
ISBN 9780803295070 (epub)
ISBN 9780803295087 (mobi)
ISBN 9780803295094 (pdf)
Subjects: LCSH: United States Indian School (Carlisle, Pa.)—History. | Off-reservation boarding schools—Pennsylvania—Carlisle—History. | Indians of North America—Cultural assimilation—United States. | Indians of North America—Education—Pennsylvania—Carlisle—History. | Indians of North America—Cultural assimilation—Pennsylvania—Carlisle—History. | Indians of North America—Pennsylvania—Carlisle—Ethnic identity—History. | Indian students—Relocation—United States—History. | Indians, Treatment of—United States—History. | Collective memory—United States. | Racism in education—Pennsylvania—Carlisle—History.
Classification: LCC E97.6.C2 C365 2016 | DDC 371.829/97074843—dc23
LC record available at http://lccn.loc.gov/2016013673

Set in Huronia by Rachel Gould.

We respectfully dedicate this book to
all Carlisle Indian School students,
their descendants, communities, and
nations, and all indigenous peoples
who have been affected by educational
campaigns of cultural genocide.

*All royalties from this volume will be paid into
the Carlisle Indian School Project Fund (housed
at the Community Studies Center, Dickinson
College) and will contribute to future Carlisle
symposia and other events and projects (such as
converting the Carlisle Farmhouse into a heritage
center) that increase and disseminate knowledge
of Indian boarding schools and preserve the
memory of the students who attended Carlisle.*

Contents

Part 6. Reflections and Responses

Illustrations

Photographs

Maps

Acknowledgments

This volume represents the research and work of numerous people down the years, many of whom will not be mentioned individually. Our especial heartfelt thanks go to all descendants who braved coming to Carlisle, Pennsylvania, to attend and contribute their thoughts and voices to discussions about Carlisle and other Indian boarding schools at the 2012 symposium. The presenters (poets, scholars, musicians, filmmakers) and the participants who shared their stories and perspectives and heard one another into speech made this an important and dynamic symposium for all involved. Without you, this volume would not exist. It has been our privilege to work on the pieces that are included in this collection. Together they represent the written legacy of the Carlisle Symposium, as well as a means to open and continue dialogue about the Carlisle Indian School, Indian "education" on and off-reservations, cultural genocide, institutions of schooling and incarceration, and the continuing effects of settler colonialism.

Thank you to the Ndé elders who permitted their people's painful story to be filmed while it was still unfolding, and who then pressed for an event to be held in Carlisle after witnessing the powerful audience response to a screening of their story, *The Lost Ones*, at a Native American and Indigenous Studies Association (NAISA) conference. They realized the time was right for these painful issues to be openly discussed and appraised. Thank you to members of the organizing committee, who responded so creatively to this call and who turned an intent into a reality (Jill Ahlberg-Yohe, Christopher Bilodeau, Joyce Bylander, Jacqueline Fear-Segal, Barbara Landis, Sharon O'Brien, Susan Rose, Stephanie Sellers, Dovie Thomason, and Malinda Triller Doran). Without funding, an event like the 2012 symposium cannot happen, so we want to thank the Central Pennsylvania Consortium (Dickinson, Franklin and Marshall, and Gettysburg Colleges) and the Department of American Studies, University of East Anglia, UK, for their generous support. We are very appreciative of Dickinson College's willingness to host this event and for the flexibility shown by staff as the numbers climbed from the expected 50 delegates to the more than 290 who eventually attended. Thanks go to Jason Illari and his staff at the Cumberland County Historical Society for so generously donating the majority of historical images in this volume and especially to Richard Tritt for his expertise and help in the Society's photo archive. Also to Chip Fox for the photographs he took during the symposium. Special thanks to Barbara Landis for escorting small groups on tours of the surviving buildings and cemetery of the Indian School throughout the symposium. Finally, our sincere thanks go to Sharon O'Brien and Steve Brouwer, who tirelessly worked to help us improve and edit some of the chapters.

JF-S *and* SDR

Introduction

JACQUELINE FEAR-SEGAL AND SUSAN D. ROSE

Close to midnight on October 5, 1879, a train drew into the railroad station in Carlisle, Pennsylvania, carrying eighty-two Lakota children from the Rosebud and Pine Ridge Indian Agencies in Dakota Territory. They were the first contingent of students sent to the newly opened Carlisle Indian School to be made the subjects of an educational experiment that would soon be extended to include Native nations across the United States and Canada.

The children had traveled over a thousand miles by river and rail, and this great distance was fundamental to Carlisle's mission. Capt. Richard Henry Pratt, the school's founder and first superintendent, was determined to remove Native children as far as possible from their families and communities, to strip them of all aspects of their traditional cultures, and to instruct them in the language, religion, behavior, and skills of mainstream white society. Pratt's objective was to prepare Native youth for assimilation and American citizenship. He insisted that in schools like Carlisle this transformation could be achieved in a generation. An acting army officer, Pratt had secured government support to establish and run this first federally funded, off-reservation Indian boarding school. Carlisle provided the blueprint for the federal Indian school system that would be organized across the United States, with twenty-four analogous military-style, off-reservation schools and similar boarding institutions on every reservation.

The federal government was entering the final stages of Native dispossession and North American conquest. By the time Carlisle opened its doors in 1879, most of the fighting was over. With Native nations now sequestered on reservations, Pratt and white Christian reformers, who called themselves "Friends of the Indian," presented the policy of education and assimilation as a more enlightened and humane way to solve the nation's intractable "Indian Problem." Yet the purpose of the education campaign matched previous policies: dispossessing Native peoples of their lands and extinguishing their existence as distinct groups that threatened the nation-building project of the United States. These destructive objectives were effectively masked for the white public by a long-established American educational rhetoric that linked schooling to both democracy and individual advancement, and by a complementary and unquestioned commitment to the American republican experiment. Pratt's main task, therefore, was to convince white Americans that his mission to transform Native children from "savagery" to "civilization" was both desirable and possible.

For Native communities Pratt's experiment at Carlisle initiated processes of diaspora, dislocation, and rupture deeper and more profound than he envisaged. These processes had many immediate impacts as well as long-term legacies. For all Native nations, physical and spiritual well-being was anchored not just within their communities, but also within the environment and land that surrounded them. When Native children were transported hundreds, and sometimes thousands, of miles to Carlisle, Pennsylvania, they were subjected to a strict "civilizing" program to strip them of their cultures; they were also forced to live in an alien place devoid of vital and familiar cultural, spiritual, and geographical markers as well as the support and succor of kin and community.

Thousands of Native children and youth would follow that first group from Dakota over the next forty years, transported from Indian agencies across the continent on rail networks that built and connected the markets of the United States. The vast majority did not assimilate into mainstream society as Pratt had envisioned but instead returned to their reservation homes, often feeling caught between two cultures. Only 758 of over 10,500 students who were enrolled at Carlisle ever graduated. Some found the school traumatic and begged to go home or ran away; others completed their Carlisle schooling but lived with stress and disturbance upon their return.

A well-known account of the difficulties many returned Carlisle students faced is that of Plenty Horses, who returned to Dakota Territory after attending Carlisle from 1883 to 1888: "There was no chance to get employment, nothing for me to do whereby I could earn my board and clothes, no opportunity to learn more and remain with the whites. It dis-

heartened me and I went back to live as I had before going to school."
Plenty Horses struggled when he returned home, trying to find his place
among his people, having been stripped of his native language and cultural traditions. As historian Philip J. Deloria notes, Plenty Horses missed
out—as did most of the students—on the essential teachings of his Lakota
education that takes place for young people between the ages of fourteen
and nineteen.[1] He was acutely aware of the cultural genocide that was
being inflicted on his people, and upon return home Plenty Horses grew
his hair long, wore traditional dress, and participated in the Ghost Dance.

Plenty Horses was there on the Pine Ridge Reservation when the
bodies of Lakota men, women, and children were dug from the snow
and buried in a mass grave after the massacre at Wounded Knee. Nine
days after this December 29th killing, on January 7, 1891, he joined some
other forty warriors who accompanied Sioux leaders to meet with army
lieutenant Edward W. Casey for possible negotiations. It was there that
Plenty Horses shot and killed Casey. During his trial, he said: "Five years I
attended Carlisle and was educated in the ways of the white man. When
I returned to my people, I was an outcast among them. I was no longer
an Indian. I was not a white man. I was lonely. I shot the lieutenant so I
might make a place for myself among my people. I am now one of them.
I shall be hung, and the Indians will bury me as a warrior."[2] In the end
Plenty Horses was not convicted of murder and was released. In order to
exonerate the soldiers of the Seventh Cavalry who conducted the massacre at Wounded Knee, the lawyers and eventually the judge declared
that a state of war had existed.[3]

This is not to say that all of the students at Carlisle had negative experiences. There is evidence in the accounts of some students and their
descendants that they made good use of their Carlisle education. And
many former students wrote to Carlisle to ask if their children could be
enrolled. It seems too that Pratt was a complex man, able to win the loyalty and lasting support of some students. When he died in 1924, his status as an army officer meant he could be buried in Arlington Cemetery,
and the words inscribed on his gravestone indicate that some Carlisle
students contributed to it: "Erected in loving memory by his students and
other Indians." Although the stories of Carlisle and its legacies are complex, the sources through which these can be tracked are very one-sided

because the official record was created and preserved by white officials. Some student letters have survived in the Carlisle archive, but very few students left any other written record.[4] Those who did wrote mostly for school publications that were under the scrutiny of white editors. On their return home, many students did not speak about their experiences, but stories that were told and passed down the generations orally often remained closely guarded within the communities; for understandable reasons they are not widely accessible. Yet it is an indisputable fact that the Indian School initiated a large-scale diaspora of Native children, and that the geo-spatial-cultural dislocation they experienced as part of settler colonialism was grounded in a new and foreign place-name that would soon become infamous in all Native communities as a major site of cultural genocide: Carlisle.

For N. Scott Momaday, the Kiowa writer, artist, and Pulitzer Prize winner, the name Carlisle carries a historical significance parallel to Gettysburg and Wounded Knee within America's national memory and history: "Carlisle, in a more subtle and obscure story than that of Gettysburg, is a place-name among place-names on a chronological map that spans time and the continent." It was in recognition of this vital importance of Carlisle in the context of Native and U.S. history that in October 2012 a symposium—"Carlisle PA: Site of Indigenous Histories, Memories, and Reclamations"—was organized and held at Dickinson College located in Carlisle, Pennsylvania. This remarkable event brought some 290 people to Carlisle, over half of whom were Native, representing thirty-six tribal nations.[5] The organizing committee wanted to create a space for descendants, storytellers, poets, musicians, oral historians, and academics to share their knowledge, stories, and perspectives about the history and legacy of Carlisle as the model for off-reservation boarding schools and Indian education. For the first time ever, Native and non-Native scholars, leaders, artists, descendants, teachers, students, and community members gathered together in the town of Carlisle, just two miles from the surviving buildings of the Indian School, to remember, explore, discuss, and evaluate this pioneering and influential institution (1879–1918).

The symposium proved to be much more than an academic conference: it became a gathering. Presentations were multigenre and included poems, memory pieces, academic analyses, stories, prayers, and songs, which encompassed and expressed multiple perspectives about Carlisle. It was a powerful experience for many; as one participant wrote: "Because of the non-academic, native structure and sessions, mingling stories with poems with videos with papers with the most heart-felt audience response I've ever seen, this symposium engaged us all as whole people: mind, heart, and spirit. Several attendees and participants spoke of "healing" as a process that took place during it, and I think that process was connected with the creation of a safe and native 'space' that was both physical and emotional."

This collection stands as the published legacy of the symposium, bringing together a range of work presented by participants that together exemplifies the importance of researching, remembering, discussing, interpreting, and assessing the complex legacies of the Carlisle Indian School within its wider historical context.

History of the Carlisle Indian Industrial School (1879–1918)

Carlisle is a major site of memory for Native peoples across the nation and in other countries, such as Canada, whose residential schools embraced both its philosophy and curriculum. Although for many, detailed knowledge and memories of Carlisle and their connections to it have been lost or deliberately erased, the name "Carlisle" still resonates in every Native community. During its thirty-nine-year history, over 10,500 students from almost every Native nation in the United States (as well as Puerto Rico) were enrolled at Carlisle. The first were deliberately recruited from tribes regarded by the government as militarily troublesome: Lakotas, Kiowas, Cheyennes. In some cases leaders and parents were persuaded to send their children to Carlisle, thinking it might provide them with a good education and so benefit their people when negotiating with whites. For other children, less choice and more coercion were involved; some were sent to Carlisle as prisoners of war.

Pratt's goal was to recruit students from every Indian agency, to universalize his experiment, and to facilitate the simultaneous obliteration of all Native cultures; at Carlisle, students were rarely placed with a roommate from the same nation, so they would be forced to speak English. Young people were brought from all over the country: California and the Carolinas, New Mexico and New York, Arizona and Alaska; the nations sending the highest number of children were the Sioux (Lakotas, Nakotas, and Dakotas) and the Chippewa (Ojibwes). Carlisle students were enrolled initially for a period of three to five years. Most did not return home during that time, and many spent far longer at Carlisle. Pratt's goal was to immerse them in the dominant white Anglo-Saxon mainstream culture. Speaking to a convention of Baptist ministers in 1883, he used the image of baptism to explain his philosophy for transforming Native children so they could be made to emulate white men and women: "In Indian civilization I am a Baptist, because I believe in immersing the Indians in our civilization and when we get them under holding them there until they are thoroughly soaked."[6]

The force and suggestion of drowning contained in Pratt's metaphor were not accidental; he believed every necessary measure should be taken to impose "civilization" through total immersion. His slogan was: "To civilize the Indian, get him into civilization. To keep him civilized, let him stay."[7] And this was the rationale for his "Outing" program. Almost all Carlisle students experienced multiple dislocations when, instead of returning home for the summers, they were sent "Out" into local communities to work for white families, typically as farmhands or maids. Some stayed Out much longer and even attended local schools. Yet even after spending many years in the East, most Carlisle students eventually returned home to their reservations. Many were caught between worlds, cultures, and languages. Cut off from the nurture of tradition, family, and community, they experienced a rupture in their affiliations, affections, and identities. For many this began a legacy of trauma and disenfranchisement that would be passed down the generations.

The federal government's support for Carlisle signaled its new and growing involvement in Indian education. Previously, Indian schools had been run by missionaries, with the emphasis on conversion. With Native nations in the West suffering progressive military defeat and their lands now forcibly incorporated within U.S. geographical boundaries, officials in Washington sought an effective way to break the intimate bonds that tied Native children to their communities, cultures, and homelands and to substitute a new loyalty to the American nation.

Prior to founding the Carlisle Indian School, Capt. Richard Henry Pratt had spent three years at Fort Marion, Florida (1875–78) guarding a group of imprisoned leaders and warriors from defeated tribes in the Southwest: Cheyennes, Kiowas, Comanches, Arapahos, and one Caddo. In a makeshift fortress school many of the young men learned to read and write, leading Pratt to conclude that education could provide the solution to the nation's "Indian problem." After they were released, Pratt took twenty-two of the younger Fort Marion prisoners to Hampton Institute, Virginia, to continue their education. But Hampton had been established as a school for black freedmen, and Pratt was loath to have Indians associated with the racial stigma suffered by African Americans. Besides, he wanted his own school, so he requested permission from the secretary of the interior, Carl Schurz, to found a school exclusively for Indians: "Give me 300 young Indians and a place in one of our best communities and let me prove it is easy to give Indian youth the English language, education, and industries that it is imperative they have in preparation for citizenship. Carlisle Barracks in Pennsylvania has been abandoned for a number of years. It is in a fine agricultural country and the inhabitants are kindly disposed and long free from the universal border prejudice against Indians."[8]

Federal officials in Washington readily granted permission for the disused barracks to be transferred from the Department of War to the Department of the Interior. The rationale for choosing cultural rather than physical genocide was that it was more humane as well as economically pragmatic. Secretary of the Interior Schurz concluded that it would cost a million dollars to kill an Indian in warfare, whereas it cost only $1,200 to school an Indian child for eight years. Likewise, a later secretary of the interior, Henry Teller, argued that it would cost $22 million to wage war against Indians over a ten-year period, but it would cost less than a quarter of that amount to educate thirty thousand children for a year.[9] As David Wallace Adams argued in his classic *Education for Extinction*: "For tribal elders who had witnessed the catastrophic developments of the nine-teenth century. . . . There seemed to be no end to the cruelties perpetrated by whites. And after all this, the schools. After all this, the white man had concluded that the only way to save Indians was to destroy them, that the last great Indian war should be waged against children. They were coming for the children."[10]

So in 1879 the Carlisle Barracks was reopened as an Indian School, with 120 federally funded Indian students from the West. This was the very site where the U.S. Army had trained the U.S. Cavalry (1838–71), which had recently enforced American settlement of the western part of the continent, fought the nations of the Indian students, and seized Native lands, incorporating them into the United States. There was a cruel irony in Pratt's choice of Carlisle as the site for the Indian School, because his reassurance to Carl Schurz at the Department of the Interior that "the inhabitants are kindly disposed and long free from the universal border prejudice against Indians"[11] neglected to mention that Carlisle was historically a key location for launching the Indian wars west of the Susquehanna River.

Established in 1751 at the intersection of Indian trails along Letort Creek, the town of Carlisle became the jumping-off point for traders and settlers heading over the Alleghenies on their way west. And as settler pressure and global conflict between England and France gave birth to the French and Indian War (1754–63), Carlisle became home to an extremely important military post, the Carlisle Barracks established in 1757. After the Revolutionary War, from 1783 to 1837, the town of Carlisle was still significant as the "frontier" gateway to the West.

Later, from 1838 until 1871, the Carlisle Barracks became the U.S. Army Cavalry School used to train officers and soldiers to fight in the Indian-American wars. When fighting moved further across the Plains, General Sherman moved the cavalry school to St. Louis. By 1879 the Carlisle Barracks appeared the perfect location for Pratt's experiment in cultural transformation. Empty, located in a quiet, rural, white community in an area that had thoroughly cleansed itself of original inhabitants a century earlier (for details, see chapter 2),[12] the barracks were only a short railroad ride from government powerbrokers in Washington DC and also close to wealthy eastern donors. In short, the school's eastern location was vital to both its educational philosophy and its visibility. Using the campus as a showcase, Pratt delighted in inviting congressmen and benefactors to Carlisle to witness the students working in classrooms and trade shops and marching in their uniforms on the parade ground to the beat of the school's military band.

From the start he was acutely alert to the promotional powers offered by the new medium of photography, and he worked closely with local photographer John Nicholas Choate to create visual "proof" of his experiment's success. These photographs, when displayed in school publications and sold as boudoir and cabinet cards, meant that thousands of Americans who never set foot in Carlisle became familiar with images of apparently civilized and educated Indian children. From the day the first students were brought in, Pratt made them subjects of the camera's lens, which recorded their arrival in traditional clothing with moccasins and feathers and subsequent transformations into scrubbed, brushed, uniformed Carlisle students. With cropped hair, tidy uniforms, and skin that was photographically enhanced to look whiter, the assumption was that these external changes had been matched by a parallel intellectual and moral transformation. The photographs were used to garner support for the school and substantiate Pratt's claim that "savage" Indians could indeed be "civilized," a radical idea for many Americans just three years after the Battle of the Little Big Horn.

During his time as superintendent (1879–1904) Pratt made the Carlisle campus a stage on which to present Indians living and working in a "contemporary" environment. New and modernized buildings and the installation of a sophisticated heating and lighting system contributed to his strategy of demonstrating to whites that Indians were fully capable of taking their place in modern America. As Deloria notes, the image of the "savage" Indian so prevalently promoted in previous years was replaced with the notion of the less threatening, "docile, pacified Indians" on their way to civilization.[13] Pratt took every opportunity to make strategic public displays of Carlisle students. The Carlisle band played at the opening of the Brooklyn Bridge in 1883, a contingent of students was sent to march at the Chicago 1893 World's Fair, and individual students whom Pratt regarded as exemplary were given posts where their so-called progress could be observed. A graphic example of this is given by Carlisle student Luther Standing Bear, who recounts how when he was sent to work at Wanamaker's in Philadelphia, he was placed on open display in the store while he was pricing jewelry: "So every day I was locked inside this little glass house, opening the trunks, taking out the jewels and putting price tags on them. How the white folks did crowd around to watch me! They were greatly surprised that John Wanamaker could trust an Indian boy with such valuables."[14]

Pratt's dismissal in 1904 signaled the start of an era when the viability of the Carlisle experiment would be increasingly brought into question. The expense of running a boarding school located in the East had always been a contentious issue, and it became increasingly controversial. Accompanied by the eugenics movement that promoted the "science" of racial inferiority, there was a growing doubt, even among American reformers, that Indians were capable of taking their place as equal to whites within the nation. Most important of all, the passage of the Dawes Allotment Act in 1887 had guaranteed that the vast Native homelands of the West could gradually and "legally" be transferred into white settler ownership. Native peoples were no longer a threat to nation building. Within a short decade, 1889–96, the West had entered the Union as seven new states: North and South Dakota, Montana, Washington, Idaho, Wyoming, and Utah. In response to the new situation, the turn of the century ushered in a change of policy in Washington. The goal of rapid assimilation, fiercely championed at Carlisle and closely linked to the perceived need to subjugate Native peoples and possess their lands, was replaced by a national Indian schooling program with a slower pace, more lowly ambitions, and requiring a much smaller budget. Reservation schools, teaching a simple and basic curriculum, were now deemed to be the best way to accommodate Indian "incapacities." The campaign for Indian citizenship was suspended.

Pratt was unwavering in his views and opinions, which ran contrary to this new course. After his dismissal Carlisle was run by a series of four superintendents—Capt. William A. Mercer (1904–8), Moses Friedman (1908–14), Oscar Lipps (1914–17), and John Francis Jr. (1917–18)—with varying degrees of success. A Senate investigation (1913–14), precipitated by the petitioning efforts of students led by Gus Welch (Anishanaabe), drew public attention to abuses and serious mismanagement at the school as well as the excessive attention and power accorded to the athletes. Carlisle's philosophy and mission were already being questioned, and the Senate investigation brought its educational procedures and practices into open and public disrepute. Out of favor and in decline, the Carlisle Indian School finally closed its doors in 1918. The War Department immediately reclaimed the Carlisle Barracks for use as a rehabilitation hospital for wounded soldiers from World War I (General Hospital 31). After the war the Carlisle Barracks housed the Medical Field Service School, and from 1946 until 1951 no fewer than six army schools were briefly located there. In 1951 the War College, the senior educational institution of the U.S. Army, relocated to Carlisle to begin the latest stage of the post's history.

During these years the surviving buildings from the Indian school were put to new and different purposes. As the campus developed, the school cemetery was seen by army officials as an obstruction to its expansion and was removed to a new and smaller plot on the outer perimeter of the post (1927). Just as the buildings and campus of the Carlisle Indian School were being rapidly changed and subsumed by the activities of the army schools, so too the reality of the Indian School faded in local historical memory. On Indian reservations across the United States, however, among Native descendants, families, and communities, the traumatic legacies of Carlisle and the boarding school experiment it spearheaded continued to have an enduring impact whether spoken of or silenced.

Reflecting on the impact of boarding schools, in 2013 attorneys for the Native American Rights Legal Fund wrote:

Cut off from their families and culture, the children were punished for speaking their Native languages, banned from conducting traditional or cultural practices, shorn of traditional clothing and identity of their Native cultures, taught that their cultures and traditions were evil and sinful, and that they should be ashamed of being Native American. Placed often far from home, they were frequently neglected or abused physically, sexually, and psychologically. Generations of these children became the legacy of the federal boarding school policy. They returned to their communities, not as the Christianized farmers that the boarding school policy envisioned, but as deeply scarred humans lacking the skills, community, parenting, extended family, language, and cultural practices of those raised in their cultural context.[15]

When the Carlisle Indian School closed its doors a century ago (1918), the institutions it spawned and its resolve to obliterate Native cultures did not die with it. In the United States, despite a brief period of apparent if romanticized respect shown Native cultures during the 1930s, the post–World War II years witnessed renewed federal determination to terminate tribal sovereignty and assimilate all Indians into the mainstream. In the face of threats to both community and culture, the boarding school memories of many survivors remained silenced and hidden. However, the late 1960s marked the beginning of a new era of Native cultural and political renaissance and resistance. This was signaled by the political activism first demonstrated at Alcatraz by the Indians of All Tribes (1969) and paralleled in literature by N. Scott Momaday's publication of *House Made of Dawn*, which was awarded the Pulitzer Prize (1969), and the beginning of what is described as a Native American Renaissance.[16] In Native communities across America, however, it would take time and courage to allow information and stories about Carlisle and its institutional legacy to surface and become acknowledged as part of a shared and painful intertribal and intercultural history. Slowly survivors, descendants, and the wider Native community began openly to address and claim these historical experiences and confront their enduring legacies as well as those responsible for implementing them.

In 2011 a coalition of indigenous groups organized the National Native American Boarding School Healing Coalition (NABS) to document "through research and oral history the extensive abuses that go beyond individual casualties to disruption of Indigenous life at every level."[17] In *An Indigenous Peoples' History of the United States*, Roxanne Dunbar-Ortiz recounts the story that Sun Elk, the first child from the Taos Pueblo to attend the Carlisle Indian School (1883–90), tells about how lessons taught at Carlisle affected him on his return to Taos society:

> They told us that Indian ways were bad. They said we must get civilized. I remember that word too. It means 'be like the white man." I am willing to be like the white man, but I did not believe the Indian ways were wrong. But they kept teaching us for seven years. And the books told how bad the Indians had been to the white men—burning their towns and killing their women and children. But I had seen white men do that to Indians. We all wore white man's clothes and ate white man's food and went to white man's churches and spoke white man's talk. And so after a while we also began to say Indians were bad. We laughed at our own people and their blankets and cooking pots and sacred societies and dances.[18]

A number of articles and books have documented the abuses that occurred at Indian boarding schools in the United States, including physical and sexual violence and corporal punishment that affected not only the children at the time but future generations as well. These schools were run by the government through the Bureau of Indian Affairs. The assistant secretary of Indian Affairs for the Department of the Interior, Kevin Gover (Pawnee),[19] made the following comments at a ceremony acknowledging the 175th Anniversary of the Establishment of the Bureau of Indian Affairs, on September 8, 2000:

This agency forbade the speaking of Indian languages, prohibited the conduct of traditional religious activities, outlawed traditional government, and made Indian people ashamed of who they were. *Worst of all, the Bureau of Indian Affairs committed these acts against the children entrusted to its boarding schools, brutalizing them emotionally, psychologically, physically, and spiritually.* Even in this era of self-determination, when the Bureau of Indian Affairs is at long last serving as an advocate for Indian people in an atmosphere of mutual respect, the legacy of these misdeeds haunts us. The trauma of shame, fear and anger has passed from one generation to the next, and manifests itself in the rampant alcoholism, drug abuse, and domestic violence that plague Indian country. Many of our people live lives of unrelenting tragedy as Indian families suffer the ruin of lives by alcoholism, suicides made of shame and despair, and violent death at the hands of one another. So many of the maladies suffered today in Indian country result from the failures of this agency. Poverty, ignorance, and disease have been the product of this agency's work.[20]

The 2007 UN Declaration of the Rights of Indigenous Peoples recognized the many abuses committed against them through "colonization and dispossession of their lands," outlined their rights (in forty-six separate articles), and made recommendations for next steps. The Declaration was heralded as a "triumph for justice and human dignity" after more than two decades of negotiations between governments and indigenous peoples' representatives. It was adopted by a majority with 143 states in favor, 4 against (Australia, Canada, New Zealand, and the United States), and 11 abstentions.[21]

While Australia, Canada, New Zealand, and the United States voted against the Declaration, they have to various degrees offered apologies for their countries' abuses against indigenous people, in part inflicted at government-run boarding schools. Formal governmental apologies in the United States, however, do not compare to those given by New Zealand and Canada (and even Australia), both of which have established Truth and Reconciliation Commissions to investigate abuses against indigenous peoples and children sent to government-run boarding schools. While U.S. president Barack Obama did issue an official apology to Native people on Saturday, December 19, 2009, when he signed the Native American Apology Resolution into law, it was closed to the media. A public reading of the apology was not held until May 20, 2010, when Senator Sam Brownback read the resolution during an event at the Congressional Cemetery in Washington DC. Only five tribal leaders were present, however, representing the Cherokee, Choctaw, Muscogee (Creek), Sisseton Wahpeton Oyate, and Pawnee nations.

Lise Balk King poignantly notes in her article for *Indian Country Today*, "A Tree Fell in the Forest: The U.S. Apologized to Native Americans and No One Heard a Sound," that a key difference between Obama's apology and Prime Minister Stephen Harper's on Wednesday, June 11, 2008, was the *public* nature of the Canadian apology. "Prime Minister Stephen Harper asked his 30 million Canadian citizens to tune in to Parliament for a live, nationally broadcast Apology to their country's First Nations. . . . He specifically addressed the government's role in assimilating Native children through church-run residential (boarding) schools, and sought a turning point in the troubled history between Native peoples and the Canadian state."[22] When Harper publically apologized for the creation and excesses of the residential school system in 2008, he brought the abuses of all Indian residential and boarding schools under international scrutiny. And the other key difference is that in Canada detailed action steps were identified to move toward repair and healing.

In 2015, after years of investigation and hearings, the Canadian Truth and Reconciliation Commission's (TRC) Report accused the residential schools of multigenerational *cultural genocide*. This report has initiated a discussion that reaches far outside Canadian boundaries. Many people both in Canada and internationally believe that this accusation should be stronger and that what happened in residential boarding schools should openly be named as genocide; some feel that there can never be full reconciliation. But the Canadian TRC findings mean that the mission and history of Carlisle are now framed within a wider international context and conversation.

Growing Interest in the Carlisle Indian School Campus

As the history of boarding schools has become more extensively and openly discussed, the Carlisle campus has drawn more attention and increasing numbers of visitors, including many descendants of students who attended the Carlisle Indian School. In 1962, as part of a wider movement to designate National Historic landmarks, the Carlisle Indian School campus was included on the national register. A museum display in the Hessian Powder Magazine (which had been the Guardhouse during Indian School days) included a short history of the Indian School. Visitors walking the grounds could find a bronze bust of Richard Henry Pratt. If they were observant, they could also read discrete labels on some of the surviving buildings describing their uses in the days of the Indian School. These markers were small and often inaccurate, and even today the sign on the Coren Apartment building in the center of the campus, where Carlisle teachers lived, wrongly informs visitors that this was a student dormitory. Nowhere was there any information about the thousands of Native students who lived and worked on the campus; evidence of the students was totally absent.

A fourteen-page pamphlet produced at the barracks in 1996 under the auspices of the U.S. Army Construction Engineering Research Laboratory provided visitors with a means to identify the surviving buildings of the Indian School. It also included a brief account of the Indian School, accompanied by photographs and dated descriptions of all the surviving buildings. A map on the final page laid out a guided walking tour of these buildings.[23] The outlined tour, however, was incomplete. Absent from both text and map was any mention or glimpse of the cemetery in either its original or its removed location. The Indian School cemetery is the only place where students are memorialized and the names of some who never returned home are inscribed. It is also the site of greatest importance and interest to many visiting descendants. Another significant exclusion from this pamphlet was the Carlisle Farmhouse. The boundary drawn around the campus on this map mirrored the one that had been marked out when the Indian School was included on the National Historic Landmark registry. It traced the buildings of the main campus, but it failed to include farmlands that had been part of the school and the surviving Farmhouse where students had trained and lived. When this Farmhouse was slated for demolition in 2010, to allow for construction of modern dwellings for army families, its omission from the protected precinct of the Indian School left it exposed and vulnerable and its historic status underrated and ignored. The Farmhouse has recently come to be recognized as a site of memory, interest, and discussion, as described in chapter 14, "Carlisle Farmhouse: A Major Site of Memory." As a result of organized protests and discussions with U.S. Army representatives at the symposium, its demolition was temporarily halted so that a more thorough investigation of its historical significance could be undertaken. Following this investigation, demolition was permanently stopped in 2014.

Gradually, the visibility of the remnants of the Carlisle campus on the grounds of the U.S. Army War College has been enhanced: a new map (merging three historic maps of the campus buildings and grounds) now reveals the location and footprint of the original cemetery (see map 2 in chapter 9); a successful campaign to erect a marker beside the cemetery railings in 2003 signals the historic presence of the Indian School to all passers-by; and regular tours of the grounds, organized by Barbara Landis and staff from the Cumberland County Historical Society, guide many visitors around the surviving remains of the Carlisle Indian School and provide factual information.[24] These factors, combined with an active demand by many third-generation descendants to know more, have contributed to a growing awareness and knowledge of this historic site of memory for both Natives and non-Natives.

Carlisle, the Symposium, and This Collection

Recordar: To remember; from the Latin
re-cordis, to pass back through the heart.

EDUARDO GALEANO

Given the importance of this site of memory, it was critical that the symposium be held in Carlisle itself. For many, like Jolene Rickard (Tuscarora), awareness of strong historical links to a school she had never visited drew her to the symposium: "As you might imagine, I have relatives that attended Carlisle and this will be a very meaningful journey for me."[25] For everyone, the very presence of the remnants of the school buildings and cemetery just two miles up the road from Dickinson College affected the ways in which this history was told, analyzed, and interpreted. These remnants shaped how participants felt and discussed the school's historical and emotional legacy. Such conversations were not just a historical exercise, but a living, moving process as participants gathered to visit the site of the Carlisle Indian School. Not only did we tour the grounds, visit the gym, and stand on the bandstand, but we also participated in blessing ceremonies at the cemetery. Direct and effective representation made by symposium delegates to officials of the U.S. Army, asking them to reexamine their decision to demolish the Carlisle Farmhouse, also meant that as discussions about the history of the school were taking place, part of the physical fabric of the school was being actively, and ultimately successfully, defended and safeguarded.

The historic significance of Carlisle is consistently acknowledged in the extensive scholarship on Indian boarding and residential schools.[26] Monographs about individual institutions published over the past thirty years unfailingly refer to the founding importance of Carlisle.[27] There are a number of books, scripted for different audiences, that focus on sport at Carlisle and in particular on football and Jim Thorpe.[28] But still missing is a work that places the Carlisle Indian School and Carlisle students at its center.[29] Building on previous writing and to fill this surprising gap in the scholarship, this book focuses specifically on the Carlisle Indian School, making visible the work and perspectives of Native and non-Native scholars, descendants, poets, and activists. This is more than a scholarly work, for the contributors to this collection reveal the continuing presence, impact, and vitality of historical and collective memory, and the enduring legacy of the Indian School. Carlisle and its history still touch the lives of many Native Americans and their communities and are also deeply enmeshed within the local and regional history of Carlisle, the national history of the United States, and the international history of settler colonialism.

Studies of settler colonialism illuminate how processes governing the settler colonial project in a wide range of nations are inherently violent and destructive for indigenous peoples.[30] As Patrick Wolfe explains, unlike traditional forms and definitions of colonialism that exploit indigenous labor and extract indigenous resources, the paramount goal of settler colonialism is the acquisition of land. Settler colonialism is therefore "premised on displacing indigenes from (or *re*placing them on) the land," and an allied objective is always the replacement of native societies. Taking his line of reasoning a step further, Wolfe argues that "the ruling logic of elimination" is the essential characteristic of the settler colonial project, which seeks always to eliminate rather than incorporate indigenous peoples.[31] In the United States, where the master narrative of the nation-state is always presented in the rhetoric of the pioneering heroics of settlers rather than the conquest and colonization of Native peoples, the Carlisle slogan, "Kill the Indian and save the man," casts a revealing light on this process. It openly articulates the cultural elimination that stops just short of physical extermination (and therefore self-characterizes as humane and Christian) and is couched in the organizing grammar of race. Viewed from this perspective, the removal of Native children to boarding schools can be seen as inseparable from the sustained and persistent national resolve to eliminate the indigenous, racialized populations that stood in the way of nation-building. Scholarship that makes connections between settler policies of self-protection and Native assimilation—through residential schools, reservations, fostering, and adoption—and the goals of the wider project lays bare both the patterns and the particulars of policies and institutions in different settler colonial societies.[32] Andrew Woolford's *The Benevolent Experiment*, a recent comparison of boarding schools in Canada and the United States in the context of settler colonialism, is of interest in this context because Carlisle is positioned at the core of its analysis.[33]

While this *Carlisle Indian Industrial School* collection is deliberately anchored in the wider historical frame of settler colonialism, it is the Carlisle students themselves and their experiences in a white-run institution far from home who stand at the heart of this volume. It is intended that their stories will draw attention to the wider campaign to destroy the vitality and autonomy of Native American cultures and lives and the federal government's determination to dispossess them of their lands by the expansion of the American nation-state. The ultimate goal of U.S. Indian policy was always the elimination, if not physically then culturally, of Native peoples as separate entities distinguishable from the rest of U.S. society.

The Carlisle Indian School contains and conveys a powerful and contentious history. Its past still haunts the present, in large part because its past has not been fully told. Haitian historian Michel-Rolph Trouillot reminds us in *Silencing the Past: Power and Production of History* that we need to interrogate history: what happened and what is said to have happened, by whom and to whom, and for what purpose.[34] While we have the official story of the Carlisle Indian School, as told primarily by Capt. Richard Henry Pratt and his staff through the various publications of the school, we have many fewer accounts by the students themselves or their families. The best known are two autobiographies by student Luther Standing Bear (Lakota), written many years after he left the school, and a teacher's account of Carlisle by the Dakota writer Zitkala-Ša, who recalled the "four strange summers" she spent teaching at an Eastern "Indian school," which was Carlisle.[35] In "The School Days of an Indian Girl" she recounts how her earlier assimilationist education had alienated her from her home culture and family.

We also find a misleading account of Carlisle in *Stiya, a Carlisle Indian Girl at Home: Founded on the Author's Actual Observations*, which appears to be an autobiographical account of the experiences of an Indian girl who returns home to her family and is horrified by their "savage" life style. Published under the mysterious pen name of Embe, it was actually authored by Marianna Burgess, whose initials, MB, make clear the identity of the author to those already in the know. Burgess was a white teacher who ran the print shop at the Carlisle Indian School. Thus, her book constitutes part of the school's propaganda campaign.[36]

Some Carlisle students never returned home to their own people to tell their stories. Others who did go home found their experiences too painful or difficult to tell, even to family and friends. Some memories were recounted privately and then passed down from generation to generation, to be carried in the living memory of Native American communities. But many stories have been lost or buried. So, while for many Native people Carlisle is a known place, others have only a vague awareness of their connections to it and scant knowledge about which of their ancestors might have spent time there. In the local Carlisle community, the memory of the Carlisle Indian School has faded. Numerous residents do not even know that it ever existed.

In large part because the legacies of the past continue to influence the conditions of the present, many Native Americans are wanting to remember and confront this difficult chapter in their histories—and the role of Indian education in understanding U.S. history. Given that "even in relation to The Past our authenticity resides in the struggles of our present,"[37] organizers of the symposium were very aware of such struggles and tensions as we planned for and engaged in the symposium. As participants, we discussed the ways in which historical memory is contested and becomes a site of cultural struggle, and we examined how dominant and alternative historical narratives and silences have affected lives and understandings.

It is useful here to acknowledge how the differing silences that surround Carlisle have had an enduring impact on how the history of boarding schools has been communicated within mainstream society and the ways in which they curtailed the potential for Native communities to research, discuss, and even know their own stories. According to Trouillot:

> Silences enter the process of historical production at four crucial moments: the moment of fact creation (the making of *sources*); the moment of fact assembly (the making of *archives*); the moment of fact retrieval (the making of *narratives*); and the moment of retrospective significance (the making of *history* in the final instance). These moments are conceptual tools . . . they help us understand why not all silences are equal and why they cannot be addressed—or redressed—in the same manner. To put it differently, any historical narrative is a particular bundle of silences, the result of a unique process, and the operation required to deconstruct these silences will vary accordingly.[38]

Whites were always in control of the historical production at Carlisle, and the resulting sources, archives, narratives, and histories handed down come from a unified perspective. Yet increasingly we are learning that the archives can be revisited to reveal hidden facts, that different voices carried in oral sources can be listened to for alternative truths, and that the "particular bundle of silences" that attach to the Carlisle narrative can be opened up and deconstructed.

We all live by the stories we tell. And stories are particularly vital to indigenous peoples, who acknowledge and embrace the importance of oral histories and storytelling, and who all too often were deceived by the written word of whites. Stories are critical for passing on history as well as for coming to terms with the past, understanding the present, and embracing the future. As Native American storyteller Dovie Thomason began her powerful performance at the symposium, she echoed the words of her grandmother: "Some stories are too painful to be told. . . . Some stories must be told."

One very painful story was the catalyst for the symposium and this anthology. It is the story of two Lipan-Apache children, known at Carlisle as Kesetta and Jack, whose fragmented histories have only recently been pieced together (see chapter 11 in this collection). While researching the biographies of individual Carlisle students, Jacqueline Fear-Segal reached out to make contact with descendants of these two Lipan Apache students.[39] The children had been sent to Carlisle as prisoners of war in 1880; their status would remain unchanged during their whole time at the school. The Lipan Apache knew nothing of the whereabouts of the children after Col. Ranald Mackenzie's attack on their village and the children's capture on what they came to call "The Day of Screams." Yet the family had kept their memory alive and continued to search for them for over a century. After reading his account of Lipan Apache history on the Internet in mid-2002, Fear-Segal made contact with Lipan Apache chairman Daniel Castro Romero Jr. The two exchanged photographs, archival information, and oral histories. In 2009, following this long conversation, Lipan Apache elders came to Carlisle from California, Texas, and New Mexico to offer Blessings so the children could be "sent home." Witnessing this extraordinary event prompted Susan Rose to work with the elders and Jacqueline Fear-Segal to create a visual record of this history and reclamation. The screening of the resulting documentary, *The Lost Ones: Long Journey Home* (2011), at the Native American and Indigenous Studies Association (NAISA) Annual Meeting in California led to a loud and determined call for a gathering at the site of the school in Carlisle. *The Lost Ones* was screened again at the symposium and was a centerpiece of the event.

In many ways the symposium and the varied perspectives presented in this collection represent a reinterpretation of the historic Carlisle "experiment" within the broader history of the United States and a fresh look at its legacies that continue to haunt the present. While differences of opinion surfaced (both between and within Native and non-Native groups), a resolve to honor the sacred memory of the children infused the symposium. There was a sense of a common commitment to face the challenges and controversies and to speak and listen to the stories and perspectives people were willing to share. While this at times became quite emotional, there was a shared awareness that the subjects under discussion were challenging, albeit in different ways for non-Native and Native people, and of great consequence. The presentations and discussions intimately touched the lives and histories of many of those present. Attendance at the symposium signaled many Native people's courageous resolve to learn and confront the facts and truths about what took place at the Carlisle Indian School—and others' resolve to listen and bear witness. The sacred space of the symposium was created by so many Native people daring to return to a place and visit an institution committed to obliterating their histories and cultures. They came to reclaim their right to tell their stories as well as expose the inaccurate, partial, and sanitized history that still dominates popular memory—a history primarily written by white people to justify the conquest and dispossession of Native peoples and the building of the American nation. The symposium opened a place for hearing legitimate voices that previously had been silenced or excluded from discussions of this history.

After an opening welcome was extended to all delegates, the Seneca Blessing "We Are One" was given by Peter Jemison. With this Blessing, Jemison created a sense of a sacred space at the opening of the symposium. The words that he spoke in Seneca and English come from the Native people known as the Haudanosaunees (also known as Iroquois or Six Nations—Mohawks, Oneidas, Cayugas, Onondagas, Senecas, and

Tuscaroras) of upstate New York and Canada. This Thanksgiving Address has ancient roots, dating back at least over one thousand years to the formation of the Great Law of Peace by a man known as the Peacemaker. Today these words continue to be spoken at the opening and closing of all ceremonial and governmental gatherings held by the Six Nations. The address always follows an order that recognizes all of Creation and is based on the belief that the world cannot be taken for granted, that a spiritual communication of acknowledgment of and thanks to all living things must be given in order to align the minds and hearts of the people with the cosmos, Nature, and one another (see the Seneca Blessing in the "Welcome"). As is the tradition, Peter Jemison first acknowledged those who had gathered and our responsibility "to live in balance and harmony with each other and all living things." We should "give greetings and thanks to each other as People," so that "our minds are one." Then thanks was given to the Mother Earth, the Waters, the Fish, the Plants, the Food, the Medicine Herbs, the Animals, the Trees, the Birds, the Four Winds, the Thunderers, the Sun, Grandmother Moon, the Stars, the Enlightened Teachers, the Creator—so "now our minds are one." This was a particularly important Blessing since the purpose of those who came to the symposium was to confront the disturbing history of the Carlisle Indian School and to begin to set the record straight. The Blessing helped remind us why we were there and with what attitude we needed to approach the difficult conversations we were about to have. In this context, the Blessing helped create not only a space in which to examine conflicting perspectives, interests, and activism, but also a site of healing.

Part 1, "A Sacred and Storied Place," opens with Pulitzer Prize–winner N. Scott Momaday's poetic essay, which engages with the terrible losses inflicted on Carlisle students and references some of the atrocities that have been meted out to indigenous peoples across the Americas. Momaday situates Carlisle within the broader postcontact span of American history, pointing out its significance for all Americans. Openly connecting the military-style gravestones in the Carlisle cemetery to similar stones that stud the landscape thirty miles south at Gettysburg, Momaday claims for Carlisle a place equal in historical significance to Gettysburg. Momaday's writing here is both political and personal as he links his own story to both community and place. Momaday gestures to some of the themes explored at the symposium and in this collection: "Names, voices, imagination, innocence, and shame. These are among elements of the Carlisle story." Tellingly, and in the spirit of the event, Momaday ends his piece by speaking openly of his own connection to Carlisle through Etahdleuh Doanmoe, the Kiowa Fort Marion artist whom Pratt made his right-hand man in the early years of school: "He was my kinsman."

Also in part 1, Christopher J. Bilodeau honors the Native nations of the Susquehanna River Valley and reminds readers of their complex relations and histories in this region before the arrival of white settlers. Tracing the development of entangling patterns of trade, military alliance, and diplomacy between the separate Native nations of America and those of Europe, this chapter also charts progressive Native land loss and community destruction, paralleled by the gradual development of a U.S. master narrative of Indian extinction. Examined through this historical lens, the cultural genocidal mission of the Carlisle Indian School can be read not just as the product of social and national forces specific to the late nineteenth century, but rather as the final unfolding of the patterns and processes of settler colonialism, whose roots are buried deep in the early history of the Susquehanna River Valley, the colonial past of America, and the foundations of the United States. By the time the Indian School was established, the Susquehannocks had been annihilated or forced to join other nations and so lost their identity as a distinct nation. Ironically, however, both the Delawares and the Shawnees, who had been forced to relocate far to the west, would be forced to send children to Carlisle to be educated in an alien culture on their own traditional homelands.[40]

The chapters in part 2, "Student Lives and Losses," explore Carlisle's "civilizing" program and its enduring effects. Over the school's nearly forty-year existence, elements of the program would change. At the start, under Pratt, few concessions were made to the undeniable fact that most students would return to their reservation homes. The drive was always toward full assimilation and citizenship, with no credence given to white Americans' reluctance to include Indians on equal terms. Starting in the early twentieth century, Carlisle's curriculum began to reflect the changed mood in Washington, with the emphasis now on teaching skills to make Indians self-sufficient and able to live on reservations and at the lower levels of society, rather than to be assimilated as equals into the American mainstream. By then Carlisle students were mostly older, and the majority had already received some schooling before arrival. However, the huge distances that they all still needed to travel to reach Carlisle, the continuation of Carlisle's outing program during the summers, and the uninterrupted assault on Native cultures meant that the fundamental experience of a Carlisle education remained unchanged. This part is framed by two poems written by Maurice Kenny (Mohawk). Both point to the loss and devastation exacted by the Carlisle program. The subject of the first is a photo-portrait of an unnamed student made by a white photographer in a medium outside the control of Native peoples. By contrast, the subject of the second is a drawing of an Osage man in full regalia, made by an Osage boy. Although McKay Dougan is living far from the source and context of the cultural regalia he has drawn and carefully colored, the boy is working in a culturally familiar medium; drawing in this pictographic style was an artistic tradition developed on the Plains. These two poems direct our attention to single, isolated individuals, who, like all Carlisle students, were forced to navigate the destructive purposes of the Carlisle program alone, without support and help from kin and community. The chapters in this part explore the different features of Carlisle's program, foregrounding the experiences of individual students. Barbara Landis returns to the theme of names. After an exploration of the personal and cultural loss experienced when Carlisle students were renamed, Landis uses the alphabetical order into which all students were slotted to select the two enrollees that begin and end the long Carlisle enrollment list: David Abraham and Otto Zotom. Landis researches the lives of these two young men so that, out of many thousands, their stories can be told and so stand in for the many student stories still waiting to be pieced together. The chapter by Louellyn White (Mohawk), "White Power and the Performance of Assimilation: Lincoln Institute and Carlisle Indian School," gives a very personal account, from the perspective of a descendant, of how both the outing system and theatrical plays in which her grandfather and many of the students acted contributed to the sustained and comprehensive performance of "civilization." John Bloom offers an account of sports at the school, a topic that most people associate with Carlisle because of the fame of Jim Thorpe. But here, too, oral histories provide a means to understand that even their sporting successes did not eliminate students' ambivalence toward Carlisle and its mission of cultural obliteration. These chapters work together to provide a powerful reminder that all Carlisle students, previously accustomed to the network of support provided by kin and community, had to leave their homes to experience a Carlisle education alone and with little preparation. This is not to say that students did not form friendships, create community, and enjoy shared activities at the school. But it is to say that this was accomplished within the strictures of an institution committed to severing their most intimate bonds to family, community, and homeland.

Part 3, "Carlisle Indian School Cemetery," lies at the heart of this collection, because today the cemetery is the only place at the Carlisle Barracks where you can see individual student names and read their tribal affiliations. The cemetery provides the most explicit and visible reminder that Native American children lived and worked at Carlisle, but that, tragically, some never went home. Although in 1927 all the graves were removed from their original location and reassembled on a smaller plot, in a different configuration, and with replacement headstones, the Indian School cemetery still has a powerful effect on all who visit. Once through the little wrought iron entrance gate, it is possible to walk between the close-set stones, read the names inscribed on them, and endeavor to come to terms with all that happened at Carlisle. The opening poem in this section, by a Spanish visitor to Carlisle and Dickinson College, Eduardo Jordá, makes clear that the poignant and powerful message delivered by this sacred site is readily intelligible even to a foreigner. Yet despite the stark and seeming simplicity of meaning conveyed by the rows of identical stones, Fear-Segal's chapter reveals that they carry a complex and hidden history that speaks to the deep historical racism of the wider American society. Standing on the oldest active army post in America, the Carlisle Indian School cemetery is a site where the histories of the United States and its indigenous populations are forever entangled. This chapter explains how the passage of the Native American Graves Protection and Repatriation Act by the United States Congress, in 1990, signaled a new respect for indigenous remains and funerary objects. Recognition that many of these had been stolen, pillaged, or buried inappropriately initiated repatriations, which for many Native communities had been long awaited. Ironically, we learn here that the Carlisle cemetery does not fall under the terms of this act. It is not classified as an Indian "burial site," because no traditional "death rite or ceremony of a culture" accompanied the children's interments; all the Carlisle children had been given Christian burial.[41]

The cemetery is thus an enduring monument to Native children's deaths far from home and the permanent cultural severance Carlisle inflicted on them. For this reason, Landis's research in identifying seven of the students buried in the Indian School cemetery, who lie under the stones marked "unknown," is healing for their families and descendants and is also welcomed by all who visit the cemetery and learn of this work. For descendants and Native visitors to Carlisle, the cemetery is a place they want to visit, although it embodies a painful past that continues to haunt the present.

The chapters in part 4, "Reclamations," contribute to the ongoing rein-terpretation of the boarding school era and to present-day challenges and developments. From an assemblage of archival fragments, in "The Lost Ones: Piecing Together the Story" Jacqueline Fear-Segal reconstructs the story of two captured Lipan Apache children who were sent to Carlisle as prisoners of war without their people's knowledge. By following the story of these two children we learn how their capture and enrollment at Car-lisle had a massive impact on their home community, both then and now. This was an extreme case because these children never returned home, but it reminds us of the many profound effects of removing young people from their communities. Fear-Segal's re-creation of the children's story is followed by a response to the story by a kinswoman of the Lost Ones. In "Necropolitics, Carlisle Indian School, and Ndé Memory," Margo Tamez (Ndé/Lipan Apache) locates and explores this recently discovered infor-mation about the lives of her ancestors within the context of current-day Ndé struggles. Writing within an Ndé epistemological and environmen-tal frame, she examines the continuing negative impact of U.S. policies toward Native nations and underscores how historical patterns of land loss, tribal disappearance, and settler colonialism continue across America up to the present day. Next, the account by Carolyn Rittenhouse (Lakota from Cheyenne River Reservation) of her removal from her Lakota fam-ily and subsequent adoptive childhood, initiated by the Latter-day Saints' Indian Placement Program, is a reminder of the persistence of Carlisle's philosophy of cultural genocide. In "Sacred Journey: Restoring My Plains Indian Tipi," Rittenhouse writes about her active retrieval of her Lakota past and engagement with her culture and community through researching, painting, and raising her Plains Indian tipi. Her personal story demonstrates her own courage and resolve as well as the possibility for cultural recuperation. This section ends with an essay about the material preservation of the Carlisle Farmhouse by Carolyn Tolman. Her chapter describes not just the history of the Farmhouse, where she lived with her family for several years, but also the campaign to save it from demolition. Tolman includes the defining moment when, during a roundtable discussion at the symposium, U.S. Army representatives were persuaded that the Farmhouse's demolition should be indefinitely postponed. At a later date the army agreed that demolition should be permanently stopped. Embodying a painful episode in all Native nations' histories, the Carlisle campus is a vital site of memory, a place where all visitors can seek to understand and confront what happened in government boarding schools. Now that the physical Farmhouse building has been saved, planning has begun for it to become a cultural center; a place where Native memories can be discussed, oral histories recorded, and some of the cultural destruction promulgated by Carlisle reversed.

Part 5 is focused on "Revisioning the Past." One of the goals of the symposium and this collection is to disseminate research and information about Carlisle. The contribution by Malinda Triller Doran, "Research Note on the Carlisle Indian Industrial School Digital Humanities Project," describes how the digitization project, organized by Dickinson College and partners, will create a comprehensive digital resource of all Carlisle archival sources that will facilitate research on this subject by descendants, scholars, teachers, and students. Anne-Claire Fisher and Paul Brawdy, in "Carlisle Indian Industrial School: Projects for Teaching," outline the capstone course they developed for trainee teachers using Carlisle Indian School as a case study. Their goal in studying this government-supported effort to assimilate and control a minority group is to encourage student teachers to use this historical example to reflect on present-day educational issues in which minority groups are engaged in unequal power relationships, both within schools and mainstream society. Dissemination of information about the Carlisle Indian School and its integration into curricula, in historically and predominantly white colleges and universities as well as tribal colleges and secondary schools across the United States, is a vital part of this project.

The final part, "Reflections and Responses," concludes the volume by bringing the reader insightful responses to Carlisle and to the symposium. Dovie Thomason (Kiowa-Apache and Lakota) contributes a powerful story written for her daughter, "The Spirit Survives." She suggests that although the Indian School cemetery embodies a painful past that continues to haunt the present, it also profoundly bears witness to the courage, resilience, and fortitude of Native peoples down the generations, as well as the enduring strength of their cultures. This resilience, Thomason insists, as well as the catastrophe Carlisle represents, needs to be known and honored. The second reflection is by a survivor, Warren Petoskey (Odawa and Lakota), who arrived in Carlisle for the symposium already painfully aware of the damage inflicted by Indian boarding schools. In "Response to Visiting Carlisle: Experiencing Intergenerational Trauma," Petoskey discusses the dark legacy of Carlisle and similar institutions that continue to affect subsequent generations. Maurice Kenny (Mohawk), who contributed two poems to this volume in part 2, offers his response to the symposium in "The Presence of Ghosts," in which he reflects on the bad spirits that haunt a guesthouse in Carlisle where he was nearly housed, and the contrasting mood and atmosphere of the symposium and the welcoming home where he eventually stayed during his visit. In "A Sacred Place" Sharon O'Brien, who now incorporates the Indian School into her teaching, reflects on the symposium's impact on herself; although she knew about the school's history, she had never previously heard it discussed by descendants of the students, and for her this was a moving as well as enlightening experience. A personal essay, "Carlisle: My Hometown," by Charles Fox, who was born to a white family in Carlisle, traces a local man's growing awareness and sensitivity to the disturbing history of the Indian School. For Daniel Castro Romero Jr., whose people lost track of two of their children (the Lost Ones) for over 130 years, the experience of Carlisle has been devastating. After the "Day of Screams" when the U.S. Fourth Cavalry attacked and killed most of the people in the Lipan Apache village on the Texas-Mexican border, a small hunting group returned to find no sign of the two children—they had disappeared. For well over a century the family never knew what had happened to the Lost Ones, but they were remembered in their oral history and at family reunions, where places were always set for them at the table. Learning from Fear-Segal in 2002 that the children had been brought to the Carlisle Indian School initiated a slow process of closure. This was completed in 2009 when Lipan Apache elders and descendants were able to come to Carlisle to offer Blessings so the spirits of the children were free to go home. Romero is determined that the story of Carlisle should be widely known, discussed, and understood. It was his and other Native people's reactions to the screening of the powerful documentary about the Lipan Apache children, *The Lost Ones: The Long Journey Home* (2011), at the NAISA Annual Meeting, and their insistence that an event should be held in the town of Carlisle, that provided the inspiration and motivation for organizing the Carlisle symposium. Romero believes that we must research and tell the stories of all the children and involve all the nations whose histories are entangled with Carlisle. Only then can the pain and damage inflicted by the school start to be addressed. This too is N. Scott Momaday's hope expressed in the epilogue: "The story of Carlisle is told on the conscience of America. We must hope and believe that there is compassion in the telling."

This too is our hope.

NOTES

1. Philip J. Deloria, *Indians in Unexpected Places* (Lawrence: University of Kansas Press, 2004), 28.
2. Robert M. Utley, "The Ordeal of Plenty Horses," *American Heritage* 26 (December 1974): 16.
3. Gary D. Solis, *The Law of Armed Conflict: International Humanitarian Law in War* (Cambridge: Cambridge University Press, 2010), 33.
4. Carlisle Indian School Student Files, Bureau of Indian Affairs, RG75, National Archives, http://carlisleindian.dickinson.edu/. Brenda J. Child's *Boarding School Seasons: American Indian Families, 1900–1940* (Lincoln: University of Nebraska Press, 1998) is a study that creatively interrogates letters written by students and parents at Haskell Institute, Kansas, and Flandreau School, South Dakota.
5. For full details, viewing, and reflections on the symposium, see "Carlisle Indian School Symposium: Site of Indigenous Histories, Memories, and Reclamations," http://blogs.dickinson.edu/carlisleindianschoolsymposium/ and "Carlisle, PA: Site of Indigenous Histories, Memories, and Reclamations," http://www.carlislesymposium.org.

6. Richard Henry Pratt, *Battlefield and Classroom: Four Decades with the American Indian, 1867–1904*, ed. Robert M. Utley (Lincoln: University of Nebraska Press, 1964), 335.

7. Pratt, *Battlefield and Classroom*, 283.

8. Pratt, *Battlefield and Classroom*, 216.

9. Robert Trennert, "Educating Indian Girls at Nonreservation Boarding Schools, 1878–1920," *Western Historical Quarterly* 13, no. 3 (July 1982): 54.

10. David Wallace Adams, *Education for Extinction: American Indians and the Boarding School Experience, 1875–1928* (Lawrence: University Press of Kansas, 1995), 337.

11. Pratt, *Battlefield and Classroom*, 216.

12. The Susquehannocks lived along the Susquehanna River and its tributaries and were the strongest tribe in the region, well able to withstand the power of the Iroquois Confederacy. Estimated by Europeans to number around six thousand at the start of the seventeenth century, within just a hundred years their numbers had been reduced to fewer than five hundred, due to disease, competition in fur trade wars with the Iroquois, and attacks by whites, the best known being by a group of Scots-Irish known as the Paxton Boys in 1764.

13. Deloria, *Indians in Unexpected Places*, 35–36.

14. Luther Standing Bear, *My People the Sioux* (Lincoln: University of Nebraska Press, 2006), 184.

15. Donald R. Wharton and Brett Lee Shelton, "Let All That Is Indian within You Die!," *Native American Rights Fund Legal Review* 38, no. 2 (Summer/Fall 2013), http://www.narf.org/cases/boarding-school-healing/.

16. Kenneth Lincoln, in *Native American Renaissance* (Berkeley: University of California Press, 1985), was the first to coin this term and to identify N. Scott Momaday as the originator of the movement.

17. "The National Native American Boarding School Healing Coalition," http://www.boardingschoolhealing.org/; Roxanne Dunbar-Ortiz, *An Indigenous Peoples' History of the United States* (Boston: Beacon Press, 2014), 212.

18. Quoted in Dunabar-Ortiz, *Indigenous Peoples' History*, 212.

19. Since 2007 Kevin Gover has been director of the National Museum of the American Indian.

20. Christopher Buck, "'Never Again': Kevin Gover's Apology for the Bureau of Indian Affairs," *Wicazo Sa Review* 21, no. 1 (Spring 2006): 97–126, http://www.jstor.org/stable/4140301.

21. United Nations Declaration on the Rights of Indigenous Peoples (2007) (*Adopted by the General Assembly, A/61/L.67 and Add.1, 13 September 2007*); "General Assembly Adopts Declaration on Rights of Indigenous Peoples; 'Major Step Forward' towards Human Rights for All, Says President," UN

press release, September 13, 2007, http://www.un.org/press/en/2007
/ga10612.doc.htm.

22. Lise Balk King, "A Tree Fell in the Forest: The U.S. Apologized to Native
Americans and No One Heard a Sound," *Indian Country Today*, December 2,
2011, http://indiancountrytodaymedianetwork.com/2011/12/03/tree-fell
-forest-us-apologized-native-americans-and-no-one-heard-sound.

23. R. Christopher Goodwin and Associates, *The Carlisle Indian Industrial School*
(New Orleans: Goodwin and Associates, 1996).

24. Jacqueline Fear-Segal, "Historic Maps of the Carlisle Indian School" (Carlisle PA: Dickinson College, 2000). The words on the marker were decided
through extensive discussion and consultation with descendants: "This
school was the model for a nation-wide system of boarding schools intended
to assimilate American Indians into mainstream culture. Over 10,000 indigenous children attended the school between 1879 and 1918. Despite idealistic
beginnings, the school left a mixed and lasting legacy, creating opportunity
for some students and conflicted identities for others. In this cemetery are
186 graves of students who died while at Carlisle."

25. Jolene Rickard to Jacqueline Fear-Segal, email, November 9, 2011.

26. Adams, *Education for Extinction*; Margaret Archuleta, Brenda J. Child, and
K. Tsianina Lomawaima, eds., *Away from Home: American Indian Boarding
School Experiences* (Phoenix: Heard Museum, 2000); Genevieve Bell, "Tell-
ing Stories out of School: Remembering the Carlisle Indian Industrial School,
1879–1918" (PhD diss., Stanford University, 1998); John Bloom, *To Show What
an Indian Can Do: Sports at Native American Boarding Schools* (Minneapo-
lis: University of Minnesota Press, 2000); Child, *Boarding School Seasons*;
Michael Coleman, *American Indians, the Irish and Government Schooling: A
Comparative Study* (Lincoln: University of Nebraska Press, 2009); Michael
Coleman, *American Indian Children at School, 1850–1930* (Jackson: University Press of Mississippi, 2007); Jacqueline Fear-Segal, *White Man's Club:
Schools, Race, and the Struggle of Indian Acculturation* (Lincoln: University of
Nebraska Press, 2007); Henrietta Mann, *Cheyenne-Arapaho Education, 1871–
1982: A Drama of Human Dimensions about Individuals, Families, Tribes, and
the Federal Government* (Niwot: University Press of Colorado, 1997); J. R. Mill,
Shingwauk's Vision: History of Native Residential School (Toronto: University
of Toronto Press, 1996); John Sheridan Milloy, *A National Crime: The Canadian Government and the Residential School System* (Winnipeg: University of
Manitoba Press, 1999); John Reyhner and Jeanne Eder, *American Indian Education: A History* (Norman: University of Oklahoma Press, 2006); Margaret
Szasz, *Education and the American Indian: The Road to Self-Determination,
1928–1973*, 3rd ed. (Albuquerque: University of New Mexico Press, 1999).

27. Amanda J. Cobb, *Listening to Our Grandmothers' Stories: The Bloomfield Academy for Chickasaw Females, 1852–1949* (Lincoln: University of Nebraska Press, 2000); Clyde Ellis, *To Change Them Forever: Indian Education at the Rainy Mountain Boarding School, 1893–1920* (Norman: University of Oklahoma Press, 1996); Mary Lou Hultgren and Paulett Fairbanks Molin, *To Lead and to Serve: American Indian Education at Hampton Institute, 1878–1923* (Hampton: Virginia Foundation for the Humanities, 1989); Sally Hyer, *One House, One Voice, One Heart: Native American Education at the Santa Fe Indian School,* (Santa Fe: Museum of New Mexico Press, 1990); Jean A. Keller, *Empty Beds: Indian Student Health at Sherman Institute* (East Lansing: Michigan State University Press, 2002); Tsianina Lomawaima, *They Called It Prairie Light: The Story of Chilocco Indian School* (Lincoln: University of Nebraska Press, 1994); Donald F. Lindsey, *Indians at Hampton Institute, 1877–1923* (Urbana: University of Illinois Press, 1995); Devon A. Mihesuah, *Cultivating the Rosebuds: The Education of Women at the Cherokee Female Seminary, 1851–1909* (Urbana: University of Illinois Press, 1993); Dorothy R. Parker, *Phoenix Indian School: The Second Half-Century* (Tucson: University of Arizona Press, 1996); Scott Riney, *The Rapid City Indian School, 1898–1933* (Norman: University of Oklahoma Press, 1999); Robert A. Trennert Jr., *The Phoenix Indian School: Forced Assimilation in Arizona, 1891–1935* (Norman: University of Oklahoma Press, 1988).

28. Lars Anderson, *Carlisle vs. Army: Jim Thorpe, Dwight Eisenhower, Pop Warner, and the Forgotten Story of Football's Greatest Battle* (New York: Random House, 2008); Kate Byford, *Native American Son: The Life and Sporting Legend of Jim Thorpe* (Lincoln: University of Nebraska Press, 2012); Sally Jenkins, *The Real All Americans: The Game That Changed a Game, a People, a Nation* (New York: Broadway Books, 2008); John S. Steckbeck, *Fabulous Redmen: The Carlisle Indian and Their Famous Football Teams* (Harrisburg PA: J. Horace McFarland, 1951).

29. Genevieve Bell's excellent but unpublished dissertation is based on extensive and systematized research on the Carlisle student record files in the National Archives. Bell, "Telling Stories out of School."

30. Fiona Bateman and Lionel Pilkington, eds., *Studies in Settler Colonialism* (London: Palgrave Macmillan, 2011); Walter L. Hixson, *American Settler Colonialism: A History* (London: Palgrave Macmillan, 2013).

31. Patrick Wolfe, *Settler Colonialism and the Transformation of Anthropology: The Politics and Poetics of an Ethnographic Event* (London: Bloomsbury, 1999), 1.

32. Coleman, *American Indians, the Irish and Government Schooling*; Annie E. Coombes, ed., *Rethinking Settler Colonialism: History and Memory in Austra-*

lia, Canada, Aotearoa, New Zealand and South Africa (Manchester: Manchester University Press, 2006); Margaret D. Jacobs, *White Mother to a Dark Race: Settler Colonialism, Maternalism, and the Removal of Indigenous Children in the American West and Australia, 1880–1940* (Lincoln: University of Nebraska Press, 2009); Linda Tuhiwai Smith, *Decolonizing Methodologies: Research and Indigenous Peoples* (London: Zed Books, 1999); Andrea Smith, *Conquest: Sexual Violence and American Indian Genocide* (Boston: South End Press, 2005).

33. Andrew Woolford, *The Benevolent Experiment: Indigenous Boarding Schools, Genocide and Redress in Canada and the United States* (Lincoln: University of Nebraska Press, 2015).

34. Michel-Rolph Trouillot, *Silencing the Past: Power and the Production of History* (Boston: Beacon Press, 1995).

35. Luther Standing Bear, *My People the Sioux* (1928); Luther Standing Bear, *Land of the Spotted Eagle* (1933); modern editions have been published by University of Nebraska Press. Zitkala-Ša, "The School Days of an Indian Girl," in *American Indian Stories, Legends, and Other Writings* (New York: Penguin Books, 2003), 87–103, first published in 1900.

36. *Stiya, a Carlisle Indian Girl at Home; Founded on the Author's Actual Observations* (Cambridge MA: Riverside Press, 1891).

37. Trouillot, *Silencing the Past*, 151.

38. Trouillot, *Silencing the Past*, 26.

39. Jacqueline Fear-Segal, *White Man's Club: Schools, Race, and the Struggle of Indian Acculturation* (Lincoln: University of Nebraska Press, 2007), 255–82.

40. From Carlisle Student Records in the National Archives it can be estimated that the Delawares sent approximately thirty-three students and the Shawnees approximately sixty-eight.

41. Native American Graves Protection and Repatriation Act, Pub. L. No. 101-601, November 16, 1990, Section 2, "Definitions."

Welcome

Drum and welcoming song by Daniel Castro Romero Jr. and Richard Gonzalez (Lipan Apaches)

Welcoming words by Susan D. Rose

We gather here today to honor those who have come before us and to acknowledge those who will come behind us, to recognize and honor those around us and beside us. We give thanks to the elders who have traveled far to be with us and to share their wisdom. . . .

Welcome to all of you who have come today. With humility, we honor the people and the nations—the Susquehannocks, the Delawares and the Lenapes, the Iroquois—who knew these lands well before Columbus touched these shores, long before the settlers came.

We welcome you to share with us and one another your stories and your vision—to teach us as we teach one another. We come here not only with open arms but with open hearts, and eyes, and ears—wanting to listen and to share—though at times it may be difficult. Let us hear one another into speech—to acknowledge painful pasts, to appreciate the accomplishments and challenges, and to envision more hopeful and peaceful futures.

Welcoming flute song by Brian Frejo (Pawnee/Seminole)

Seneca Thanksgiving Prayer "We Are One" by Peter Jemison (Seneca)

The People

Today we have gathered, and we see that the cycles of life continue. We have been given the duty to live in balance and harmony with each other and all living things. So now, we bring our minds together as one as we give greetings and thanks to each other as People.

Now our minds are one.

The Earth Mother

We are all thankful to our Mother, the Earth, for she gives us all that we need for life. She supports our feet as we walk about upon her. It gives us joy that she continues to care for us as she has from the beginning of time. To our Mother, we send greetings and thanks.

Now our minds are one.

The Waters

We give thanks to all the Waters of the world for quenching our thirst and providing us with strength. Water is life. We know its power in many forms—waterfalls and rain, mists and streams, rivers and oceans. With one mind, we send greetings and thanks to the spirit of Water.

Now our minds are one.

The Fish

We turn our minds to all the Fish life in the water. They were instructed to cleanse and purify the water. They also give themselves to us as food. We are grateful that we can still find pure water. So, we turn now to the Fish and send our greetings and thanks.

Now our minds are one.

The Plants

Now we turn toward the vast fields of Plant life. As far as the eye can see, the Plants grow, working many wonders. They sustain many life forms. With our minds gathered together, we give thanks and look forward to seeing Plant life for many generations to come.

And now our minds are one.

The Food Plants

With one mind, we turn to honor and thank all the Food Plants we harvest from the garden. Since the beginning of time, the grains, vegetables, beans, and berries have helped the people survive. Many other living things draw strength from them, too. We gather all the Food Plants together as one and send them a greeting and thanks.

Now our minds are one.

The Medicine Herbs

Now we turn to all the Medicine Herbs of the world. From the beginning, they were instructed to take away sickness. They are always waiting and ready to heal us. We are happy there are still among us those special few who remember how to use these plants for healing. With one mind, we send greetings and thanks to the Medicines and to the keepers of the Medicines.

Now our minds are one.

The Animals

We gather our minds together to send greetings and thanks to all the Animal life in the world. They have many things to teach us as people. We see them near our homes and in the deep forest. We are glad they are still here, and we hope that they will always be us. With one mind, we greet and thank the Animal life.

Now our minds are one.

The Trees

We now turn our thoughts to the Trees. The Earth has many families of Trees who have their own instructions and uses. Some provide shelter and shade, others with fruit, beauty, and other useful things. Many peoples of the world use a Tree as a symbol of peace and strength. With one mind, we greet and thank the Tree life.

Now our minds are one.

The Birds

We put our minds together as one and thank all the Birds who move and fly about over our heads. The Creator gave them beautiful songs. Each day they remind us to enjoy and appreciate life. The Eagle was chosen to be their leader. To all the Birds—from the smallest to the largest—we send our joyful greetings and thanks.

Now our minds are one.

The Four Winds

We are all thankful to the powers we know as the Four Winds. We hear their voices in the moving air as they refresh us and purify the air we breathe. They help to bring the change of seasons. From the four directions they come, bringing us messages and giving us strength. With one mind, we send our greetings and thanks to the Four Winds.

Now our minds are one.

The Thunderers

Now we turn to the West where our Grandfathers, the Thunder Beings, live. With lightning and thundering voices, they bring with them the water that renews life. We bring our minds together as one to send greetings and thanks to our Grandfathers, the Thunderers.

Now our minds are one.

The Sun

We now send greetings and thanks to our eldest Brother, the Sun. Each day without fail he travels the sky from east to west, bringing the light of a new day. He is the source of all the fires of life. With one mind, we send greetings and thanks to our Brother, the Sun.

Now our minds are one.

Grandmother Moon

We put our minds together and give thanks to our oldest Grandmother, the Moon, who lights the nighttime sky. She is the leader of women all over the world, and she governs the movement of the ocean tides. By her changing face we measure time, and it is the Moon who watches over the arrival of children here on Earth. With one mind, we send greetings and thanks to our Grandmother, the Moon.

Now our minds are one.

The Stars

We give thanks to the Stars who are spread across the sky like jewelry. We see them in the night, helping the Moon light the darkness and bringing dew to the gardens and growing things. When we travel at night, they guide us home. With our minds gathered together as one, we send greetings and thanks to all the Stars.

Now our minds are one.

Fig. 1. Entrance to Carlisle Indian School from Pratt Avenue, c. 1915. Photo by Maynard J. Hoover. Cumberland County Historical Society, Carlisle PA. 304C.

The Enlightened Teachers

We gather our minds to greet and thank the Enlightened Teachers who have come to help throughout the ages. When we forget how to live in harmony, they remind us of the way we were instructed to live as people. With one mind, we send greetings and thanks to these caring Teachers.

Now our minds are one.

The Creator

Now we turn our thoughts to the Creator, or Great Spirit, and send greetings and thanks for all the gifts of Creation. Everything we need to live a good life is here on this Mother Earth. For all the love that is still around us, we gather our minds together as one and send our choicest words of greetings and thanks to the Creator.

Now our minds are one.

Closing Words

We have now arrived at the place where we end our words. Of all the things we have named, it was not our intention to leave anything out. If something was forgotten, we leave it to each individual to send such greetings and thanks in their own way.

And now our minds are one.

Part 1   A Sacred and Storied Place

1

The Stones at Carlisle

N. SCOTT MOMADAY (KIOWA)

Here are six rows of children. How
Symmetrical the gray array.
The names are dim and distant now.
We come and go, and here they stay.
Please pray they rest, and bless each name,
Then reckon innocence and shame.

Some of the stones bear no names. They are the tombs of the unknown
children, those who died here between 1879 and 1918 during the tenure of
the Carlisle Indian Industrial School. They were American Indian children,
and they came from far away, from places with American names—Piqua,
Chinle, Tahlequah, Bimidji, Nespelem, Oraibi. Moreover, in the course of
time and renovation the graves were removed from their original placement; the current tombstones are new, and many no longer mark the graves
of those whose names they bear. The "tombs of the unknown children"
is a sad but accurate designation.

Names are especially important in Native American culture. Names and
being are thought to be indivisible. One who bears no name cannot truly
be said to exist, for one has being in his name. His name stands for him; it
is his shield. I am Tsoai-talee, therefore I am. In this context we see how
serious is the loss of one's name. In the case of the tombstones at Carlisle
we are talking about the crime of neglect and negation. We are talking not
only about the theft of identity, but indeed the theft of essential being.

I am Tsoai-talee. "Rock tree boy." I am Tsoai-talee of the Kiowa nation.
I was given that name by Pohd-lohk, also called "Kiowa George," an elder,
a chief, and an arrow maker. Before I was a year old my parents took me
to Devil's Tower, Wyoming, on the apron of the Black Hills. It is a sacred
place in Kiowa tradition. Tsoai, the Rock Tree, is a monolith that rises

above the timbered banks of the Belle Fousche River. In conformation it closely resembles the stump of a tree, but it is an immensity that has to be seen to be believed. It rises a thousand feet from base to summit. It is a mile around at the base. When the Kiowas migrated from the Yellowstone some hundreds of years ago, they camped in the Black Hills and of course encountered the rock tree. They must have been struck dumb. What was it? How did it come to be? How was it to be accommodated to the human condition? A story must be told. From the time Man acquired language, all the answers to all the questions in the world have been contained in story.

Eight children were there at play, seven sisters and their brother. The boy pretended to be a bear, and he chased his sisters, who pretended to be afraid. They ran through the woods. Then suddenly a strange and terrible thing happened. The boy was turned into a real bear. The sisters were truly terrified, and they ran for their lives, the bear after them. They came upon a very large tree stump. The tree spoke to them, "Climb upon me, and I will save you." They did so, and the tree began to grow. The bear came to the tree, but the sisters were beyond its reach. The bear reared against the tree and scored the bark all around with its claws. The sisters were borne into the sky, and they became the stars of the Big Dipper.

For a moment think of the story, and think of what purpose it serves. It explains the origin and being of Tsoai, the great monolith that is strange and unique and profound in nature. Never again will it be the unspeakable unknown. By means of the story has Tsoai come into the sphere of Man's perception. It now belongs to us. Moreover the story relates us to the stars. We have kinsmen in the night sky. Like the sisters we are borne into infinity and immortality. Do you hear what I am saying about the story? Story is the farthest reach of the imagination. It is the breath of God.

And the story of Tsoai is the story of my name. I am Tsoai-talee. I am the boy who turned into a bear.

We have come together in a sacred and storied place, a place made sacred by sacrifice, and by the investment of men, women, and especially children in a critical chapter of American history. Isn't it a stroke of irony that another sacred place is nearby, one where the very fate of our nation was determined? These footnotes, these chapters in their respective ways, define the American experience. Carlisle, in a more subtle and obscure story than that of Gettysburg, is a place-name among place-names on a chronological map that spans time and the continent, names such as San Salvador, Mankato, Canyon de Chelly, the Little Bighorn, Sand Creek, Tenochticlan, and Wounded Knee, among others.[1]

But what truly distinguishes Carlisle is a politics of ambiguity and a policy of moral confusion. What are we to think of Richard Henry Pratt? In a biographical sketch on the Internet there is this sentence: "The legacy of Pratt's boarding school programs is felt by modern Native American tribes, where he is often remembered not as a champion for Native American rights but as leader of a cultural genocide that targeted children." The founder and superintendent of the Carlisle Indian Industrial School is an enigma, and a frightening one at that. His motto, "Kill the Indian and save the man," suggests the tension of a wounded intelligence. This curious formula is at best a contradiction in terms. Man and Indian are separated by a gratuitous bias that sadly informs the whole record of white-Indian relations. The Indian is not a man; he is an inferior creature who can become a man only if his natural identity is destroyed. The bias is given a similar expression in the old byword, "The only good Indian is a dead Indian." If Richard Henry Pratt was possessed of good intentions in his missionary zeal, they were negated by the imposition of mottos and clichés.

We must imagine Carlisle. It is a kind of mythic memory in the American mind. Perhaps it is an extension of the Wild West, which is so gaudy and predictable in the dime novels and stock Hollywood films. Here we have yet again the never-ending conflict between the cavalry and the Indians, removed to the Wild East. The crucial difference, of course, is that the Indians who take the field are not fabled warriors like Geronimo or Crazy Horse or Sitting Bull. They are children. They are those who lie beneath the stones of Carlisle.

Imagine the children. They have no choice and no advantage whatsoever. They are helpless and afraid. They are brought here by force, and in a matter of days they are dispossessed of their names, their dress, their religion, their language, their childhood, their culture, their identity, their human being.

How could they live through such an experience? As a testament to human will and endurance, many did; it was no doubt a bare survival. There was a curious and perhaps unforeseeable backlash to the boarding school experiment. In it there were the seeds of Indian unification.

Diversity has always been a principal element of the Indian world. The children who came to Carlisle were divided from each other in obvious and significant ways. They came from many different worlds, they spoke many different languages, they had different systems of belief and ceremony, different histories, economies, philosophies, political and military organizations—in short, different ways of seeing themselves and the world around them. Carlisle inadvertently created the necessity of ethnic integration, of bonding, of being Indian. It was the mere matrix of survival.

In her landmark study, *White Man's Club*, Jacqueline Fear-Segal considers the voice of the Man-on-the-Bandstand, an instrument that was played relentlessly on the hearing of the Carlisle children.[2] I quote, "Although he worked to furnish the children with an inner voice of conscience, he could never be sure that this would not be drowned out by older, deeper Indian voices."

The "older, deeper Indian voices" are those that were heard exclusively in the hearts and minds of the Carlisle children. They were the voices of tradition and tenure, a tenure of thirty thousand years on the North American continent, indeed of origin in the mist of timelessness. The voices were spoken in a hundred different languages, but they were universally intelligible in the inviolable underworld of the children's essential existence. They were the "they say" of the Native spirit.

Haw
They say
They say there was Raven
They say there was Raven his talons in the sun
And light splashed upon the stones
And light grew up among the stones
They say the cold informed it
It could not be broken
But they say the light fell from Raven's hands
Light was broken and rang upon the stones
And then cold splinters of light could be heard
Ringing and popping in the six directions
Light broke upon the darkness even as
Words broke upon the silence

First light first words
Haw
That is what they say
The sight and sound of origin
The north and night of origin and all became
They say
And it was made sacred in the saying
They say
We have always had words they say
Always
Always
Words
They say
They say
First light
First words
They say
Raven sang a throaty song
Shhh shhh shhh
Breaks the dawn in stillness
Shhh shhh shhh
In wondrous colors
Shist
The eldest wind lowing
Shhh shhh shhh
In wondrous colors
Seal
The first sky like sealskin
A hide scraped for drawing
A plane luminous with glitter
Drawn with light
Shhh shhh shhh
In wondrous colors
Mica
Then were mountains thrown away
On the sky standing still forever

Cradling the dawn
Drawn with light
Berries bleeding on the sun
Shhh shhh shhh
In wondrous colors
Salmon
A sky of silver and violet
Shot through with red and orange
Raven was not only ancient but original, of the
Very essence of origin, having being before all others.
Raven had heft and sheen, had the Northern Dawn
And lightning about him. Above all, Raven had spirit,
Was spirit, the force that held all the threads of
The world together in the weaving of Creation, in a whole
Design, in a balance of beauty and being. And to these
Were added mischief and magic. For these were threads
In the fabric of origin. These also were things of the
Shaman. In the name of Raven there is proportion, there is
Beauty, there is meaning, there is mischief, and there is
Magic. Shaman is the Raven's name. Raven is one with the
Name, the Word. For words, like Raven, wheel and hover and
Soar and glide. They soothe and rend. They turn and strike.
They cast shadows that cannot be caught and held. In patterns of
Shade on the snow, Raven plays with foxes.
Therefore
We praise the Raven
We fear the Raven
We revere the Raven
For his knowing
For his guile
   Oo ae la keshla
   Oo ae la keshla
   Oo ae la keshla
   Oo ae la keshla
For his guile
Haw

Names, voices, imagination, innocence, and shame. These are among the elements of the story of Carlisle. Carlisle is a storied place.

I wrote a play about Carlisle, titled *The Moon in Two Windows*. I would like to tell you a little about the play and then give you an excerpt from it, as a closing to my introduction for this collection.

It is a screenplay, and so the locations are varied. Most of the action takes place at the school. The principle characters are Richard Henry Pratt and Luther Standing Bear. Jim Thorpe plays a part, as do several other well-known Indians. A little girl, Grey Calf, called "Grass," is a ghost. She has died on the train that brought the first children to Carlisle. Pratt is horrified that Grass has died, and in his panic he orders his aide Etahdleau to bury the body secretly. Etahdleau does so, but he keeps her doll and eyeglasses. All the children know what has happened, but when Grass comes among then from time to time as a ghost, they accept her without question.

There is a scene in which Luther and Etahdleau talk:

LUTHER: Have you seen Grass?

ETAHDLEAU: Not today.

LUTHER: You know, I thought I saw her in the room tonight, earlier, when we were in the meeting—came in and stand in the darkness for just a minute or two. And then she was gone.

ETAHDLEAU: She is everywhere, and nowhere.

LUTHER: She does not see very well, I think.

ETAHDLEAU: I know. I have her glasses. I will give them to her.

Then we see Indian Field, the athletic field at Carlisle. It is a beautiful, bright day, and in the distance two figures—a man and a child, holding hands. Now and then the little girl skips and hops, and we hear the faint sound of laughter. We approach a little closer, and the little girl is in her tattered dress, and the sun glints upon her glasses. The man takes both of the girl's hands and swings her round and round.

In a later scene Pratt, late at night, is at home. He has fallen asleep in his easy chair. He twitches, apparently dreaming. A figure in silhouette appears in the doorway. He looks up, blinking.

PRATT: Who's there? . . . you? (*It is Grass. She stares at him through her Glasses. The light is such that the lenses reflect it. Otherwise She is in shadow, dimly visible.*) What is it? What do you want?

GRASS: I have come to forgive you.

PRATT: Forgive? Me? What are you . . . talking about?

GRASS: You dishonored my death. You threw me away. You buried me without a name, as if I had not lived. It was shameful.

Pratt is in a cold sweat. He does not know if he is awake or if he is dreaming.

PRATT: No, no . . . I don't know . . . what you're talking about.

GRASS: It doesn't matter. I have earned my death. I am going home. I forgive you.

Pratt blinks. This is beyond him. His expression goes from fear to anger.

PRATT: You forgive me? Why, why, how dare you! I don't want your forgiveness. I have done nothing to be forgiven! How dare you!

Grass is perfectly calm, serene.

GRASS: The warriors and the chiefs have brought medicine for me. And they will soon bring medicine for you. Do not be afraid. Be at peace. They will bring you sage and sweetgrass. When they come, and you see them, how beautiful and fierce they are in their wet paint, you will grow peaceful, won't you? When you hear their cries and their honor songs, when you hear the beating of their horses' hooves, you will be peaceful, won't you? And when they touch you and then let you go, you will be peaceful, won't you? I forgive you. Aiyee!

And she is gone.

In the final scene, Pratt and Luther come together for the last time. Following the Carlisle–Army football game of 1912 they meet in New York City to visit and reminisce. Luther is a grown man. Pratt has grown old.

PRATT: Remember . . . well, you remember.

LUTHER: I remember it all, Captain. Everything. I do remember. I remember, as a little boy on the train, I saw the moon in the window where I sat. And then, a few minutes later, I saw the moon in the window on the other side of the train. It seemed to me that the moon had flown across the sky. I was frightened.

PRATT: Isn't that funny? It happens to me, too. There are many turns in the road, isn't that so? You had been turned around without knowing it. You were disoriented.

LUTHER: There was more to it than that, I think. The moon in two windows. It is a strange thing, somehow, an unnatural thing. What you Christians call a miracle.

PRATT: What is natural, I wonder. The natural world you lived in was hopeless. The miracle was that you escaped it. I like to think that I had something to do with bringing about that miracle. With the help of others—and with God's help above all—I saved those I could.

LUTHER: Richard, have you been to the cemetery?

PRATT: What? The cemetery?

LUTHER: At the school. The graves of the children. Many people go there now. They bring flowers and ribbons—sometimes tobacco and cornmeal, pollen. Have you gone there?

PRATT: You have to understand that the young people who died there were beyond help. They were dying before they left the camps. We must think of the ones who didn't die, the many hundreds who lived. They are healthy, happy human beings. And they produce healthy, happy children of their own. They are well-adjusted Americans. They are . . .

LUTHER: Civilized.

PRATT: Yes, indeed, civilized. (*Pratt slowly gets to his feet. He has grown feeble with age.*) I must go, Luther. Shake my hand. It was wonderful to see you again.

Luther stands and takes his hand.

LUTHER: Goodnight, Captain Pratt, and goodbye.

Dissolve to: Exterior, Arlington National Cemetery. Day. Luther stands at Pratt's grave. On the simple headstone are the words:

RICHARD HENRY PRATT

ERECTED IN LOVING MEMORY

Exterior. Carlisle cemetery. Day. Luther and his son Stone walk among the stones. They are the only ones there.

LUTHER (VO): The Indian Industrial School at Carlisle was a kind of laboratory in which our hearts were tested. We were all shaped by that experience. Some of us were destroyed, and some were made stronger. I believe that; I know it to be true. Captain Pratt, and others after him, came for the children and took them away. For every one of them, for every single child, it was a passage into darkness. It was a kind of quest, not a quest for glory, but a quest for survival. They were all brave; they did a brave thing. Those who died on the journey were especially brave, and their bravery is signed here in stone. Theirs is the sacrifice that makes sacred this ground. But they were all brave, those who lived and those who died; all were marked by Carlisle. We were children who ventured into the unknown. And if again my father told me to go away from my Indian home into an alien world that I could not have imagined, I would do it. I would go, as all of us did, with all the love and courage in my heart. I would do a brave thing.

Father and son go out of the cemetery and walk on the grounds of the school. As they approach Indian Field, Stone pulls at his father's hand, and they stop and stand still. Stone points to two figures, distant on the field, a man and a child. The man takes the child by both hands and swings her round and round.

END OF PLAY

A footnote: Etahdleau, who, as a specter, swings Grass round and round, was a Kiowa. He was one of the prisoners who were taken to Fort Marion in chains. He went with Pratt to found the Carlisle Indian Industrial School and became Pratt's trusted friend and assistant. He was Luther Standing Bear's friend, too. He married at Carlisle and returned to his Indian home, where he died of a disease that must have been incipient at Carlisle. He was my kinsman.

I think of Luther's final speech in the play, and these words stand out in my mind: Carlisle. *They came for the children and took them away. . . . It was a passage into darkness.*

Fig. 2. Indian School cemetery after blessing ceremony for Jack Mather (his name is incorrectly inscribed on stone as "Martha"), 2009. Photo by Steve Brouwer.

With love, humility, and remembrance, we come among the stones at Carlisle.

Aho.

Notes

1. These are all names of places where whites committed terrible atrocities against indigenous populations of the Americas.
2. The Man-on-the-Bandstand was the editorial persona of the school newspaper, the *Indian Helper*, which gave advice and instruction to the children. The bandstand stood at the center of campus, and the all-knowing imaginary man was actually Marianna Burgess, a white woman who ran the print shop at the school and edited the *Indian Helper*. The quote is from Jacqueline Fear-Segal, *White Man's Club: Schools, Race, and the Struggle of Indian Acculturation* (Lincoln: University of Nebraska Press, 2007), 218.

2

Before Carlisle

The Lower Susquehanna Valley as Contested Native Space

CHRISTOPHER J. BILODEAU

The establishment of Carlisle's infamous Indian School in 1879 ushered in a new era in Indian-white relations in the mid-Atlantic region. But Carlisle, Pennsylvania, and its surrounding area has a deep Native history, as archaeological research shows that Indians lived in the Susquehanna River Valley for at least eleven thousand years before the influx of European settlers.[1] The valley's inhabitants, the Susquehannocks, at various times lived, traded, and warred with surrounding Native groups such as the Lenni Lenapes to the east, the Piscataway and Mattawomans to the south, and the powerful Iroquois Confederacy to the north. As Europeans began to settle in the region in the early seventeenth century, their presence and goods attracted indigenous groups for diplomatic engagement and trade, creating new tensions and exacerbating old ones. The European colonies of New Netherland, New Sweden, New York, Maryland, Virginia, and eventually Pennsylvania would irrevocably change the dynamic of the history of the Susquehanna River Valley, drawing to the valley Native nations like the Nanticokes, Shawnees, and Conoys and creating a region of striking Native diversity, intricate military alliances, and complicated trading arrangements.

But in the early decades of the eighteenth century, Europeans increasingly gained the power to dispossess Indians of their lands in the valley, often with the aid of the dominant group in the wider region, the Iroquois. Using intimidation, forced migration, or, as seen most glaringly in the aftermath of the Seven Years' War, outright destruction and murder, Europeans rapidly turned the valley into an area hostile to Native peoples. An intratribal alliance of Indians on the Ohio frontier coalesced in the 1760s to foment an uprising—known as Pontiac's Rebellion—to rid the region of white settlers, but it failed to stem white settlement or the virtual eradication of the region's Native peoples. Even if pockets of Natives continued to live in the region, their communities had been devastated, and their stories became increasingly invisible and ignored in the records.

The Carlisle Indian School casts a dark shadow across the area's past, obscuring both the thousands of years when it was Native space and the much shorter period of Native and imperial interaction. Viewing the Indian School within the broader history of the region enables us not only to explore and understand the complex history of Native relations in the Susquehanna Valley after the arrival of white settlers, but also to trace the area's transformation from Native to white space. Native populations of the area were totally dispossessed of their lands, which were progressively taken by white settlers. This dispossession was accompanied by a narrative of Indian extinction that resounded throughout white American society during the nineteenth and twentieth centuries.[2]

Pennsylvania was once Indian Country. Paleo-Indian artifacts dug up along the banks and islands of the Susquehanna River provide tangible archaeological evidence of the material cultures and movements of the peoples who once lived there.[3] They tell us that the southern area of the Susquehanna River Valley was inhabited for a short period of time by a relatively unknown group, labeled by archaeologists the "Shenk's Ferry People," who were either removed or absorbed by a more powerful nation, the Susquehannocks. These Indians lived on the northern branch of the Susquehanna River until at least 1550, but sometime before 1570 they left their villages and migrated southward to what is now Lancaster County, Pennsylvania.[4] Iroquoian speakers of Mohawk origin, the Susquehannocks had separated from the Mohawks in roughly 1300 AD. Most scholars have argued that the Iroquois Confederacy of what is now upstate New York—made up of the Senecas, Cayugas, Onondagas, Oneidas, and Mohawks—pushed them southward, while others have suggested that sixteenth-century European explorers and traders drew them to the region of the Chesapeake. Whatever the reasons for their migration, the Susquehannocks began to spread up and down the Susquehanna River, creating small villages and at times clashing with other Native groups in the mid-Atlantic region. During the late sixteenth and early seventeenth centuries, three to four thousand Susquehannocks inhabited between nine and twelve palisaded villages on both sides of the Susquehanna. Women farmed corn, beans, squash, and tobacco, while men fished and traded. By the 1640s their population had reached about six thousand.[5]

Numerous other groups moved through the region, however, as the river provided routes for trade and communication. From the north, the Iroquois traveled down the river to trade and fight with Indians to the south. From the east, the Lenni Lenapes inhabited the southern Delaware River Valley while the Munsees inhabited the valley in the north. North of those groups lived the Mahicans.[6] Various Native groups to the west in the Ohio River Valley, such as the Shawnees and the Eries, accessed the Susquehanna by smaller branches of water and portages, as did other groups even further west.[7] The Piscataway Indians inhabited the Potomac River Valley, and the Nanticokes resided on the eastern shore of Chesapeake Bay. All told, the Susquehanna Valley was a space of significant Native diversity and movement.

When Europeans settlers arrived in North America during the early seventeenth century, population movement on the Susquehanna would increase. English explorers and settlers traveled into the mid-Atlantic region starting in the 1580s and settled on the James River in 1607. The French sailed down the St. Lawrence River and founded Québec in 1608. The Dutch established Fort Orange in New Netherland in 1624, trading extensively with the Mohawks. The Swedes created New Sweden on the Delaware River in 1638 on lands claimed by the Dutch, and Maryland was created by George Calvert, the First Baron Baltimore, in 1632, with colonists arriving in 1634. All of these groups, Native and European, shared in the history of the lands where Carlisle was eventually located.[8]

From their river valley villages, the Susquehannocks traded and fought with many of these different peoples throughout the ensuing decades, but they also worked to create alliances with European traders to guarantee their access to knives, axes, and guns, the riches brought by trading pelts.[9] In the 1620s and 1630s the Susquehannocks attempted to gain a monopoly on trade goods from the Swedes on the Delaware River and clashed with the Lenapes, only resolving their differences by 1638.[10] But the Susquehannocks and the region's other Natives were no longer hunting simply for subsistence but to supply the European market, and they began to confront a shortage of animals. They moved outside their traditional hunting lands to find more furs, and so they quickly came into conflict with other Native groups. By the 1640s it was clear that access to both European goods and the furs they could trade for them was fueling conflicts between competing Natives in the region.[11] However, the Susquehannocks remained very powerful and even built a massive central town near what is now Columbia, Pennsylvania, with three thousand people living in a palisaded area of thirteen acres. As long as they had access to Swedish traders and the arms and goods they provided, the Susquehannocks were the most formidable group—Native or European—in the Susquehanna Valley region.[12]

However, competition from the north proved troublesome for their dominance in trade. As they were trying to establish themselves as middlemen between New Sweden and western Native peoples who had little access to European goods, the Mohawks were trying to do the same thing with New Netherland at Fort Orange, and the growing tensions between the two Indian nations both reflected and nurtured the rivalry between the two European colonies.[13] The Iroquois Confederacy would eventually war with almost every Native nation in the Northeast as they attempted to gain control over the fur trade and replace their mounting losses with captives. Recognizing the difficulty of fighting such a formidable enemy to the north and facing an increasingly powerful Maryland to the south, the Susquehannocks brokered peace with the colony of Maryland in 1652.[14]

But officials in New Netherland proceeded to revamp the geopolitical situation in the region in a way that brought the Susquehannocks within their diplomatic and economic fold. In Europe the Dutch went to war with England in 1652, and New Netherland officials therefore wanted to keep tensions high between English Maryland and the Susquehannocks. Additionally, they watched the Swedes confiscate lands along the Delaware River that they believed were part of their colony. Therefore they attacked and evicted the Swedes from the Delaware Valley in 1655, ending forever Sweden's colonial ambitions in North America, and created New Amstel at what is now New Castle, Delaware. This act devastated the Susquehannocks, as it removed their most reliable and trustworthy trading partner and source of European goods. Fearful of Dutch anger if they allied themselves solely with Maryland, the Susquehannocks were forced to negotiate for peace with New Netherland in 1658. That peace ameliorated relations between the Susquehannocks and the Mohawks, who began to work together against other nations, even the other tribes within the Iroquois Confederacy. They succeeded impressively between 1658 and 1662, as the Susquehannocks used arms acquired from the Mohawks both to fight the other four nations of the Iroquois and take control of Delaware Valley trade with the now dominant Dutch.[15]

But the Susquehannocks had difficulty maintaining this position throughout the 1660s as Native conflicts overlapped and conflated with European imperial rivalries, especially the rivalry between the Dutch and the English. Furs, especially beaver fur, which was highly valued in Europe as the raw material for making hats, became the first North American trade commodity. Competition for this trade provoked alliances and brutal wars between Native nations and the different European nations, as well as population displacements and annihilation. The diplomatic and military pressures on not only the Susquehannocks but all of the region's Native peoples were relentless and were periodically intensified by epidemic disease. Smallpox, brought by Europeans, hit the Susquehannocks in 1661 and the Iroquois in 1662. Its spread temporarily stemmed non-Mohawk Iroquois depredations against the Susquehannocks, but the Iroquois Confederacy clearly was reaching its limit in its capacity for war. When eight hundred Senecas, Cayugas, and Onondagas besieged the Susquehannocks' home fort in May 1663, they retreated after only one week. That battle would prove to be the last large Iroquois attack on the Susquehannocks, as rounds of smallpox continued to ravage both nations. Simultaneously, Mohawks attacked the Sokoquis in what is now western New England, only to suffer retaliations from Indians of that region, and the Oneidas attacked Indian groups in the Chesapeake Bay region in 1660, angering Maryland officials. But even as the separate members of the Iroquois Confederacy staggered under this level of combat, their Susquehannock rivals also found it difficult to remain in the field, burdened by the constant fighting.[16]

Nonetheless that fighting continued and, in fact, was exacerbated by imperial transformations in Europe. Louis XIV came of age in France in 1663 and immediately took an aggressive posture toward the enemies of New France, and the English temporarily conquered New Netherlands in 1664. Both of these events severely limited the possibilities for European trade and alliance for many Indian groups in the region. The Mohawks, who had relied so much on Fort Orange in their economic and political life, found their world transformed. They contacted the English immediately for talks of peace and found the new governor of New York, Richard Nicolls, receptive. But other Indian groups continued their enmity toward the Iroquois, and 1666 proved to be a year of great violence. The Mahicans, newly supplied allies of New France, rekindled war with the Mohawks. The French joined the Dutch in the renewed Anglo-Dutch War by razing Mohawk towns and destroying their supplies. And the Susquehannocks played their part in the bloodshed, annihilating an Onondaga army. Governor Nicolls attempted to create a pan-colonial, pan-Indian peace, but failed, and the entire Iroquois Confederacy feared decimation. In 1670 the Onondagas wanted revenge against the Susquehannocks so badly that they murdered a Susquehannock leader on a peace mission to the Cayugas. An expanding European market system, Native competition for a share in this trade, and imperial rivalries had all combined to recast loyalties and power structures of the Delaware and Susquehanna river valleys by the middle of the seventeenth century.[17]

All this warfare had crippled Indian groups throughout the northeast, the Susquehannocks included. So even as the Iroquois sustained staggering losses, their enemies the Susquehannocks could not take advantage. That situation allowed English colonial officials in Maryland and, especially, in New York to push ahead with their various and at times conflicting imperial agendas for control of lands and waters of the Delaware and Susquehanna regions.

In the 1670s Maryland officials attempted to secure their vision for the region first but would find only disappointment. The colony's leadership came up with a two-pronged strategy to enhance their status and power. First, colonial officials invited the Susquehannocks to move from the Susquehanna Valley to Maryland lands, away from Iroquois depredations. To those officials' delight, the exhausted Susquehannocks agreed, moving into an abandoned Piscataway fort at the first falls on the Potomac River in February 1675. That created the possibility for the second diplomatic maneuver, approaching the Iroquois with talks of peace. If they achieved that, Calvert and Maryland's leadership hoped they would have clear access to Delaware Bay and the Atlantic Port they so desired. Their plan collapsed in November 1674 when an English fleet took New Netherland, placing all of the Delaware Bay, including diplomatic channels to the Iroquois, under the Duke of York. Maryland officials had succeeded in bringing the Susquehannocks closer into their orbit, however, and their migration south opened up the Susquehanna Valley entirely.[18]

As good as that move might have been for Maryland, it plunged the Susquehannocks unknowingly into the disastrous politics over land in neighboring Virginia, and their misfortune provided a diplomatic opportunity for Maryland's new rival, New York. Only seven months after they moved to the Potomac region, the Susquehannocks were attacked in their fort by vengeful Virginia militiamen who raided the wrong Indian group. The subsequent Susquehannock reprisals against frontiersmen and women would play their role in the calamity that was Bacon's Rebellion in 1675 and 1676. The attacks on Indians by white settlers eager for land, and the failure of Virginia's colonial government to protect their Indian allies from those settlers, convinced the Susquehannocks that moving south could not provide the peace they had hoped for. However, their suffering opened the door for New York and its astute new governor, Edmund Andros, to win the Susquehannocks away from Maryland. After consulting with the Mohawks to make sure they supported his plan, Andros invited the Susquehannocks to move back to the Susquehanna Valley, away from Maryland's influence. Eager for peace, some Susquehannocks began to do this, migrating back to their old fort on the Susquehanna River, and others moved along the Delaware River to live with the Lenapes.[19] Maryland officials were shocked at being so outmaneuvered and, with the help of the Piscataway and Mattawomans, attacked the reinvested Susquehannock fort, hoping a decisive victory would allow Maryland more access to Delaware Valley lands.[20]

Andros heard of these machinations and responded with a series of diplomatic moves that led to the Covenant Chain, which enhanced New York's standing among the English of New England, the English of Maryland, and the various Indian groups in the region, especially and most importantly the Iroquois Confederacy. He sent a message to the Susquehannocks, repeating his offer for them to come to New York under his protection, and the Susquehannocks and the Iroquois eventually came together in peace negotiations at the Lenape village of Shackamaxon early in 1677 and again later that year at Albany. Soon afterward Susquehannocks began to move back north to live among numerous Iroquois groups, while others decided to move east among the Lenapes.[21] This once powerful nation was now fragmented.

But the real achievement of the peace at Albany in 1677 was the creation of the Covenant Chain between the English and the Iroquois. The Covenant Chain was a series of Indian-English alliances that could be then connected to other Indians in the region, institutionalizing a peace that had previously been so hard to achieve in the Northeast. Every Native group increased its strength with the Covenant Chain, but the Iroquois gained the most. Certain important nations in the region, such as the Mahicans and the Lenapes, could be recognized within the covenant, thus gaining for the Iroquois protection to the east and southeast, and the absorption of the Susquehannocks into Iroquois villages added a substantial number of warriors to the confederacy's ranks.[22] With their now bolstered connection to the confederacy, gained in part through a masterful diplomatic use of Susquehannock migration, New York officials became the most powerful European players in Indian affairs throughout the Susquehanna, Delaware, and Hudson valleys, affecting the course of both Indian and colonial policies.[23]

Just at the moment when New York became the paramount colony in the mid-Atlantic, William Penn received grants to lands that would become Pennsylvania and Delaware from the king's brother, the Duke of York. Unlike Calvert, Penn would pursue a deft diplomacy strategy that enabled the new colony to acquire Native lands: he dealt directly with the Indians, engaging them in peaceful negotiations and purchasing land only from them, and he hoped that good relations with Indians would lead to protection for his fledgling colony. Pennsylvania presented a transformative, dynamic force for Native peoples and European empires in the mid-Atlantic as the seventeenth century came to a close, one that reorganized the history of settlement and Native life in the Susquehanna Valley.[24]

Maryland and New York leaders were taken aback by the creation and rapid growth of Pennsylvania. Thomas Dongan, the recently appointed governor of New York, wanted to make sure Penn stayed out of the Susquehanna Valley, as did Lord Baltimore. Its location was crucial to access to the fur trade of the interior, and Dongan wanted to maintain some kind of control over those lands, no matter how tenuous. He developed a scheme that would have a grave impact on Indian peoples throughout the region for decades to come. It rested upon the notion that the Susquehannock migration northward to live among the Iroquois in 1677 had been the outcome of a military defeat and not diplomacy, even though there is no evidence that the migration was understood as such at that time. If it was interpreted as a military defeat, then the Iroquois could claim Susquehannock lands along the Susquehanna River Valley, and Penn would have to approach the Iroquois Confederacy, and not the Susquehannocks, to purchase them. Dongan then persuaded the Iroquois to reject any land sales in the Susquehanna Valley to Penn's commissioners, who arrived in 1683, and to grant himself the rights to the entire valley. The arrangement solidified New York's influence and expanded Iroquois power in the region. After Dongan retired and moved back to Ireland in 1696, Penn paid him £100 for the grant to access lands in the Susquehanna Valley—a sum so small that both Penn and Dongan probably thought the grant illegitimate.[25]

Susquehannock relations with Pennsylvania were initially positive. In 1700 William Penn visited Conestoga, where they had moved from Iroquoia in 1693, and received a deed to lands "which are or formerly were the right of the People or Nation called the Susquehannagh Indians."[26] Penn followed this land grant by inviting them to Philadelphia to finalize an agreement of amity and goodwill between the two groups, which was signed in 1701. The Susquehannocks clearly hoped that continued good relations with Pennsylvania would lead to a constant supply of cheap, and growingly necessary, goods, which might allow them to achieve the success they had found in their trade and diplomatic relations with the Swedes and Dutch in previous decades. Penn had finally succeeded in purchasing lands in the Susquehanna River Valley, and, at a price, the Susquehannocks had gained a powerful and peaceful ally.[27]

William Penn also attempted to entice a series of Indian groups into Pennsylvania's sphere as conduits for trade in furs but also as a buffer against potentially hostile Indians to the interior. Those who arrived in the 1690s transformed the Susquehanna River Valley in important ways. After the Susquehannocks returned from Iroquoia in 1693, the Shawnees, Lenapes, Conoys, Nanticokes, and even some Senecas joined them in multiethnic Indian villages that ran up the eastern side of the Susquehanna

River by 1700. Many of these Indians had suffered greatly from disease, warfare, and dislocations that came from European trade. The Conoys and Nanticokes were splinter groups from the Mattawoman and Piscsataqua nations, respectively, of the Chesapeake region. The Shawnees and Delawares—a new group made up of Lenapes and Munsees who identified with the river from which they came—were highly fragmented by the turn of the eighteenth century and were reduced to paying tribute to the Iroquois to maintain their standing along the Pennsylvania frontiers. But the area gave them a measure of needed independence.[28]

By 1725 the river had numerous multiethnic villages up and down both banks. Mostly they were made up of Shawnees and Delawares, but also included were Susquehannocks, Senecas, Conoys, Nanticokes, Tuscaroras, and Tutelos. Conestoga became the biggest of these multiethnic villages, but another large center was at Paxtang, near what is now Harrisburg. By 1730 two other villages were on the western bank, about twenty miles east of where Carlisle would be: one called Geneptukhanne, resting on the Conodoguinet Creek, which fed into the Susquehanna, and another village of Shawnees that sprang up at New Cumberland, on Yellow Breeches Creek, founded by a French-Shawnee trader named Peter Chartier. The people of these villages created new networks of interaction that rested upon the foundations of older ones. The Susquehanna River Valley had been transformed into a valley of hybrid cultures.[29]

Pennsylvania officials, of course, wanted to take advantage of the economic opportunities that all of these Indians presented to the colony. Provincial secretary James Logan, who was the Penn family's representative in the colony from 1699 to the 1730s, was a crucial presence in interior relations with Indians. He worked for Pennsylvania against the potential encroachment of traders, officials, and settlers from New York and Maryland, all the while trying to carve out a space for his own gain. Another was a Frenchman named James LeTort, a trader connected with Logan who worked for the Quakers in Philadelphia. In 1719 Logan ceded a large amount of land on the Susquehanna River to LeTort, who set up a trading post on a small creek that fed into the Conodoguinet Creek. LeTort Creek, which runs through Carlisle and lands where the Carlisle Barracks would be built, was populated at this time by Shawnees, who maintained a number of small villages on the river. The trader would remain at that location until roughly 1727, when the Shawnees were forced westward, toward the Ohio Country.[30]

The location on LeTort Creek would be an attractive meeting point between Philadelphia commercial interests and Native hunters, especially Shawnees, who brought deerskins to market from the Ohio Valley.[31] Logan, in concert with his Iroquois allies, attempted to use that trade to command an outsized reach into the Susquehanna Valley, turning his white traders into de facto deputies, interpreters, informants, and even diplomats, granting those that pleased him prizes of land and aid for their services. Since 1690 the Iroquois had allied with many Native groups, even creating some relations of dependency with many of the numerous Indian nations migrating into the region. The Shawnees and the Delawares refused to maintain a dependent relationship with the Iroquois, creating instead the Shawnee-Delaware village of Paxtang, and that independence led to tension. Beginning in 1721 Logan and the Iroquois Confederacy began to place diplomatic pressure on all of the Indians on the Pennsylvania frontier to recognize the Iroquois as the "spokesmen and political superiors" in any interaction with white leadership in Philadelphia, continuing what was by then a tradition of cooperation between the Iroquois and white colonial leadership to gain hegemony over the Delaware and Susquehanna region.[32] Many Indians were threatened by this pressure and began to remove themselves from the Susquehanna River Valley, establishing themselves on the Allegheny and Ohio Rivers to the west. By 1731 Shawnees and Delawares had created more than six new towns there with an estimated four to five hundred men and their families. It was at that time that traders like James LeTort moved westward as well to take continuing advantage of Indian trade.[33]

As the Shawnees and Delawares were pushed out of the region in the 1720s, white settlers moved in, creating other kinds of troubles for Indians in the region. The first settlers to the western shore of the Susquehanna began arriving by the 1720s and contributed to the problems that oppressed the Shawnees and Delawares. Many of these newcomers squatted on the land, drawn to the good soil of the valley. Those that settled in what would become Carlisle were initially attracted by LeTort's trading post. The post also brought other traders, many of them unlicensed, who traded liquor to the Indians. A vast majority of these people were Scots-Irish, from Protestant Northern Ireland, looking for economic opportunity or religious freedom, and they established humble farms, taverns, and rude homesteads. But the paths to success were difficult for these people. They had trouble securing lands, which were controlled by colonial leaders such as Logan, and they suffered from prejudice against their Scots-Irish heritage, which barred them from more firmly established colonial settings. Roughly four hundred white families lived west of the Susquehanna River by 1731, at the outermost edge of colonial Pennsylvania, squatting among Native groups that stayed within the valley. They eked out lives based on subsistence agriculture, foraging, and hunting, and often engaged in troubling behavior such as excessive drinking and violence. And they utterly relied on Indian aid to survive.[34]

But in the 1730s, as many Indians fled the region for lands westward, the world of the Lower Susquehanna River Valley was becoming increasingly a white colonial space. That was good for officials in Philadelphia, who wanted control over Pennsylvania's frontier lands. William Penn died in 1718, leaving his sons John, Richard, and, especially, Thomas the opportunity to claim interior lands as firmly as they could, which they eventually did in 1746. Thomas Penn attempted to quell violent outbursts between Maryland colonists and Pennsylvanian squatters over the control of land in 1734 by creating settlements based on illegal "licenses," or temporary titles to land. Penn recognized these licenses as temporary, knowing he needed to purchase the lands outright from the Indians who owned it. But he went against his father's practice of approaching individual Indian nations and their leaders, and instead, like many New York officials before him, he opened discussions with the Iroquois Confederacy, which claimed the lands west of the Susquehanna River. By doing so, Penn and his officials wanted to destroy any claims maintained by the Shawnees and the Delawares, and the Iroquois were only too happy to be recognized as the main power in the region.[35] He realized his wish in October 1736, when he signed a treaty with twenty-three Iroquois in Philadelphia. Penn exchanged trade goods for approximately two million acres—roughly forty-one thousand square miles—much of it on the lower Susquehanna, thereby gaining "formal control" of Cumberland Valley and the legitimacy to formalize the border with Maryland. In 1750, with the creation of Cumberland County, the sixth county in Pennsylvania, formal government was set up in the area for the first time.[36] Carlisle was created a year later, at the point of LeTort's abandoned trading post.[37]

Once Thomas Penn and his brothers secured the region of the Susquehanna Valley on paper, they then wanted to exercise more control over the land itself. Thomas Penn recognized the importance of the Natives in the region to this plan, and their reliance on trade goods.[38] But his dreams of developing the region indicated how marginal the Indians and the fur trade would later become. He had visions of this frontier territory sprinkled with roads, trading posts, and white-inhabited villages. As proprietor he immediately began to make arrangements for setting up townships, locating county seats with an eye toward colonial stability, and planning economic investment to set up commercial centers. He hoped that the Scots-Irish would move away from their rougher, more precarious lifestyle and transform into orderly, productive colonial subjects. He then designed the town of Carlisle in a grid pattern with a central square and a sense of order for stability and control, even if it was inhabited with groups deemed unruly, like the Scots-Irish.[39]

That tension between white leadership and the colonists who would settle in the district in the 1750s only became more pronounced as the process of settling Carlisle proceeded, and it entangled those Native peoples who remained in the area. Many of the region's white settlers simply ignored the claims made by the 1736 treaty signed in Philadelphia. They hotly challenged surveyors and their Philadelphia superiors who attempted to clarify the boundary of Cumberland County, eliciting a response equally heated. These officials believed that the squatters on lands west and north of the boundaries marked in the 1736 purchase had no right to inhabit them, were setting up disorderly settlements, and were connecting more to the Indians than to Philadelphia. Some Indians liked the squatters even less. At treaty negotiations in Philadelphia in 1749 the Ohio Seneca leader Canasatago claimed that some of these poor whites were moving into Indian hunting territories and should be removed by Pennsylvania at once. Other squatters seemed to work well with Indians in the region and insisted that they had occupied the land with Indian consent—a claim that mortified the proprietors even more, as it simply removed any control colonial officials had over the land.[40] Pennsylvania officials tried to evict the squatters, but many refused to leave, and new settlements continued to spring up past the 1736 treaty boundary.[41]

With the constant influx of Scots-Irish settlers and the growing migration of Indians away from them, many areas in Cumberland County became dominated by whites, and by the early 1750s the town of Carlisle had become solidly Scots-Irish. As such, the concerns there focused less on conflicts between Indians and whites and more on conflicts between whites who wanted to settle the land and whites who wanted to control the lands where those whites settled. But Carlisle's commercial interests were squarely connected to the Ohio Valley, to the fur and deerskin trade and the Native peoples who facilitated it, so Carlisle became a site of social, commercial, and political contact with western Indians, even as it was increasingly a space in which white concerns were paramount. An Indian-white conference at Carlisle in 1753, attended by Benjamin Franklin, highlighted how white elites from Philadelphia used a language of exoticism and barbarism to marginalize Ohio Valley Indians. Franklin labeled the group of Mingos, Delawares, Shawnees, Miamis, and Wyandots as inebriated, rowdy, and savage. "Their dark-colour'd bodies," he wrote, "half naked, seen only by the gloomy light of the bonfire, running after and beating one another with firebrands, accompanied by their horrid yellings, form'd a scene the most resembling our ideas of hell that could well be imagin'd." He mused that their addiction to alcohol might be the way to destroy them, as "It has already annihilated all the tribes who formerly inhabited the sea-coast." Even when Indians were present in Carlisle, whites like Franklin and others were beginning to write them out of the landscape. This rhetoric of the "vanishing Indian" encouraged—even insisted upon—their gradual dissipation and future annihilation. And the narrative of Indian barbarism would get so elaborate and popular in the ensuing years and decades that it became instrumental in legitimating the dispossession of Indian lands.[42]

The Indians would return to the region the year after that conference, but for entirely different purposes, and within a transformed political landscape. The Seven Years' War started in 1754 in the Pennsylvania backcountry, with George Washington's ill-fated attempt to wrest Fort Duquesne from the French and his crushing defeat at Fort Necessity. English military leadership, led by General Edward Braddock, would attempt to make amends in western Pennsylvania, only to suffer catastrophe at the hands of a smaller yet much savvier French and Indian force.[43]

But crucially, the Albany Conference also occurred in 1754, in which the Iroquois Confederacy stunned the Delawares and other Indians of the region by controversially selling their lands.[44] The commissioners from Pennsylvania—Lieutenant Governor James Hamilton, Richard Peters, and John Penn—had all been instructed to purchase the remaining lands that rested within Thomas Penn's charter from the Iroquois delegates. Some of these lands were claimed by the colony of Connecticut, and their efforts to make good on those claims spurred Pennsylvania officials to use their ties with the Iroquois to claim the lands before Connecticut could. That territory was enormous, and in two parts: the Wyoming Valley, inhabited by eastern Delaware and Mahican Indians who lived in and around Moravian missions; and a larger tract of land that stretched from the Susquehanna River to the Ohio Valley, inhabited by western groups of Delawares. The Iroquois claimed to speak for all of the Indians that lived on these lands, and none of those groups sent any delegates to the conference. The decades-long strategy of relying on the Iroquois for the sale of lands in the Susquehanna and Delaware River valleys and for control over the region's peoples paid off yet again for an English colony, as Philadelphia officials and the Iroquois signed an agreement that ceded those lands to Pennsylvania. This treaty infuriated the affected Delawares in the regions, who were incredulous that the Iroquois had sold their lands from under them and that the English had agreed to it. The treaty utterly destroyed any remaining Delaware-English amity that had been built up over the years, and the growing tensions between Great Britain and France over the Ohio Valley simply provided a convenient pretext for Delaware anger. As the English interpreter Charles Thomson stated in 1759, the Albany Purchase "ruined our interest with the Indians, and threw those of them, especially to the westward of us, entirely into the Hands of the French."[45]

These tensions, and their connection with the Seven Years' War, would have a profound impact on the region around Carlisle. Delaware Indians began to attack western Pennsylvania settlements, even those on the Susquehanna River itself, which terrified Carlisle's residents. One raiding party, made up of mostly Shawnees and Delawares, raided white villages in the region in the hopes of reclaiming lands that the Iroquois had traded to Pennsylvania, and the inhabitants of Cumberland County decried them as "a Powerful Army of Cruel Merciless and Unhuman Enemies."[46] As Daniel K. Richter has noted, the personal relationships between Indians and white settlers in the region that had been built up over years did not ameliorate the possibilities for searing violence but instead gave them a harsher cast, as "ethnic conflicts can become most ruthless when the parties have long lived side by side and know each other well." Richter writes that when "Delawares, Shawnees, and others took up arms, therefore, they did not engage in random acts of violence or broad strategic sweeps. Instead, they struck very specific targets, at particular homesteads of Euro-Americans who had settled on the lands the Six Nations had sold out from under them."[47]

It was during this time that Carlisle became a center for whites fleeing exposed Pennsylvania settlements and soldiers running to defend the region. White refugees flooded the town in waves. The Assembly and Provincial Council of Pennsylvania noted that western townships like Carlisle were receiving "Men[,] Women[,] and Children who had Lately Lived in great affluence and plenty reduced to the most extreme poverty and distress."[48] Carlisle soon became one of the western-most towns in Pennsylvania, and by the end of the war in 1763 it was on the frontier's edge.[49] The colony's government sent troops for the region's defense, but only reluctantly, as the pacifist Quaker leadership in Philadelphia refused to stoutly defend and expand the colony's frontiers. That refusal rankled many settlers, who thought the provisions that came from the east were not enough, and the continuing violence on the frontier induced panic.[50] But even as Carlisle tipped precariously on the edge of war, the town also thrived in ways that other towns in the region did not, as refugees and a variety of military personnel flooded its streets and increased its population. Roughly 6,400 British troops under Brig. Gen. John Forbes began to reside there permanently in 1757, and although their presence created some tension with the local residents, they also brought Carlisle the benefits of security and economic gain. Because the town was threatened but never attacked, Carlisle was able to successfully solidify its standing in the region, undermining Indian attempts at reclaiming land in the Susquehanna Valley.[51]

But those years of Indian raiding led to a new kind of virulent Indian-hating among whites. Settlers continued to fear Indian attacks in the Susquehanna Valley well into the 1760s, especially in 1763, when the Delaware prophet Neolin and the Ottawa warrior Pontiac spread a spiritual and military message of pan-Indian sovereignty against white encroachment.

Pontiac's Rebellion gave rise to renewed Indian attacks in the Pennsylvania frontier, which only fed anti-Indian sentiment. White settlers felt besieged, and some struck out in murderous ways. A group of fifty-seven Scots-Irish men traveled to Conestoga and killed six Indians that lived under the protection of the Quaker leadership in Philadelphia on December 14 of that year, and two weeks later a group of whites dubbed later the "Paxton Boys" descended upon Lancaster and murdered the rest of the Conestoga Delaware and Susquehannock men, women, and children, highlighting the disturbing lengths to which racist white settlers would go to eliminate Indians from the region. For whites, the Paxton Boys' raid rendered the Susquehannocks essentially extinct, as it removed any substantial Indian presence on the lower Susquehanna River Valley and so opened these lands for white settlement. Yet white settlers fostered a rhetoric of Indian barbarity and legitimate retaliation, which became fundamental to the rise of a new kind of vicious racism in the late eighteenth century.[52]

The rise of this form of Indian-hating transformed Carlisle. Racism against Indians became a litmus test for political positions and social views and was crucial to the creation of a distrustful and prejudicial attitude toward outsiders in general—whether Indians from the west or Philadelphia elites from the east. By 1768 Carlisle was a town intensely wary of foreigners and resolutely inhospitable to Native peoples.[53] This sentiment only became more entrenched as the Indian population of the region declined. The Susquehannocks, possibly 5,000–7,000 strong in 1600, were either absorbed into the Iroquois Confederacy or destroyed by 1763.[54] The Shawnees had migrated from the region completely by the mid-1700s.[55] The roughly 11,000 Lenape and Munsee Indians of the Delaware River in 1600 were reduced to roughly 3,200 Delawares who migrated westward and ultimately were forced to sign away their rights to all their lands east of the Mississippi in 1820.[56] Many of those Indians who had moved into the area from the south, such as groups of Conoys and Nanticokes, decided to join the Delawares in western Pennsylvania and Ohio in the late 1760s and 1770s.[57] The decline of Native peoples, and the rapid demographic growth of Scots-Irish and other settlers of European descent in the region, allowed whites throughout Pennsylvania to ignore and denigrate the dwindling Indian population.[58]

The growing insularity of Carlisle in the aftermath of the Seven Years' War and the subsequent expunging of Native peoples from the history of the region, even as certain Indians remained, rendered Pennsylvania's complicated history of ethnic and cultural trading and migration invisible and eventually unknown. The thousands of years when Native peoples forged their own destinies in the Susquehanna River Valley were entirely overlooked. The complex period of fluctuating cooperation and competition that is sketched in this chapter became subsumed into a simple, two-stranded narrative of white triumph in conjunction with Indian conquest and disappearance. To the growing white population, the Indians who continued to live on the Lower Susquehanna River after the horrific massacre at Conestoga in 1763 seemed at best irrelevant or at worst an unwelcomed affront to the finality that act was supposed to signify. Those Natives—small in number, often separated from white society and living in tiny groups—continued to survive in a region that ignored them throughout the late eighteenth century, into the nineteenth, and after. They remain invisible, underresearched, and little known.[59] Today, Pennsylvania is one of the few states where there are no reservations and no state or federally recognized Indian tribes.[60]

When the Indian School opened in 1879 and Captain Richard Henry Pratt brought the first contingent of students to Carlisle from the Pine Ridge and Rosebud agencies in Dakota Territory, they were viewed by locals as strange, exotic, and savage. Hundreds of townspeople who had never knowingly seen an "Indian" eagerly flocked to the railroad station to inspect the "savages" for themselves. For those unable to join the throng, the reporter from the *Carlisle Valley Sentinel* provided a full, descriptive account of the children: "All possessed the large black eye, beautiful pearl-white teeth, the high cheek-bone, straight-cut mouth and peculiar nose." Signaling the town's support for the Indian School and its mission, he explained, "Our citizens are greatly interested in the school, and we know Captain Pratt will be heartily seconded in his good work by our citizens."[61] For this reporter and his readers, "Indians" were associated with the West, not Pennsylvania, and their presence in the town seemed so peculiar that Pratt was quickly forced to build a high fence round the school to stop the curious from coming to stare. The narrative of Indian extinction was by this time so deeply entrenched in the local population

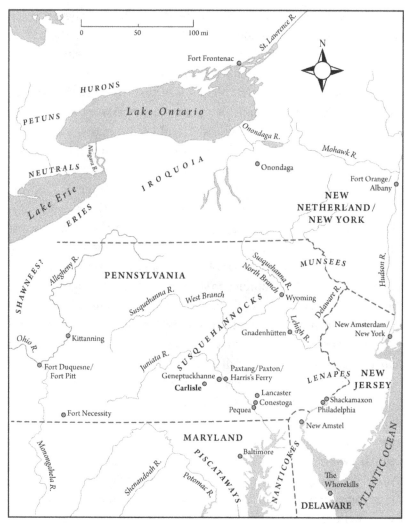

Map 1. Historical map of the Carlisle region showing lands of Native nations, 1600–1763. Map by Erin Greb Cartography.

that the Carlisle Indian School could be welcomed as a purveyor of "civilization" for the Indian tribes of the West, and its intrinsic links to the Indian destruction and disappearance that had once been played out in Carlisle and the surrounding region could go unremarked and unrealized. As the *Sentinel* reported, the people of Carlisle could see themselves as willingly contributing to the commendable tasks of civilizing and nation building.

1. David J. Minderhout, *Native Americans in the Susquehanna River Valley* (Lewisburg PA: Bucknell University Press, 2013), 3.
2. What follows is an essay of historical synthesis. Anyone familiar with the historiography of Indian-white relations in what would become the state of Pennsylvania will recognize how indebted this essay is to the work of Francis Jennings, Daniel K. Richter, and Judith Ridner. See specifically, for Francis Jennings, "Glory, Death, and Transfiguration: The Susquehannock Indians in the Seventeenth Century," *Proceedings of the American Philosophical Society Proceedings* 112, no. 1 (1968): 15–53, and *The Ambiguous Iroquois Empire: The Covenant Chain Confederation of Indian Tribes with English Colonies* (New York: W. W. Norton, 1984); for Daniel K. Richter, see *The Ordeal of the Longhouse: The Peoples of the Iroquois League in the Era of European Colonization* (Chapel Hill: University of North Carolina Press, 1992), and *Trade, Land, Power: The Struggle for Eastern North America* (Philadelphia: University of Pennsylvania Press, 2013); and for Judith Ridner, *A Town In-Between: Carlisle, Pennsylvania, and the Early Mid-Atlantic Interior* (Philadelphia: University of Pennsylvania Press, 2010).
3. For archaeological material, see John Witthoft, "A Paleo-Indian Site in Eastern Pennsylvania: An Early Hunting Culture," *Proceedings of the American Philosophical Society* 96, no. 4 (1952): 464–95. See as well Robert E. Funk, "Post-Pleistocene Adaptations," 16–27; James A. Tuck, "Regional Cultural Development, 3000–300BC," 27–43, especially 37–39; James E. Fitting, "Regional Cultural Development, 300BC to AD1000," 44–57, especially 52–56; and Dean Snow, "Late Prehistory of the East Coast," 62, all in *Northeast*, ed. Bruce Trigger, vol. 15 of *Handbook of North American Indians*, gen. ed. William C. Sturtevant (Washington DC: Smithsonian Institution, 1978).
4. Daniel K. Richter, "The First Pennsylvanians," in *Pennsylvania: A History of the Commonwealth*, ed. Randall M. Miller and William Pencak (University Park: Pennsylvania State University Press, 2002), 27, 30. See as well Jay F. Custer et al., "Data Recovery Excavations at the Slackwater Site (36LA207), Lancaster County, Pennsylvania," *Pennsylvania Archaeologist* 65 (March 1995): 19–112. The name "Susquehannock" comes from a blending of the term "Sisku," which is the Algonquian translation of the Iroquois-French term "Andastes," and "hanne," or stream. So "Susquehannock" is the Algonquian term that means "the people of the river of the Andastes." See Francis Jennings, "Susquehannock," in Trigger, *Northeast*, 362–63.
5. John Witthoft, "Ancestry of the Susquehannocks," in *Susquehannock Miscellany* (Harrisburg: Pennsylvania Historical and Museum Commission, 1959),

32; Peter C. Mancall, *Valley of Opportunity: Economic Culture along the Upper Susquehanna, 1700–1800* (Ithaca NY: Cornell University Press), 30–31; and George P. Donehoo, *Indian Villages and Place Names in Pennsylvania* (Harrisburg PA: Telegraph Press, 1928), 215–16.

6. Gunlög Fur, *A Nation of Women: Gender and Colonial Encounters among the Delaware Indians* (Philadelphia: University of Pennsylvania Press, 2009), 5–6; Richter, *Trade, Land, Power,* 159; and Amy C. Schutt, *Peoples of the River Valleys: The Odyssey of the Delaware Indians* (Philadelphia: University of Pennsylvania Press, 2007), 43.

7. Paul A. W. Wallace thinks that the Black Minquas and the Eries are two distinct groups; Francis Jennings is not so sure. See Wallace, *Indians in Pennsylvania,* 2nd ed. (Harrisburg: Pennsylvania Historical and Museum Commissions, 1993), 13, 15; and Jennings, "Glory, Death, and Transfiguration," 17.

8. Jennings, "Glory, Death, and Transfiguration," 17; Daniel K. Richter, *Before the Revolution: America's Ancient Pasts* (Cambridge MA: Harvard University Press, 2011), 124, 131, 138–39, and 150; Jennings, *Ambiguous Iroquois Empire,* 115–17; Gunlög Fur, *Colonialism in the Margins: Cultural Encounters in New Sweden and Lapland* (Leiden: Brill, 2006), 92; Karen Ordahl Kupperman, "Scandinavian Colonists Confront the New World," in *New Sweden in America,* ed. Carol E. Hoffecker et al. (Newark: University of Delaware Press, 1995), 89–111.

9. For a compelling argument that emphasizes continuity at the time of European contact, see Neal Salisbury, "The Indians Old World: Native Americans and the Coming of Europeans," *William and Mary Quarterly* 53, no. 3 (1996): 435–58.

10. "Issack de Rasière to the Amsterdam chamber of the West Indian Company, 23 September 1626," in *Documents Relating to New Netherland, 1624–1626, in the Henry E. Huntington Library,* trans. and ed. A. J. F. Van Laer (San Marino CA: Henry E. Huntington Library and Art Gallery, 1924), cited from http://www.rootsweb.ancestry.com/~nycoloni/huntdocf.html; "Relation of Captain Thomas Yong, 1634," in *Narratives of Early Pennsylvania, West New Jersey, and Delaware, 1630–1710,* ed. Albert Cook Myers (New York: Scribner and Sons, 1912), 38; "Affidavit of Four Men from the *Key of Calmar,* 1638," in Myers, *Narratives of Early Pennsylvania,* 87; and Thomas Campanius Holm, "Description of the Province of New Sweden . . . ," *Memoirs of the Historical Society of Pennsylvania,* 14 vols., ed. Peter S. Du Ponseau (Philadelphia: McCarty and Davis, 1834), 3, part 1: 158. Francis Jennings speculates that the Lenapes might have paid tribute to the Susquehannocks as a diplomatic guarantee against Lenape intrusions on Susquehannock hunting grounds,

but that fact remains unclear. See Jennings, "Glory, Death, and Transfiguration," 19–20.

11. Ridner, *Town In-Between*, 17; Jennings, "Glory, Death, and Transfiguration," 17. For an argument that outlines a clear break between before-contact and after-contact societies for Indians, see James Merrell, "The Indians' Old World: The Catawba Experience," *William and Mary Quarterly* 41, no. 4 (1984): 538–65. This dynamic would turn into the devastating Beaver Wars of the seventeenth century, as accessing furs to gain firearms, shot, cloth, and alcohol would dominate the economic and political worlds of northeastern North America. See Alan Taylor, *American Colonies* (New York: Penguin, 2005), 111–13.

12. Jennings, "Glory, Death, and Transfiguration," 17, 20–22. The warrior estimate of 1,300 warriors from one village in 1647 comes from Paul Rageneau, "Relation of 1647–1648," in *The Jesuit Relations and Allied Documents*, ed. Reuben Gold Thwaites, 73 vols. (Cleveland OH: Burrows Brothers, 1896–1901), 33:129. See also J. Frederick Fausz, "Merging and Emerging Worlds: Anglo-Indian Interest Groups and the Development of the Seventeenth-Century Chesapeake," in *Colonial Chesapeake Society*, ed. Lois Green Carr, Philip D. Morgan, and Jean B. Russo (Chapel Hill: University of North Carolina Press, 1988), 76–77.

13. Jennings, "Glory, Death, and Transfiguration," 22, 24–25, and Jennings, *Ambiguous Iroquois Empire*, 102.

14. Richter, *Ordeal of the Longhouse*, 61–62; Neville B. Craig, ed., *The Olden Time . . .*, vol. 1 (Cincinnati OH: Robert Clarke, 1876), 225–30; Richard White, *The Middle Ground: Indians, Empires, and Republics in the Great Lakes Region, 1650–1815* (New York: Cambridge University Press, 1991), 1–10; Marian E. White, "Erie," in Trigger, *Northeast*, 415–16; and Jon Parmenter, *The Edge of the Woods: Iroquoia, 1534–1701* (East Lansing: Michigan State University Press, 2010), 80–81.

15. Jennings, "Glory, Death, and Transfiguration," 23, 25–26; Fur, *Colonialism in the Margins*, 225–26; Richter, *Before the Revolution*, 262; Jennings, *Ambiguous Iroquois Empire*, 122, 155; Parmenter, *Edge of the Woods*, 111–12.

16. Parmenter, *Edge of the Woods*, 111, 115. See as well two volumes of Thwaites, *Jesuit Relations*: "Relation of 1662–1663," 48:77–79, and "Relation of 1663–1664," 49:147–49. See also "Andreis Hudde, to Director Stuyvesant, Altena, 29 May 1663" and "William Beekman to Director Stuyvesant, Altena, 6 June 1663," in E. B. O'Callaghan, ed., *Documents Relative to the Colonial History of the State of New York . . .*, 15 vols. (Albany NY: Weed, Parsons, 1856–87): 12:430–31 (hereafter cited NYCD); "Assembly Proceedings, 27 September 1663," *Archives of Maryland*, 1:471–72; "By the Leiuetenennet Generall, 17 November 1663," *Archives of Maryland*, 3:489; "Torture of Two Oneida Prisoners by the Pascastoways, 9 June 1664," *Archives of Maryland*, 3:501; "War with Senecas,

27 June 1664," *Archives of Maryland*, 3:502; and Colin G. Calloway, *The Western Abenakis of Vermont, 1600–1800: War, Migration, and the Survival of an Indian People* (Norman: University of Oklahoma Press, 1990), 70–72.

17. Jennings, "Glory, Death, and Transfiguration," 29–30; and "Relation of 1668–1669," Thwaites, *Jesuit Relations*, 52:147, 175–77.

18. Lovelace became New York's second governor in 1668. See Michael Kammen, *Colonial New York: A History* (New York: Scribner, 1975), 79; Jaap Jacobs, *The Colony of New Netherland: A Dutch Settlement in Seventeenth-Century America* (Ithaca NY: Cornell University Press, 2009), 103–4; John A. Monroe, *Colonial Delaware: A History* (New York: KTO Press, 1978), 68–70; and Jennings, "Glory, Death, and Transfiguration," 31–34.

19. Jennings, "Glory, Death, and Transfiguration," 34–37; Edmund S. Morgan, *American Slavery, American Freedom* (New York: W. W. Norton, 1975), 250–58.

20. Jennings, "Glory, Death, and Transfiguration," 37–38.

21. "Captain John Collier to be Commander in Delaware and His Instructions, 23 September 1676," *NYCD*, 12:556–58; Jennings, "Glory, Death, and Transfiguration," 39.

22. Jennings, "Glory, Death, and Transfiguration," 44; Richter, *Ordeal of the Longhouse*, 136–37.

23. "Captain Randolph Brandt to His Lordships, 17 May 1680," *Archives of Maryland*, 15:283–84, and "Captain Randolph Brandt to His Lordships, 1 June 1680," *Archives of Maryland*, 15:299–300; and "Lord Baltimore's Instructions to Henry Coursey and Philemon Lloyd, 15 May 1682," *Archives of Maryland*, 17:98.

24. Joseph E. Illick, *Colonial Pennsylvania: A History* (New York: Scribner's, 1976), 1, 29; Jennings, "Glory, Death, and Transfiguration," 45–48.

25. Jennings, "Glory, Death, and Transfiguration," 33, 49; Jennings, *Ambiguous Iroquois Empire*, 226–30, 235.

26. "Widaagh and Andaggy-Junkquagh to William Penn, September 13, 1700," in *Pennsylvania and Delaware Treaties, 1629–1737*, ed. Donald H. Kent, vol. 1 of *Early American Indian Documents: Treaties and Laws, 1607–1789*, gen. ed. Alden T. Vaughan (Washington DC: University Publications of America, 1979), 1:99 (hereafter cited as *EAID*).

27. Jennings, "Glory, Death, and Transfiguration," 50; "Articles of Agreement between William Penn and the Susquehannah, Shawoneh and North Patomack Indians, April 23, 1701," *EAID*, 1:101–4.

28. James H. Merrell, *Into the American Woods: Negotiators on the Pennsylvania Frontier* (New York: W. W. Norton, 1999), 35, 107; Taylor, *American Colonies*, 269; David L. Preston, *The Texture of Contact: European and Indian Settler*

Communities on the Frontiers of Iroquoia, 1667–1783 (Lincoln: University of Nebraska Press, 2009), 125.

29. Ridner, *Town In-Between*, 18–20, Michael McConnell, *A Country Between: The Upper Ohio Valley and Its Peoples, 1724–1774* (Lincoln: University of Nebraska Press, 1992), 9–15.

30. Evelyn A. Benson, "The Huguenot Le Torts: First Christian Family on the Conestoga," *Lancaster County Historical Society Journal* 65 (1961): 92–103; Samuel P. Bates et al., *History of Cumberland and Adams Counties, Pennsylvania* (Chicago: Warner, Beers, 1886), 8.

31. Ridner, *Town In-Between*, 21; Charles Callender, "Shawnee," in Trigger, *Northeast*, 630; Eric Hinderaker, *Elusive Empires: Constructing Colonialism in the Ohio Valley, 1673–1800* (New York: Cambridge University Press, 1997), 22–25; quote on 22; Daniel H. Usner Jr., *Indians, Settlers, and Slaves in a Frontier Exchange Economy: The Lower Mississippi Valley before 1783* (Chapel Hill: University of North Carolina Press, 1992).

32. Hinderaker, *Elusive Empires*, 25–27.

33. Hinderaker, *Elusive Empires*, 27, 29–30, 31n51; Richard White, *Middle Ground*, 186–222.

34. Ridner, *Town In-Between*, 21–23; D. W. Thompson, ed., *Two Hundred Years in Cumberland County* (Carlisle PA: Hamilton and Historical Association of Cumberland County, 1951), 18–19.

35. Ridner, *Town In-Between*, 23–24, 26–27, Sally Schwartz, *"A Mixed Multitude": The Struggle for Toleration in Colonial Pennsylvania* (New York: New York University Press, 1987), 87–88.

36. "The Six Nations to the Proprietaries for the Susquehanna Valley, October 11, 1736," in Kent, *Pennsylvania and Delaware Treaties*, 438; Ridner, *Town In-Between*, 27, Jennings, "Glory, Death, and Transfiguration," 50.

37. "Thomas Cookson to Governor [James] H[amilton], Lancaster, March 1, 1749," in *Pennsylvania Archives*, ed. Samuel Hazard (Philadelphia: Joseph Severns, 1853), 2:42–44; Ridner, *Town In-Between*, 29–31; I. Daniel Rupp, *History and Topography of Dauphin, Cumberland, Franklin, Bedford, Adams, and Perry Counties* (Lancaster PA: Gilbert Hills, 1846), 386–87, William Cronon, *Changes in the Land: Indians, Colonists, and the Ecology of New England* (New York: Hill & Wang, 1983), especially chapters 2 and 3.

38. *Minutes of the Provincial Colonial Records of Pennsylvania*, 10 vols. (Harrisburg PA: Theo. Fenn, 1851–52), 4:91 (hereafter cited as MPCRP); Ridner, *Town In-Between*, 27.

39. Ridner, *Town In-Between*, 27–28, 33, 39.

40. "Canassatego's Speech on Behalf of the Six Nations, July 7, 1742," MPCRP,

4:570; Ridner, *Town In-Between*, 44, 46; Preston, *Texture of Contact*, 135–36, 139; Bates et al., *History of Cumberland and Adams Counties*, 15–16.

41. Ridner, *Town In-Between*, 46–48; various documents in MPCRP, 5:435, 438, 440–49, 479; Silas Wright, *History of Perry County, in Pennsylvania* (Lancaster PA: Wylie & Griest, 1873), 9–10. For a broader work on Croghan, see Nicholas B. Wainwright, *George Croghan, Wilderness Diplomat* (Chapel Hill: University of North Carolina Press, 1959).

42. Benjamin Franklin, *The Autobiography of Benjamin Franklin*, ed. Louis P. Masur (Boston: Bedford's/St. Martin's, 2003), 127–28.

43. Fred Anderson, *Crucible of War: The Seven Years' War and the Fate of Empire in British North America, 1754–1766* (New York: Vintage, 2000), 11–107.

44. Paul Moyer, "'Real' Indians, 'White' Indians, and the Contest for the Wyoming Valley," in *Friends and Enemies in Penn's Woods: Indians, Colonists, and Racial Construction in Pennsylvania*, ed. Daniel K. Richter and William Pencak (University Park: Pennsylvania State University Press, 2004), 225–26; Francis Jennings, *Empire of Fortune: Crowns, Colonies, and Tribes in the Seven Years' War in America* (New York: W. W. Norton, 1988), 101–6; Jane T. Merritt, *At the Crossroads: Indians and Empires on a Mid-Atlantic Frontier, 1700–1763* (Chapel Hill: University of North Carolina Press, 2003), 172–73; Preston, *Texture of Contact*, 116–46; Richter, *Trade, Land, Power*, 155–76; Kevin Kenny, *Peaceable Kingdoms Lost: The Paxton Boys and the Destruction of William Penn's Holy Experiment* (New York: Oxford University Press, 2009), 50–61; for the entire treaty, see EAID, 2:331–46, and for the deed of lands, see 346–47.

45. Moyer, "'Real' Indians," 225–26; Jennings, *Empire of Fortune*, 102–4, 263–81; Charles Thomson, *An Enquiry into the Causes of the Alienation of the Delaware and Sawanese Indians from the British Interest* (London: J. Wilkie, 1759), 77; Julian Boyd and Robert J. Taylor, eds., *The Susquehannah Company Papers*, 11 vols. (1930–71), 2:i–xvi, 2–5, 11.

46. Ridner, *Town In-Between*, 81; "Petition of the Inhabitants of Cumberland County to Gov. James Hamilton, July 15, 1754," MPCRP, 6:130–31; Merritt, *At the Crossroads*, 176–85; Peter Silver, *Our Savage Neighbors: How Indian War Transformed Early America* (New York: W. W. Norton, 2008), 60–71; Matthew C. Ward, *Breaking the Backcountry: The Seven Years' War in Virginia and Pennsylvania, 1754–1765* (Pittsburg: University of Pittsburg Press, 2003), 60–70.

47. Richter, *Trade, Land, Power*, 171.

48. Ridner, *Town In-Between*, 82; quote from "Report of Benjamin Chew, et al, to the Governor and Council, April 21, 1756," Penn Papers, Assembly and Provincial Council of Pennsylvania, Historical Society of Pennsylvania, 82, cited in Ridner.

49. "Col. Henry Bouquet to Gov. James Hamilton, Carlisle, 13 July 1763," in Thompson, *Two Hundred Years in Cumberland County*, 32.

50. Ridner, *Town In-Between*, 83–85. For the Carlisle Fort, see William Hunter, *Forts on the Pennsylvania Frontier, 1753–1758* (Harrisburg: Pennsylvania Historical and Museum Commission, 1960), 436–50.

51. Ridner, *Town In-Between*, 87–89. Brigadier General Forbes received and wrote correspondence that is filled with comments about the potential diplomatic possibilities and problems of the Cherokees. See, for examples, John Forbes, *Writings of Gen. John Forbes*, ed. Alfred Proctor James (Menasha WI: Collegiate Press, 1938), 81, 91–93, 256–57.

52. Anderson, *Crucible of War*, 267–85; for Pontiac, see Gregory Evans Dowd, *A Spirited Resistance: The North American Indian Struggle for Unity, 1745–1815* (Baltimore: Johns Hopkins University Press, 1992), 23–46; Hinderaker, *Elusive Empires*, 144–61; Krista Camenzind, "Violence, Race, and the Paxton Boys," in Richter and Pencak, *Friends and Enemies*, 201–20; Merritt, *At the Crossroads*, 267, 272–83, 292; John Dunbar, ed., *The Paxton Papers* (The Hague: Martinus Nijhoff, 1957), 3, 58–59; Silver, *Our Savage Neighbors*, 73–94, especially 83–85.

53. Ridner, *Town In-Between*, 94–95, 109–10.

54. This estimate remains provisional, as it is based only on the *Jesuit Relations* document that claims one village could support 1,300 warriors in 1657; see note 12 above. The estimate does sound plausible, however, as the Susquehannocks were able to present a formidable foe to a group as large as the Iroquois Confederacy. See William Brandon, *The American Heritage Book of Indians*, gen. ed. Alvin Josephy (New York: American Heritage, 1961), 188–89.

55. Charles Callender, "Shawnee," in Brandon, *American Heritage Book of Indians*, maps on 623 and 631.

56. Ives Goddard, "Delaware," in Trigger, *Northeast*, 214.

57. David J. Minderhout, "Pennsylvania's Native Americans: History Timeline," in *Native Americans in the Susquehanna River Valley, Past and Present*, ed. David J. Minderhout (Lewisburg PA: Bucknell University Press, 2013), 49; and Christian F. Feest, "Nanticoke and Neighboring Tribes," in Trigger, *Northeast*, 246.

58. Merritt, *At the Crossroads*, 261–62.

59. This topic—on Indians in central Pennsylvania after the Seven Years' War—has yet to find its historian. For cursory discussions of these survivors, see David J. Minderhout and Andrea T. Frantz, *Invisible Indians: Native Americans in Pennsylvania* (Amherst NY: Cambria Press, 2008), 67, and Minderhout's essay "Native Americans in the Susquehanna River Region: 1550 to Today," in Minderhout, *Native Americans*, 90–91. A talented group of historians has written on Indians who lived "behind the frontier" in New England in the eighteenth and nineteenth centuries, and their work stands as a model for other regions. See Daniel R. Mandell, *Behind the Frontier: Indians in Eighteenth-Century Eastern Massachusetts* (Lincoln: University of Nebraska

Press, 1996); Daniel R. Mandell, *Tribe, Race, and History: Native Americans in Southern New England, 1780–1880* (Baltimore: Johns Hopkins University Press, 2008); Jean M. O'Brien, *Dispossession by Degrees: Indian Land and Identity in Natick, Massachusetts, 1650–1790* (New York: Cambridge University Press, 1997); Jean M. O'Brien, *Firsting and Lasting: Writing Indians out of Existence in New England* (Minneapolis: University of Minnesota Press, 2010); David J. Silverman, *Faith and Boundaries: Colonies, Christianity, and Community among the Wampanoag Indians of Martha's Vineyard, 1600–1871* (New York: Cambridge University Press, 2005); and numerous essays in Colin G. Calloway, ed., *After King Philip's War: Presence and Persistence in Indian New England* (Hanover NH: University Press of New England, 1997).

60. The Eastern Lenape Nation of Pennsylvania is a nonrecognized community. They run the Lenape Cultural Center in Easton, Pennsylvania.

61. *Carlisle Valley Sentinel*, October 10, 1879, 5.

Part 2   Student Lives and Losses

3

Photograph

Carlisle Poem—Who Is This Boy?

MAURICE KENNY (MOHAWK)

I hear ancient drums in the eyes
see dances on the mouth

why is this teenage boy
stiff in the shutter
punishment, pain on the cheek
loss in folded hands

who is this boy . . . nationless
nondescriptive in an army uniform
devoid of hair-feather, fetish, and paint

stiff young sapling rising from some eastern wood
straight as a Duwamish totem
tall as a southwestern mesa pueblo
collar so tight it proclaims a hanging
no pemmican or jerky or parched corn
in the clenched fist that your mother
gave to eat on the road to Pennsylvania
where Delawares once built Longhouses
made fires, loved in furs, fished rivers
praised the Creator for boundless beauty

who is this boy . . . hair cut, tongue cut
whose youthful warrior braids lay heaped
    on the barber's floor
spine straightened by Gen. Pratt's rules of order

ancient image scattered over forested hills
so many leaves from a dying apple tree

who is this teenage lad with eyes cold
    in utter fear
mouth vised and shut of prayer and song
whose thin legs tremble within the army trousers
arms quiver in dread of the un-expected
(an instructor standing off from the flash
of the insensitive camera demanding compliance)

there should be a flute to his lips
making songs, music of love
there should be a lance in his grip to take home game
there should be a future on the roll of his dark cheek
there should be a vision quest in his spirit
a name given for honorable deeds
a drawing of the deed on stretched skin
    of the winter count/calendar

he stands before the photographers
amalgamated in uniform and shaved head
he stands compromised before his teachers
all that is left to him which is him . . .
beaded moccasins below the cuffs of his pants
but the bead work so faint in the photo
his great Nation cannot be fathomed
(it can be guessed that probably the supply room
ran out of army shoes the morning
his wagon arrived at the boarding school)

who is this lad
he has no name.
no land.
no Nation.
Is he Jim Thorpe. Louis Tewanima.

Where was he born. When was he born.
Who is his father. His uncle. His siblings.
Who was his mother who suckled him at breast.
Is this boy entombed in the unmarked grave
    of the Military Institute
which won so many wars by bringing
so many proud children to their young knees.

I listen for the drum in your eyes
wait to see the dance on your mouth
all I hear are your bitter cries
    of anguish

He has no name
only a reflection

his is one of the many spirits
Chief Seattle prophesied
would forever roam this once
free and beautiful land
and that always the Gen. Pratts
would be aware of the ghosts.

this photograph . . .
a reminder
of this nameless boy
who is he . . .
my grandfather

(For Geary Hobson and Paula Olinger)

Fig. 3. "Before" photograph: Chiricahua Apaches as they arrived at Carlisle from Fort Marion, Florida, November 4, 1886. Front row, left to right: Clement Seanilzay, Beatrice Kiahtel, Janette Pahgostatun, Margaret Y. Nadasthilah, and Frederick Eskelsejah. Second row: Humphrey Escharzay, Samson Noran, and Basil Ekarden. Third row: Hugh Chee, Bishop Eatennah, and Ernest Hogee. Photo by John N. Choate. Cumberland County Historical Society, Carlisle PA. 12-24-01 (US-46).

Fig. 4. "After" photograph: Chiricahua Apaches four months after their arrival at Carlisle, March 1887. Front row, left to right: Humphrey Escharzay, Beatrice Kiahtel, Janette Pahgostatun, Bishop Eatennah, and Basil Ekarden. Second row: Ernest Hogee and Margaret Y. Nadasthilah. Third row: Samson Noran, Frederick Eskelsejah, Clement Seanilzay, and Hugh Chee. Photo by John N. Choate. Cumberland County Historical Society, Carlisle PA. 12-25-01.

4

The Names

BARBARA LANDIS

As I stand at the podium, speech at hand, ready to introduce two people who have worked closely with me in my endeavors to get the Carlisle Indian School student enrollment names to the Native nations, I look out into the audience and suddenly realize I can't speak. I am looking into the eyes of all those descendants with whom I've been emailing for twenty years without meeting them, and now they are real. Their relatives' names are imprinted in my brain. Names of memory. Names of history. Names of reclamation. I know their ancestors' stories, or parts of their stories. And now they are real. The virtual descendants' group I have created is suddenly here in this auditorium, and I am overwhelmed by their presence.

In 1991 I first became familiar with the Carlisle Indian Industrial School collections when working as a library assistant for the Cumberland County Historical Society in Carlisle, Pennsylvania. My duties included answering inquiries from descendants of students who had been enrolled at the school. The Historical Society archives houses the most complete collection of Indian School newspapers, publications, and photographs in the country. The staffer who had been handling descendants' requests retired, and so I became the de facto answerer of those inquiries. These inquiries revealed the stories of historical figures heretofore unknown to me. I wondered how thousands of Native youngsters could have passed through my community from 1879 to 1918 and yet remain invisible, with the exception of one notable athlete, Jim Thorpe. I resolved to expand my own awareness about the Carlisle Indian School and began to seek out books on federal Indian policy, American Indian history, biographies of notable Native Americans, and encyclopedias of Indian events. I was amazed and surprised by how widely shared the Carlisle experience is by American Indians across the United States, while it is absent in mainstream American history.

My understanding of the Carlisle Indian School expanded in the early 1990s when I developed a website—www.carlisleindianschool.org—devoted to my newly found interest. I wrote an online history of the school based on a series of lectures I presented online in 1993. I added biographical pages, bibliographic pages including primary and secondary sources, samples of transcribed publications, news of relevant speakers and events, and links to outside pages tied to American Indian boarding school and assimilation themes. Within a few years I had amassed a long list of email correspondents who had direct connections to the Carlisle Indian School through these web pages.

As I made connections with descendants through the Internet, I became informed by those voices that had direct links to Carlisle Indian School students. These were the sons, daughters, nieces, nephews, and grandchildren of the Carlisle names. I was able to pass on bits of information about individual students from the school newspapers. In return, my correspondents shared snippets of knowledge about their relative(s) who had spent years in training at Carlisle. I began to recognize many of the Carlisle names in the archives, which were now becoming linked to family stories. As the students' names were becoming familiar to me, I resolved to make them available to the nations.

My work took on new meaning in 1995 when an Australian anthropologist visited the Historical Society. Genevieve Bell had created a database from the 8,856 Carlisle Indian School student folders housed in the National Archives. She had the names, or most of the names, of the Carlisle Indian School students. Her lists were based on the only primary source information available (apart from the actual family stories) containing biographical and administrative data: the student records found in file 1327 of Record Group 75 in the National Archives.[1] Prior to this, I had independently begun to develop web pages and had come upon a website listing all the Carlisle names indexed in the CCHS collection.[2] Bell agreed the lists should be combined, and graciously gave me her names with the stipulation that they be freely accessible to descendants looking for information about their ancestors. Combining those names from the National Archives with the Historical Society's card catalog of names, and weeding out the duplicates, was an ambitious project that took several years to complete. Bell's and my goal was to organize the lists by nation and make them accessible to the nations. We ultimately decided the pages should not be publicly linked, out of respect for those tribes for whom names should not be easily accessible.[3] The list constituted the most comprehensive listing of Carlisle students ever made, and the World Wide Web would become the ideal venue for providing access to those names, which in many cases had been *lost* to their own people.

I realized that the school publications were valuable sources for gathering the names, and so I began transcribing the weekly *Indian Helper* newspaper for a growing online list of Carlisle Indian School descendants. Email clearly offered an efficient form of networking, and my lists of *Helper* subscribers quickly grew to hundreds of descendants. First emailed in 1995, during the centennial of the *Indian Helper*'s original publication, the files were blind copied under the title, "History a Hundred Years Ago." Recipients eagerly awaited the emails that often included glimpses into their ancestors' daily routines at the school.[4]

Not long after I began the *Helper* transcriptions I met Dovie Thomason, a Kiowa-Apache / Lakota storyteller. Dovie had long been interested in the residential boarding school stories and was especially supportive of the web page project. She gave the financial support of her organization, the Viola White Water Foundation, to help cover my costs when creating dozens of web pages, not only making the names accessible to the nations, but also facilitating uploaded biographical sketches of students. Information from descendants' inquiries began to flow into my emails. The website quickly expanded as more pages developed and hundreds of descendants and researchers were networking via the web. In 2004 Thomason developed and added a story to her repertoire, "The Spirit Survives," based on her own journey connecting Carlisle to her family's history and experience (the story is included here in chapter 17).

Today, my www.carlisleindianschool.org pages include 10,595 names representing most Native nations, although this number changes as more research is done. The tribal tally begins with five Abenaki students and ends with five Zuni Pueblo students, A to Z, bookending the 10,595 (at this writing) names from over five hundred nations.

Many Carlisle Indian School students enrolled under their Anglicized names. But that was not the case with the very first group of students to arrive at Carlisle from the Rosebud and Pine Ridge Sioux Agencies in South

Dakota close to midnight on October 5, 1879. The National Archives records show sixty-six young people ranging in age from seven to twenty-seven in that first group of Lakota Sioux children. Their fathers bore the names of men we recognize, straight out of the pages of Black Elk's accounts of the Battle of the Greasy Grass—American Horse, White Thunder, Hollow Horn Bear, Chips, and Milk. This was the first group of youngsters destined to embark on a program designed to strip them of their traditional identity, beginning with the replacement of their Native names.

Just as Adam named his subjects in the Garden of Eden in order to exercise dominion over them, so did the Carlisle administrators rename those first children from the Sioux agencies. Luther Standing Bear describes the very process in his book *My People the Sioux*. Shortly after they arrived, students were asked to approach the blackboard showing a list of Christian names. A boy named Ota Kte, who was the son of Standing Bear, walked up to the blackboard and pointed to the name "Luther." Thus, Ota Kte, translated to English meaning "Plenty Kill," became Luther Standing Bear. A girl, whose Lakota name translated into English as "Take the Tail," pointed to the name "Lucy." Being the daughter of Pretty Eagle, she became "Lucy Pretty Eagle." Neither of these Rosebud Sioux students returned to their communities after having spent their requisite time at Carlisle. Luther was scheduled to return after three years' time, but he secured employment at John Wanamaker's Department Store in Philadelphia, where he worked an additional fifteen months past his scheduled time for departure from the Carlisle Indian School. He returned to the Rosebud Agency in early July 1885. Lucy Pretty Eagle, on the other hand, who had been enrolled for a period of five years, did not survive past her first complete year at the school. She died within three months and three weeks of her arrival.

Genevieve Bell divides the Carlisle names into three enrollment waves. The first students who arrived between 1879 and 1890 were recruited to ensure the cooperation of their resisting parents and grandparents. The second cohort (1890–1904) consisted of students who had received at least four years of previous schooling, and the third cohort (1904 through the school's closing in 1918) were orphans, troublemakers in the agency schools, second-generation offspring of former Carlisle students, or athletes recruited for their athletic ability. Most male students came through the experiment with a certificate in a trade—farming, woodworking, masonry,

Fig. 5. First students to arrive at the Carlisle Indian School. Sioux Indian boys from Rosebud and Pine Ridge Agencies, October 6, 1879. The man on the far left is Capt. Richard Henry Pratt. Photo by John N. Choate. Cumberland County Historical Society, Carlisle PA. PA-CH1-309B #03.

Fig. 6. First students to arrive at the Carlisle Indian School. Sioux Indian girls from Rosebud and Pine Ridge Agencies, October 6, 1879. The woman on the far left is Miss Sarah Mather; the man on the right is interpreter Charles Tackett. Photo by John N. Choate. Cumberland County Historical Society, Carlisle PA. PA-CH1-309B #01.

tinsmithing, printing; female students were all trained in the domestic
arts—sewing and laundry or housekeeping. Some of the girls later went
on to teaching colleges or nursing schools in neighboring counties.

Nellie Robertson (Sisseton Sioux) was one of the girls who trained to
teach. Her name would become closely associated with the historical
record of the Indian School, and she would spend more than forty years
at Carlisle. Nellie came to the Indian School in November 1880 from her
home in South Dakota and then reenrolled for an extended stay. She graduated in 1890, after serving multiple Outings in homes in the Philadelphia
area. Her final Outing was spent at the West Chester Normal School in
West Chester, Pennsylvania, and after completing the teaching program
she was hired as an employee of the Carlisle Indian School. Nellie then
served as administrative assistant to every superintendent, starting with
Pratt, from 1896 through 1918. Her initials appear in the signature of
nearly all the correspondence found in the student folders of the school
records. After graduation from West Chester and during her employment
at Carlisle, Nellie married Wallace Denny (Oneida), the assistant disciplinarian and subsequent athletic director of the school. Hers is the longest
known tenure in Carlisle, and her associations were the most far reaching

of any student or administrator of the school. When the Indian School closed, it was Nellie Robertson Denny who rescued a large number of the school records and secured their survival by ultimately giving them to the National Archives, via the Bureau of Indian Affairs. These records have now been digitized and made accessible to the public.[5] Thanks to this Sisseton Sioux woman, there is a treasure trove of school records available to descendants, researchers, and academics today.

Each enrollee has his or her own unique story, but I here use the serendipity of the alphabet to tell the stories of two of them. Alphabetically, the first student listed on the Carlisle enrolment roster of 10,595 names is David Abraham (Odawa), from Michigan, and the last student listed is Otto Zotom (Kiowa), from Oklahoma.[6] Like Nellie Robertson, but unlike many others, both Otto Zotom and David Abraham were enrolled with the names with which they arrived.

David Abraham was a nineteen-year-old orphan from Petoskey, Michigan, who arrived in Carlisle in 1889. Seven years earlier, Otto Zotom, from the Kiowa Comanche and Wichita Agency, had been recruited to Carlisle by his brother, Paul Zotom, a former Fort Marion prisoner and ledger artist. Abraham graduated from Carlisle in 1900 and married fellow student Margaret Wilson, a Shawnee girl who graduated with the class of 1905. Zotom never graduated.[7] David Abraham's and Otto Zotom's backgrounds could not have been more diverse, and yet their Carlisle years gave them the distinct experience of a boarding school education that was shared by so many other Native children. Coincidentally, these two students, the first and last to be listed on Carlisle's register of names, knew one another and sang together in the school choir.[8]

Information taken from the Carlisle Indian School publications, when combined with evidence from the National Archive student cards assembled on the Bell database, enables us to begin our "A–Z" glimpse into the lives of the first- and last-named students listed alphabetically on the Carlisle roster.

The August 16, 1889, issue of the *Indian Helper* reported two groups of prospective Indian students, including Odawas, arriving from the Midwest at exactly the same time as the Little Traverse Band of Odawa lost their status of federal recognition, making clear the direct link between Native land dispossession and the schooling of Native youth. These groups were

Fig. 7. The Tin Shop at Carlisle Indian School, where students were taught cutting and soldering in the trade of making tinware, c. 1902. Photo by Frances Benjamin Johnston. Cumberland County Historical Society, Carlisle PA. JO-04-12.

Fig. 8. Girls measuring, cutting, and fitting in a sewing classroom, c. 1902. Photo by Frances Benjamin Johnston. Cumberland County Historical Society, Carlisle PA. JO-01-10.

recruited by Alfred Standing, the school disciplinarian, who "had authority to get 100 students from Michigan and Minnesota to Carlisle" that
summer.[9] Among them was nineteen-year-old David Abraham (Odawa),
who had left his home in Petoskey on the shore of Lake Michigan that
hot August 7 morning. After two days' travel he and his peers arrived at
the train station in Carlisle, Pennsylvania. Their tribal identification was
shown in the records and in the school newspapers as "Chippewa."[10] They
settled into Carlisle's daily routine, waking to the trumpet call of Reveille,
keeping their rooms neat, going to breakfast, lunch, and supper at the calls
of the bells and the shrieks of the whistles, attending classes in academic
and vocational instruction, taking music and elocution lessons, and retir-
ing at night to broadcasted trumpet strains of Taps.

David Abraham was known for his musical talent, both as a singer and
as a member of the band. His beautiful tenor voice singled him out for
solo parts during school concerts and performances. Within two years of
arrival he gave a comic performance before the entire student body on
the occasion of the anniversary of the founding of Carlisle, as reported in
the November 7, 1890, issue of the *Indian Helper*:

> Last Saturday night being the Eleventh Anniversary of the opening
> of the Educational Department of our school, scenes of those early
> days were reproduced upon the stage. . . . The school scenes, the first
> of which told the story of the trials of the first day when all the pupils
> were in blankets and knew no English, kept the five hundred lookers-
> on in a roar of laughter, the real enactment of which [arrival] . . . was
> anything but funny . . . and the best impersonator of [an arriving Indian]
> was David Abraham, but every one of the sixteen boys and girls in the
> school did his or her part beautifully.

Although none of the original blanket-clad first enrollees would have
been among the audience viewing the farcical rendition of their arrival,
many Carlisle alumni subscribed to the weekly *Indian Helper* and may
not have found this account of the students' arrival amusing. The surviving photographs of that first group of boys and girls from the Rosebud
and Pine Ridge Sioux Agencies show anything but comical scenes. Their
stunned faces testify to the trauma of displacement.

Fig. 9. Carlisle Indian School graduating class of 1900. David Abraham (Odawa) is in the second row from the bottom, fifth from the right. Photo attributed to John N. Choate. Cumberland County Historical Society, Carlisle PA. 11-A-10.

David Abraham also played solo E-flat alto clarinet in the Carlisle band, under the direction of the highly regarded Oneida composer Dennison Wheelock.[11] The first report of his athletic prowess can be found in another school newspaper story, which reports that he took second in the barrel race during Carlisle's annual Fourth of July games, in 1890.[12] The following spring he broke the school record for the pole climbing race, having climbed twenty feet in eight seconds![13]

David Abraham's first Outing experience was with a farmer named August Blackwell, in Pennington, New Jersey. According to information from his student card in the National Archives (collated on Bell's database), Blackwell employed eight Carlisle boys to work on his farm between the summers of 1890 and 1902. Most of these students were being trained as farmers, including David Abraham, who lived on the Blackwell Farm during the summer of 1891. Shortly after his return to Carlisle, he was listed on the baseball roster as a substitute left fielder. His subsequent Outings occurred after three uninterrupted years in residence at the school. Abraham's enrollment for five years was completed by that time, but instead of returning to his home community in Michigan, he spent one twenty-month Outing term with Mrs. Ella Hart, in Davisville, Pennsylvania, and then, starting in October 1896, spent the next two years working for her relatives in Hatboro, Pennsylvania. The November 29, 1895, issue of the *Helper* reported, "David Abraham is in from his country home for a Thanksgiving visit, looking better than we ever saw him." Coincidentally, his future wife, Margaret Wilson (Shawnee), also spent a year on Outing in Hatboro, the year after David Abraham graduated from Carlisle. He married Margaret Wilson after her graduation in 1905.

David Abraham was one of the few students who did not return to his home community after graduation. Answering a Carlisle survey in 1907, he reported back to the school that he and Margaret were living in Hatboro. Their first child, Wilson, had been born there in 1906,[14] and Abraham was working as a shipping clerk for a company in nearby Philadelphia. Richard Henry Pratt's replacement, Moses Friedman, was not an army officer but a civil servant. Between 1909 and 1913 he conducted a series of systematic surveys to collect information about the students after they had left the school. This was to substantiate the success of the Carlisle program by providing evidence of where they lived, their marital status, the property they owned, and their general well-being. David and Margaret Abraham responded to these surveys, reporting in 1909 that they had moved to Shawnee, Oklahoma. Margaret was a member of the Absentee Shawnee Tribe. Her allotment became the site of their farm, located in Shawnee, and David Abraham's occupation was listed as "shipping clerk and traveling salesman."[15] Their responses to further surveys in 1914 and 1915 showed that the Abrahams were still in Shawnee and that David was working for the Atchison, Topeka and Santa Fe Railroad. By 1914 they had two sons.[16]

However, it appears that David Abraham may have regretted leaving Hatboro for his wife's reservation in Oklahoma. In a letter to school secretary Nellie Robertson Denny he wrote: "When a non-reservation school student comes home and is ready for his trade and hunts for work white people size the Indian up and know he is an Indian, he has no work for him. It is no wonder the students from non-reservation school get so discouraged and are once more back to their old Indian ways. They are better off in the East because people in the East take more interest in them than they do here."[17] This same lament, repeatedly found in other student correspondence in the National Archive student records, speaks to the obvious failure of Pratt's goal of assimilation. As willing as students were to make their way into the white world, job opportunities off the reservation were scarce. According to the 1920 census, the Abrahams were still in Shawnee, with three sons, ages thirteen, nine, and seven, and David was listed as a laborer.

In contrast to David Abraham's interest in keeping connected with Carlisle, the last student listed alphabetically on the Carlisle student name roster, Otto Zotom, did not respond to any surveys. In fact, we know little of his whereabouts after leaving the Carlisle Indian School. We do know that he was recruited to Carlisle in 1882 by his older brother, Paul Zotom, who had been one of the Kiowa prisoners held at Fort Marion, Florida. When released after three years, Paul Zotom was sent back west to his community by Pratt to recruit further Kiowas for the newly established Carlisle Indian School. Otto Zotom had a younger brother, Owen Yellow Hair, who had been recruited and enrolled at Carlisle before him.

Owen Yellow Hair arrived as a teenager in the second group of Carlisle Indian School recruits on October 27, 1879, exactly three weeks after Pratt had enrolled the first group of students from the Rosebud and Pine Ridge Sioux Agencies. Owen's Carlisle experience paved the way for the enrollment of Otto, who entered the Indian school on August 31, 1882, two months after his older brother Owen's departure. Otto Zotom was only twelve years old upon arrival, and Paul Zotom was listed as guardian.[18] The three brothers were nephews of Etahdleuh, who with Paul had become one of the accomplished Fort Marion Prison ledger artists.[19]

Otto Zotom was enrolled for a five-year-term and was scheduled to return to the Kiowa Comanche and Wichita Agency in the summer of 1887, but similar to David Abraham's and many other students' experience at Carlisle, he stayed an additional four years. According to his school record card, twelve-year-old Otto entered grade one for his first term in 1882, with no previous schooling at the time of his enrollment. By the time he left in 1891, he had completed grade seven and had been sent on an Outing every summer between 1882 and 1887. There is very little information about Otto Zotom's experience at the school, save for the news of him almost winning the corn husking contest at the lower farm in October 1887, as reported in the *Indian Helper*.

Fig. 10. Otto Zotom (Kiowa), c. 1882. Photo by John N. Choate. Cumberland County Historical Society, Carlisle PA. PA-CH1-038c.

Although fewer than 7 percent of the Carlisle Indian School population graduated, people often assumed that returned students had graduated, and newspaper articles frequently referred to students as Carlisle graduates regardless of whether they had passed the necessary examinations. Probably the most famous example of this mistake, as well as one that illustrates the complexities associated with Carlisle student names, is the case of the Brulé Lakota Plenty Horses. At Carlisle, Plenty Horses, the son of Living Bear, was enrolled under the name Plenty Living Bear. He attended Carlisle from 1883 to 1889 and then went home to the Rosebud Sioux Agency. Two years after his return, he was arrested for murdering a cavalry officer in revenge for the officer's complicity in the massacre at Wounded Knee. The trial of Plenty Horses was covered by the weekly *Indian Helper*, as well as the monthly *Red Man* and *Helper* magazines. The evidence was complicated, but the school was able to deny the charges that Plenty Horses was a Carlisle graduate, because no student named Plenty Horses had ever graduated from Carlisle. That was technically true, since Plenty Horses had been enrolled under the name of Plenty Living Bear, and Plenty Living Bear had not technically graduated. Plenty Horses was ultimately exonerated of the crime of murder because of the ruling that the conditions surrounding the killing represented a state of war. Had Plenty Horses been found guilty, so too, by implication, would have the cavalry officers who massacred dozens of innocent Indians at Wounded Knee.[20]

The names on the Carlisle roster represent a broad mix of nations, cultures, and experiences. Tribes represented from the United States include the Stockbridge, Munsee, Coeur D'Alene, Spokane, Choctaw, Pueblo, Mohawk, Umatilla, Tlinget, Haida, Penobscot, and Abenaki tribes, and hundreds more. There are also more than sixty members of the so-called "Porto Rican" tribe, because, in 1898 during the Spanish–American War, General Nelson Miles recruited young adults from these islands; eight of them would go on to graduate from the Carlisle Indian School. Also recruited during this era was a young Filipino boy, Engracias Baculi, who was at Carlisle for three months.

By the beginning of the twentieth century, sports had taken hold at Carlisle, and winning football and track teams were the direct consequence of recruiting athletes from feeder reservation and mission schools on or near the reservations, as well as the other off-reservation schools, such as Haskell, Chemawa (which, incidentally, predates the founding of Carlisle by several months), Chilocco, Albuquerque, Santa Fe, and the nineteen additional schools modeled after Carlisle. And, of course, it was in the realm of sports that we find the best-known name associated with the Carlisle Indian School: Jim Thorpe.

Jim Thorpe (Sac and Fox) was recruited from the Haskell Indian School in 1907. He would become famous for his success in the pentathlon and decathlon events in the 1912 Stockholm Olympics, and he also played on the Carlisle football team, which featured many other well-known Carlisle athletes: Alex Arcasa (Colville), Joe Guyon (Chippewa), Bruce Goesback (Arapaho), Robert Hill (Tuscarora), William Hodge (Klamath), Roy Large (Shoshone), Gus Lookaround (Menominee), and Stansill "Possum" Powell (Cherokee).[21] Many descendants talk about their grandparents who played ball with the likes of these players. The Carlisle football players drew large crowds and substantial gate receipts and became the source of Carlisle's name recognition. Theirs are the names people universally associate with Carlisle. They are the names that bring a kind of magic to Carlisle, because they were larger than life, performing legendary feats. They beat the Army team when they played at West Point in 1912, and a limping Dwight Eisenhower had to be carried off the field after Jim Thorpe tackled him. And they beat Ivy League teams—Harvard, Dartmouth, Brown, Columbia, Cornell, and Penn—in games that were covered by the national press.

Yet despite the magic associated with the names of Carlisle's well-known sports heroes, the subject of names at the school is, as we have seen, far more complicated. It cannot be separated from the broader Carlisle mission to destroy Native cultures and assimilate Native youth. Many descendants still do not know the names of their ancestors who attended the school, and few have full awareness of what these students' lives were like when living thousands of miles from home. Based in the town of Carlisle, my research and work to get the names of students to the Native nations has been a twenty-year-long effort to restore some of the familial connections that were broken when children were taken away from home to have new clothes, religions, values, and names forced on them at Carlisle.

Always, it is links to families and communities that make the research live, and this is why I was so moved to meet so many descendants at the symposium. I want to end this chapter with a story that illustrates the importance of research on the Carlisle names. Nowhere in the archival resources dedicated to Carlisle Indian School history is the issue of student names more problematic than in the Indian Cemetery, now located at the eastern end of the Carlisle Barracks. The stones at Carlisle include dozens of misspelled names and misspelled nations, and among the neatly landscaped rows of military-issue headstones are thirteen Carlisle Indian school student graves marked "Unknown" (see chapter 10 for details of the "Unknowns").

In August 2012, the letter I received from an elder (see below) confirmed my belief that names need to be discovered and preserved. Mary Jones, along with her husband Willard and daughter Eleanor Hadden, had discovered on a visit to Carlisle in 1997 that there was no headstone in the cemetery for their relative Mary Kinninook. They returned to Carlisle in 2000 for a commemorative Powwow to honor Carlisle Indian School children. On this second visit they took photographs of the campus, and Mary Jones wrote that one of these photographs was of the hospital, which was where her grandmother's sister, Mary Kinninook, had died. Mary was buried in the school cemetery. However, because there was no death certificate or news of the death reported by the state of Pennsylvania, it was assumed by Alaskan agency officials that Mary Kinninook had returned to Alaska. Mary Jones wrote:

> Grandma got a letter from the Territory of Alaska inquiring of Mary's whereabouts. To them, it's like she just disappeared. I found this correspondence after Grandma died, so when I answered Juneau, their reply was—there was such a time lapse that they just closed the files. I believe the old hospital became some kind of living quarters. No picture of Mary, just bits of information. A half sheet of her being in the hospital states she died Christmas day, apparently alone.
>
> Grandma had mentioned her sister, Mary, who went to Carlisle then dying there being buried there. No grave marker. As the Kininnook family was in the Saxman Church session books, it showed Mary being baptized there with a final notation in the "remark" line the date and place where Mary died—Carlisle Indian School. Imagine the hundreds of other Indian children with similar stories.[22]

This sad commentary, by a living relative and namesake (Mary Jones) of a child buried under an "Unknown" stone at Carlisle, represents a dramatic illustration of the importance of knowing all the Carlisle names. As we gather the names and the stories behind them, we celebrate the respect given by the relatives, who hold the names in their hearts. The Carlisle Indian School names endure, and, hopefully, more stories about them will emerge as relatives make their personal discoveries after the records become more available.

NOTES

1. Bell organized a database of statistical information from National Archives Records Administration (NARA) Record Group (RG) 75, File 1327. Included

in the Folders of File 1327 are the official documents of the school; any correspondence kept between school, agent, and parents or guardians; photographs; original enrollment applications, which include lineage, blood quantum, home agency or address, and physician's report; Outing Reports including patrons' names and locations and students' dates of service; runaway information; number and sex of siblings; and occasional follow-up surveys of the students' whereabouts after 1910. Folders hold different documentation, and some only contain the enrollment cards. These folders may be photocopied by writing to NARA and are also available online at the Carlisle Indian School Digital Resource Center: http://carlisleindian.dickinson .edu/.

2. The website http://members.aol.com/carlisle/ is no longer viable. The site included a listing taken from the index of the Linda Witmer book *The Indian Industrial School* (Carlisle PA: Cumberland County Historical Society, 1993). That listing was compiled by CCHS volunteer Charles Maclay, who transcribed the card catalog listing developed by volunteers at the CCHS and used by patrons for research. This is the list that Landis merged with Bell's list, weeded out the duplicates, and then sorted by nation and posted online.

3. The archivist for the Oglala Lakota Tribal College explained the importance of protecting Lakota names of those who have passed away. To print them out, stack them up under a pile of papers, or to throw them away into a wastebasket would be disrespectful. "We do not treat our names in that way."

4. Email from Dale Besette to Barbara Landis, July 4, 2002. "Hi Barbara, Having a lot of trouble with computer, e-mail, etc. Would you be good enough to put me back on your list for the Carlisle Indian School newspaper? Just love reading abt. the old days and what it was like for my grampa when he was at Carlisle as a boy. Thank you Barbara. Lots of love. Dale Bessette, Winsor, Ontario, Canada."

5. Carlisle Indian School Digital Resource Center, http://carlisleindian.dickinson .edu.

6. This number of 10,595 is fluid and will be constantly changing as new names are discovered or duplicates are deleted. The changing number can be tracked at Carlisle Indian Industrial School (1879–1918) Tribal Enrollment Tally, http://www.epix.net/~landis/tally.html.

7. Of the 10,595 recorded names, 758 graduated. Genevieve Bell, "Telling Stories out of School: Remembering the Carlisle Indian Industrial School, 1879–1918" (PhD diss., Stanford University, 1998; UMI #9908713, Ann Arbor MI, June 1998), 402.

8. *Indian Helper* 9 (October 18, 1889): 2. David Abraham sang tenor. Otto Zotom sang bass.

9. *Indian Helper* 6 (September 20, 1889): 3.

10. Chippewa and Ottawa are used interchangeably in the Carlisle Archive to identify students enrolled from the agency at Petoskey, Michigan.

11. *Indian Helper* 7, no. 7 (October 23, 1891): 2.

12. "Second Barrell Race," *Indian Helper* 45, no. 5 (July 11, 1890): 3.

13. "Pole Climb," *Indian Helper* 6, no. 29 (March 27, 1891): 4.

14. Wilson Abraham, 1910 Census and Voter list, Earlsboro Township, Pottawatomie County OK, Ancestry.com.

15. NARA RG 75, File 1327, Folder 5384.

16. NARA RG 75, File 1327, Folder 5384.

17. NARA RG 75, File 1327, Folder 5384.

18. NARA RG 75, File 1328, Record B6-97.

19. Karen Daniels Petersen, *Plains Indian Art from Fort Marion* (Norman: University of Oklahoma Press, 1972).

20. N. Scott Momaday, "The Man Made of Words," in *The Remembered Earth: An Anthology of Contemporary Native American Literature*, ed. Geary Hobson (Albuquerque: University of New Mexico Press, 1981), 102–3.

21. John S. Steckbeck, *Fabulous Redmen: The Carlisle Indians and Their Famous Football Teams* (Harrisburg PA: J. Horace McFarland, 1951), 137.

22. Email from Mary Jones to Barbara Landis, August 22, 2012.

5

White Power and the Performance of Assimilation

Lincoln Institute and Carlisle Indian School

LOUELLYN WHITE (MOHAWK)

The connection between my family's story and the Carlisle Indian School's history drew me to the Carlisle Symposium. My paternal grandfather, Mitchell Aronhiawakon White, was born in 1889 on the Akwesasne (St. Regis) Mohawk reserve and died in 1975.[1] I have fond memories of sitting on his lap while he played a harmonica, tapping his feet to the music. Sometimes he would clap his hands and do a jig around the room. He seemed to possess a natural gift for music that had been honed while he was at the Carlisle Indian Industrial School, where he played clarinet in the school's marching band. He was there at the same time as Jim Thorpe and had a "ringside seat" to Thorpe's football games; it's quite possible a friendship developed between them.[2] But there were only a few stories about my grandfather and Carlisle, and those I learned from my father because Grandpa "just didn't like to talk about his time at Carlisle."

In contrast, my father, who grew up during the Great Depression hunting muskrats for food, attending only elementary school, and later joining the army, always talked about Carlisle with a sense of pride. He would pound his fists on the table and say: "The goddamn white man took everything, but he can't take away your education." My father saw education as a way out of poverty—and for his family—that started with Carlisle. My grandfather, his brother John White, my paternal grandmother's sister Genevieve Jacobs, and several other relatives attended the school during the years 1900–1914.[3] My feelings about Carlisle are quite mixed. On one hand, I partially attribute my own educational journey to Carlisle, because had my family not attended, the value of education may never have been passed on to me. But the cost of education at Carlisle meant that my family lost some of their culture, language, and identity. I am also cognizant of and sensitive to those survivors of boarding and residential

Fig. 11. Mitchell (on left) and John White, c. 1906. From John White's personal Carlisle Indian School scrapbook. Courtesy of Louellyn White.

schools who suffered physical, emotional, and sexual abuse at the hands of school authorities. The experiences of Indian boarding school students were complex; they varied greatly depending on when and where they went to school and the current administration and government policies of the time. A common factor they shared, however, was that they were all a part of a grand colonial project whose mission was to civilize, assimilate, and "kill the Indian to save the man." Like the thousands of Indian children who survived residential schools, my grandfather was a part of that grand experiment designed to eradicate his identity as Onkwehonwe.[4] Carlisle wasn't successful at completing wiping out all that was Mohawk in my family, because they continued to identify as Mohawk, retained some semblance of the language, maintained strong connections with their family on the reserve, and passed on Mohawk cultural values to succeeding generations.

I had been researching my family at Carlisle for several years, and one night, after staying up late transcribing documents, I lay in bed thinking about my grandfather and all he must have endured as a young child far away from his home and family, leaving behind his Mohawk culture and sense of identity. That night I had a dream about my grandfather. I told him I wanted to know everything there was about Carlisle, and I asked him: "Grandpa, what do you want them to know?" He said, without hesitation and quite to the point: "Tell them we didn't have a *choice*." By "choice," I think he meant that as a child, neither he nor his family made the conscious *choice* to give up their culture and language at an institution designed to assimilate Indian children into white society.

The U.S. Department of Indian Affairs collected Native children from across the United States, including reservations in New York, in a benevolent attempt to help them escape the "ignorance and heathenism" in their communities.[5] There were 352 Mohawks who went to Carlisle,[6] and the majority were from the St. Regis reservation. Some students, like my grandfather and his brother, were sent to Carlisle from the Lincoln Institute, a boarding school in urban Philadelphia that had its start in 1866 as a home for white orphaned children of Civil War soldiers.[7] It was turned into a school for Indian children by Mrs. Mary McHenry Cox in 1882, drawing hundreds of children from various tribal nations.[8]

At both Carlisle and Lincoln my family members encountered the "Outing" system, one method of assimilation into white society started by Carlisle's founder and superintendent, Richard Henry Pratt. Thousands of Indian children spent their summers with local white families, where Pratt thought the added exposure would complement what they learned during the school year: "No school can give home training on a small scale as the Indian should learn it in order to become Americanized."[9] Some Outings started during the summer months were extended to include the rest of the year, with students attending local public schools.[10] The Outing program also served to benefit local non-indigenous families and businesses through exploitation in the form of cheap child labor.[11]

Outings served another purpose as well: by occupying students during the summer months, Outings prevented the children from returning to their families and their reservations, where it was feared they would return to their traditional lifestyles or, as it was described, "go back to the blanket." Instead, they were submersed in the dominant white American culture throughout the entire year with the aim that they would acquire the American values of industry and thrift. According to Pratt, the main purpose of the Outing program was to help Indian children "learn English and the customs of civilized life."[12] Photographs of Carlisle girls, working in kitchens and sitting on the porches of their white Outing patrons, demonstrated the "socially elevating" aspects of the program through immersion in the "refined homes and families, where the pupils are received."[13]

But there was a contradiction between the outward appearance of the assimilated Indian living in white society and the ways in which such a program simultaneously ensured Indians' inferiority. The Indian could be like the white man in dress and behavior, but the occupation and social status of the Indian would never be equal to that of this white counterpart. The children were mostly trained to be domestic servants and farm laborers, not teachers or lawyers.

My grandfather was trained in agricultural skills at Carlisle. This agricultural training began on the school's own farms, both those bordering the school grounds and off-site. Boys who worked in the dairy stayed in the school's old farmhouse and ate their meals there.[14] Working the land was seen to be of great importance to the white American way of life. Even in an era of industrialization, for Indians, Americanization meant becoming a farmer. So Pratt thought Indian children would benefit by spending summers "among our farmers to gain practical knowledge for managing their own farms."[15] If the Indian could learn such skills, he would be "just as good a hand at all the various employments of the farm as the White man."[16]

My grandfather worked on dairy farms in rural Pennsylvania and New Jersey during his Outings and was subject to the Outing rules. Proper conduct during Carlisle's Outings was strictly enforced, forbidding pupils from going to nearby cities like Philadelphia and to public parks unless accompanied by a member of their Outing family. Evening and Sunday excursions were also discouraged, while church and "Sabbath school" were required.[17] Carlisle's school policy required two years of attendance before going on Outing. An Outing agent filed reports of children's health, working conditions, and progress.[18] Females were often placed with families to assist in childcare and household duties.

Despite the potential for exploitation, Pratt believed that all Indian children on Outing should be treated like family members and not as servants. As long as Indians could be properly assimilated into white society, Pratt believed they could be as industrious as the white man. At the beginning of the Outing program, Carlisle refused to place the children for work in cities like Philadelphia or in locations where they could become trapped in menial occupations. However, Pratt later relented, and Indian children were eventually placed in various factories like the nearby Hershey Chocolate factory. Later, some were sent as far away as Detroit to work in the Ford automobile plant, and others went to work in area resorts.[19]

While on Outing, my grandfather, like other students, was provided with clothing and books, but he had to pay for his own board. Wages were modest at $1 to $15 per month, and records indicate that my grandfather earned $11 for his Outing work in July 1909.[20] A portion of money students earned was used for personal expenses, and the remainder was sent to the school and deposited into personal savings accounts. Money from their personal accounts could be withdrawn once per month. "Interest bearing certificates of deposit" were also issued and held until the children left school.[21] Thriftiness went hand in hand with Pratt's plan of introducing ideas of individuality and private property. Part of student training at Carlisle emphasized important American values like earning and saving money, as well as spending it wisely. Strict rules were in place for how Outing students could access and spend their earned money:

> Do not allow the free use of money. Advise and assist in the purchase of clothing and other necessaries, which charge up at the time. Give a small amount of spending money occasionally if asked for, but if it is spent for useless articles withhold it and advise me. Pupils are expected to save at least 75% of their wages when regularly at work. After two weeks trial, talk with pupils and correspond with me about wages, which are to commence when pupil is received, but what is customary in your vicinity for like service should determine the matter. When returning to the school give enough money for transportation and send the balance to me by mail.[22]

Students, however, didn't always receive their pay in a timely fashion A letter from my grandfather to the school superintendent dated October 1910 reads: "Dear Mr. Friedman,[23] your letter arrived and I was so disappointed about the money I wrote for last week. . . . I am still asking you to send me the $20.15, for if you don't I will surely have to go on a farm again and lose my job. You may think I'm spending money foolishly, but I am not. I am making every penny count and worked hard for it. Yours truly, Mitchell White."[24]

My grandfather wrote to the school at least twice asking for the hard-earned money he made from working on a farm. He had already left Carlisle and was doing what he had been trained to do—work, earn money, and participate in the American economic and social structure. He also indicated in his letter that he needed his money to buy a suit for his new job. It is unclear what his new job was, but he was still in Pennsylvania and by that time a young adult. But like a child asking his parents for an allowance based on good behavior, he had to justify how he was going to spend his money.

This provides one example of the overarching power Carlisle authorities held over Indian students, who were denied agency in how they earned, saved, and spent their wages. Students had to make special requests to withdraw their earnings, indicating what they intended to purchase with their money while promising to avoid frivolity and the purchasing of "useless articles." Such strict rules about money management were meant to teach students to become self-sufficient farmers and homemakers who would become good and productive citizens.[25]

Pratt wanted his school to do more than educate students for subordinated forms of employment; he wanted to change their very consciousness and sense of tribal identity. One method used to erase Native history was to superimpose a dominant white narrative by engaging students in theatrical performances such as *The Captain of Plymouth*, a comic opera by Seymour S. Tibbals and Harry C. Eldridge based on Longfellow's poem "The Courtship of Miles Standish." The play was first performed by Carlisle students for Carlisle students, teachers, and staff with subsequent showings open to townspeople and invited guests, including reporters from Philadelphia.[26] It was also performed by students in nearby Harrisburg at the Majestic Theater.[27] In March 1909, performances ran for three evenings. One night drew an audience of over a thousand people, all potential financial donors to Carlisle's mission. Most likely the show was popular among white audiences because of its acceptance of the narrative of white superiority.

Doubtless Tibbals and Eldridge, in creating an opera featuring white settlers and Indian adversaries, did not imagine Indians playing both roles. Given the white-dominated system of early twentieth-century entertainment, they must have imagined white actors taking on these identities.

But in Carlisle, the reverse happened: Indian students took on both roles. So *The Captain* required those Indian students cast as settlers to act white, while those cast as Indians had to adopt the white-constructed stereotype of the Indian as savage. Thus, Carlisle students were "performing whiteness" not only when learning English and reading Longfellow or laboring in white homes and industries, but also on stage when they were acting the parts of settlers and savages for both Indian and white audiences.

My great uncle, John White, an "educated Indian" and soloist, had a prominent role in the play as one of the original colonists at Plymouth, named Elder Brewster. According to a report in the Indian School newspaper, he sang "with a force, volume, and precision that was a joy to hear."[28] Photographs from the play show him and other students dressed in Pilgrim hats and colonists' clothing while those Carlisle students playing the stereotypical role of Indians were dressed in feathers, buckskin, and war paint. John White, as Elder Brewster, opened the play with a line that encapsulates the contentious history of Indian and white relations and replaces the fact of conquest with the image of settlement: "[This] land is settled for

Fig. 12. Cast of *The Captain of Plymouth* on stage. The musical was presented March 29, 30, 31, 1909. John White is in the second row, tenth from left. Photographer unknown. Cumberland County Historical Society, Carlisle PA. PA-CH3-117.

the benefit of the church."[29] The character of Miles Standish, or the "Captain," led the newcomers in settling Indian land.[30] Standish was lauded for his abilities to face "wild beast[s] and savages without fear."[31] By replacing the realities of conquest with the euphemistic term "settlement," this play reflected the larger society's denial of Indian history, Indian claims to the land, and white violence. In the love story between Standish and Priscilla (a maiden Pilgrim), Standish was taken captive by a band of Pequot Indians. In exchange for his freedom, Standish declared that he would marry Chief Wattawamey's daughter, the "Indian princess."[32] The play's script overtly characterizes Katonko, the "Indian Princess," and Indians in general as "the very beginning as it were of the race problem." Standish's solution to Katonko and "the race problem"—"Let's segregate her."[33]

Instead of segregating Indians and the newly arrived Europeans, however, Standish chooses to kill the Indians. Amid battle cries and "Indian yells," Standish, while used to the "killing ways of Indians," was in "hand to hand combat with twenty blood thirsty redskins. . . . I had slain nineteen of them. . . . That last one begged so pitifully for his life that I spared him."[34] Standish then adds, "To kill the festive Indian, I my head with tactics cram, I've fairly earned my title of Uncle Sam."[35] Joining the killing festivities, another Pilgrim states that he hasn't "killed an Indian for twenty-four hours."[36]

As the play continues, Standish makes it clear that he "will never wed the Indian," Katonko.[37] He is then held captive and tied to a tree while "savage" Indian "braves" danced and sang, threatening to roast him at the stake. "Weird Indian music" played when the "Indian braves" entered the stage singing: "a great and mighty chief arose, the chief of all the Pequots . . . build a fire they must burn . . . hatred of the Pequots."[38] The "braves" also sang "Indian Ghost Dance," ridiculing the real-life practice of the Ghost Dance: "We don our airy featherettes . . . throw ourselves in a spooky dance . . . we are a group of most select and dandy ghosts . . . the finest lot that any tribe can boast."[39]

Eighty-four Carlisle students played the parts of Indian "braves and squaws," soldiers, sailors, Puritan men, and maidens.[40] Claude Maxwell Stauffer, music director at Carlisle, staged and conducted "Captain of Plymouth," choosing the play for its "civilizing influence." He stated: "If Oscar Hammerstein can spend $1 million dollars to civilize Philadelphia, we could spend a few weeks for the same civilizing influence on the wards of the nation."[41] An article in the school newspaper added: "Indians are capable of taking up the White man's burden. Before long these Aborigines will realize how superior to their peaceful tribal ways are the manners of Church choirs and other amateur musical organizations."[42]

Contradictions exist between the messages conveyed in the play and the lives that Carlisle students were required to lead. The school promoted assimilation, but the play created a stark dichotomy between white and Indian, civilized and savage, and did not suggest that this gap could ever be bridged. The school was attempting to bridge the gap but would do so only by requiring students to leave any semblance of Indianness behind in their day-to-day lives. While the school seemed to promise equality if the students assimilated to white values, customs, and behaviors, the play signaled to both the public and the students themselves that "savage Indians" were inferior to white Americans. *The Captain* was instrumental in demonstrating to Indian children "that their subjugation was an inevitable consequence of historical progress."[43] Additionally, the public was reminded that Indians could leave "savagery" behind them while embracing a civilized lifestyle: "It cannot be forgotten that these are aborigines and these not only their first steps in an art foreign to their race, but what is virtually the first steps of the race in that direction."[44] While Indians could adopt the dominant society's art form (a comic opera) as an expression of civility, the audience was reminded that they were racially marked, and so their inferiority would remain. In a sense, then, the play may have offered a more realistic view of white-Native relations than did the ideology of the school.

Captain seeks to instill the master narrative of white America's manifest destiny. America was a vast expanse of empty land just waiting for European Christian conquest. The play's romanticized views of Plymouth colony disregarded the decimation of the indigenous populations of America through the introduction of disease and warfare. The play encourages the false notion that the East Coast was a vast tract of empty land waiting for the arrival and settlement of Europeans, when in fact by the time of the *Mayflower*'s arrival epidemics from germs introduced by Europeans had already wiped out 90 percent of the local indigenous population.[45] European traders followed by settler colonists would forever change the lives of indigenous peoples.

Public performances such as *The Captain of Plymouth* were meant to impress the audience and were "carefully orchestrated to demonstrate to the public and, more importantly, the Indian Bureau, that Carlisle was successfully molding Indians into productive and loyal citizens."[46] Dressed up in colonial garb while spouting lines that praised settler colonialists and damned the "savage" Indians who were in their way, students entertained white audiences by performing a version of the master narrative of settler colonialism.

By having indigenous children portray the beginning of U.S. colonialism, taking the roles of settlers and savages, the Indian School performance of *The Captain of Plymouth* reveals the contradictions in the goals of Carlisle. Students were taught that they could improve themselves by

Fig. 13. Ninth-grade class schoolroom at the Carlisle Indian School, c. 1902. The lesson on the blackboard is named "Hiawatha's Children." Photo by Frances Benjamin Johnston. Cumberland County Historical Society, Carlisle PA. JO-02-09.

embracing dominant American values and becoming productive members of American society—but they could do so only by leaving any remnants of indigenous identity behind. Whether they were taking on the role and characteristics of their oppressors and enacting "assimilation" or performing Indian stereotypes created by whites, Indian actors, like my great uncle, must surely have struggled with these painfully conflicting roles and identities. "Kill the Indian to save the man," Richard Pratt famously said; the play, like the school, left no room for my uncle to be both an Indian and a man.

Indian schools often used white-authored narratives about Indians to socialize children into accepting inferior roles. At Carlisle the children were taught Longfellow's *Song of Hiawatha* (see fig. 13). At Lincoln, the boarding school in urban Philadelphia that my grandfather and his brother attended, students were made to perform the same poem.[47] It was first published in

1855 and depicts a romanticized tale of Indian peoples through its main character, Hiawatha.[48] The epic poem features mystical stories of spirit beings and various animal characters, while the protagonist Hiawatha takes on the fictional role of a prophet with magical powers. The legend spans the birth of Hiawatha, from his childhood adventures to his eventual courtship of his love, Minnehaha. The tale ends when Hiawatha accepts Christianity from the "Black Robes" after which he disappears in his canoe, rowing off into the sunset.[49]

The poem became very popular in its day for its portrayal of the noble savage and the vanishing Indian. "Hiawatha" became a national folk hero acted out by school children across the country. Plays, recitations, drawings, paintings, statues, parodies, cartoons, music, and film all endlessly featured the white man's construction of the noble savage. Like the Wild West shows of the time, *The Song of Hiawatha* was highly influential in shaping American ideas about Indians. The scholar Alan Trachtenberg describes how "vast audiences rushed to Indian performances—Wild West shows, dances in the Southwest, and in the East and Midwest, popular performances by Indians themselves of staged versions of the irresistible cadences of the most famous poem in English written by an American, Longfellow's putative Indian epic, 'The Song of Hiawatha.'"[50]

On September 24, 1884, children at the Lincoln Institute dressed in stereotypical Indian costume and performed a theatrical spectacle of *The Song of Hiawatha*. They entertained a large audience with segments of the poem including "The Indian Home," "Indian Lullaby," "Hunting," "Ambush," and "Lover's Advent," among others. Indian children performing *The Song of Hiawatha* were performing expressions of Indianness according to the expectations of white society. The generic white man's Indian who lived in a wigwam, hunted bison, and ate wild rice was an acceptable representation of Indianness in the eyes of white audiences. Likewise, performing a generic version of the vanishing Indian was a safe and controlled depiction of Indianness whereby there was no individual or authentic tribal expression. Indians played Indians, not members of specific tribes. Not only were they pretending to be someone they were not, but they were also endorsing a white-constructed version of "the Indian."

Hiawatha, as a construction of white imagination, depicted the vanishing Indian as conquered by the white race. *The Song of Hiawatha* ends with the character of Hiawatha accepting the white savior's message of salvation after which he disappears into the sunset, reflecting the nation's ideas of the vanishing Indian. The fact that the hero departs just as the white man arrives is symbolic of the "powerful nationalizing force with ideas of race and white supremacy . . . and of America's manifest destiny."[51] After all, it was the demise of the Indian that made possible the expansion of America.

Indian students required to perform assimilation, whether by participating in the Outing program or performing narratives like *The Captain of Plymouth* or *The Song of Hiawatha* were witnessing displays of white power to construct reality. The vanishing of Hiawatha reflected the goals of the Indian School: to erase Native identity and history and replace it with the "assimilated" Indian who adopted more civilized, white ways. The children's lives would never be the same.

Some boarding school students never returned to live in their home communities, including John White. After graduating from Carlisle in 1909 he stayed in Pennsylvania and lived the rest of his life near Harrisburg working at a printing press—a skill he learned at Carlisle. John White was a "success" story of Carlisle as he was one of the few graduates of the institution. Genevieve Jacobs enrolled at Carlisle in 1916 at around sixteen years of age and left after two years in 1918, the same year the school closed. Genevieve also did not return to her reservation, and she eventually settled in Syracuse, New York, where she raised a family and died at age thirty-nine from cancer. My grandfather eventually returned to Akwesasne, but he had left the reserve as a young child and returned as a man who had grown up in a foreign and sometimes hostile environment. Carlisle could never replace a nurturing home life or the love and cultural grounding of family. The discrepancies in the records make it difficult to determine the exact dates he was at Lincoln and Carlisle, but he left his home sometime between the ages of five and eight and stayed at Carlisle until he was about twenty-one years old. Unlike his brother John, he never graduated from Carlisle. I don't know the exact circumstances of how or why my family went to these institutions, but I do know that it made a significant impact on their ability to learn and transmit the Mohawk language and culture to future generations. My grandfather rarely spoke Mohawk to his children, and both he and my grandmother became devout

Catholics. They moved from Akwesasne to central New York State for better economic opportunities and raised their children there.

My family was denied agency and had little choice in being subjected to the power of colonialism, whether by remaining in poverty on the reservation or by attending colonizing institutions designed to eliminate all traces of indigeneity. They were subjected to degrading displays of the savage warrior and the vanishing noble savage, inculcated with a white value system that sought to keep them inferior to non-Indians, and lived out their lives under the control and domination of colonial powers.

Whether their attendance in government-sponsored Indian boarding schools was forced or not, families were not enabled to make conscious and informed choices about how their children would be educated, raised, and treated. Families were rarely aware of the short- and long-term impacts these institutions would have on their children. The consequences of cultural loss and identity confusion—not to mention inadequate nutrition, disease, overcrowding, and abuse in many of the institutions—would devastate generations to come. As a descendant of Carlisle Indian Industrial School survivors, I feel a sense of responsibility in unearthing and reclaiming my family's stories. Their stories have been silenced for over one hundred years, and I aim to bring their voices alive. This chapter represents the beginning of my effort. It is through the act of discovery and of telling their stories that I am reclaiming the sense of agency that they were denied.

NOTES

1. Akwesasne is bisected by the border between the United States and Canada. New York State, Ontario, and Quebec fall within its territories. Over the years the name St. Regis has fallen out of use to some extent while the original Mohawk name of Akwesasne (Land where the partridge drums) has become more popular.

2. In 1999 *Indian Time* (Akwesasne's newspaper) reprinted an article submitted by Beatrice Jacobs, "Friend of Great Thorpe Recalls Carlisle Days with Famous Athlete." The article is about my grandfather Mitchell White. The article claims that Mitchell White and Jim Thorpe developed a close friendship at Carlisle Indian School. I have never heard any stories about this friendship, but it certainly could hold some truth.

3. Not much is known about Genevieve Jacobs and her time at Carlisle other than a couple of photographs of her that appear in Linda Witmer, *The Indian*

Industrial School: Carlisle, Pennsylvania, 1879–1918 (Carlisle PA: Cumberland County Historical Society, 2000). One of the photos shows Genevieve and another student named Honey Sweet, lying in the grass. Witmer later interviewed Honey Sweet, one of the last remaining survivors of Carlisle, who told her the two girls were best friends and were inseparable. Genevieve Jacobs's sister, Elizabeth Jacobs, would later marry Mitchell White, my grandfather. Much of the information known about John White was obtained from his personal scrapbook.

4. *Onkwehonwe* is a Mohawk concept that refers to the "Original People."

5. U.S. Department of the Interior, Office of Indian Affairs, *Annual Report of the Commissioner of Indian Affairs: General Survey of the Field* (Washington DC, October 1, 1892), 43, https://ia800302.us.archive.org/12/items/usindianaffairs 92usdorich/usindianaffairs92usdorich.pdf.

6. Barbara Landis, "Carlisle Indian Industrial School (1879–1918) Tribal Enrollment Tally," http://home.epix.net/~landis/tally.html.

7. According to the 1892 *Annual Report of the Commissioner of Indian Affairs*, children from the St. Regis reservation were sent to the Lincoln Institute beginning in 1884 at the request of Principal Chief Alexander Ransom. Letters from children at Lincoln attest to the "ignorance and poverty" on the reservation and to their inability to read and write English before attending the institution. Little is known about the Lincoln Institute, which is often confused with Lincoln University. Formerly known as the Ashmun Institute, Lincoln University was the first postsecondary institution for African Americans ("Explore PA history," http://explorepahistory.com/displayimage.php ?imgId=1-2-16B8). The Lincoln Institute discussed here was entirely separate. Also note that the names "Lincoln Institute" and "Educational Home" appear to have been used interchangeably.

8. Bob Goshorn, "Ponemah: Land of the Hereafter," *Bulletin of the Radnor Historical Society* 4, no. 7 (1987): 14–15; Department of the Interior, *Annual Report of the Commissioner of Indian Affairs, 1889–90*, Executive Documents of the House of Representatives, 51st Cong., 1st Sess., Congressional Series Set (Washington DC, 1889), vol. 2, part 5, 317–20.

9. *Carlisle Indian School Catalogue* (Carlisle PA: Carlisle Indian Industrial School, 1912), 28, http://www.archive.org/details/cu31924097741130.

10. Genevieve Bell, "Telling Stories out of School: Remembering the Carlisle Indian Industrial School, 1879–1918" (PhD diss., Stanford University, 1998), 166.

11. Robert A. Trennert, "From Carlisle to Phoenix: The Rise and Fall of the Indian Outing System, 1878–1930," *Pacific Historical Review* 52, no. 3 (1983): 267–91.

12. Bell, "Telling Stories out of School," 169.

13. *Indian Industrial School* (Carlisle PA: Carlisle Indian Industrial School, 1895),

62, https://archive.org/details/indianindustrial00unit_0. This is a publicity brochure that includes a collection of Carlisle Indian Industrial School photographs.

14. Carolyn Tolman, "The Farmhouse at Carlisle Barracks: Carlisle Indian School Farmhouse; A Major Site of Memory," https://sites.google.com/site/thefarm houseatCarlislebarracks/.

15. Richard Henry Pratt, *Battlefield and Classroom: Four Decades with the American Indian, 1867–1904*, ed. Robert Utley (Norman: University of Oklahoma Press, 2004), 193.

16. *Indian Industrial School*, 1895, 60.

17. Bell, "Telling Stories out of School," 169.

18. *Carlisle Indian School Catalogue*, 1912, 28–29.

19. Bell, "Telling Stories out of School," 198; Trennert, "From Carlisle to Phoenix,"1983.

20. National Archives and Records Administration, RG 75, Entry 1327, Box 70, File #3476.

21. *Carlisle Indian School Catalogue*, 28.

22. Pratt, MSS S1174, Box 30, Folder 815, c. 1900; qtd. in Bell, "Telling Stories out of School," 169.

23. Pratt was no longer at Carlisle in 1909. His replacement was Superintendent Moses Friedman.

24. National Archives and Records Administration, RG 75, Entry 1327, Box 70, File #3476.

25. Bell, "Telling Stories out of School," 169.

26. "The Captain of Plymouth—A Comic Opera," *Indian Craftsman* 1, no. 4 (May 1909): 47.

27. Barbara S. Lee, "Racial Resolutions in *Uncle Tom's Cabin* and *The Captain of Plymouth*: Acculturation through Drama at Carlisle Indian Industrial School, 1909–1910" (MA thesis, Lehigh University, 1999), 30.

28. "Captain of Plymouth," *Indian Craftsman*, 48.

29. Seymour S. Tibbals and Harry C. Eldridge, *The Captain of Plymouth: A Comic Opera*, script (Franklin OH: Eldridge Entertainment House, 1908), 10.

30. Standish arrived on the *Mayflower* and was a founder of the Plymouth Colony. Nathaniel Philbrick, *Mayflower: A Story of Courage, Community, and War* (New York: Penguin, 2006). He was popularized through the book *The Courtship of Miles Standish* by Henry Wadsworth Longfellow, which fictionalized much of Standish's character. Tudor Jenks, *Captain Myles Standish* (New York: Century, 1905).

31. Tibbals and Eldridge, *Captain of Plymouth*, script, 6.

32. *The Captain of Plymouth: A Comic Opera in Three Acts: As Part of the Com-*

mencement Exercises, 1909, program (Carlisle PA: Carlisle Indian School Press, 1909), 2.

33. Tibbals and Eldridge, *Captain of Plymouth*, script, 20.
34. Tibbals and Eldridge, *Captain of Plymouth*, script, 19, 81, 19.
35. Seymour S. Tibbals and Harry C. Eldridge, *The Captain of Plymouth: A Comic Opera*, vocal score (Franklin OH: Eldridge Entertainment House, 1908).
36. Tibbals and Eldridge, *Captain of Plymouth*, script, 19.
37. Tibbals and Eldridge, *Captain of Plymouth*, script, 23.
38. Tibbals and Eldridge, *Captain of Plymouth*, script, 15, vocal score, 62.
39. The Ghost Dance began in the late 1800s when the prophet Wovoka, a Paiute Indian, received a vision signaling a return of ancestral spirits to join the living. It was thought the Ghost Dance would bring peace and unity among Indians while preparing them to rise up from white oppression. James Mooney, *The Ghost-Dance Religion and Wounded Knee* (New York: Dover, 1896); Robert M. Utley, *The Last Days of the Sioux Nation* (New Haven CT: Yale University Press, 2004). Since the practice involved resistance to the "white man," authorities at Carlisle sought to dismantle any notions of truth or adherence to the practice. Tibbals and Eldridge, *Captain of Plymouth*, vocal score, 61.
40. *Captain of Plymouth*, program, 3.
41. "Captain of Plymouth," *Indian Craftsman*, 47.
42. "Captain of Plymouth," *Indian Craftsman*, 47.
43. Lee, "Racial Resolutions," 33.
44. Tibbals and Eldridge, *Captain of Plymouth*, script, 48.
45. Neil Salisbury, "Squanto: Last of the Patuxet," in *The Human Tradition in Colonial America*, ed. Ian Kenneth Steele and Nancy Lee Rhoden, vol. 1 (Wilmington DE: Scholarly Resources, 1999).
46. Lee, "Racial Resolutions," 29.
47. The Lincoln Institute, at 324 S. 11th St., Philadelphia, was where the Indian girls were housed and educated. Three miles away, at the corner of 49th St. and Greenway, was the boys' residence. Department of the Interior, *Annual Report, 1889–90*, 317–20; Rev. E. F. Wilson, "My Wife and I," *Our Forest Children: And What We Want to Do with Them* 3, no. 4 (Shingwauk Home, Owen Sound ON, 1889): 24–26. A summer location was also established in the country to escape the heat of the city. The Lincoln Institute eventually became a home for homeless orphaned boys between the ages of five and fourteen. In 1915 it merged with the Educational Home Organization, and in 1922 it merged with the Big Brother Association. Goshorn, "Ponemah."
48. Hiawatha is a fictional character based on legends of the Ojibwes and other Native peoples. The name "Hiawatha," however, is borrowed from the Iro-

quois historical figure who helped found the Iroquois Confederacy. See Alan Trachtenberg, *Shades of Hiawatha: Staging Indians, Making Americans, 1880–1930* (New York: Hill and Wang, 2004), 81. Longfellow borrowed much of his material from ethnographer Henry R. Schoolcraft, who served as U.S. Indian agent in 1822. See Richard G. Bremer, *Indian Agent and Wilderness Scholar: The Life of Henry Rowe Schoolcraft* (Mount Pleasant: Clarke Historical Library, Central Michigan University, 1987).

49. Henry Wadsworth Longfellow, *Hiawatha: A Poem* (Chicago: Reilly and Britton, 1909), 194–98, http://openlibrary.org/books/OL24240059M/Hiawatha.

50. Trachtenberg, *Shades of Hiawatha*, xxiii.

51. Trachtenberg, *Shades of Hiawatha*, xii.

6

The Imperial Gridiron

Dealing with the Legacy of Carlisle Indian School Sports

JOHN BLOOM

A longtime mentor and scholar who pioneered critical work on the Carlisle Indian School once said that it was her goal to write a history of the institution that never once mentioned Jim Thorpe.[1] Such sentiments are entirely understandable. Thorpe's iconic memory represents a larger history of sports at the institution, and Carlisle Indian School sports have driven the institution's public narrative for over a century. In fact, the public history of sports at Carlisle is so powerful that it can extinguish the recognition of almost all of the rest of the school's pasts and meanings. Even worse, the inspiring stories of triumph and success associated with the Carlisle football and track teams can easily mask the fundamental pain and destruction created by assimilation policies. That is one of the reasons why both the symposium held at Dickinson College in the fall of 2012 and this publication are so important.

Not only does the history of sports at the Carlisle Indian School tend to dominate and smother all other discussions about the school, but scholars interested in generating critical discussion about Native American education and assimilation efforts find the topic of sports to be highly problematic. On the one hand, they see the very mission of the boarding school system as violent, arrogant, and harmful socially and psychologically. Even if operated well, boarding schools served destructive purposes, and for the most part, they were not even operated very well.

On the other hand, the sports programs at Carlisle were remarkably successful. The school produced champion football teams and world-class track athletes who won Olympic medals and made the "Carlisle Indians" internationally recognized for their athletic prowess. It is difficult to reconcile these two images with one another—of victimized indigenous boarding school students with triumphant masters of the gridiron. For sports fans eager to celebrate a set of Indian athletic heroes who overcame long odds, it might be easier to simply disregard the pain caused by institutions like Carlisle, while for critics of boarding schools, it might be easiest to treat sports as an adjunct to the history of these institutions—an interesting story, but separate from the serious issues that historians of Carlisle must confront.

Anyone interested in the history of the Carlisle Indian School, however, must confront both its oppressive character and its successful athletic programs, not as separate entities, but as two dimensions intricately linked to one another. The "Carlisle Indians"—that is, the athletes who competed under the school's name, most successfully between 1894 and 1914—were more than just the public face of the school. Sports grew to become an essential part of the Carlisle Indian School in ways that would reverberate throughout the boarding school system long after Carlisle closed its doors in 1918. A careful examination of Carlisle's famed sports teams exposes the school's imperialistic mission as much as its triumphs, while a critical examination of the schools themselves illustrates that sports were a centrally important part of students' lives.

The Imperial Gridiron

In the United States we tend to take for granted that schools provide the organizational hub for amateur athletics, but this was not always the case. While team sports among college students existed as far back as the colonial period, as the nineteenth century progressed, they were difficult to regulate, generated sensational passions, and could be exploited for commercial gain. Victorian educators favored individual exercises like gymnastics for men and women as part of a larger program to elevate moral character, virtue, and discipline.[2]

After the Civil War college men began to embrace team sports in ways that school administrators could not entirely control. In addition, the nature of higher education began to change away from a liberal arts model and toward the development of managerial, middle-class subjects for an industrial economy. Male students particularly embraced the extraordinarily violent sport of football, and educators did not see this game as entirely out of step with the new direction of their institutions. Brian Ingrassia, drawing upon the work of Gail Bederman, illustrates how the rise of football corresponded with a change in ideas of manhood. While Victorian men were expected to be virtuous and emotionally restrained, postbellum men had to learn to compete in a newly aggressive market, demonstrating their *masculinity*—or elemental, physical toughness and manliness—as much as their moral virtue.[3]

Ingrassia shows that until the end of World War I, most college and university leaders embraced the public relations opportunities created by the spectacle of football. The early game was certainly bloody and dangerous, not infrequently resulting in player deaths. Yet educators found in football an outlet for the kind of teamwork, discipline, and toughness that were required of men in a heartless world where, as ex-footballer Tom Buchannan famously opines in Fitzgerald's *Great Gatsby,* "if we don't look out the white race will be—will be utterly submerged."[4]

Like late nineteenth-century educators, Carlisle Indian School founder Richard Henry Pratt was slow to embrace football for his school. Such a violent, passionate game seemed to counter his goals of demonstrating that Indians could be civilized. Yet, as Matthew Bentley observes in his doctoral dissertation on the promotion of manliness at Carlisle, Pratt understood that football could serve a function for Indian students that would be the opposite of what it meant for Ivy League college students. A Yale man might find in football a chance to demonstrate masculine toughness and assurance that in an imperial world he could uphold the "White Man's Burden." For a Carlisle Indian, however, the display of restraint and sportsmanship in the aggressive game of football would demonstrate that a "savage" game could produce civilized Indians—that Indian males could be trained to become what white, Anglo-Protestants would recognize as virtuous, morally upright men. The very spectacle that football was becoming could serve to demonstrate Pratt's assimilationist goals better than any other public demonstration he could imagine.[5]

In a now somewhat famous passage from his memoir, *Battlefield and Classroom,* Pratt recalls banning students from playing football during the early 1890s after learning of a Carlisle player who badly injured his leg. When students confronted him and demanded that he allow the students to form a team, Pratt relented but demanded two conditions. First, no Carlisle player could return a "slug" from an opponent, even if it seemed justified. Second, the players should commit themselves to defeating the "biggest football team in the country" in the span of "two, three, or four years."[6]

These two demands nicely summarize Pratt's understanding of how football could help him accomplish his goals, while also illustrating a core tension in scholastic sports that continues to this day. In fact, as Carlisle's team came closer to accomplishing the second goal over the subsequent years, they departed, at least in spirit, from the first. While Carlisle teams almost always controlled their "slugging," their most impressive victories began only after the hiring of Glenn S. "Pop" Warner as coach, a leader who elevated winning over moral virtue. Warner was known to have freely used profanity, expressed fits of temper, and enjoyed achieving a win through variously expansive interpretations of the rules (such as the hidden ball trick employed against Harvard in 1903). After the 1903 season, Warner resigned over a conflict with a player and with Pratt, who also resigned later that year. Warner returned to coach before the 1907 season though, and with weak leadership of the school in the post-Pratt era, he was free to operate his team with virtually no oversight. It was during these years that Carlisle was able to defeat the biggest football teams in the country.[7]

During Pratt's years, though, demonstration of Carlisle's "civilizing mission" took precedence over victories. Pratt subscribed to the idea that assimilation up a stepladder of civilization was a scientific fact, and he was not alone in his beliefs. In fact, Pratt was only one of a large and influential body of elites in the United States who subscribed to ideas like those of social theorist Lewis Henry Morgan's taxonomy of civilizations. Morgan advanced the idea that civilizations rather than races existed along an evolutionary hierarchy, with "savagery" as the most primitive, "barbarism" as the next step up, and "civilization" as the ultimate form of human society.[8] According to Morgan, "civilized" peoples could elevate the "savages" that they encountered as civilizations expanded to rule over increasingly remote parts of the world. However, they needed to do so through systematic processes of gradual assimilation.

It is not surprising that sports would become a primary means by which to demonstrate the theory and practice of social evolution. As Susan Brownell has illustrated in her brilliant collection of scholarship on the 1904 Olympics in St. Louis, the rise of sports in the late nineteenth century interfaced with the rise of anthropology during this same era. Sports provided a way to place "primitive" imperial subjects on display, such as during the Montreal "Indian Games" in 1860 when indigenous lacrosse teams played before British royalty, or when Mohawk lacrosse teams toured Europe between 1868 and 1883, or when Dahomean visitors from Africa raced against French athletes in the 100-kilometer steeplechase during the 1893 Chicago World's Fair.[9] At many of these events anthropologists measured the athletes who provided data that scientists used to demonstrate either inherent biological distinctions or evidence of social progress. The 1904 Olympics, held in conjunction with the Louisiana Purchase (Centennial) Exhibition in St. Louis, was perhaps the most overt example of this use of sports. W. J. McGee, the founding president of the American Anthropological Association, created the anthropology displays that were a centerpiece of the Exhibition. Non-European, indigenous peoples from around the world set up camps and residences that represented a hierarchy of civilizations. Pygmies from the Congo were established at the bottom of a hill upon whose peak organizers had constructed a mock boarding school for Native Americans. These visitors competed against highly trained athletes from Europe and North America in standard Olympic sports. Ethnologists and anthropologists used their inferior performances as evidence of racial subservience.[10]

As soon as Carlisle's football team began to play before a paying public, they were a special kind of curiosity that presented a dramatically vivid illustration of Morgan's, and Pratt's, ideology. In 1895, when Carlisle played the New York YMCA in the Polo Grounds on Thanksgiving, fans who came expected to experience a Wild West show. According to Sally Jenkins, they were somewhat disappointed. "Apart from their darker complexions," she writes, "the Carlisle players were indistinguishable from any other collegians." Jenkins writes that a woman in the stands commented, "'Oh, dear me . . . are those the Indians? Why, they don't look any different from our boys."[11] This is exactly the kind of impression that Pratt wanted the football team, and other athletic squads who performed publicly, to make. In fact, it was not uncommon for Indian school sports teams from around the United States in the late nineteenth and early twentieth centuries to be included in world expositions and fairs that publicly presented narratives of human progress and civilization. In 1901 the Pan-American Sports Carnival in Buffalo opened with a baseball game between the Carlisle Indian School and Cornell University, and their football teams played in the same festival later that fall.[12]

Fig. 14. Jim Thorpe and players of the 1912 Carlisle football team. Left to right, front row: Charles Williams, Peter Calac, Elmer Busch, Joe Bergie, William Garlow, Joe Guyon, Roy Large. Back row: Alex Arcasa, Stancil "Possum" Powell, Gus Welch, Jim Thorpe. Photo by A. A. Line. Cumberland County Historical Society, Carlisle PA. 317A #11.

In the early twentieth century, Morgan's ideas became less influential. Federal policy makers under President Theodore Roosevelt believed that nonwhite races were essentially inferior peoples. Unlike Morgan, they believed that no amount of schooling could elevate a dark-complexioned people from a "savage" state. It was under such policies that Pratt resigned in 1904, and that Warner returned to Carlisle, less intent upon demonstrating the success of assimilationist policies and more focused upon winning games. The most impressive seasons for the Carlisle Indian School football team were between 1911 and 1913. During this stretch they won thirty-eight games against three losses. They defeated some of the strongest powerhouse teams of the era such as Harvard, Pennsylvania, and Brown, often by large margins. During these seasons Jim Thorpe emerged as a superstar, and before the 1912 season he won the gold medal in both the pentathlon and decathlon at the Olympic Games in Stockholm.

Yet success on the gridiron and the Olympic track had a price. Thorpe had played semiprofessional baseball in North Carolina, which violated the rigidly amateur ideal that the International Olympic Committee had established. They stripped Thorpe of his medals—only well after Thorpe's death did they return them to his family. Toward the end of the 1913 football season 276 students led by football star Gus Welch signed a petition calling for an investigation into the school's management. A congressional investigation into corruption at Carlisle exposed wretched conditions for most students while football players were well fed and housed. The scandal forced the school's superintendent, Moses Friedman, to resign. Although Warner continued to coach for one more year, he left after a poor 1914 season. The scandal was a central factor in the closing of the school in 1918.

In fact, criticism of the Carlisle football team dated back to 1907, when it first started to achieve widespread success against major college foes. Major newspaper sportswriters penned stories accusing the team of engaging in professionalism. The accusations achieved even more merit when the famed Native American doctor, and Pratt defender, Carlos Montezuma penned a nationally published editorial accusing Warner of improperly handling team funds and of paying players.[13] Journalist Sally Jenkins, who has written perhaps the most comprehensive history of the Carlisle football team, understands much of this to have emanated from an implicitly racist newspaper media that held Carlisle to a double standard, noting that "the accusations against Carlisle could have been made against any school, then or now."[14] She continues, "So long as the Indians lost to the Ivies, they were considered a legitimate opponent. But now that they'd won, they were suddenly illegitimate. It smacked of another equation."[15]

Jenkins is absolutely correct to point out the hypocrisy of those leveling accusations against the Carlisle football team once it began to win (and to point out that a number of sports writers defended Carlisle at the time as well). Yet in noting that most schools were also guilty of similar crimes, Jenkins misses a key difference. At major colleges and universities in the early twentieth century, football had become a public face for powerful institutions that were developing for the benefit of major business interests, the federal government, and affluent white student populations. By contrast, Carlisle's successful football team provided a satisfying public image to an institution that was, at best, shamefully mismanaged and corrupt and, at worst, that directed acts of cultural genocide.

Jenkins also rightly asserts that students like Welch who signed the petition calling for Warner's resignation, and who testified against Warner before Congress, were motivated in large part by anger over the repeal of Thorpe's medals. Yet the depth of their response, and the willingness of Welch to testify before Congress (along with the abandonment of the team by most of its star players after the 1913 season), also suggests that their upset had deeper roots. Their action was perhaps one of the first to raise before the general public a protest by athletes of color over exploitation within white-dominated sports. It opened up the question of who was truly served by the success of the Carlisle Indian School football team. While the heroes of the Carlisle gridiron certainly filled students with pride, its football victories were symbolic. Few non-athletes who attended Carlisle attained the success of Frank Mount Pleasant, Jimmy Johnson, and Gus Welch, who went on to successful careers in dentistry, law, and coaching, respectively. In fact, what athletes did provide was entertainment for paying white spectators, and a distorted reflection of a school's misguidedness and corruption. Nevertheless, sports were not just about exploitation and problematic colonial representations. The success of the Carlisle Indian School sports teams provided a touchstone for students who often defined memories and lore that they connected to their experiences in boarding school.

Sports and the Lives of Students

When asked about social life at Carlisle, Lucy Logan Griggs (Sac and Fox) struggled to recall any. "Well, on Sundays was the only time that we had social. Well, Saturday night I guess some of them went to the dance." In her oral history transcript stored with the Doris Duke Oral History collection at the University of Oklahoma, she then remembers, "We had these sports. Oh! By the way, I want to mention Jim Thorpe here. That's where he was and he learned all his sports at Carlisle. Course it was really . . . everybody went all out for sports." Griggs then goes on to discuss dances, band concerts, and an afternoon social. It is as if the memory of sports triggered a memory of social life that she had trouble recovering before she mentioned it.[16]

According to the background information provided on the front of the transcript, Griggs was sixty-four years old at the time of the interview in

May 1969. She also recalls that she was thirteen years old when she arrived at Carlisle after both of her grandparents and her father had died. Since she was born sometime between May 1904 and June 1905, she would have arrived in Carlisle at the earliest in 1917, at least four years after the height of the Carlisle football program and Jim Thorpe. In fact, by 1917 the sports teams at Carlisle were all but eliminated, and by August 1918 the school had shut its doors forever.

A similar management of narrative time informs an interview with John Alonzo (Laguna), who played lacrosse at the Carlisle Indian School. Alonzo remembers spending most of his free time in the school gymnasium as a student. When lacrosse arrived as a spring sport, he was determined to make the team, and he did. He proudly remembers scoring a goal against the Naval Academy in his first game. He also recalls scoring two goals against the University of Pennsylvania at Franklin Field and playing against the Brooklyn Athletic Club. When asked, Alonzo affirmed that defeating white opponents provided extra satisfaction, and for an example he discussed a victory over a team from Toronto. "They beat everybody in Canada and so they scheduled their games with all these colleges down the Atlantic seaboard." Alonzo recalls that the Canadians were "overconfident," but when they came to play the Indians, "Carlisle just walked away from them" with a victory. When asked, however, if he played in that game, he said no, that it actually took place "before my time."[17]

These stories are not told to suggest that Griggs and Alonzo were being dishonest or misleading. In fact, they show quite the opposite. Griggs never actually says that she attended with Jim Thorpe, or that she watched the most famous football teams play. Similarly, Alonzo is clear that he was not enrolled at Carlisle when the lacrosse team defeated a group of cocky Canadians. Instead, their narratives suggest that sports were a part of a public memory for Carlisle Indian School students, not just for an audience of white sports fans or for scientific racists. For both of these two former students to have been able to recall the memories of athletic success in such a pronounced way suggests that sports victories were part of Carlisle student lore, and that they held special meanings for many former students.

Former students and their children almost always mention sports in oral history interviews that were conducted with them. For example, Alonzo remembered that for students, "sports was about the main attraction at

Carlisle."[18] Charlie "Hobo" Atsye, who arrived at Carlisle in 1913, remembers playing football on the second team, called the "Hot Shots," with Jim Thorpe. "The Indians were real good," he remembers. "Always beating the whites."[19] A woman identified as Mrs. George Serracino remembers of her parents, "The reason why we think they liked Carlisle so much is because there were many students attending Carlisle who made a name for themselves in sports. They are proud to have known and have gone to the same school where such great names as Jim Thorpe, Gus Welch, and Frank Hudson went to school." Serracino singles out her uncle, Frank Hudson, known as the greatest drop kicker in the game of football.[20] Asked about the Carlisle football team, John Alonzo said that he still had a photograph of the players and could name every one. He proudly states, "I know practically all of the football players that played on that squad."[21]

At the same time, in oral history interviews former students and their relatives also could use sports to pivot toward critical insights. Delia Waterman (Oneida), who became an activist who worked to organize fellow Oneidas to fight for land claims on ancestral territory, expressed particularly sharp criticisms of the school.[22] When she came to Carlisle, she states, "the only one I was interested to know was Jim Thorpe." Yet she also remembered there being two brothers named the Godfrey Boys for whom football brought tragedy. "They was a good six feet maybe, and one of the brothers got hurt, broke his nose. Whether it was attended to, or he didn't get the attention or something, but it ran, he got an infection. Killed him. I think that was from a broken nose."[23]

Not only does Waterman recall a sports story that ended in the death of a player, but she implies that he might have survived had school officials not neglected the student. She also reflected upon what she felt was the exploitation of Native American athletic fame. In her mind, when Native athletes from Carlisle became too successful, they were "pulled back down off the ladder," perhaps referring to athletes like Jim Thorpe, who in cinema and literature was often portrayed as a fallen star and tragic hero.[24]

While sports at Carlisle may have provided an image of pride and success for Native Americans, Waterman even reflected upon this respect quite critically, particularly with regard to race. She remembers that the town of Carlisle was racially segregated during the time that she attended the Carlisle Indian School. Her memories are accurate. Carlisle School

District, in direct violation of an 1881 state law, fully segregated its student population by race through the early twentieth century, and segregated primary schools until 1948.[25] She remembers that in theaters African Americans had to sit in the balconies, and that when walking down a sidewalk, "the colored people had to step off the sidewalk and let you pass." Yet, she recalls that if any Indian students were subject to such treatment, "that was an insult."[26]

She related the plight of Carlisle athletes to that of Ira Hayes (Pima), one of the six Marines photographed by Joe Rosenthal raising the American flag over Iwo Jima during World War II. After the war Hayes became an alcoholic and died of alcohol poisoning in 1955. When asked if Hayes died because of "personal weakness," Waterman said no. "Because when he first came back, he was so famous they wanted him here and there. And he didn't think it was anything to him to be shown into big banquets and all that. He didn't believe in that. There was other things he was more interested in. Something for his people. He wanted water irrigation on his reservation."[27]

While John Alonzo's reflections upon Carlisle Indian School sports were more positive than Waterman's, even his praise of the school was couched in criticisms. When asked why the federal government closed the school, he stated that Carlisle stayed open "as long as General Pratt was living." In fact, Carlisle closed several years before Pratt died, but Alonzo's mistake does emphasize his larger point. He saw Carlisle as the kind of avenue for Native American success that Pratt had envisioned, so closing the school, for him, reinforced the idea that white society only wanted Indians to fail. "In fact, I think, Congress didn't want Indians to get too smart at the time. Keep the Indians from getting ahead. Keep the Indian on the reservation." In addition, Alonzo also remembers some of the more corrupt aspects of Carlisle sports, even as he told stories of Carlisle's athletic heroes, recalling that the University of Pennsylvania hired Frank Hudson to play in a game against Harvard.[28]

Alonzo can be forgiven for his cynical ideas about the closing of the school. Indeed, having aggressively used football to promote the school for two decades, Carlisle's administration in 1914 quickly turned toward portraying big-time sports as sources of temptation and iniquity. In June 1914 the school journal, the *Red Man*, printed an article titled "The Temptations of an Athlete," anonymously authored by "One of Them." The author recounts his own disillusionment with sports, stating that the moral standards of coaches were low, and that athletes must associate with unsavory persons who are "foul-mouthed and evil minded."[29] It seems that this transformation of the athlete from hero and role model to moral degenerate even influenced school investigations of students.

During the summer of 1915 a female student returned to Carlisle from her Outing assignment in Bala Cynwyd, a suburb of Philadelphia.[30] She was pregnant. Immediately the school discharged her. Despite this, the superintendent at the time, Oscar Lipps, decided to investigate the circumstances of her pregnancy, for she claimed to have been raped during her Outing. The matron of the home where the student worked was outraged. She accused the student of fabricating the rape story, and in a letter to Lipps she suggested that the real father was a Carlisle Indian School student. "She was very fond of one of the young men in the foot-ball squad and wrote to me on Nov. 23rd of her delight at having been his selected one to go to the Penn-Indian game in Phila," the matron writes. The student's file, in fact, contains a letter from a football player from a road trip with the football team. He writes, "I cannot think of anything else but my little girl," and signs "xxxxxxx and then some."[31]

In the end, the Outing manager could find no evidence that the female student was lying. He wrote, "Last evening I had [the female student] over in my room for about an hour, but I failed to get any other story from her, than that story which she had already told others. The child adheres to this story in such a way that we cannot doubt her word."[32]

The story of this student reveals a great deal about how the federal Indian boarding school system had developed into a perverse exercise in both power and neglect by the second decade of the twentieth century. As much as some may have tried to accuse her of sexual immorality by having an affair with a football player, their accusations were no more valid than those they wished to discredit. As Jenkins illustrates, it also demonstrates how boarding school sports had become a foil for the more general incompetence of boarding school administrators, and how the very success of Native American athletes could actually be used against Native Americans.

In an oral history interview, Grace Thorpe, one of Jim Thorpe's daughters by his first marriage to fellow Carlisle student Iva Miller, states, "Dad told me once that his happiest years were spent at Carlisle. . . . I know that there is a lot of talk today, and a lot of writing about how terrible the Indian boarding schools are, but my mother and father never had anything wrong to say about them, and I don't either. I went to them too."[33] Thorpe's positive feelings about Indian boarding schools are but one piece of evidence that understanding the role of sports at the Carlisle Indian School is no straightforward matter. Yet one should be cautious not to confuse the success of Grace's father, and of other boarding school athletes, with a naive and uncritical celebration of sports at the school. Through sports, Carlisle's founders inadvertently stumbled upon a form of popular culture that students often were able to claim as their own. During an era when Native Americans were, on many levels, thoroughly defeated, such triumphs were no doubt important. Neither the Carlisle Indian School nor their football teams returned any land to the students' tribes and nations, nor water rights to the Pima, nor fair pay and justice to an abused student. Yet they were a core aspect of the school's history. Sports established a prism that refracted a powerful image of the Carlisle Indian School. It is one that is impossible to ignore, and for this reason alone, it is vital to critically discuss this image.

NOTES

1. Lonna Malmsheimer, professor emerita of American studies, Dickinson College, and author of seminal work analyzing Carlisle Indian School photographs.
2. Brian M. Ingrassia, *The Rise of Gridiron University: Higher Education's Uneasy Alliance with Big-Time Football* (Lawrence: University Press of Kansas, 2012), 14–23.
3. Ingrassia, *Rise of Gridiron University*, 40–70; also see Gail Bederman, *Manliness and Civilization: A Cultural History of Gender and Race in the United States, 1880–1917* (Chicago: University of Chicago Press, 1995). Matthew Bentley's doctoral thesis applies this idea directly to the history of football at the Carlisle Indian School. See Matthew Steven Bentley, "'Kill the Indian, Save the Man': Manhood at the Carlisle Indian Industrial School, 1879–1918" (PhD diss., University of East Anglia, 2012).
4. F. Scott Fitzgerald, *The Great Gatsby* (New York: Scribner, 2003), 13.
5. See Bentley, "'Kill the Indian'"; also see John Bloom, *To Show What an Indian*

Can Do: Sports at Indian Boarding Schools (Minneapolis: University of Minnesota Press, 2000), 12–18; Sally Jenkins, *The Real All Americans: The Team That Changed a Game, a People, a Nation* (New York: Doubleday, 2007), 120–24.

6. Richard Henry Pratt, *Battlefield and Classroom: Four Decades with the American Indian, 1867–1904*, ed. Robert M. Utley (New Haven CT: Yale University Press, 1964), 317–18.

7. Jenkins, *Real All Americans*, 227.

8. See Frederick Hoxie, *A Final Promise: The Campaign to Assimilate the Indians, 1880–1920* (Lincoln: University of Nebraska Press, 1984), 17–18.

9. Susan Brownell, introduction to *The 1904 Anthropology Days and Olympic Games: Sport, Race, and American Imperialism*, ed. Susan Brownell (Lincoln: University of Nebraska Press, 2008), 17.

10. Brownwell, introduction, *1904 Anthropology Days*, 14–15.

11. Jenkins, *Real All Americans*, 134–35.

12. Mark Dyreson, "The 'Physical Value' of Races and Nations: Anthropology and Athletics at the Louisiana Purchase Exposition," in Brownell, *1904 Anthropology Days*, 139.

13. Carlos Montezuma, "Carlisle's Athletic Policy Criticized by Dr. Montezuma," *Chicago Sunday Tribune*, November 24, 1907.

14. Jenkins, *Real All Americans*, 244.

15. Jenkins, *Real All Americans*, 245.

16. Lucy Dogan Griggs (Sac and Fox), oral history interview transcript, interview and transcription by Peggy Dycus, May 7, 1969, Doris Duke Collection, University of Oklahoma Western History Collections.

17. John Alonzo (Laguna), oral history interview transcript, October 1976, interview by DeWitt Clinton Smith III, Carlisle Indian School Papers (1876–2007), MC 2008.4, Box 1, Folder 15.

18. Alonso, oral history, 1976.

19. Charlie "Hobo" Atsye, oral history interview transcript, June 22, 1973, interview by DeWitt Clinton Smith III, Carlisle Indian School Papers (1876–2007), MC 2008.4, Box 1, Folder 15.

20. Mr. and Mrs. George Sarracino, oral history interview transcript, July 1, 1973, interview by DeWitt Clinton Smith III, Carlisle Indian School Papers (1876–2007), MC 2008.4, Box 1, Folder 15.

21. Alonzo, oral history.

22. Glenn Coin, "Oneida Land Crusader Delia Waterman Dies; Woman Who Helped Lead the Struggle to Reclaim Ancestral Land Was 102," *Syracuse Post-Standard*, April 24, 2003.

23. Delia Waterman (Oneida), oral history interview transcript, December 10,

1976, interview by DeWitt Clinton Smith III, Carlisle Indian School Papers (1876–2007), MC 2008.4, Box 1, Folder 15.

24. John Bloom, "No Fall from Grace: Grace Thorpe's Athlete of the Century Campaign for Her Father," in *Native Athletes in Sport and Society*, ed. Richard King (Lincoln: University of Nebraska Press, 2005), 228–44.

25. See Mark Blashford, Nick Bloom, Daniel Mootz, Jason Smith, and Eugene Stockton-Juarez, "Segregation's Last Stand," Carlisle High School student presentation for National History Day, May 2008.

26. Waterman, oral history.

27. Waterman, oral history.

28. Alonzo, oral history.

29. John Bloom, *To Show What an Indian Can Do: Sports at Indian Boarding Schools* (Minneapolis: University of Minnesota Press, 2000), 29; One of Them, "The Temptations of an Athlete," *Red Man*, June 1914, 438–40.

30. Pratt had created the Outing program early on in his tenure as an opportunity for students to work for white families as farm workers or domestics during the summer months when school was out of session.

31. National Archives Records Administration (NARA), Record Group (RG) 75, File 1327 Carlisle Indian School Student Records, Folder 364, Box 8.

32. NARA, RG 75, Box 8.

33. John Bloom, "No Fall from Grace," 240.

7

Waste

MAURICE KENNY (MOHAWK)

A Native Lad's Etching
He stands tall, this young Osage lad with potential to be a great
   warrior for his people;
he stands in full regalia: head gear, breast plate
of bone, shield with hanging feathers, with more feathers blowing in
   afternoon winds . . . all painted in brilliant colors: maroon of grass,
   blues of morning; his
moccasins the shades of sunset and eve. Handsome in anyone's world,
   but just
a lad, a boy of some years to seventeen . . . Why would General Pratt,
   master
of the boy's school, care concerning his age, let alone the year he
   painted this portrait at so young an age.
But who cares: the army, the government,
his teachers at the Army School? But possibly by a now famed poet—
   Marianne Moore.

Now it might be wondered where rests his bones, this child named in
   English McKay Dougan . . . the signature
written in red crayon on his canvas, a lad who may have developed into
a Vincent Van Gogh or Winslow Homer
. . . had the General cared that he would learn more than how to
   change wagon wheels,
or polish horse saddles, or sweat
in weeded gardens for Eastern tables.

Was McKay's gift spooned encouragement to pick up the brush and
   canvas

Fig. 15. Drawing of an Osage warrior by McKay Dougan (Osage), c. 1883. Cumberland County Historical Society, Carlisle PA. FMPI-01-03-32-15.

of hide or rock, to scan the western sky.
Still rumbles the Boarding School's whispers that no he was not. If
    they refused to record his age, what can time and history think.

His plan was to be a warrior for his people. Yet he was just a kid who
    might be hunting squirrels for his mother's soup kettle,
or playing rolling stone with other lads.

No, a talent withering on the vine,
eaglet shorn of wings. Indians shouldn't sing,
or dance, or draw designs of the sky, waters below, mountain peaks of
    winter dressed in purple snow, paint Earth
in autumnal shades, a pretty face
of a blushing girl or a husky stag downed
by his arrow. Of no import to the Army.
No reason why this lad with this silly name when probably he
    should have been
called "Boy with Colors," or "Lad
Standing with Lance," or just plain "Youth with Vision." The rich
    talent, vibrant imagination, sense of time stymied at the open
    door . . . who cares,
who cared, Gen. Richard Pratt whose sight
was to change these savage children to Christian angels who would
    learn how to change a wagon wheel instead
of roaming free the plains of this great land?
McKay, but is it preferred to name this lad Boy of Vision, perhaps
    was wise sufficiently to know this was the way
to preserve not just his blood, his nation of Osage, but the world he
    had known and then disappearing, before his view.

But who cares! Should it be asked?

(Enrolled at Carlisle 6/9/1882. Sent
home because of illness 7/6/1885.)

(For Ari and Jan)

Part 3   *Carlisle Indian School Cemetery*

8

Cementerio indio

EDUARDO JORDÁ

Tuvieron que comer pan, que les sabía a tierra.
Y queso, que tampoco les gustaba.
Y leche, que les daba náuseas.
Y soportaron la áspera lana de los uniformes,
y los cuellos tan duros como sogas,
y las botas lustradas con betún
—porque no había allí grasa de búfalo—,
que a todos les desollaban los pies,
ya que los mocasines estaban prohibidos.

Y debieron cortarse el pelo
—su gran vergüenza, su peor deshonra—,
y ver cómo quemaban sus chaquetas
de piel, y los fetiches y amuletos
que sus madres les dieron en el tren
que ya se los llevaba de sus tierras.
Nacieron para ser como las águilas,
pero ahora tendrían que ser cuervos.

Y estudiaron comercio, álgebra, religión,
hicieron el saludo a la bandera,
y respondieron: "Sí, capitán Pratt"
con palabras que herían sus gargantas
como la escarlatina o las paperas,
añorando los baños en el río,
el humo de los tipis, el regalo
de un caballo, o aquel grito de guerra
de su hermano mayor
en un amanecer en las llanuras.

Y escribieron sus cartas a sus padres:
"Por favor, mi querido padre,
mándame el arco con las flechas,
cuida bien a mi pony,
y dile a mi hermano Cuatro-Perros
que me escriba pronto.
Volveré dentro de dos años
si el capitán Pratt quiere."

Nacieron para ser como las águilas,
pero ahora tendrían que ser cuervos.

Y tuvieron que usar unas palabras
que no existían en sus lenguas,
palabras sin sentido
como la frase "yo estoy solo,"
una frase imposible en sus idiomas,
pero que ahora era tan real
como un escalofrío en un camastro
en cuanto se apagaba la luz del dormitorio.
Y palabras como "útil," "honor," "patria,"
"civilizar," "bandera," "mantequilla."
"Ya soy un chico útil," pensaban confundidos,
reprimiendo las lágrimas,
mientras abrillantaban los zapatos
o se ponían los tirantes del boxeo.

Y desfilaron
cada domingo por el pueblo,
al son de las trompetas y trombones
que les hacían morirse de miedo.
También tenían miedo de las niñas
con gruesas faldas y gruesos corpiños.
Y a las niñas les daban miedo ellos,
con sus gruesas casacas
y sus cuellos tan duros como un hueso.

Nacieron para ser como las águilas,
pero ahora tendrían que ser cuervos.

Abe Lincoln, hijo de Antílope,
cheyenne,
17 de enero de 1880.
Hayes, hijo de Viernes,
arapahoe del norte,
15 de abril de 1882
(y no sé bien por qué, pero a Hayes lo imagino
mirando desde aquí
a un jilguero en un poste del telégrafo
justo antes de caer enfermo).
Kate Rosskidwits, wichita,
10 de enero de 1882.
Isabel Kelcusay, apache,
25 diciembre 1884.
Y al fondo cinco tumbas
con la misma inscripción: "Desconocido."

Algunos ya llegaron muertos en el tren
que los traía del oeste.
Otros aquí murieron.
Paperas, sarampión, viruela, fiebres,
tuberculosis, neumonía:
cualquier cosa podría haberlos matado.
El profesor Lippincott dirigía
las honras fúnebres,
y por aquí resuenan sus palabras
si aún somos capaces de escuchar:
"La civilización y la cultura,"
"Debéis ser útiles y buenos ciudadanos,"
"El Gran Espíritu que aquí se llama Dios,"
y cosas por el estilo.

Nacieron para ser como las águilas,
pero aquí aprendieron a ser cuervos.

Y ahora sólo quedan
las lápidas que asoman entre el césped,
con una flor roja, una sola,
que no sabemos quién les ha dejado,
y la hierba que crece y crece, indiferente,
y que murmura encogiéndose de hombros:
"Ellos no están,
pero yo sigo aquí."

Mientras miro sus tumbas,
y cae la lluvia helada, y un camión
pasa a toda pastilla,
y se oye un cornetín en el cuartel,
y un veterano de Irak monta guardia,
ellos están rezando por nosotros
al sol, o al Gran Espíritu, o a Dios,
o al vacío, o a la hierba que susurra.

Nacieron para ser como las águilas,
y acabaron muriendo como cuervos.

[Translation by Mark C. Aldrich]

Indian Cemetery

They had to eat bread, and it tasted like dirt.
And cheese, which was not to their liking either.
And milk, which made them nauseous.
And they put up with the rough wool of the uniforms,
and collars as stiff as rope,
and boots shiny with polish
—there was no buffalo fat there—
that blistered their feet
because moccasins were prohibited.

And they had to have their hair cut
—the biggest shame, the greatest dishonor—

and see put to the flames their animal skin jackets,
and the amulets and other sacred objects
their mothers had given them on the train
that took them from their land.
They were born to be like eagles,
but now they would have to be crows.

And they studied commerce, algebra, religion,
they pledged allegiance to the flag,
and answered, "Yes, Captain Pratt,"
words that burned in their throats
like scarlet fever or mumps
as they yearned for swims in the river,
the smoke of the teepees, the gift
of a horse, or older brother's
dawn war cry on the plains.

And they wrote letters to their parents:
"Please, dear father,
send me the bow and arrow,
take care of my pony,
and tell my brother Four Dogs to write soon.
I will return in two years
if Captain Pratt wishes it."

They were born to be like eagles,
but now they would have to be crows.

And they had to use some words
they did not have in their languages,
words without meaning,
like the expression, "I am lonely,"
a senseless phrase in their tongue,
but now, in the bunk bed, as real
as the onset of shivering
when the barrack lights are turned off.

And words like "useful," "honor," "homeland,"
"civilize," "flag," "butter."
"Now I am a useful boy," they thought, confused,
suppressing their tears
as they shined their shoes
or put on their boxing gloves.

And on Sundays they marched
through town to the sound
of trumpets and trombones
which scared them to death.
They were also afraid of the girls
with their thick skirts and thick bodices.
And the girls were afraid of them,
the boys' thick dress coats
and their necks as hard as bone.

They were born to be like eagles,
but now they would have to be crows.

Abe Lincoln, son of Antelope,
Cheyenne,
January 17th, 1880.
Hayes, son of Friday,
Northern Arapaho,
April 15th, 1882.
(And I don't know why, but I imagine
Hayes looking out at a goldfinch
on a telephone pole
before falling ill.)
Kate Rosskidwits, Wichita,
January 10th, 1882.
Isabel Kelcusay, Apache,
December 25th, 1884.
And in the back, five tombs
with the same inscription: "Unknown."

Some were already dead when they arrived
on the train that brought them from out west.
Others died here.
Mumps, measles, smallpox, fevers,
tuberculosis, pneumonia:
anything could have killed them.
Professor Lippincott led the funeral rites,
and around here his words still ring out
if we can manage to listen:
"Civilization and Culture,"
"You must be useful and good citizens,"
"Here the Great Spirit is called God,"
and so on.

They were born to be like eagles,
but now they would have to be crows.

And now all that is left
are the tombstones sticking up out of the lawn,
each one with a single red flower,
left by someone unknown to us,
and the grass that grows and grows, indifferent,
murmuring, shrugging its shoulders:
"They are gone,
but I am still here."

As I contemplate their tombs,
a freezing rain falling,
a truck speeding by,
and an Iraq veteran keeping watch,
they pray for us,
to the sun, to the Great Spirit, or to God,
or to the void, or the whispering grass.

They were born to be like eagles,
and they ended up dying like crows.

9

The History and Reclamation of a Sacred Space

The Indian School Cemetery

JACQUELINE FEAR-SEGAL

Today it is still possible to visit the Carlisle Indian School cemetery, walk between the stones, and read the names on nearly two hundred identical markers standing in six, neat rows. Small and well kept, this rectangular graveyard looks like a military cemetery, except for the Indian names on the stones. The cemetery faces out onto the road flanking the entrance to the Carlisle Barracks, now home to the U.S. Army War College. Since 9/11, all traffic visiting the post has been screened and directed around huge, protective concrete slabs before entering the grounds on a road that runs beside the Indian cemetery. The blue and gold marker of the Pennsylvania Historical and Museum Commission, mounted on a high pole beside the cemetery railings, informs passers-by of the history of the Carlisle Indian Industrial School and its intention "to assimilate American Indians into mainstream culture." Only visitors on foot will notice a much older plaque, screwed to a boulder beside the little wrought iron entrance gate, which tells them, "The original Indian Cemetery was located to the rear of the grandstand on Indian Field. In 1931 the graves were transferred to this site." Although the date given is incorrect (it should read 1927), this snippet of the cemetery's history raises many questions. And interrogation of the history of the site reveals not only removal but also hidden patterns and reverberations of racial exclusion, segregation, erasure, and appropriation.

In his stringent analysis of how history is inscribed on the landscape by plaques and monuments, James W. Loewen, in *Lies across America*, admits to avoiding cemeteries because tombstones can convey biography, but they rarely reflect civic discourse.[1] The mute record carried by the Carlisle cemetery defies this claim. It reaches beyond the realm of both biography and civic discourse, and the same is true of cemeteries at other Indian boarding schools.[2] The cemetery is the only place at the Carlisle

Barracks where you can read the names of individual students, who stand in for the thousands of Indian children, from nations across the United States, who were enrolled in Carlisle's assimilation program. The cemetery is a tangible link to the children who lived at the school but never went home. At the same time, it is also the surviving physical manifestation of a white discourse about race and dispossession. Exploration of the racial politics that governed burial patterns at the Carlisle Indian School lays bare the processes by which dead Indian children, and the land they occupied, became indivisible from Indian dispossession and the construction and inscription of national patterns of racial definition.

The Carlisle cemetery carries an account of the school's history not found in the official record. Parts of it can to be pieced together from a range of different sources: maps, charts, surveys, school newspapers. Surprisingly, photographs provide no useful evidence. Although the school's founder and first superintendent, Captain Richard Henry Pratt, commissioned hundreds of photographs to publicize the children's advance from savagery to civilization and trumpet improvements to the campus, no single photograph of the old cemetery survives, and it is likely that none was ever taken.[3] Pratt was not keen to draw attention to the school's high mortality rate. It is only possible to discover where the cemetery was situated on the campus by scrutinizing surveys drawn up to facilitate the laying of water and sewer pipes, and overlaying these on engineering maps made by the U.S. Army. In this way, we can locate the cemetery at the northern extremity of the campus, as well as chart its expansion from a small triangular shape to a large rhombus (see map 2). Such records made by whites were created for practical not public purposes, yet if rescaled and superimposed using Photoshop, they reveal previously undisclosed evidence not only about the cemetery's location but also about the school's burial practices.[4] Shrouded from public view, the history of the Carlisle Indian School cemetery is central to understanding the wider history of the school, the national campaign for Indian assimilation it spearheaded, and the racialization of Native people to which it contributed.

Not all the children who died while in the East were buried in the school cemetery. Those who passed away while working on local farms during the summer or on longer Outing placements were often not brought back to Carlisle for burial. Although little research has been done on this topic,

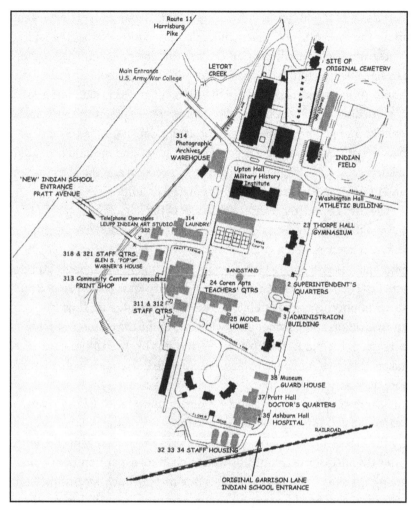

Map 2. Surviving buildings of Carlisle Indian School showing location of Indian School cemetery before its removal in 1927. Gray indicates surviving buildings. Black indicates buildings of the Indian School no longer standing. The calculated site of the original cemetery is marked on this present-day map by rescaling and photoshopping historical maps. © Jacqueline Fear-Segal.

it seems likely that across Pennsylvania and beyond, small local cemeteries hold the remains of children from the Indian School. (The story of a Lipan Apache student who died in Lahaska, Pennsylvania, and is buried in the Lahaska Quaker cemetery is explored in chapter 11, "The Lost Ones: Piecing Together the Story.") Many more children were sent home to the West to die. Indeed, as the high death rate at Carlisle became a subject of fierce criticism, Pratt very deliberately started to send sick and dying children back home to die in their communities. In 1881 fourteen children were "returned to homes on account of sickness," and in 1885 thirty-six "on account of failing health or mental weakness."[5] The lengthening lines of gravestones in the school cemetery to the north of the Carlisle campus represented only a truncated record of Carlisle deaths. Investigation of the history of the cemetery also reveals that its very creation and existence challenged the school's declared mission to prepare Indian children to find a place in white society.

Spatial Politics of Burial

The dead Indian has always been an alluring and enduring trope. Spirits of dead Indians haunt the literature as well as psyches of white Americans.[6] Decisions about where dead Indians should be laid to rest, what ceremonies should accompany their burial, how and whether they should be memorialized, and if they had a right to "rest in peace" were inseparable from the ongoing geopolitical campaign to seize Indian lands and expunge Indian cultures. Analysis of these processes exposes the dynamic and interconnected role played by white land claims and constructions of race in the creation, demarcation, segregation, obliteration, and reorganization of spaces for the dead. Such analyses make it possible to understand patterns of burial, as well as disputes over interment, as physical and symbolic contests about property, power, racial privilege, and status.

The spaces that are given to the dead are, as Philippe Ariès reminds us, "the identifying mark of a culture."[7] Land lies at the hub of Indian-white relations in the United States. In public memory the Paxton Boys' savage massacre of Susquehannocks in 1763 is long forgotten, and Pennsylvania boasts a lustrous reputation for having treated the colony's Indian tribes fairly and commendably in land negotiations. Yet even in this apparently exemplary state, all Indian lands had been progressively and systematically incorporated into the white body politic, and Indian negotiators' pleas to be allowed to hold onto diminutive tracts had been overridden. By the mid-eighteenth century, whites controlled both government and lands in Pennsylvania. (For an examination of Native dispossession, see chapter 2, "Before Carlisle: The Lower Susquehanna Valley as Contested Native Space.") Then suddenly and unexpectedly, in the final quarter of the nineteenth century, a new Indian "demand" for land was asserted: children who died at the Carlisle Indian School required burial.

Through interment, the dead make claims on the land. The need to lay a body to rest in a small plot has a quotidian familiarity that often veils its political and historical specificity. The United States came into being at a time of significant change in social and political consciousness. This was matched by a critical shift in attitudes toward personal mortality in both Europe and America. The new individualism brought "an enhancement of the sense of self-value" and a new emphasis on commemoration and memorialization of the dead. A prosperous and self-confident wealthy class that surrounded itself in the trappings of luxurious domesticity in life also sought to stretch its power and influence beyond the grave. Paris was at the forefront of this movement and built three new extensively landscaped cemeteries outside the city walls. The most famous was Père Lachaise (1804), where grand avenues and serpentine walks offered the Parisian bourgeoisie a consciously Elysian setting to purchase plots for family monuments and mausoleums. This cemetery's success rested on economics and intense marketing as much as aesthetics. For the first time, burial was not in the control of church authorities; anyone with money could invest in a plot of land for perpetual memorialization. Though the property owner might be mortal, the fact as well as the display of owner-ship could continue forever.[8]

Père Lachaise gradually became the economic and aesthetic model for cemeteries across Europe and America. Many American towns opened new leafy, landscaped cemeteries on their perimeters, the most famous being Mount Auburn outside Boston. Americans had no need to contest the powers of an established church, but these privately owned premises offered a welcome solution to the problems of overcrowding and public health. Simultaneously, and significantly for the argument here, they pro-vided a site where prominent white local families and individuals could purchase plots on which to build imposing monuments, to undyingly confirm their wealth, status, and racial exclusivity.

In Carlisle, the new Ashland Cemetery on the eastern perimeter of the town was one such site. Ashland gave the Boslers, Hendersons, and other prominent Carlisle families the opportunity to invest in well-situated burial plots. Through the economics and, as later shown, the racial politics of interment, their social and political identities became strengthened and, quite literally, permanently built into the landscape. Death became a potent means to assert physical and symbolic property rights, as well as spatially and visually to legitimate personhood and power. Poorer members of the white community were not excluded but had to satisfy themselves with smaller, less prominent plots. African Americans, however, were specifically banned from Ashland. To the north of the city, Carlisle's small black population continued to bury its dead in a diminutive, intensely used area.[9] Well-entrenched social-racial hierarchies thus determined not only who should be buried where and how, but they also visually and geographically inscribed acceptance of these class- and race-determined practices. In Carlisle in the 1880s, Indians had not yet been included in this racial division of space. Yet the founding of an Indian School in the midst of this confident and well-established town presented an interment problem no one had anticipated. Its solution would expose and confirm entrenched patterns of racial segregation, openly position Indians on the nation's chromatic scale, and physically inscribe on the landscape their nonwhite status.

Racial Politics of Burial

Less than seven weeks after the initial group of Indian students had been brought to Carlisle, on November 26, 1879, the first child died at the school.[10] Local press accounts and the records of St. John's Episcopal Church confirm that the same day a service was held in the Indian School chapel, before the body of Amos LaFromboise, a thirteen-year-old Dakota boy from Sisseton Agency, was taken to Ashland Cemetery. Following prayers at the graveside, at which the Rev. W. C. Leverett officiated, he was buried in the government-owned plot at Ashland.[11]

To Carlisle's superintendent, Captain Richard Henry Pratt, Ashland must have appeared an obvious and convenient place to inter the child. The cemetery lay in Carlisle's East Ward, just a mile south of the school.[12] The government had purchased a 540-by-32-foot plot in December 1865. It lay along the western perimeter of the cemetery on what became known as United States Avenue. Here, five hundred unknown veterans of the Battle of Gettysburg had been buried in a huge trench grave.[13] A dozen named veterans lay under individual stones at the opposite end of this government site, and in the central area, over fifty burial sites remained vacant.[14]

Possibly there were murmurings and disquiet among the local population about this Indian burial in a cemetery used by Carlisle's elite. Certainly Pratt was very keen to gain official endorsement for his action. The day after Amos LaFromboise was laid to rest in Ashland Cemetery, Pratt wrote to the War Department requesting "to be informed whether the Burial Ground at that place is available for the interment of Indian youth who may die while attending that school." His enquiry initiated a flurry of correspondence between the quartermaster general, the adjutant general, the judge advocate general, and the secretary of war, all of who displayed some confusion and, between them, took more than two months to arrive at a decision. To begin with, the adjutant general was not sure whether Indian children *could* be buried at Ashland Cemetery and wrote to the quartermaster general: "It seems not to be allowed in the deed. Whether interment of red men would violate the grant or no, I am not able to decide. Possibly the Executive could make a new deed covering the case. The War Department should not object, unless it endangers its property rights."[15]

Adjutant General Townsend's initial wavering and unsteadiness points to the high degree of ambiguity surrounding this issue and the need for interpretation of existing legal documents. He airs the possibility of drawing up a new deed but is quite explicit that the property rights of the War Department should not be endangered, thus signaling that property ownership was an important factor in the decision-making process. Ultimately, however, the judgment handed down rested on a clear racial designation and a positive answer to the question of "whether interment of red men would violate the grant or no." The judge advocate general was called on to make the final decision, and he informed the War Department:

The deed in this case conveys to the United States the "exclusive and entire right of interment and sepulture" in a certain burial lot of the Ashland Cemetery in said Carlisle, "to have and to hold"—as it is added—"for the burial of such <u>White persons</u>" as the grantee may admit to be buried there: In my judgment these last words constitute a <u>condition</u> annexed to the grant, that the premises shall be used for the burial of White persons only; and I have therefore to express the opinion that the interment therein of an Indian would not be legally authorized.[16]

This judge's definitive interpretation of a preexisting deed both reflected and furthered a racial definition of Indians. In the judgment he handed down, Indians were constructed as nonwhite; even in death they were forced into segregation. This recapitulated existing black/white patterns of cemetery spatial use and embraced Indians in an all-too-familiar racial attribution of space. While the adjutant general had raised the possibility of creating "a new deed," the judge advocate general chose instead to rule out this possibility and to focus his decision on a clause that had been added to the original deed, limiting burial in Ashland to "White persons." So Indian children, who had been brought to Carlisle to be instructed how to live like whites, were now legally barred from lying alongside them in death and openly categorized as nonwhite.

History of the School Cemetery

In Washington, discussion of this case had dragged on for more than two months when, in Carlisle, on January 17, 1880, a second Indian boy died. This time Pratt did not organize a burial in Ashland Cemetery. Instead, the sixteen-year-old son of the Cheyenne leader Antelope, who had been renamed Abe Lincoln, was buried in a plot of open farmland to the north of the campus, close to an area marked "Old Burial Ground" on historic maps of Carlisle Barracks. This interment marked the unceremonious opening of the Indian School cemetery. When Pratt later received word that "under the grant the U.S. cannot inter *Indians* in . . . Ashland Cemetery," it seems clear that he must have had the body of Amos LaFromboise, who had been buried in Ashland, disinterred and reburied at the recently opened school cemetery, because records of the cemetery include the name of Amos LaFromboise.[17] On the cemetery plot map, he lies alongside the Cheyenne boy, Abe Lincoln. Within just three months of its establishment, the Carlisle Indian School had opened its own discrete, segregated cemetery. A legal judgment about the Indian's nonwhite racial identity had been built into the landscape of an institution dedicated to educating Indian children to join white society.

Nevertheless, Pratt used burials and the design and layout of this cemetery to further his Americanizing program, subsuming the bodies of the dead within the school's purposes. The children were all interred with Christian prayers and laid to rest in an east-west position, according to Christian tradition. While it could never match the landscaped glories of Ashland, efforts were made to beautify the school cemetery, and the school children were recruited into American practices of mourning and commemoration. The *Indian Helper* noted that "girls are raising funds for the decoration of school graves . . . and are contemplating buying rosebushes and other growing plants for the school cemetery."[18] There is no evidence that any Indian families or community members were ever present at interments or that they were permitted to carry out their own traditional ceremonies. The extensive range of nations on Carlisle's enrolment list meant that practices surrounding death in the children's home communities varied enormously. To Pratt this was irrelevant. He signed a contract with Ewings, a local firm of undertakers, to deal with all the practicalities of death, according to white values and practices.[19]

The graves of the children were made to resemble those of whites. Identical rectangular headstones extended in an ever-growing line, scoring the landscape with a sad record of the Native American diaspora Carlisle had precipitated. Eight stones the first year, ten more the next, and ninety-six within the first decade.[20] Each stone gave name, nation, and age. Its location in the cemetery recorded the chronology of death; Lakota lay beside Cheyenne, Ponca next to Pueblo, Kiowa alongside Wichita, in an intertribal pattern that scrambled the children's geographies, histories, and backgrounds. The cemetery stood as the physical manifestation of a composite, monolithic, white-created Indian identity. Yet it also accurately bore witness to the children's recent pasts: their multitribal schooling at Carlisle and, in death, their exclusion, as Indians, from the white society they were being trained to emulate and join. Eight surviving stones from the cemetery, which together span burials between the years 1883 and 1900, suggest that during the Pratt years the children were all memorialized with identical markers.[21] Only one stone was different. No marker in this cemetery more powerfully conveyed the complex racial anomaly represented by this site and the intensification of an individual's social and racial status in death than "the stone of gray granite . . . erected by the Young Men's Christian Association" at the grave of Thomas Marshall, a year after his death.[22] This stone embodied the central contradiction of the Carlisle Indian School: that Native students who were being educated for assimilation into mainstream society were, nevertheless, consistently constructed as nonwhite. Marshall's stone is examined in closer detail below, but to fully appreciate its significance we need to know more about the life of Thomas Marshall.

Thomas Marshall

A talented Lakota from Pine Ridge, Marshall arrived in Carlisle in 1895, not as a student of the Indian School, but to study at Dickinson Preparatory School. From here he would progress to become an undergraduate in Latin and science at Dickinson College, winning an entrance prize in his freshman year. To support himself at Dickinson Marshall lived at the Indian School, where he worked in the storehouse as janitor, and then in his junior year as tutor in charge of the small boys' dormitory.[23] Thomas Marshall's intellectual and personal qualities had been evident to white teachers from his early years. After he graduated from White's Manual Labor Institute in Wabash, Indiana, in 1894, the superintendent of this Quaker institution, Oliver H. Bales, immediately began to seek funds to enable Thomas Marshall to continue his education. This was no easy task, because among officials in Washington there was a growing resistance to giving any support to Indians who sought education beyond the elementary level. In a letter to the superintendent of Indian schools, William Hailman, Bales outlined Marshall's academic and personal qualities and talents: "He will have completed Rhetoric, Algebra, and three books of Caesar's Commentaries by the last of June, having taken in thoroughly the lower branches in their order. At odd times he has acquired a useful proficiency in shorthand and type-writing. He studied Book-keeping, and showed, during two months of responsible charge of our Account Books and office work, a remarkable aptness and application of the principles. He is a good bass singer, performs well on various brass instruments, and renders organ voluntaries with fine effect."[24]

Bales went out of his way to convince the superintendent that his own support for Marshall was less to do with the young man's Indian status than "on account of his worthiness, superior natural ability, integrity, and attainments." The school superintendent concluded by noting that, even though "all his early associations were among the Sioux Indians. . . . He is however, to all appearance, Caucasian."[25] Bales deemed Marshall's supposed non-Indian, or "white," physiognomy not only worthy of mention, but an additional attribute, likely to qualify him for educational funding from the superintendent of Indian schools. In short, Bales suggested that Marshall should be given support because his combined abilities and looks meant that he could successfully "pass" in the white world.

Thomas Marshall's Carlisle student card records his Indian blood quotient as one quarter.[26] Whatever the accuracy of this information, it is clear that while at Dickinson Marshall chose not to accentuate his Indian looks. In his photographic portrait he is shown sporting a moustache, and in a photograph of the Dickinson class of 1900, taken during their sophomore year, Marshall blends unremarkably with his white classmates.[27] He appeared to carry his Indian identity with both ease and humor. In a Dickinson compilation of "Junior Statistics," individual undergraduates published pithy answers in response to a set of five questions. In Marshall's entry, he playfully claimed and subverted white stereotypes of Indians: "Name: Thomas P. Marshall; Forte: Reserve; Past: In a Wigwam; Present: At the Indian School; Future: With his Squaw; Greatest Need: Less Modesty." The joke about "his squaw" had specific resonance, because Marshall was engaged to the Yankton Sioux writer and musician Zitkala-Ša (aka Gertrude Simmons), who from 1897 to 1899 was a teacher at the Indian School.[28] Like Simmons, Thomas Marshall functioned effectively in the white world, although unlike her, he was a committed Christian. A leading light of the Indian School's YMCA, he acted as its president and represented Carlisle at national meetings. Marshall appears to have moved easily between the white-run Indian world of the Carlisle School and the privileged white world of Dickinson College, but it was alongside Indian students that he would lie in death.

Thomas Marshall never graduated from Dickinson College. He died suddenly, on April 23, 1899, from a disease diagnosed as "malignant" or "black measles." Tellingly, it was his Indian home in Dakota that officials at the Indian School immediately identified as the source of the illness, blaming a contaminated letter from Indian Country for his death. Flying in the face of today's medical knowledge about the transmission of infectious diseases, an announcement in the *Indian Helper* was adamant, "He got the disease through a letter from home where two of his family have died recently of measles. The case is completely isolated, and we do not fear any epidemic."[29] The Dickinson College community was stunned to hear of Thomas Marshall's sudden death. His class met to issue formal resolutions to express their grief, and at a memorial service on the campus Dickinson's president gave a eulogistic address.[30] Yet there was never any suggestion that Thomas Marshall should be buried anywhere but in the Indian School cemetery. The serendipity of his date of death placed Marshall beside an eighteen-year-old Cheyenne boy, Reuben Tahpeos/ Tahpers/Tapios, in the second line of stones that was already extending across the graveyard.

The following year, however, the YMCA broke with Indian School practice. Instead of the normal rectangular stone, giving name, tribe, and date of death, they erected a huge granite rock to memorialize Thomas Marshall. In so doing they signaled his special status in a manner more familiar at Ashland. In height and mass this stone dwarfed all the other students' stones, setting Marshall apart from his "Indian" neighbors. On the front face of the stone, the intertwined letters of "YMCA" publicized and commemorated the organization as well as Thomas Marshall's life. Unlike all the other stones in the cemetery, however, this one was graced with a year of birth as well as of death, mimicking white practice and suggesting a certainty in the record normally unavailable to Indians. Significantly, no mention was made of Marshall's Lakota origins; through this omission, the commemorations on his stone had erased Thomas Marshall's Lakota identity. If not for its telltale location in the Indian School cemetery, Thomas Marshall's grave might easily have been mistaken for the final resting place of a white man. In death, as in life, he had been made to "pass." To the north of the Carlisle campus, on a hillside that sloped from the school's blacksmith shop and other utilities toward the city's refuse dump, this huge granite boulder stood as both a commemorator of Thomas Marshall's life and a monument to white insistence that Indians should resemble but remain separate from Whites.

The Indian Cemetery after Closure of the School

By the time Pratt was removed from office in 1904, Carlisle's mission to educate and assimilate Native children in a single generation was being called into doubt in Washington. The 1914 Senate investigation into financial irregularities and abuse at the school would bring damning details to public attention.[31] In 1918 the Carlisle Indian School was closed by the government. The remaining students were sent home or dispersed to other Indian schools, and the buildings of the Carlisle Barracks were handed back to the U.S. Army for wartime medical service as U.S. General Hospital Number 31. Two years later, an army medical field service school was opened at the post. Many of the buildings that were then occupied by the military had been constructed using Indian labor, and some had even been financed out of the children's earnings. Yet only the names engraved on the surviving headstones in the school cemetery provided a cryptic record of over ten and a half thousand Indian children from across the United States who had lived, studied, and worked there for nearly forty years.

The army medical school officially rejected the Indian School cemetery as a suitable burial site for whites who died on the post. In the field medical school quartermaster's judgment, it was "solely an Indian Burial Ground."[32] So arrangements were made for the post to use the Ashland Cemetery, where it was estimated there was "sufficient room on the [government] plot to take care of the requirement of this station for years to come."[33] Over the next decade, the Indian cemetery fell into a state of disrepair.[34] Then, as the medical school grew, the graves were seen as an obstacle to the expansion of the post. In 1926 the commandant at the Carlisle Barracks, Surgeon General Ireland, made an unofficial request to have "the Indian interments, now in the middle of Carlisle Reservation, gotten out of the way." His proposal stands as a reminder that, unlike those buried in Ashland, the Indians did not own the land on which they were interred; they had not bought the right to rest in peace. Clearly unaware of the Indian cemetery's history, Ireland suggested "the Government plot in Ashland Cemetery" as his site of preference to receive the remains.[35] Once again, however, forty-six years after the first denial, Indian children were refused burial in Ashland. This time the reasons had shifted: the decedents could not be buried in the government plot at Ashland because they had no "military, naval Marine Corp or Coast Guard Service," and, more practically, it was noted that with only fifty unused burial sites available in the government plot, there was insufficient space to accommodate all the children's remains.[36] Insistent that "the future development of the post will require the site now used for the interment of the Indian dead," General Ireland secured permission to have the cemetery razed and "removed from the present site to the north-east limits of the reservation, or elsewhere."[37]

The "New" Indian Cemetery

The last student buried had not been in his grave a decade when work began to relocate the school cemetery to a small, rectangular plot, measuring 180 by 55 feet, on the outer perimeter of the post.[38] Removal began in the July heat of 1927, as soon as permission had been granted. The local newspaper gave an account of the work under a headline that highlighted not the Indian children, but the unpleasantness of the task: "Removing Bodies of Carlisle Indians: Men at Army Post Have Gruesome Job." Inaccurate facts about the cemetery were given, with the first burial erroneously dated 1882. The cemetery's controversial beginnings went unmentioned, and its creation was attributed to Indian parents' lack of concern for their dead children. "When an Indian would die, he was buried in the Indian School graveyard, unless the remains of the student were claimed by relatives." The Indians' presence in Carlisle was given a cursory and benign explanation: "At one period there were 1,000 Indians here, wards of the nation, receiving an education." The bulk of the article was a narrative of mystery and horror, supplying titillating details alongside ghoulish particulars about the state of the bodies:

> The excavators found a skull with a bullet hole in it. It was the skull of an Indian who committed suicide years ago while in Carlisle. He had been in poor health and it is believed grew despondent. Only a bit of flesh was found on one side of his body. All of the bodies disinterred so far are skeletons. Some of the clothing worn was found to be in a remarkably good state of preservation. Coffins crumbled when handled to any extent. A necktie and a pair of shoes were still in excellent condition. In one of the coffins was found a diamond ring. In one casket,

Fig. 16. Indian cemetery at the Carlisle Indian School, c. 1933, after being removed from its original location. All the stones were replaced with standard military stones, except the larger stone, which is that of Thomas Marshall (Yankton Lakota). Photographer unknown. Cumberland County Historical Society, Carlisle PA. 12-09-05.

which contained the body of a girl, the hair was separated from the skull, but it was of luxuriant growth and in good condition.[39]

In place of the old cemetery, a "building for officers' use and occupancy" was constructed.[40] The cemetery's relocation thus repeated an age-old pattern of Indian dispossession and the assertive inscription of white ownership on the landscape.

The transfer of the cemetery scrambled and erased part of the history of the school as well as a painful chapter in Indian-white relations shared by every tribe in the United States.[41] The original cemetery had grown up slowly, over forty years. Lying in five uneven rows, most of the deceased children had a standard headstone, although some of the later graves only had wooden markers.[42] Despite the absence of any photographs of the cemetery, studying a plot map drawn up at the time of removal in conjunction with the students' Carlisle record cards discloses the sequential pattern by which the cemetery grew from the middle. Four, long, parallel lines of graves stood on lands belonging to the original army post site that Pratt took over in 1879. A fifth short line of eight stones was added, at an acute angle to the first line; these last interments were on farmland deeded to the school in 1887.[43]

When the cemetery was relocated, the chronology of the children's deaths was lost. Their remains were reburied in random order, to fit the neat, symmetrical pattern of the new space. None of the original standard-issue headstones accompanied the children. Instead, their new graves were marked with soldiers' stones. Two miles down the road, at Ashland Cemetery, two different styles of military stone had been used to mark the graves of Civil War veterans: one with a shield embossed on it, the other with a cross.[44] The Indian children were all given the stone with a cross. Standing in six, tight, even, rows, these new, white, army-issue stones, simultaneously cleansed, standardized, militarized, and Christianized them. Only Thomas Marshall, his stone transported from the old cemetery to stand splendidly alone in the central plot, was permitted continuity in his memorialization. His stone proclaimed, in its grey granite and privileged position, the special status reconferred on him, although its cryptic engravings continued to pose perplexing questions about his identity and the basis for his interment in an Indian cemetery. Ironically, Marshall's unique stone, which rendered his Lakota identity invisible, was and still remains the single surviving visible feature connecting the new Indian cemetery to the original school burial ground.

Erasure and Appropriation

When they died, none of the Indian children was a citizen of the United States;[45] yet in burial most lost their Indian designations and were memorialized under recently acquired American names—Abe Lincoln, Henry Jones—or sometimes new "Christian" names coupled to translations of a parental name—Charles White Shield, James Foxcatcher. In the process of removing and remarking the cemetery, more of their fragile and changing identities was expunged and lost. All except Marshall lost their original headstones. The age of each individual, which had been etched onto the original stones, was omitted from the new markers. One effect of this was to reduce the poignant impact of so many young deaths. Nations, dates of death, and even new American names were often mistranscribed. A

Lipan Apache boy (whose story is explored in chapter 11) was known at the school as Jack Mather, but his stone in the new cemetery reads "Jack Martha."[46] On the original stone of John Bull, who died at age fifteen of tuberculosis after spending little more than a year at Carlisle, his nation is spelled the traditional way, Gros Ventre; on his new marker the stone mason has carved "Grosvontre."[47] Margaret Edgar, from Acoma Pueblo, who died in August 1885 after just one year at the school, has no details on her new stone apart from her name.[48] Some of the dead children were "lost" altogether, so thirteen graves in the new cemetery are marked "unknown."[49]

The removal of the cemetery instigated other losses and confusions. The child listed as being buried in plot D12 on the chart of the old cemetery drawn up at the time of removal is Samson Noran, a Chiricahua Apache who was one of the children from Geronimo's band. An orphan of sixteen, he was brought to Carlisle in 1888 as a prisoner of war from Fort Marion. He died of tuberculosis in March the following year.[50] Yet there is no stone for Samson Noran in the new cemetery, and in plot D12, where the chart indicates he should have been buried, stands a stone marked with the single word "Earnest." Only one child named Ernest/Earnest is recorded as having been buried in the school cemetery.

This was Earnest Knocks Off, son of the Brulé leader White Thunder, from Rosebud Agency, and one of the first children to arrive at the school. Earnest White Thunder had begged to go home with Spotted Tail, when this famous Brulé leader visited Carlisle. Spotted Tail was outraged at what he saw. He condemned Carlisle's military regime—the children's drilling, their "soldier uniforms," and his youngest son's incarceration in the guardhouse—and took his own children away.[51] Spotted Tail wanted to take all the Sioux children home with him, but this was forbidden by officials in Washington. While his train was standing in Carlisle station, Earnest White Thunder stowed away, but he was quickly discovered and taken back to the school. Prevented from leaving, Earnest subsequently fell ill. According to a letter Pratt wrote to his father, Earnest was sent to the hospital, where he refused all medicine and food. He died in December 1880, at the age of thirteen, after just two months at Carlisle, and was buried in plot D29 in the recently created school cemetery. The chart of the new cemetery indicates that Earnest was reinterred in plot C12, and,

Fig. 17. Ernest White Thunder (Brulé Lakota), 1880. Photo by John N. Choate. Cumberland County Historical Society, Carlisle PA. CS-CH-019.

indeed, on this site stands a stone that reads, "Ernest, Son of Chief White Thunder, Sioux, December 14, 1880." It appears that Ernest White Thunder is memorialized twice in the new cemetery, and if this is the case, it is grimly ironic because Luther Standing Bear, in his first autobiographical text, *My People the Sioux*, writes that the boy's father made a specific request for a headstone, which Standing Bear claims was refused: "Of course his father, Chief White Thunder, was very angry that he had not been notified that his son was even sick, and he stopped off at the school, en route to Washington, where he was going with the expectation of being appointed head chief at Rosebud Agency. White Thunder said he wanted the body of his son sent home, but if the authorities would not do that, they might at least place a headstone over his grave. Neither request was ever granted."[52] That two headstones might have been erected for the same child and none for another reflects the disorder and carelessness that must have accompanied the cemetery's removal.

In its new location, facing out onto Claremont Road, the new school cemetery was now far from the main site and unconnected even by a path to the medical field service school. Conveniently out of the way, it was ignored and rapidly fell into a state of disrepair. Then a dispute about who was responsible for its maintenance broke out between the Department of the Interior (holding jurisdiction over the Indians) and the War Department (holding jurisdiction over the Carlisle Barracks). The argument revolved around the question of whether the Indian cemetery could be defined as a post cemetery, even though it contained no military personnel.[53] Once it had been determined that the military was indeed responsible for the cemetery's upkeep, it was reclaimed by the army and renovated to reflect its military status. Old wooden posts and a woven wire fence, marking the cemetery's boundary, were torn down and replaced by a concrete curb and wrought iron railings. Spare capacity was also identified, and the cemetery was now officially determined to be able to accommodate 229 bodies.[54] On January 21, 1935, the first non-Indian was buried in the new Indian cemetery: the infant son of an officer serving at the post.[55] Over the next thirty years all burials in this cemetery were of whites. Their graves were marked with the same plain white, cross-embossed, veteran-style stones that had been given to the dead Indian children. This did not indicate an end to patterns of racial segregation, but rather that the transfigured

Carlisle Indian School cemetery was now being claimed and occupied by the U.S. Army.

Gradually, the remaining plots were filled, mostly by infants and children of officers serving at the post, but occasionally a white adult was also given space. Staff Sergeant Bruno Verano, from Pennsylvania, who was serving in the medical department, buried two sons in the cemetery in less than two years. When a few years later, in 1945, he too died, aged forty-two, he was buried in Row F close to his two sons. By this time an arrangement was in place for military personnel who died at the Carlisle Barracks to be buried in Ashland Cemetery. But for Bruce Verano, the Indian cemetery offered a way to perpetuate patriarchal family ties, and the Veranos have the privilege of being the only family with two generations interred in the cemetery.

When, in 1951, the Carlisle Barracks became home to the U.S. Army War College, the campus rapidly expanded to fill the vacant lands of the whole military reservation and engulfed the Indian cemetery. A new road was built to connect the main campus to Clarement Road, so the cemetery now stood beside the busy back gate entrance of the War College. To the outsider, the cemetery did not look out of place here, because at first glance it so thoroughly resembled a military cemetery. Occasionally Indian people who knew about Carlisle and its history came to pay their respects.[56]

As the Indian children's presence in Carlisle receded into history, the cemetery became incorporated into a romanticized, sanitized, white version of events. It became a site to commemorate Indian nobility and mourn tribal disappearance, without confronting the problematic mission of the Carlisle Indian School. Staff and children from the barracks, as well as locals who visited the cemetery, often left trinkets and coins on the graves. On May 19, 1983, an eighty-one-year-old retired master sergeant living in nearby Mechanicsburg went one step further. He paid a visit to the adjutant at the barracks to gain permission to be buried in the Indian School cemetery. Clarence F. Barr had retired in 1946 after working at the Carlisle Barracks for eighteen years doing a variety of jobs, including cook and military police officer. In his early years, it is likely that he was one of the workers who assisted in moving the graves to their new site.[57] During his years at Carlisle Barracks, Barr must have noted white burials taking place in the relocated cemetery, the last interment being in 1957. After that, for almost thirty years, all military personnel and their families were buried at Ashland. Nevertheless, Clarence Barr was granted his wish. He died on August 23, 1984, and five days later the front page of the *Harrisburg Patriot* reported, "Retired Master Sgt. Clarence F. Barr was laid to rest with full military honors in the Indian Cemetery at Carlisle Barracks."[58] With this burial, the new Indian cemetery was declared closed. In August 2005, however, June Wagner Barr claimed her right to be buried alongside her husband, and her inscription was added to his stone. The Barrs' gravestone stood as a final marker of appropriation; a white military man and his wife taking the last space.[59] In one of history's symmetric ironies, a white man had chosen burial in an Indian cemetery that had only been established because Indians were not permitted to be buried alongside whites.

Barr's motivations for choosing an Indian cemetery as his final resting place must have been complex. Although he had most likely helped move the bodies of dead Indians, Barr had no connection with living Indians, since he arrived at the Carlisle Barracks too late to see the Indian School in operation. His wife, however, is reported to have explained: "He always liked Indians. He studied their ways. He read a lot about them."[60] One of the local papers echoed this rationalization in its headline to an article about his funeral, which celebrated the fulfilment of his desire to be interred in the cemetery: "His Wish: Old Soldier Buried among Friends."[61] By portraying the dead Indian children as Barr's "friends," the copywriter at the *Harrisburg Patriot* implied that Barr had established a connection, not with any of the real Indian children who had died while attending the government boarding school, but rather with his own romantic version of Indians. The journalist catalogued a dozen tribes—Apache, Sioux, Cheyenne, Paiute, Oneida, Washoe, Commanche, Youkton, Shawnee, Seneca, Pawnee, Chippewa, Arapahoe—and copied down some of the most "Indian-sounding" names from the headstones—Friend Bear, Dora Morning, Charles Whiteshield, Titus Deerhead, Herbert Littlehawk, Young Eagle, Percy Whitebear, Almeda Heavyhair, Nannie Little Robe. He used this exotic "evidence" to demonstrate how, through burial in the Indian cemetery, Barr had, quite literally, found his place among children whose "markers provid[ed] a directory of noble Indian heritage." This ultimate appropriation of Indian land, accompanied by a narrative of "playing Indian" at its most macabre, was of keen interest to the local community, and Barr's funeral was given extensive coverage in the press. It was the front-page story in the *Harrisburg Patriot* and also a major news item inside the *Carlisle Sentinel*. The *Sentinel* published a page-wide photograph showing solemn and tearful relatives sitting on fold-up chairs beside the open grave in the cemetery, with the armed honor guard standing at attention behind. This spectacle of military esteem and family sorrow provided an unthreatening way for the local community to integrate the history of the Indian School into its own narrative. It served to displace attention from the Indian children and the Carlisle Indian School's mission of cultural genocide, and to relocate it within the white community. It allowed an assuaging narrative, in which whites were positioned as the principle sufferers of grief, and an old soldier's desire for burial alongside his "friends" was presented as both a triumph for Barr and a solemn but sanitized and safe connection, across the years, to the days of the Indian School. The *Sentinel* reported: "Then taps sounded. The mournful notes sounded across the barracks grounds—all the way back to 1879. 'It's what he always wanted,' Mrs. Barr said."[62]

The significance of this funeral to Indian-white relations within the community was emphasized again fifteen years later, in 1999, when plans for an Indian powwow, to honor the children who had been brought to Carlisle, prompted a past president of the Pennsylvania Poetry Society to suggest that the "festival," as he called it, might wish to use a poem he had written about the Barr funeral. The words of his poem made no reference to the obliteration of Indian cultures that the Indian School had championed, but instead painted a rosy picture of unity between the two races. For many whites, the cemetery was not a place that encouraged grappling with a problematic past nor acknowledgment of the existence of living descendants of the schoolchildren, but instead provoked mournful nostalgia and a romanticizing of dead Indians.[63] And for some, an Indian ghost story and Halloween-style haunting of one of the school's surviving buildings, persistently linked to a Sioux girl who died at the school in 1884, offered a gripping yet trite way to deal with complex emotions and questions raised by the legacy of the Indian School and the existence of an Indian cemetery in their midst.[64]

Reclaiming the Carlisle Indian School Cemetery

Within Native communities, there was growing determination to uncover the truth about Carlisle and its program and to ensure that the children who never went home were respected and honored. Starting in the 1970s, on the Saturday before Memorial Day, without fanfare or publicity, representatives from the American Indian Society of Washington DC would regularly visit the cemetery to pray and place new flowers on all the graves.[65] Gradually, among Native peoples across Indian Country, a new awareness of the centrality of boarding schools and Carlisle to their shared histories was emerging. A widespread resolve to confront the legacies of Carlisle was accompanied by the realization that very few had ever visited the old campus. On Memorial Day weekend of 2000, this was to change.

For the first time since the Carlisle Indian School closed its doors in 1918, Native Americans from across the United States journeyed to the town of Carlisle in the hundreds to assemble on the grounds of the Carlisle Barracks for Powwow 2000: Remembering the Carlisle Indian School. The powwow was organized jointly by a committee of Native peoples and members of the local community to honor the former Carlisle students and their families. It was part of the 250th commemoration of Cumberland County. From California, New York, Florida, New Mexico, South Dakota, Maryland, and as far away as Alaska they came, their car and camper license plates in the campground north of the town reading like a geography of the United States. Most had never before visited the town of Carlisle or the school; many had a relative who had been a Carlisle student; all came to pay tribute to the children who had been taken from their homes and brought to Carlisle to learn the white man's ways.

A key focus for many Native visitors was the traditional ceremonies for the children in the cemetery. For the first time ever, on the morning of May 28, 2000, sacred Native American rites were practiced openly on the grounds of the Carlisle Barracks.[66] On a damp overcast morning a group of about fifty people gathered beside the gate of the Indian School cemetery. The mood was reverent, and people spoke easily and quietly to each other, but there was also a general feeling of diffidence. No one was quite certain what was going to happen. The different tribes with ancestors buried in the cemetery each had their own rites and rituals for mourning the dead. In death as in life, these children had been forced together. As a result, their descendants were now all powerfully connected to the school that had forced itself into their respective histories. The order and symmetry of the stones in the cemetery belied the story of rupture and disarray of which the descendants were all aware.

Standing beside the ceremonial pit, where the fire of cedar and hemlock burned strongly near the entrance to the cemetery, Wayne Cave explained to the group that he was going to conduct a spirit-releasing ceremony. This was a Lakota rite, to help the spirits pass to the other side; it had never been performed for these children. When the drummer began his steady beat, it was the first time this sound had ever been heard at the Carlisle Barracks. The ceremony was for all the children, but the buffalo meat offered to the spirits gave it both a cultural and regional character. Appropriately, Thomas Marshall's outsized stone at the central plot, transported from the original cemetery, was made a representative grave for much of the ceremony. Tobacco leaves, carried round the cemetery and placed on every stone, with a larger amount to bless the "unknowns," served as a reminder of a cultural tradition shared by all tribes. The air was heavy from burning sage when the family from Alaska stepped forward to continue the ceremony. Willard Jones made clear that the Tlinglit also shared the tradition of "feeding the spirits." But, he explained, "We are people of the sea, so the offerings we have brought are dried salmon, haddock and seaweed." Everyone present was there to mourn lost children, and Willard invited them all to join the Tlinglit ceremonial. One by one the mourners took a small handful of the sea products from the proffered bag and dropped them onto the fire of cedar and hemlock boughs. Gradually, they formed a close circle around the fire. Gathered together to honor and grieve, the occasion was, as N. Scott Momaday observed later, something like a "give-away": generous, inclusive, and encompassing.

Throughout the weekend, although all the subsequent powwow events took place on the adjoining field, the cemetery remained a central focal point for everyone. No one left without paying their respects. Throughout both days, individuals and groups drifted away from the stalls and dancing to walk between the little white stones and read the names engraved on them. For many it was a shock to recognize some of the names of the dead, or to see their tribal label chiseled onto a marker. By the end of the weekend, gifts of coins, toys, candy, beadwork, and sweet grass had been left on many of the graves. Beside the stone of a Pawnee boy, a long, severed plait of hair and pair of scissors indicated that someone was in deepest mourning.

The drums beat all weekend. Their heartbeat pulse accompanied music, singing, and dancers' swaying regalia that came from the length and breadth of America. Grass dancers, traditional dancers, jingle-dress dancers,[67] shawl dancers: men, women, and children all danced to honor the children who were taken to Carlisle to learn the white man's ways, and, in particular, for the ones who never went home.

The rupture experienced by the children who had been taken from their homes recurred in different ways for those of later generations who had returned to revisit Carlisle. For many students, years away from the nurture of family and community had left them emotionally scarred and unready for the responsibilities of adulthood. After attending the pow-wow in Carlisle, Jim West (Cheyenne) was prompted to write an honest, open letter to his niece while journeying home to New Mexico. He paid tribute to his grandmother: "Rena's heart is not 'on the ground' and her strength is a great legacy to us all." But he also recognized the "chasm that has made it difficult for your Father and I to know how to be an extended family with our cousins." He identified "Rena's experience at Carlisle" as "another link in the chain of dysfunctionality that runs through our family."[68] For many, the loss of life marked by the cemetery was matched by a deep awareness of so much more that had been lost and that could never be reclaimed.

The powwow had been organized to honor the children and to help acknowledge the truth that is always a prerequisite for healing and reconciliation. Despite the pain intrinsic to the event, Powwow 2000 was also a triumphant moment. Native American people had returned to reclaim the grounds of the Carlisle Barracks. As Jim West wrote to his niece: "We prayed that day in languages that had been forbidden. We wore buckskins covered in beadwork, shawls, and all forms of traditional regalia, which had been taken from the students of Carlisle, our Grandparents and Great Grandparents. We were still dancing that day on the grounds of the school that was going to "kill the Indian and save the man" and had long since disappeared. It was a good day."[69]

Not since the school's closure had Indian people assembled on the grounds of the Carlisle Barracks. Never before had they danced openly to the beat of the drum or publicly performed ceremonies of mourning and remembrance. They came to reclaim a facet of their histories and to mourn and dignify the sacrifice made by the dead children who never returned home, as well as the many survivors who are testimony to the failure of a deliberate program of cultural erasure. For this brief period, Indian people were able to repossess the space where the remains of their kin are interred and to enact ceremonies, forbidden at the time of their deaths, that would safeguard both them and their living descendants.

Living Site of Memory

Powwow 2000 marked the start of a progressive, Native reclamation of the Indian School cemetery as a living site of memory. Sage, sweet grass, tobacco, and other gifts left on the graves provides evidence that visitors come regularly and that individual students are mourned and honored. In May 2009, a Lipan Apache boy, who had been lost to his people for over a century, was welcomed home with a spirit-releasing ceremony (for the story of "the Lost Ones" see chapter 11). Increasing numbers of Native people now make the journey to Carlisle to tour the grounds of the barracks, inspect the remaining school buildings, and, without fail, visit the cemetery. Barbara Landis from the local historical society often acts as their guide.[70] Many institutions, such as Milwaukee Indian School and the American Indian Leadership Program at Penn State, make regular visits to the campus, and their students are aware of how Carlisle and the institutions it spawned are an integral part of their histories. On one such tour, a Penobscot congressional intern noted with disquiet the paucity of visible evidence on the campus to honor and validate the thousands of Indian children who once lived at the Carlisle Barracks. This observation prompted Barbara Landis to initiate an Internet campaign to authorize, finance, and erect a historical marker that would draw public attention to the site of the school and honor all the students who attended.[71] The boundary of the cemetery was chosen as the most noticeable and appropriate site.

The ceremony to dedicate the Carlisle Historical Marker (August 31, 2003) once again brought Native peoples from across America to the Carlisle Barracks. A smaller, more focused event than Powwow 2000, it created a rare public space for personal recollections and stories about the Indian School. Many of those present had actively participated in the process of writing the words for the marker and planning the day's events. Through online introductions and discussions they had come to know one another, and they constituted one of the very first Carlisle descendants' groups.

When the podium and microphone were set up outside the cemetery railings, the space was claimed with reverence, respect, and assurance. The historical marker signaled public recognition of the importance of Carlisle, and its dedication provided an occasion for those most affected by the school's history to voice their thoughts, feelings, and stories. Many of the people who took the microphone that day came forward to speak publically for the first time about the impact of Carlisle on their families. Ory Cuellar (Absentee Shawnee), daughter of Andrew Cuellar (1898–2002), who had been the last surviving Carlisle student, explained how despite its obvious flaws, the Carlisle program had given her father, his three brothers, and one sister valuable training that helped them in later life. Rick Harrison (Osage) explained how his family links to Carlisle stretched back to 1890, when his grandfather, Ben (Mon-kah-sah), had arrived at Carlisle at age nineteen.[72] An outstanding student, Ben went "out" to the country for two summers and completed his full five-year term. Rick's father, Benjamin, however, who was sixteen when he arrived at Carlisle, ran away after just three months and made his way back to Pawhuska, Oklahoma, a journey of over a thousand miles. Rick Harrison described this escapade and then read out the angry letter Carlisle's superintendent had sent to the Osage agent, after the latter had failed to track down Rick's father and return him to Carlisle.

While there was a great deal of humor on display during the day, many of the speakers' stories were spiked with pain and anguish. Chuck Penoi, from Laguna Pueblo, recalled his grandfather, Mark Penoi, who arrived at Carlisle at age fourteen and stayed at the school eleven years. Graduating with a group of twenty-five in 1896, Mark Penoi experienced the full force of the Carlisle program, including seven summers spent away from home, working on Outings in local Pennsylvania communities. Eventually returning home to Oklahoma, he married a Cherokee woman and had a family. But Chuck Penoi described his grandfather's Carlisle years as an emotionally scarring time that rendered his grandfather ill-prepared for parenthood. This incapacity introduced emotional dysfunction into the Penoi family, which would be passed down and suffered by subsequent generations. For Chuck Penoi, recalling his grandfather's Carlisle story reawakened bitter memories and strong feelings, recognized and understood by everyone present. It was an emotional day. By telling their stories and sharing some of the humorous and positive memories, as well as the pain, rupture, and dysfunction that Carlisle brought to their families, Carlisle descendants ensured that the experiences of their ancestors would actively contribute to the history and understanding of the school. The Carlisle story telling would continue, long after everyone returned home.[73]

In Carlisle the Indian School cemetery might embody a history of racial exclusion, segregation, erasure, and appropriation, yet despite having been removed, renovated, regimented, and militarized, it remains a sacred place where the memory of the children who died as well as the survivors can be honored. Its poignant power as a living site of memory continues to be felt by all who visit.[74]

NOTES

1. James W Loewen, *Lies across America: What Our Historic Sites Get Wrong* (New York: New Press, 1999), 458, in which Loewen gives only one tombstone an entry, 230–34.
2. For an illuminating possibility for comparisons with Carlisle, see chapter 7, about the cemetery at Sherman Institute, in *The Indian School on Magnolia Avenue: Voices and Images from Sherman Institute*, ed. Clifford E. Trafzer, Matthew Sakiestewa Gilbert, and Lorene Sisquoc (Corvallis: Oregon State University Press, 2012), 159–72.
3. On three occasions I have been given or sent photographs that purported to be of the Indian School cemetery, but on close examination none matched what we know about its layout and position.
4. The original location of the cemetery and features in the surrounding landscape were established by Fear-Segal using Photoshop to rescale and merge information from three maps: (1) Survey map of "United States Indian Industrial School for Proposed Borough Sewer," 1884, Cumberland County Historical Society (hereafter CCHS); (2) "Map of the United States Barracks," 1909, National Archives and Records Administration, Washington DC (hereafter NARA), Record Group (hereafter RG) 77 subgroup b, Records of the Office of Chief Engineers, held at Carlisle Barracks; (3) Water and Sew-

age map of U.S. General Hospital Number 31, Carlisle PA, October 18, 1918, NARA, Construction Division, War Dept. See map 2 in this chapter to view the results of this merger.

5. Pratt, "Second Annual Report," in Carlisle Indian School, *Eadle Keatah Toh*, October 1881, and "Fifth Annual Report," in Carlisle Indian School, *Morning Star*, vol. 2, September 1884.

6. Renee L. Bergland, *The National Uncanny: Indian Ghosts and American Subjects* (Hanover: University Press of New England, 2000); Coll Thrush, *Native Seattle: Histories from the Crossing Over Place* (Seattle: University of Washington Press, 2008); Colleen E. Boyd and Coll Thrush, eds. *Phantom Past, Indigenous Presence: Native Ghosts in North American Culture and History* (Lincoln: University of Nebraska Press, 2011).

7. Philippe Arès, *The Hour of Our Death* (New York: Alfred Knopf, 1981), 476.

8. Chris Brooks, *Mortal Remains: The History and Present State of the Victorian and Edwardian Cemetery* (Exeter, UK: Wheaton, 1989), 7.

9. In Carlisle, an African American burial ground, the Lincoln Cemetery Memorial Park, was established before the Civil War at 101 West Penn Street. In the 1970s, as part of an urban renewal program, it was razed and turned into a children's playground. Today, a small plaque can be seen, commemorating the African Americans still buried there.

10. Amos LaFromboise, Carlisle Indian School Student File no. 116, NARA, RG 75.

11. St. John's Episcopal Church, "Carlisle Record of Burials," no. 231, 196; *Carlisle Sentinel*, November 28, 1879; *American Volunteer*, December 4, 1879; *Carlisle Herald*, December 4, 1879.

12. F. W. Beers, *Atlas of Cumberland County, Pennsylvania, from Actual Surveys* (New York: F. W. Beers, 1872), 41, 42, 46.

13. Quartermaster R. C. Bower to the Quartermaster General of the Army, November 28, 1921, NARA, Records of the Quartermaster General, RG 92, Entry 225, Consolidated Correspondence File, Box 275, Folder "Carlisle Barracks Cemetery," 1879–1880. A copy is held at the U.S. Army Military History Institute, Carlisle (hereafter MHI).

14. Assistant H. J. Conner to Quartermaster, Medical Field Service School, Carlisle Barracks, July 25, 1923, "Carlisle Barracks Cemetery," 1879–1880, MHI.

15. Adjutant General E. D. Townsend to Quartermaster General, December 1, 1879, "Carlisle Barracks Cemetery," 1879–1880, MHI.

16. Judge Advocate General H. M. Dunn to Secretary of War Alexander Ramsey, January 20, 1880, "Carlisle Barracks Cemetery," 1879–1880, MHI. Underlining is included in the document.

17. Adjutant General E. D. Townsend to Richard Henry Pratt, January 28, 1880, "Carlisle Barracks Cemetery," 1879–1880, MHI.

18. Carlisle Indian School, *Indian Helper*, May 5, 1900.

19. Author's interview with William Ewing, March 16, 2000, Carlisle PA.

20. For official death figures, see Pratt, "Annual Reports," in U.S. Bureau of Indian Affairs, *Annual Reports of Commissioner of Indians Affairs* (Washington DC: Government Printing Office, 1880–1904).

21. The surviving eight "recovered tombstones" are stored at the Military History Institute, Carlisle PA.

22. *Indian Helper* 15, no. 33 (June 15, 1900): 3.

23. *Indian Helper* 11, no. 37 (June 19, 1896): 3; *Indian Helper* 12, no. 39 (July 9, 1897): 3; *Indian Helper* 13, no. 52 (October 14, 1898): 3.

24. Oliver H. Bales to William N. Hailman, Supt. of Indian Schools, March 15, 1895, Thomas Marshall File, Dickinson College Special Collections.

25. Olive H. Bales to William N. Hailman, Supt. of Indian Schools, March 15, 1895.

26. Thomas Marshall, Carlisle Indian School Student File no. 161, NARA, RG 75.

27. Thomas Marshall "Portrait," C-82, CCHS Photographic Collection; "Class of 1900," in *Microcosm* 9, no. 100 (Wilmington DE: M. Rogers Press, 1898).

28. Simmons had attended White's Institute at the same time as Marshall, and from July 1897 until January 1899 she taught at the Carlisle Indian School.

29. *Indian Helper* 14, no. 26 (April 21, 1899).

30. Dickinson College, *Dickinsonian*, Friday, April 28, 1899.

31. *Carlisle Indian School: Hearings before the Joint Commission of the Congress of the United States*, 63rd Cong., 2nd sess., pt. 2 (Washington DC: GPO, 1914), http://archive.org/stream/hearingsbeforejo01unit#page/n3/mode/2up.

32. Field Medical School Quartermaster, Carlisle Barracks, R. C. Bower to Quartermaster General of the Army, Washington DC, November 28, 1921, "Carlisle Barracks Cemetery" file, MHI.

33. P. M. Ashburn, Colonel, Medical Corps, Commandant, to Quartermaster General, Washington DC, December 13, 1921, "Carlisle Barracks Cemetery" file, MHI.

34. "Some twenty-six graves are marked with wooden markers, which have rotted off and should be replaced with standard markers." K. J. Hampton to Quartermaster, Medical Field Service, Carlisle Barracks, June 20, 1927, "Carlisle Barracks Cemetery" file, MHI.

35. Mitchill at Office of the Quartermaster General, Memorandum for Cemeterial Division, September 17, 1926, "Carlisle Barracks Cemetery" file, MHI.

36. B. F. Cheatam, Major General, the Quartermaster General, memorandum to the Surgeon General, September 18, 1926, "Carlisle Barracks Cemetery" file, MHI.

37. Surgeon General, memorandum for the Quartermaster, January 19, 1927, "Carlisle Barracks Cemetery" file, MHI.

38. Isaac Longshore was buried in the Indian School cemetery on June 27, 1918. The *Carlisle Evening Sentinel*, June 26, 1918, and author's interview with

Andrew Cuellar (oldest surviving graduate of Carlisle), August 3, 2000, confirm Longshore's death and burial. The cemetery plot size is given in War Dept., Q. M. C. Form no. 117, Carlisle Barracks PA, Building No. 79, Cemetery, 1931, "Carlisle Barracks Cemetery" file, MHI.

39. *Harrisburg Patriot*, July 14, 1927.

40. *Carlisle Sentinel*, July 14, 1927.

41. *Carlisle Sentinel*, July 14, 1927; Major George Sandrock, Medical Corps, Carlisle Barracks, to Commanding General, Baltimore MD, November 6, 1934, and War Department Memorandum for Cemeterial Division, September 17, 1926, both in "Carlisle Barracks Cemetery" file, MHI.

42. K. J. Hampton to Quartermaster, Medical Field Service, Carlisle Barracks, June 20, 1927, "Carlisle Barracks Cemetery" file, MHI.

43. Map of Military Army Post [in negative], Carlisle PA, showing boundaries of proposed purchase of Henderson Tract, 1918, CCHS. Research on patterns of burial was conducted by Jacqueline Fear-Segal and Barbara Landis in 1999–2000 by using plots maps and visits to the cemetery.

44. These Civil War stones are still standing at Ashland Cemetery.

45. Citizenship was conferred unilaterally on all Indians by the federal government in 1924.

46. Jack Mather, Old Cemetery plot A33, New Cemetery plot C1.

47. The eight surviving stones from the original cemetery expose just a few of these mistakes. These stones belong to the following children [in order of death]: Leah Road Traveller, Arapaho; Warren Painter, Sioux; Lena Carr, Pueblo; John Bull, Gros Ventre; Thomas Suckley, Mandan; Mattie Ocumma, Cherokee; Fred Senoche, Sac and Fox; Tomiccouk, Alaskan.

48. Margaret Edgan, Old Cemetery plot B14, New Cemetery plot B23.

49. See chapter 10 in this collection, "Death at Carlisle: Naming the Unknowns in the Cemetery."

50. Alicia Delgardillo, *From Fort Marion to Fort Sill: A Documentary History of the Chiricahua Apache* (Lincoln: University of Nebraska Press, 2013), 213.

51. Richard Henry Pratt, *Battlefield and Classroom: Four Decades with the American Indian, 1867–1904*, ed. Robert Utley (New Haven CT: Yale University Press, 1964), 239. Spotted Tail later allowed his children to return.

52. Luther Standing Bear, *My People the Sioux* (Lincoln: University of Nebraska Press, 1975), 159.

53. Major George Sandrock, Medical Corps., Carlisle Barracks to Commanding General, Baltimore MD, November 6, 1934, "Carlisle Barracks Cemetery" file, MHI.

54. War Department Q. M. C. form no. 117, Carlisle Barracks, Building No. 79 [Cemetery], June 1941, NARA, RG 77, "Carlisle Barracks Cemetery" file, MHI.

55. Herbert Rasmussen, F40, Plot map of new cemetery, November 7, 1947, "Carlisle Barracks Cemetery" file, MHI.

56. After seeing photographs I took of the cemetery at a conference presentation in 2000, Grayson Noley (Choctaw), who was in the audience, informed me that when he visited the Carlisle Cemetery in the 1980s, it was unkempt and dilapidated. *Death, Identity and Place* panel, American Indian Workshop, Swansea, UK, 2006.

57. *Carlisle Sentinel*, August 29, 1984.

58. *Harrisburg Patriot*, August 29, 1984.

59. On August 29, 1984, the *Harrisburg Patriot* had reported, "Mrs. Barr may be buried next to her husband if she so wishes." Nearly a quarter of a century later, she was laid to rest with her husband, in plot 28, row F.

60. *Harrisburg Patriot*, August 29, 1984.

61. *Harrisburg Patriot*, August 29, 1984.

62. *Carlisle Sentinel*, August 29, 1984; *Harrisburg Patriot*, August 29, 1984.

63. L. J. Reho, "The Burial Grounds," manuscript in CCHS.

64. Barbara Landis, "Putting Lucy Pretty Eagle to Rest," in *Boarding School Blues: Revisiting American Indian Educational Experiences*, ed. Clifford E. Trafzer, Jean A. Keller, and Lorene Sisquoc (Lincoln: University of Nebraska Press, 2006), 123–30.

65. The American Indian Society (AIS) of Washington DC is composed of Indian peoples, from many different tribes, who have moved to the DC area; see http://www.aisdc.org.

66. Native people who visited the cemetery often performed ceremonies, but these were private, unpublicized events.

67. Carolyn Rittenhouse tells her story of cultural reclamation in chapter 13 and gives details of how her daughter danced with a jingle dress at the Carlisle Powwow.

68. Jim West to his cousin Karin, May 29, 2000, with permission.

69. West to Karin, May 29, 2000.

70. Barbara Landis works as the Indian School biographer at the Cumberland County Historical Society. She leads tours of the Indian School and has helped hundreds in their efforts to research ancestors and their links with Carlisle.

71. For discussions leading up to the dedication of the historical marker, see "Historical Marker for the Carlisle Indian School," http://home.epix.net/~landis/markplan.html.

72. Ben Harrison spent four years at Haskell, an off-reservation boarding school in Lawrence, Kansas, before attending Carlisle. "Student in 1985 at Indian

School: Ben F. Harrison Saw His Granddaughter Graduate from Haskell," *Lawrence Daily Journal-World,* May 24, 1945, 2.

73. Dovie Thomason, a native storyteller, attended the marker dedication with her daughter, Samantha, and three generations of the Sickles family whose histories are entwined with Carlisle. It inspired her to write the story *The Spirit Survives,* which is published for the first time as chapter 17 in this collection.

74. Recently, descendants of some of the children buried in the cemetery have come together to request that the remains of their ancestors be sent home. On May 10, 2016, representatives of the U.S. Army traveled to the Rosebud Agency, South Dakota, to meet with the Rosebud Tribal Council and representatives of other Plains tribes whose children were sent to Carlisle more than a century ago. The army agreed to begin the process to enable Carlisle students' remains to be repatriated, with the army paying the full cost. This is likely to be a painful, sensitive, and difficult process, but for the very first time there is official acknowledgment that the wishes of families to have their children returned should be respected.

10

Death at Carlisle

Naming the Unknowns in the Cemetery

BARBARA LANDIS

When I first saw the cemetery at Carlisle, filled with rows of children's graves, I noticed that thirteen of them were marked with the same worrying and uninformative word: "Unknown." Who were these children, I wondered. Where did they come from? What were their names? I decided it would become part of my work as the biographer of the Carlisle Indian School at the Cumberland County Historical Society to try to find out who these missing children were. This essay presents the results of my search, as well as more general information I uncovered about deaths at the Indian School.

The Carlisle Indian School cemetery is located at the very eastern edge of the Carlisle garrison, near what was once identified as the "back gate." Now, due to strict U.S. Army security imposed since 9/11, every vehicle entering the Carlisle Barracks has to drive past the cemetery. Although the cemetery takes up a tiny footprint compared to its original size and location (see chapter 9 for details of the cemetery's removal), it stands as a memorial to 192 students who died while at the school. We know that bodies were moved from the site of the original cemetery in 1927, because the local Carlisle newspaper published an article describing that gruesome process.[1] We know too that old headstones were replaced with standard government-issued limestone markers, similar to the military markers found at Gettysburg and Arlington National Cemeteries. But the stones in the Indian School cemetery do not show ages, dates of birth, or, in some cases, even dates of death. A walk through the graveyard also reveals variant spellings of student names and nations, and it appears that most of these errors were introduced when the graves were relocated, new headstones carved, and their layout randomly altered. A plot map drawn up at the time of removal lists the interred students' names, but some did not have

Fig. 18. "Unknown" gravestone in Indian School cemetery, 2015. Photo by Susan Rose.

markers.[2] So in the Carlisle Indian School cemetery today, interspersed among the six rows of markers, are thirteen stones inscribed with only that single word: "Unknown."

Focusing on the cemetery and the students buried in the cemetery, we can discover information that adds pieces to the puzzle of the Carlisle Indian School's history.[3] Official documentation is sparse; there are no government records giving details of either the burials or the moving of the cemetery. Information about student deaths, however, can be gleaned from the 8,856 Carlisle student files in the National Archives and Records Administration (NARA) in Washington DC, from obituaries in the school newspapers, and from local church records. The database created by Genevieve Bell from the NARA Carlisle student files brings us organized statistical information and details about the numbers and identities of children buried at Carlisle. Recently the digitization of the Carlisle Indian School student files has made it possible to access these individual student records online.[4] When these sources are interrogated alongside Carlisle newspapers and other publications, much is revealed about student deaths at Carlisle, which was a topic officials did not wish to publicize.

Just the existence of these 192 graves in a cemetery on the school grounds lays bare the deeply troubling practice of interring pupils at Carlisle, rather than returning them home to their families. There is no correspondence in the archive to suggest that Pratt gave parents or other family members the option to reclaim the children's bodies or their possessions. Nor do we know anything about their last days or their last wishes, apart from a few references in the weekly newspapers. In Luther Standing Bear's autobiographical book, *Land of the Spotted Eagle*, we hear about student deaths at Carlisle from a firsthand witness. He wrote from the perspective of one of the very first students who left home knowing nothing of the world he was entering. Determined to design a new kind of vision quest for himself by traveling miles away to Carlisle, he embarked on a rite of passage in which he fully anticipated the possibility of never returning home: "I remember when we children were on our way to Carlisle School, thinking that we were on our way to meet death at the hands of white people, the older boys sang brave songs so that we would all meet death according to the Lakota code—fearlessly."[5] Standing Bear's fears that he would be killed may have been misplaced, but the dread faced by his relatives and friends back home that they would never see their children again proved very real. Standing Bear returned home, but large numbers of his Rosebud Sioux friends and relatives would die while at Carlisle and be buried in the school cemetery. During the first seven years of the Carlisle experiment, at least nine burials were of children who had come from Luther Standing Bear's home community at the Rosebud Agency.

Three of the girls from Rosebud, Maude Little Girl, Dora Her Pipe, and Rose (no surname; daughter of Long Face), and two of the boys, Ernest White Thunder and Dennis Strikes First, had traveled with the fifteen-year-old Luther to Pennsylvania, as members of the first group of Carlisle enrollees; their ages ranged from twelve to eighteen years. They arrived together, around midnight on October 5, 1879, and just fourteen months later, Maude and Ernest passed away on the same day. The school newspaper reported: "It was a sad and mysterious coincidence by which two of our pupils were taken from us by death on the night of the 13th of December, both of them being from the same agency and the same band of Sioux."[6]

They were the children of powerful and respected leaders, Swift Bear and White Thunder, and their deaths on the same day were of particular concern back home at the Rosebud Agency. But as with many other Carlisle stories, we have only the administrative narrative to provide clues about what happened. From this we learn that White Thunder's only son, Ernest, had become depressed and staged a hunger strike a year after his arrival, and that he lingered for two months, before succumbing to death. We know a similarly small amount about Maude's death. In keeping with the accepted practice of deflecting responsibility for student deaths, the Carlisle school newspaper reported that Maude Swift Bear had arrived at the school in poor health: "[She] was a bright, impulsive, warm-hearted girl, much loved by her school mates. She came to the Training School suffering from diseased lungs, and so had not strength to resist pneumonia which seized her. She was the first girl to die here, and the first Sioux out of more than ninety connected with the school. Funeral services were conducted by Professor Lippincott, and the double burial is one which will never be forgotten by those who witnessed it."[7]

But deaths among the first group of students, who had been Luther's traveling companions from the Rosebud Agency, did not end there. The next two to die were the daughters of Brave Bull and Long Face. Maggie-Stands-Looking reported Dora Her Pipe's illness in a home letter to her father, American Horse. She wrote to American Horse to ask him to tell Brave Bull that the latter's daughter had "been a little sick, but is most well now." But Dora passed away three months later. That same month, Rose, the daughter of Long Face, also died. These girls' deaths came in April 1881, just three months after news reached Rosebud Agency that Ernest White Thunder and Maude Little Girl had passed on the same day. One can only begin to imagine how the tragic news of these losses from so far away was received. But the bad news did not end there.

Rosebud lost another child to illness contracted at Carlisle when Dennis Strikes First, a son of Blue Tomahawk, died on January 19, 1881, of "Typhoid Pneumonia." Dennis was "a bright studious, ambitious boy, standing first in his class, and of so tractable a disposition as to be no trouble to his teachers. Two of his sisters had recently died at the agency of similar disease so that Blue Tomahawk's family is indeed bereaved."[8]

September 1883 marked more tragedy for the Rosebud group, with the news of the death of Spotted Tail's daughter, Gertrude. She passed away while on Outing with Miss Bender of Byberry, New York. Gertrude died of pneumonia and, according to her obituary, had been prone to consumption. She was the second of Spotted Tail's children to die in the East that year, and at home on the Rosebud reservation, three more of Spotted Tail's children had died within the same period. It is worth noting that in Gertrude's case, her remains were interred in the Byberry Cemetery.[9] This stands as a bleak reminder that there were more Carlisle deaths than are represented by the stones in the cemetery.

A further four Rosebud Sioux children never returned home. Two passed away within a month of each other, in September and October 1884, and two more in May and June 1886. These were the children of Hollow Horn Bear, Foot Canoe, Bear Paints Dirt, and Pretty Eagle.

The Indian cemetery at Carlisle holds the remains of an additional nine Sioux pupils who came from other Sioux communities in the West. Twelve-year-old Alvan, the son of Roaster, died in March 1882. Luther Standing Bear told of this death in a letter home. He wrote to his father, Standing Bear: "Day before yesterday one of the Sioux boys died. . . . He was a good boy always. So we were very glad for him. Because he is better now than he was on Earth. I think you may be don't know what I mean. I mean he has gone in heaven. Because he was a good boy everywhere."[10]

Herbert Good Boy, from the Pine Ridge Agency, who had arrived at the school at the age of sixteen and distinguished himself by being elected president of the Young Men's Christian Association, had been at the school a full ten years before succumbing to pneumonia in October 1895. He too is buried in the Indian School cemetery. Cora Price, a Cheyenne River Sioux girl, passed away in April 1896, after having been at Carlisle only four months. Two members of Charging Shield's family, Fannie and Wallace, passed away within fourteen months of each other. The other Sioux children buried there are fifteen-year-old Warren Painter, son of Bear Paints Dirt, seventeen-year-old Richard Morgan, a Yankton boy who had come to Carlisle from the Fort Peck Agency in Montana, and fourteen-year-old Edward Upright, son of Wanatah and from Sisseton Agency in Dakota Territory. In total, there are nineteen Sioux students buried in the Carlisle Indian School cemetery and a twentieth Sioux, Thomas Marshall (for his story, see chapter 9, "The History and Reclamation of a Sacred Space"), who lived at the Indian School and looked after the small boys dormitory while he was attending Dickinson College.

The children of many nations, many communities, and many families also lie in the school cemetery. The greatest numbers of deaths for a particular nation are the Chiricahua Apache prisoners of war, associated with Geronimo's capture. Prior to their arrival at Carlisle, these Apache prisoners had been incarcerated at Fort Marion in St. Augustine, Florida, under the most devastating of circumstances. There were only two privies for over five hundred prisoners, sanitary conditions were horrendous, and the fort was dark and dank. Eleven of these young Apache prisoners of war arrived early in February 1884, fifteen more in the winter of 1886, and seventeen more the following spring; most of the burials in the Indian cemetery are from this particular group. Almost all of these deaths are attributed to tuberculosis, although one child, Titus Deerhead, was memorialized in the December 1885 issue of the *Morning Star* as having died of epilepsy.

When word got out among the Apache prisoners-of-war in Florida that children would be sent to Carlisle, there were a spate of marriages to ensure family intactness.[11] Despite this, young married people were sent to Carlisle, and as a consequence, babies were born at the school. Two

Fig. 19. Katie Irvine Kinzhune and Eunice Suisson, Chiricahua Apache babies at the Carlisle Indian School, December 25, 1886. Photo by John N. Choate. Cumberland County Historical Society, Carlisle PA. SA-05.

Apache babies born to prisoner-of-war couples in the fall of 1887, Eunice Suisson and Katie Kinshoe, were tracked through the school's weekly *Indian Helper*s from the time of their births until their deaths. The babies' first teeth, the first donning of short pants, first gifts from visitors, and first photograph sessions were all chronicled in the *Indian Helper*. Photographs of one of the babies, Eunice, were given as a premium for new subscribers to the newspaper. Sadly, both babies lived only a short time. Katie Kinshoe died in the summer of 1888. Her obituary appeared in the July 27, 1888, issue of the *Indian Helper*:

> DIED.—On Friday, July 13, at the Carlisle School, Katie Kinshone, aged nine months. Katie was one of the Apache babies born to parents at the school who were brought from their prison home at St. Augustine, Fla., a year ago last spring. On Monday she was taken sick with enlargement of the liver, and later, Pneumonia set in which ended her life. All was done to save her that human skill and loving care could do. She was a bright child, greatly loved and will be mourned by all who remember her sweet smile and charming ways.

The following spring, baby Eunice passed away. "Our little Eunice had all that care and attention could give, and yet she was taken from us. The disease from which she suffered went to her brain and for two days she lay in a stupor from which she was not able to rally. On Sunday afternoon she was buried and many a heart sank in sorrow as the pretty little white coffin, covered with the choicest flowers and containing the remains of our beloved baby was lowered in the grave."[12] Even after Eunice's death, the *Indian Helper* offered her photograph as a reward for securing three new subscriptions to the paper and continued doing this until the Thanksgiving issue eight months later.

The *Indian Helper*'s keen interest in the lives of these two Chiricahua Apache babies moved from fascination to macabre, but the newspaper's concern also inadvertently carries vital information about the identities of two "unknowns" in the cemetery. The newspaper's description of their burials in the Indian cemetery is evidence that they were definitely interred there. Yet there are no stones in the cemetery marking the graves of babies Katie and Eunice, and this enables us to attribute two of the "unknown" markers in the cemetery to Eunice Suisson and Katie Kinshoe. This means that we can decrease the number of unknown Carlisle Indian School graves from thirteen to eleven.

The sad story of these Chiricahua Apache babies opened a new avenue for my research on the Indian School cemetery. If these babies had been buried in the school cemetery but their markers had not survived (so that their names were not listed and then reinscribed on new stones when the cemetery was removed), there was a possibility that the identities of other "unknowns" could also be discovered. Evidence might not be forthcoming in the official record, but outside sources could perhaps also provide crucial information.

My second research finding again focused on the Chiricahua Apaches. Documentary data, gathered by Fort Sill historian Gillett Griswold, records the deaths at Carlisle of the wife and baby of an Apache prisoner of war, Talbot Goday.[13] The couple was among the prisoner group arriving at the school on April 30, 1887, and their baby was later born there. According to Griswold, both mother and child died at Carlisle and were buried in the school cemetery. No date is given for their deaths, but it is reported that the grieving father returned to Mount Vernon Barracks in 1890. As there are no stones bearing their names in the cemetery, it is safe to assume that they are two more of the "unknowns," which then reduces the number of unknown markers from eleven to nine.

Careful scrutiny of the Bell database and the digitized online records allows for in-depth study of the Carlisle data from the student files in the National Archives, providing more detail of numbers of deaths at the school. The compilation of student entries shown as "died at school" provided the basis for a comparison of National Archive (NARA) student folders with published cemetery lists found in the collections at the CCHS. There are five entries in Bell's "Reason for Departure" column simply noted as "Death." Listed among these is Henry Rose, an Alaska Native who arrived at the school on October 15, 1903, at age seventeen. He had six Outings from June 1904 through July 1907. Henry was removed from his last Outing in Lititz, Pennsylvania, due to illness. He died and was buried in the Carlisle Indian School Cemetery August 4, 1907. There is no stone identifying him, so we can bring the number of unknowns in the cemetery from nine to eight.

Some information about student deaths can also be discovered in official documents. Pratt included reports of mortalities in his *Annual Reports to the Commissioner of Indian Affairs*, and these add to the body of information we have about the numbers of deaths at the school during the early years. His first report, dated October 5, 1880, reveals the deaths of ten children: "We have lost by death six boys, and have heard of the death of four others returned to their agencies."[14] In order to corroborate this report, the NARA records from Bell's database show eight known burials in the Indian cemetery before October 5, 1880, contradicting the official report of only six deaths. It is possible that Pratt was only reporting the deaths of those students physically present on the campus when they died, disregarding those who died over the summer months on Outing.[15]

Subsequent years' comparisons of the official reports and information in the Bell database reveal other contradictions in the numbers of deaths, hinting that these mortality statistics were probably underreported. The reports do, however, provide information about students who were returned home due to illness. In the report of October 1881, Pratt writes:

Returned to homes on account of sickness: fourteen. For other reasons, four (two of whom were former Florida prisoners). By death, ten. Making a total of twenty-eight, and leaving us this date 267 [students enrolled] and of those returned to the agencies four have died. During the late winter and early spring both measles and scarlet fever were epidemic in this vicinity, and came into the school in spite of a strict quarantine. A number of the deaths reported occurred from these diseases. Our present condition of health is excellent. We have but one pupil whose health is a matter of concern, and none who are not able to attend their meals.

From the fifth Annual Report dated September 12, 1884:

Sanitary Condition.

The general health of the school has been better than in any previous year. Very few cases of acute diseases of malignant character occurred. Four (4) girls and two (2) boys died all from disease of long standing. Thirty-six were sent home on account of failing health or mental weakness. A number of these have died. An epidemic of mumps passed through the school in November, December and January. There were one hundred and sixteen (116) cases. All recovered without any serious complications resulting. Our greatest trouble is tubercular disease and scrofula, these being the diseases most prevalent among Indians. Our best health results have been among those placed out in families. Nearly every pupil so placed added increased health to the other gains.

Of the total number of burials at Carlisle, it seems that all but twelve were deaths during the Pratt years. After his dismissal, on June 30, 1904, four students died that same year, four died in 1905, and four more in 1906. However, no burials were publicly reported in the school papers after 1904, even though the NARA records provide evidence of eight more deaths occurring before the school's closing in 1918. While the latest death date to appear on any stone or in any record for the Indian cemetery is December 7, 1906, the last known reported death and burial in the cemetery was a very public suicide on school grounds in the weeks after the school was closed down in the summer of 1918 and was reported in the local press.[16] Isaac Longshore, a despondent former student, was buried among his former peers; however, there is no stone bearing his name. This brings the present number of "unknowns" to seven.

The most recent discovery of the identity of an "unknown" came about because the student's descendants had a record that she had died while at Carlisle Indian School and had been buried in the cemetery. They came to visit her grave but could not find her name on any of the markers in the cemetery. Willard and Mary Jones, Tlinget and Haida elders from Alaska, came to Carlisle to participate in the ceremonies organized for Powwow 2000. This event was a tribute to the children who had been sent away to Carlisle, as well as to those who had died there, and was attended by descendants from across the United States.[17] At a ceremony in the cemetery Willard and Mary Jones shared the story of Mary's great aunt, Mary Kinninook, who came to Carlisle on October 24, 1903, at the age of eight, died December 28, 1908, and was buried in the school cemetery. There is no stone marking Mary Kinninook's grave. This discovery brings the present number of "unknowns" from seven to six.

This means that over the past fifteen years, seven of the names of children buried in the Indian School cemetery and marked as "unknown" have been discovered. By nation they are Henry Rose and Mary Kinninook, Alaskan; Eunice Suisson, Katie Kinshoe, Talbot Goday's wife and his infant daughter, Chiricahua Apache; Isaac Longshore, Sac and Fox. Through the pages of the weekly *Indian Helper* newsletters, Annual Reports, death certificates, and the determined quest of one Alaskan Native family, these names have been reclaimed.

Deaths of children at faraway off-reservation schools brought sadness and grief to many Native communities, with the Sioux and Apache nations especially hard hit. These deaths, the enforced Christian burials far from home with no opportunity to conduct the necessary traditional ceremonies, and the lack of proper information and records about what had happened leave unhealed wounds and lingering griefs as part of the boarding school legacy. As more of the school's history is discovered and discussed, it is to be hoped that all the remaining six "unknowns" in the Carlisle cemetery will be identified and named.

It is important to remember, however, as we seek to fill in the remaining names of the six unknowns, that there may be other children buried at Carlisle who never even received a gravestone marked with "Unknown." I hope that the search to recover the past will someday include these children— the unknown "unknowns"—so that their stories can be known and they can take their place in the evolving history of the school and its legacy.[18]

NOTES

1. *Newville Valley Times*, August 18, 1927, front page.
2. "Plot map of graves/names in removed cemetery," manuscript created by Humer et al., in CCHS Archives, n.d.
3. It must be recognized that there were other children who passed whose remains were returned to their home communities.
4. Carlisle Indian School Digital Resource Center, http://carlisleindian.dickin son.edu/.
5. Luther Standing Bear, *Land of the Spotted Eagle* (Lincoln: University of Nebraska Press, 2006), 217.
6. Carlisle Indian School, *Eadle Keatah Toh* 1, no. 8 (December 1880/January 1881): 3.
7. Carlisle Indian School, *Eadle Keatah Toh* 1, no. 8 (December 1880/January 1881): 3.

8. Carlisle Indian School, *Eadle Keatah Toh* 1, no. 8 (December 1880/January 1881): 3.

9. Philadelphia PA Death Certificate Index, 1803–1915, Ancestry.com.

10. Luther Standing Bear's March 31, 1882, letter on the death of Alvan was reprinted in Carlisle Indian School, *School News* 2, no. 11 (April 1882): 4.

11. Ruth McDonald Boyer and Narcissus Duffy Gayton, *Apache Mothers and Daughters: Four Generations of a Family* (Norman: University of Oklahoma Press), 104–5.

12. Carlisle Indian School, *Indian Helper* 4, no. 30 (March 15, 1889): 3.

13. Alicia Delgadillo, *From Fort Marion to Fort Sill: A Documentary History of the Chiricahua Apache* (Lincoln: University of Nebraska Press, 2013), 102.

14. First Annual Report of the Indian Training School, Carlisle Barracks, Carlisle PA, October 5, 1880, *Eadle Keatah Toh* 1, no. 7 (November 1880): 1.

15. The Outing Program was a feature of the "civilization" program that was developed at Carlisle by which students were sent *out* into non-Native homes where they worked for a nominal wage, boarding with host families and attending church and Sunday school and, in some cases, public schools year round with their non-Indian siblings.

16. *Carlisle Evening Sentinel*, June 26, 1918.

17. Powwow 2000: Remembering the Carlisle Indian School was organized by the 250th Anniversary Committee of Cumberland County.

18. In June 2016 a team of archival researchers from Dickinson College who are working with the newly digitized Carlisle archive found documentation for two more Carlisle Indian School students who were buried in the Indian cemetery but for whom there are no stones: Fred Warbonnet (Rosebud Sioux) and Wilson Carpenter (Seneca). This brings the number of unknown stones from six to four.

Part 4   Reclamations

11

The Lost Ones

Piecing Together the Story

JACQUELINE FEAR-SEGAL

Col. Ranald Slidell Mackenzie's ferocious 1873 attack on three large Lipan Apache, Mescalero Apache, and Kickapoo villages inside the Mexican border near Remolino left many Native people dead. Two Lipan Apache children were captured, made prisoners of war, and later transported across the continent, from Texas to Pennsylvania, to be enrolled at the Carlisle Indian School. Their parents and community knew nothing of their whereabouts. The Lipan Apaches never heard from their children again, and their loss initiated a period of distress and mourning that lasted more than a century. The Lipan Apaches' long search and vigil would only begin to draw to a close in 2002, when they at last heard from Jacqueline Fear-Segal about where their children had been taken all those years before. Closure was finally reached in 2009, after Lipan Apache elders were able to visit the children's burial sites for spirit-releasing ceremonies. The beginnings of the story of the "Lost Ones" were first pieced together and published in *White Man's Club*, and it was subsequently made the subject of a documentary: *The Lost Ones: Long Journey Home.*[1] When this film was screened in California, at the Native American and Indigenous Studies Association in 2011, it elicited a powerful response and a call for a symposium to be held in Carlisle so that this story and the legacy of the Indian boarding school system could be openly addressed in the very place where the Indian School had operated. The story of the Lost Ones lies at the heart of this collection and was the inspiration for the Carlisle Symposium.

These Lipan Apache children who were forcibly transported to Pennsylvania were just 2 among more than 10,500 Native children who were sent to Carlisle to be enrolled at the Indian School during its nearly forty-year existence. Very few of their stories have ever been told. While all were unique, the lives of the Lost Ones are especially noteworthy because these students were classified as "prisoners of war" during their whole time at the school, and all contact with their people had been broken.[2] Enrolled in 1880, shortly after the school first opened, the Lost Ones were known at Carlisle Indian School as Kesetta and Jack.

The children had spent their early days living on the Texas-Mexico border, where their people had been subjected to repeated attacks by American soldiers who were fighting to open the region to white settlement. After Colonel Ranald Mackenzie's Fourth U.S. Cavalry crossed the border into Mexico, attacked their band, and massacred almost everyone, soldiers found the children hiding in the bushes and took them prisoner. From that moment, all links to their culture and their past were abruptly and permanently severed. They lived for a while with a military family, traveling between different forts in the West. Then, when the Carlisle Indian School opened, Mackenzie sent his two juvenile "prisoners of war" to Pennsylvania; neither of them would ever return home or see their people again. Jack died of tuberculosis seven years later at about age seventeen and was buried in the school cemetery. Kesetta, however, remained on Carlisle's student list until shortly before she died at age thirty-nine, still officially a prisoner of war; she was the school's longest registered student.[3]

This painful, tragic story reveals the educational campaign to obliterate Native cultures at its most brutal. Research in the written and photographic archival record, Lipan Apache oral histories, and the commitment and generosity of a large number of people have enabled the two separate chapters in the children's story to be joined. It is assembled here and presented as a means, firstly, to show some of the impacts of Carlisle's "civilizing" mission; secondly, to explore the people, processes, and sources (both written and oral) that enabled the story to be pieced together; and finally, to demonstrate the vital importance of descendant communities knowing and sharing the truth about what happened to their ancestors at Carlisle and other institutions it spawned.

In many ways, these children appeared to be ideal subjects for Carlisle's experiment. They were already completely cut off from the influence of family and community, and the split in their lives perfectly matched the savage/civilized binary so integral to the Indian School's ideology. Their culturally unencumbered status seemed to offer a perfect test case for a school intent on obliterating all traces of students' tribal pasts and training individual Indian children for assimilation into mainstream America. But things did not go as school officials anticipated. Like many students, Jack fell victim to disease and died. And Kesetta did not shine in a manner the school could acknowledge. Instead, she lived and worked on the fringes of white society and died a "fallen" woman. Her short life of drudgery embodied Carlisle's and the government's educational campaign at its most pitiless.

Tracing and constructing the life story of any Carlisle student is challenging, and those of Kesetta and Jack are no different. Fragments must be pieced together from an assortment of disparate sources: written, photographic, and oral. The written record—Indian School newspapers, augmented by Carlisle student records in the National Archives—is vital for basic facts, but it yields a patchy, brittle account, often telling more about the "civilizing" mission of the school than the children's feelings or reactions. Occasionally individual students do speak from the written record; a letter that Jack penned to Pratt from his new home in Fort Augustine, Florida, brings a welcome human touch. Nowhere, however, is there any record of words that Kesetta wrote or spoke. In the Carlisle archive she is utterly silent. Yet despite this, her story can be partially recovered. Although she left no written record of her life, when she died she left behind her three-year-old son, Richard Kasetta. While Kesetta's student file in the National Archives contains only a series of enrollment cards, with stark facts charting her many years at the school and her "Outings," Richard's file is much more robust and carries a wealth of information about both him and his mother. Inevitably, this official record ends abruptly in 1918, when the Carlisle Indian School was closed. But Kesetta's story is carried forward because her son continued to live in the town of Carlisle. Oral accounts recorded in the 1980s with townspeople, as well as more recent interviews, made it possible to track Kesetta's continuing story through local people's memories of her son. The most momentous of all discoveries in my efforts to recuperate Kesetta's story, however, came as the result of an Internet search for details of Lipan Apache history. This led quickly to an email correspondence with her great-great-nephew in Texas, Daniel Castro Romero Jr., the Lipan Apache General Council chairman. In response to information I sent him about Kesetta and Jack's lives in Carlisle, Romero revealed how continually and secretly, across four generations, the Lipan

Apaches had mourned and memorialized the Lost Ones. Although they never knew where their children had gone, the Lipan Apaches had kept their memory alive by annually retelling their story at family reunions and incorporating it into their oral history. For the Lipan Apaches, receiving the news that the Lost Ones had been taken east and enrolled at Carlisle Indian School was painful, but also comforting. The knowledge elucidated their loss and enabled a vital connection to be made between the separated Texan and Pennsylvanian histories of their Lost Ones' lives, bringing the possibility of closure.

Most descendant communities of Carlisle students grapple with the corrosive effects of the school's assimilation program and the associated consequences of cultural genocide. For the Lipan Apaches, however, the Carlisle legacy was experienced as a profound and incomprehensible loss, made worse by total absence of information. So for the Lipan elders, once they learned the whereabouts of their Lost Ones, it was critically important to travel to Carlisle to perform the sacred ceremonies that would enable the spirits of their buried ancestors to be reunited with their Lipan Apache kinsfolk. While waiting for an occasion to make this journey, the elders were keen for me to tell them everything I had learned from the archives about the lives of Jack, Kesetta, and her son Richard, although much of this information was raw and painful.

After their capture, the Lipan Apache children lived entirely within parameters defined by whites. The series of white-assigned last names they carried during their lives (for Kesetta: Smith, Lipan, Roosevelt; for Jack: Smith, Lipan, Mather) reflected and matched the deracinated existence forced upon them. After just a few years in Carlisle's classrooms, Kesetta was sent on Outing and spent her adult years working in a succession of white homes as a paid servant. She lived a larger proportion of her life in Pennsylvania and the surrounding area than in her native Southwest.[4] The Carlisle Indian School represented the most enduring continuity in her life. All ties to her Apache people had been forcibly cut, yet her continuing links to the Indian School signaled her uninterrupted white-designation as Indian; this designation would persist down the generations, to be reinscribed on her half-white son. The trauma and rupture that characterized Kesetta's life meant that for her little resistance and only minimal autonomy was possible.

Yet on the other side of the continent, fighting for their physical and cultural survival, the Lipan people defied and withstood the fracture initiated by the U.S. Army when they had captured Kesetta and Jack and taken them east. Purposefully and secretly, down four generations, they kept the children's memory alive. For whites, the erasure of Kesetta and Jack's Indian identity was never complete. For the Lipan Apaches, it never began.

From the moment their children were taken by the U.S. Army the Lipan people desperately sought news and information about them, but they never heard from the children again and never found out where they had been taken.[5] During all the long years Kesetta was registered at Carlisle, her people were in crisis. For decades they struggled to confront the devastating power of the U.S. Army and defend their lands and lifestyle. Raids up and down the border and relentless assaults by troops meant that Lipan Apache numbers and power rapidly dwindled. They numbered several thousand at the beginning of the century, but by the 1880s they had been reduced to a handful of bands with a few dozen members. Some clusters of Lipans pulled back over the border and merged with the population of Mexico, others mixed with the population of Texas, and a small group moved onto the Mescalero Reservation in New Mexico. Shrunken in number, defeated and subjugated, the Lipan Apaches reluctantly adapted to the dominant power of the United States. But Jack and Kesetta's people never forgot their stolen children. The intensity of their loss, and the silence that followed, only served to deepen the memory.

Collusion between violence and silence can nurture the will to contest grand patterns and overall schemes of history, as Helena Pohlandt-McCormick has argued in her work on South Africa. In such cases, Pohlandt-McCormick suggests, acts of speaking, or doing, can actively create what she describes as "landmarks of memory."[6] In the nineteenth century the Lipan Apaches had neither the strength nor the will to publicly correct the U.S. master narrative and the larger American grand pattern of history, but they did have the motivation and means to protect and secure their own. At secret annual remembrances, they retold events surrounding the kidnapping of their children, who became known as the Lost Ones. Creating and progressively enforcing a "landmark of memory," they ensured that their people's knowledge of the children was kept alive and passed down orally through four generations.[7] Among the Apaches the only place it is believed appropriate to mention a lost family member's name is family reunions. Utterly private, the "hidden transcripts" of these family gatherings ensured that Jack and Kesetta, although never again seen by their own people, maintained their place within Lipan collective memory.[8]

Kesetta was born in about 1867 and, based on his size in surviving photographs, Jack probably a few years later. This was shortly after their small band, led by their father, Ramon Castro, had been forcibly moved to the newly established Fort Griffin, near Albany, Texas.[9] By the 1870s the Lipan Apaches' principal enemies had become American settlers, backed by cavalry stationed at numerous forts across the region. Fort Griffin was part of this new line of defense, built to protect stage and mail lines as well as settlers and provide a base for troops fighting to subdue the tribes of the Southern Plains. The Lipan Apaches based at this fort were considered prisoners of war, but like the Kiowas and Comanches, they continued to make raids on the Texas frontier. Colonel Ranald Slidell Mackenzie, who had earned a formidable reputation commanding cavalry during the Civil War, arrived on the Texas frontier in 1869 to take command of the Fourth Cavalry. Mackenzie would play a decisive role in the history of many Native peoples, including Kesetta and Jack and their band. Ordered by President Grant to ignore Mexican sovereignty and strike the Indian villages lying south of the border at Remolino,[10] Mackenzie crossed the Rio Grande on May 17, 1873, and attacked three villages under cover of darkness. Military historian Robert Wooster writes, "The action at Remolino was more akin to a massacre than a battle as the Indian warriors were away hunting when the attack occurred."[11] It was judged a bold success by the army.[12] By the Lipan Apaches it was remembered forever as "the day of screams." Stories of the horrors of that night were passed down from generation to generation. And the screaming did not end there. After the assault Ramon Castro discovered that his two young children had been taken prisoner by the soldiers.[13] For many years, desperate at this loss and what he interpreted as the deliberate theft of his children by the U.S. government to test his loyalty, his band continued to fight American troops ferociously. He never saw his children again.[14]

The children began a life with whites that was characterized by progressive rupture, loss, and movement. Now named Kesetta and Jack Smith, for about four or five years the children traveled around with the cavalry, from Fort Clark to Fort Duncan back to Fort Clark in Texas and then on to Fort Hays in Kansas. It appears that they had been "adopted" by a member of the Fourth Cavalry who played in the band, Charles Smith, and his wife Mollie. Their itinerant lives can be traced by following the movements of the Fourth Cavalry Band, listed meticulously on a Commissioner of Pensions record card.[15] A report in Carlisle's *Morning Star* confirms this part of their history, stating that "they became children of the regiment, and for four years lived with it, moving from post to post as the regiment changed stations."[16] We know what the children looked like at this time because in the personal archives of the Smiths' granddaughter, Celeste Sorgio, there is a photograph of them. A handwritten description on the back reads, "Kesetta and Jack Smith, taken in Hayes City, Kansas, February '80," and an added note, "We get a school report and a letter from them every month and they always address Mollie (my wife) as dear 'Mama.'" The picture shows the children blank faced and dressed for the occasion in their Sunday best.[17] It may have been made as a memento for the Smith family before Jack and Kesetta were taken from them and transported from the Southwest forever, on the orders of Colonel Mackenzie.[18]

Nearly a century later, Sorgio found the photograph in her grandparents' papers. Wanting to find out more about these children, who had once been part of her family, she sent a copy of the image to the Cumberland County Historical Society. Barbara Landis, Indian biographer of the Carlisle Indian School, thus became alert to the Lipan Apache children and carefully filed their image. This serendipitous event deposited the children's photograph from the Southwest in the same archive as their Carlisle photograph, which would later provide the vital visual link to prove the children's identity. Identified on the back of their Hayes City photograph as "Jack and Kesetta Smith," just one month later, in March 1880, they were enrolled at the Carlisle Indian School as Jack and Kesetta Lipan. Their changed names signaled a further disruption of their identities. But when laid alongside the photograph taken of the children at the Carlisle Indian School, the February 1880 picture provides indisputable evidence of who they are.

At Carlisle, however, the progressive erasure of their past continued,

Fig. 20. Kesetta and Jack "Smith" (Ndé/Lipan Apaches) in Kansas, 1880. Photographer unknown. Courtesy of Jacqueline Fear-Segal.

and even their sibling relationship was disregarded when Kesetta became known officially at the school as Kesetta Roosevelt. It is unclear where the name Roosevelt came from, but it is easy to track the origin of Jack's new name. He was "adopted" by an old friend of Pratt's from St. Augustine, Miss Sarah Mather, and became known at Carlisle as Jack Mather.[19] "Roosevelt" and "Mather" severed the children's connection to each other as well as to their own people, the Lipan Apaches. Their new names also wiped clean the bureaucratic slate; in administrative terms their lives had "started again" when they were sent to Carlisle. On her student card, Kesetta is recorded as having been born in Kansas. She had traveled to Carlisle from Fort Hays in Kansas, and so Kansas was recorded as her official place of origin, not Mexico or Texas, where she had grown up and witnessed the killing of her mother and many of her people.[20]

Fig. 21. Kesetta and Jack "Lipan" (Ndé/Lipan Apaches) in Carlisle, 1880. Photo by John N. Choate. Cumberland County Historical Society, Carlisle PA. CS-CH-047.

Conducting a full medical examination of Kesetta on her arrival at Carlisle, staff discovered three large scars: one on her forehead and two on the front and back of her shoulder. When questioned, Kesetta reportedly told them these were left from wounds inflicted by a stone her mother had used to try to kill her, "so as to keep the white men from getting me in the fight." Full details of this story were published in the school paper to exemplify, not the desperation and fear of a Lipan mother when confronting the U.S. Cavalry on the "day of screams," but rather as evidence of Indian savagery on realizing the "result of the battle would be against them."[21]

When Kesetta arrived in Carlisle, she was about thirteen years old. If she had remained with her Lipan Apache people, this would have been a very important time for her. An elaborate dance and feast would have been given as part of a ceremony to celebrate her womanhood in a sacred way. But Kesetta never wore the clothes specifically made for an Apache girl's puberty ceremony nor listened to the women's wisdom passed down to her by elders. Instead, she donned the regulation girls' uniform of Carlisle and learned to drill and march.[22]

Jack

The few details we have about Kesetta and Jack's lives at the school are garnered from snippets of information appearing in Carlisle's publications. Colonel Mackenzie apparently took an interest in Jack and wrote him letters, but this connection to the officer who had ordered the massacre of his people did not last long. In a Carlisle publication we learn how "the great calamity that has befallen General Mackenzie, in the loss of his mind, deprives Jack of his friend and guardian." From the Indian School paper we also learn that when playing with his friends, while making and using bows and arrows, Jack seriously injured his right index finger; seven months later it was amputated by the school doctor.[23]

After four and a half years at the school, Jack, a young man of about sixteen, was sent on the long journey by land and sea, via Philadelphia, New York, and Savannah, to make his home in St. Augustine, Florida, with Miss Mather. His own account of his first days in St. Augustine, written in a letter to Pratt, was published in the *Indian Helper*. He writes how he found the town strange, the Florida oranges tasty, and the flies troublesome. The highlight of his day, however, must have stirred memories of his old life. He describes with pride how "this morning I went out riding with Miss Mather."[24]

Sarah Mather was by this time a woman of nearly seventy. Originally from New England, she attended Mount Holyoke for a year, where she earned a teaching certificate. With her lifetime companion, Miss Rebecca Perrit, she then moved to St. Augustine, and in the 1850s they built a house in the center of town, on King Street, and opened a boarding school for young ladies.[25] Their school closed down during the Civil War. When Pratt arrived in town in 1875, in charge of the warriors and leaders from the southwestern tribes imprisoned at Fort Marion, he enlisted these two experienced teachers. Along with half a dozen others, they would instruct the younger Indian prisoners at the fort and thus participate in the first stage of Pratt's educational experiment. Four years later, when Secretary of the Interior Schurz gave Pratt authority to establish the Carlisle Indian School, Sarah Mather, at the age of sixty-three, enthusiastically accompanied Pratt on his trip to Dakota to help recruit Sioux girls. The experiment in Carlisle had been approved in Washington, "provided both boys and girls are educated in said school." They returned together to Carlisle with eighty-four pupils, including twenty-five girls.[26] After helping the school in its early days, Sarah Mather returned to Florida, but she continued to retain a close interest in developments at Carlisle and made frequent visits to the school. She took a shine to Jack, and as he had been removed from his own family and community, nothing stood in the way of her making him her adoptive son.

When Jack moved to Florida, Sarah Mather found him local jobs. St. Augustine was a tourist town for northerners seeking winter sun, and for a time he was employed in a local hotel, receiving a wage of $1.25. Later his pay went up when he became apprenticed to a carpenter.[27] But for Jack, the most momentous event of his three years in St. Augustine must have been the arrival in town of nearly five hundred Apache prisoners of war. The U.S. Cavalry was gaining the upper hand in the Southwest, subduing and capturing the raiding Apache bands that whites regarded as the scourge of the region and transporting them to Florida. In September 1886 Geronimo, the famous Chiricahua Apache warrior, was also captured. For both Apaches and Americans this was a major event. It ended the last Native resistance, allowing the Southwest to be claimed for American settlement. Geronimo and sixteen other chiefs and warriors were transported east and for security were imprisoned separately from their people at Fort Pickens in Pensacola, Florida. The Chiricahua Apache prisoners stayed in St. Augustine for a year. In the streets of St. Augustine the Apache language was regularly heard, as the Indians walked about the town in groups, sold their wares, or visited the photographic studio on St. George Street to have their portraits taken.

Living in the center of town on King Street, Jack Mather would certainly have encountered them. For the first time since his own capture more than a decade before, he would have heard his mother tongue spoken openly, and perhaps he also understood it. From gossip in the town and perhaps discussion in his own home, he would have learned that one hundred and eight of the Chiricahua Apache children, classified as prisoners of war like himself, would also share his destiny and be taken to Pennsylvania, to be enrolled at the Carlisle Indian School.[28]

Jack Mather's own story would end in Carlisle. In January 1887, having been diagnosed with tuberculosis, Jack Mather made the same long journey back north to Carlisle, leaving behind the balmy climes of Florida for the freezing temperatures of a Pennsylvania winter. In the school hospital he joined a sizeable group of sickly children of all ages.[29] Two weeks after his return, on Sunday, February 5, 1888, Jack Mather died and was buried in the school cemetery.[30] Evidence confirming the end of his short life is misleading: his present-day marker is incorrectly inscribed with the name "Jack Martha," and the map, drawn up in 1927 before the cemetery's removal and relocation, calls him by the same misspelled name.[31] Only the brief notice in the *Indian Helper* the week following his death ("Died of consumption Jack Mather, an old pupil of Carlisle, for two years past in Florida") confirms that this is the same Lipan Apache boy who had been brought to the school as a prisoner in 1880.

Kesetta

At the time of her brother's death, Kesetta Roosevelt was not at Carlisle but in Norfolk, Virginia, where she had been living with and working for a white family, the Paxtons, for almost five years, while still registered as a student at Carlisle. She was listed continuously on the Carlisle enrollment records, from March 1880 through April 1903 (apart from a short, three-year break between 1892 and 1895), a period of over twenty-three years. Most of those years were not spent in Carlisle's classrooms, but working for white families in the region. After two years at the school, Kesetta spent the summer with a family in Lancaster, Pennsylvania, as part of the Outing system.[32] The following year when her school term finished, now aged about sixteen, she was sent to live with the Paxton family in Schuylkill County, Pennsylvania.[33] After almost three years with the Paxtons, Kesetta returned to the Indian school. That week, in the *Indian Helper*, there was a cryptic comment suggesting that she was not considered one of Carlisle's star pupils. "Kesetta Roosevelt is with us again. She stayed at her place nearly three years, and SOME of the time she did well."[34] Yet the Paxton family was clearly pleased with her. The following April she returned to Schuylkill Haven to look after their growing family. Six months later, when the family moved to Virginia, they took Kesetta with them. Pratt had to give his permission for this move; not only was Kesetta a charge of the school, but she was still classified by the War Department as a prisoner of war.[35]

In 1892, after twelve years on the Carlisle enrollment list, Kesetta was officially discharged from the school for the first time. She was now a young woman of about twenty-five, and she continued to work for the Paxton household. Had nothing changed, there would have been no record of her later life, and all trace of her might have been lost. Like so many other ex-Carlisle students, she might have disappeared untraceably into the local population. But Kesetta decided not to spend the rest of her days in Norfolk, Virginia. With no known community to return to in the West, her only home base was the Indian School, and in 1895 she returned to Carlisle. Twenty years after Kesetta left the Paxton family, in 1916, the father of that household, Joseph Paxton, would make an attempt to reestablish contact with Kesetta, and his letter gives a suggestion of why she might have left the family. Explaining that Kesetta's last letter to his family had been sent in 1901, from a Baltimore address, Paxton wrote to the school requesting more recent details of her whereabouts. He recalled with affection how she had been "very fond of [his] children when they were smaller." Reflecting on the reason for her leaving his household, he concluded that it was because the circumstances had changed and explained that his "family was quite large and as the children grew up and left home, she became dissatisfied and wanted to go back to Carlisle."[36]

Kesetta left the Paxtons in December 1896. She arrived back at the Carlisle Indian School just two weeks before Christmas, on the coldest day of the season, when the thermometer registered one degree above zero and the first snow covered the ground.[37] Once again she was formally reenrolled as a pupil, for the usual period of five years. Her registration card looked no different from any other, despite her advancing years, but the *Indian Helper* used her return as an opportunity to publicize one of Carlisle's policies of encouraging students to remain in the East to live independent lives: "Miss Kessetta [*sic*] Roosevelt, who has been her own woman in the East for the past ten years, independent of the school, is now visiting with us.[38]

Kesetta was now almost thirty. After the relative stability of twelve years spent with the Paxton family, her life became less secure and more itinerant. She provided for herself by working as a domestic, on a series of Outings recorded on her student cards.[39] Three years working for a Pennsylvania family in Willow Grove were followed by a placement further afield with the Bishops in Columbus, New Jersey. When the Bishop family moved from Columbus to Trenton the following year, they took Kesetta with them.[40] A month later, however, Kesetta left their household and returned to Carlisle. This time she was sent out to work in Delaware, with a Mrs. A. W. Powell, but she stayed only a year before being sent to her fateful placement with a Mrs. Bishop in Baltimore, Maryland. It looked as if this was to be Kesetta's last official Outing placement from Carlisle. Noted as being "self supporting," she was discharged from the school in June 1902. Three months later, however, just one year after going to live with the Bishop family in Baltimore, Kesetta was back at Carlisle. The record is unclear as to whether this was the same Bishop family she had left two years previously, but indisputable was the fact that when Kesetta left Baltimore and returned to Carlisle, in October 1902, she was nearly three months pregnant. No named individual is identified as the father in the record, but he is recorded as being "white."[41] Her condition was not yet noticeable, and the *Red Man and Helper* unsuspectingly reported her presence on campus: "Kesetta Roosevelt, one of our Apache students who has been living in a country home for years, is with us on a visit." In November the Outing officer sent her back to the Powells, the family in Delaware for whom she had worked before she went to

Baltimore.[42] She was not with them for long. When her predicament became obvious, Kesetta was sent to the Rosine Home in Philadelphia, an institution run by the Quakers for those who were described at the time as "fallen women."

On Kesetta's Carlisle student card, the reason for her discharge was falsely recorded as "Time out." This was a phrase generally applied to children who left Carlisle after the prescribed five-year period. Kesetta's story, as we have seen, was quite different. Originally registered at the school in 1880, she was signed-up for the third and final time in October 1902; she was then thirty-five years of age, but her original status was still not forgotten, and on her card she continued to be designated as "prisoner." For Kesetta, ever since she had been taken from her Texas home, Carlisle Indian School had represented the single continuity in her life; the place to which she had always returned. But on April 1, 1903, she was discharged from Carlisle for the last time, and it seemed as if Kesetta Roosevelt's lengthy association with the school had finally come to an end.

On May 22, 1903, in the Rosine Home in Philadelphia, Kesetta Roosevelt gave birth to a boy. Helped by the women of the Rosine Home, she found work in Lahaska, a town just north of Philadelphia, and moved there with her infant son, Richard. In 1905, while she was living in Lahaska, twenty surviving members of the Lipan Apache Band of Texas were moved onto the Mescalero Indian Reservation, although another small group of Lipan Apaches, including Ramon Castro's band (Kesetta's family), was not among them.

In the winter of 1906 Kesetta fell fatally ill with consumption. During the last five weeks of her life she was nursed by the wife of a local accountant, Elizabeth Slotter. For Slotter, this was a business arrangement. She presented her bill for caring for Kesetta, and also a separate bill for looking after and boarding her son, to the accountant of Kesetta's estate, who was also her own husband. All monies were paid. Between them, J. Titus Slotter and Elizabeth Slotter received $75 dollars from Kesetta's small estate for their services rendered at the end of Kesetta's life. The sum represented a quarter of the money in the estate. Kesetta had worked until the last week of her life, and when she died $15 was still due to her in wages. A further $283.68 was also still held in her account at the Indian School from her previous earnings.[43] So she left behind a diminutive estate for her son, which also constitutes a financial strand by which we are able to track her story in the archival record.

Kesetta Roosevelt ended her days in a town where she would have been known only as an Indian woman with an illegitimate child; the complexity and intricacies of her early life, in Mexico, Texas, and Kansas, and then her later years in Virginia, New Jersey, Delaware, and, of course, Pennsylvania, had been completely obscured. At the Carlisle Indian School, which had been Kesetta's home base for most of her life, her "disgrace" inevitably imposed a total silence about her death. Ironically, in the edition of the school newspaper where her death should normally have been reported, a story about another "dead Indian" was published. An anonymous donor had given $1,000 to locate the gravesite of the Indian chief after whom his city, Kokomo, Indiana, had been named, in order that he could to erect a monument to commemorate him. Chief Kokomo, whose true story was unknown and who had been dead for over sixty years, could safely be appropriated to enhance and romanticize the narrative of a booming U.S. city.[44] Kesetta Roosevelt, whose story was known only too well, had been dropped from Carlisle's record. The school newspaper did not report her death or the details of her burial. A $6.00 gravestone, funded out of her own estate, marked her lonely burial place in the Quaker cemetery in Lahaska, Pennsylvania.[45] Only through her son are we able to follow her story. His existence meant that despite the obscurity of her life, she had left behind a living record. When her life ended, her story continued.

Richard

Richard was a little over three and a half years old when his mother died. During the final weeks of Kesetta's illness he was looked after by Elizabeth Slotter. He then returned to his place of birth, the Rosine Home in Philadelphia.[46] Six months later, Melosina Diamant, the president of the Rosine Home, filed an application for Richard Roosevelt to be enrolled at the Carlisle Indian School. In the space where the form enquired why no "adequate education" could be provided at the child's home, Rosine's matron, Margaret Rich wrote, "Not a proper Institution for a boy his age." She also confirmed Richard's identity as "Indian," verifying that he was "known and recognised in the community in which he lives as an Indian."[47] Richard was being sent back to where his mother had come from. It was twenty-seven years since Kesetta Lipan had been enrolled for the first time at the Carlisle Indian School. Two-thirds of her short life had been spent there, or working in the surrounding white community, and all this time she had experienced no contact with her people. Her infant son never enjoyed any connection with the Lipan Apache community. Yet on his application form, although he was officially acknowledged to be half-white, Richard was categorized as "Indian," and on August 13, 1907, he was enrolled at the Indian School.

Richard Roosevelt had no legal guardian, and the cost of appointing one was judged too prohibitive by the attorney responsible for administering his mother's estate. So the sum of $111.73, due to him as her "only heir," was passed directly to Moses Friedman, the superintendent of the Carlisle Indian School; and so, like his mother, Richard became a ward of both the government and the Indian School. Although all links to her people had been deliberately severed, on her son's Carlisle student card, Richard was recorded as being a member of the Lipan Nation.[48]

Richard Roosevelt was too young to be listed among the new students entering Carlisle in August 1907. But the week after his arrival on campus this four-year-old had caused enough excitement for the school paper to note that "Richard H. Roosevelt is very popular among the large girls."[49] Enrolled as "Richard Roosevelt" and also publicly referred to by this name, inexplicably Richard's name was changed. On his student card, in all correspondence relating to his mother's estate, and later in progress reports from the school, he is called "Richard Kasetta," or different spellings of this name: Kesetta, Kasetti, Kasitti, Kissitti.[50] At this time, Indians were not citizens and so were not included on the white register of births, deaths, and marriages, so Richard's changed name appears not to have been accompanied by any legal formalities. Whether consciously or not, the white official who decided to alter his name from Roosevelt to Kasetta had coupled Richard to the single unchanging element of his mother's designation: her first name.[51] But in so doing, this official had also dislocated the obvious last-name link between mother and son, made the connection between the two of them more obtuse, and ensured that her story and his ancestry were made harder to track. This might have been a deliberate attempt to veil the stigma that was attached to illegitimacy at this time. Nevertheless, when researching this story, because Kesetta

Fig. 22. Richard "Kissitti," the baby of the Indian School at age four, in his Carlisle school uniform, c. 1907. Photo by Leupp Studio. Cumberland County Historical Society, Carlisle PA. 13-25-03.

in any of its spelled forms is a distinctive name, it signaled a possible relationship between Kesetta Roosevelt and Richard Kasetta. The connection needed to be established and verified, and for this task the documents in Richard Kasetta's Carlisle student file at the National Archives were indispensable. This connection, first noted by Genevieve Bell, who laboriously made a spread sheet of all Carlisle student record cards during research for her excellent dissertation, drew me to read Richard's complete student file in the National Archives, and this confirmed beyond any doubt that "Richard Kissitti" was indeed Kesetta Roosevelt's son.[52]

Young, orphaned, with no links to any Indian nation but powerful links to the Indian School, Richard Kasetta had a status at Carlisle that was, from the beginning, out of the ordinary. Within five months of arriving at the school he was no longer residing in the dormitories with other students but had been taken home to live with a white family in town, Mrs. Martha Sharp, who was at this time sixty-seven, and her daughter and son-in-law, Mary and Jack Culbertson. Martha Sharp had lived in Carlisle for over thirty years. Her daughter Mary was matron of the Teachers' Club at the Indian School, and in 1898 Mary married the son of a local businessman, John Purviance Culbertson.[53] This union was to be of critical importance to the future life of Richard Kasetta. Jack Culbertson, as he was known, had friendly links to the school and often accompanied the young boys on walks or demonstrated some of the magician's tricks for which he had become widely renowned locally.[54] He had grown up in the neighboring town of Chambersburg and was from a well-established family. In Carlisle he bought a substantial plot of land to the north of the town, bordering the Conodoguinet Creek, where he would develop Bellaire Park, a pleasure amenity for the residents of Carlisle, with rafts, water slides, a bathing house, canoes, and a huge dance hall. When little Richard Roosevelt arrived at the Carlisle Indian School in 1907, this venture was still in its infancy. When he joined the family, Martha Sharp and Jack and Mary Culbertson lived in a sizeable townhouse—133 West Pomfret Street—where Richard was given his own room on the second floor; from then on, this became his home. When old enough, he started in the kindergarten class at the local Hamilton Elementary School, just two blocks away, and later went on to attend the Carlisle High School. Family snapshots show him swimming in the creek at Bellaire Park, playing outside his house, and standing in posed groups with Martha Sharp in the Pomfret Street yard.[55] They reveal a childhood very different from the institutionalized life of other children at the Indian School.

Yet Richard Kasetta continued to live under the auspices of the Indian School. After nine months in his new home, when he fell ill, he returned there to be nursed in the school hospital.[56] Once back on Pomfret Street, he was visited by school officials, who regularly reported his situation and progress to the superintendent. When the 1910 census was filed, Richard Kasetta was included on the list of Indian School students, described as a "ration Indian." This was a pattern that was to characterize the whole of his life. Living with many of the trappings and benefits of white society, his identity was nevertheless consistently inscribed as "Indian." At the school he was claimed as a mascot from the very beginning and paraded in his miniature military or army uniform. When he was sick he was described in the school newspaper as "our Carlisle baby."[57]

His mascot role became more pronounced as the school's football team rose to prominence on the national gridiron. The year 1912, when Richard was nine, was a triumphant year for the school. The Carlisle Indians beat West Point, Louis Tewanima brought back an Olympic bronze for running at the Stockholm Olympics, and Jim Thorpe also won his infamous gold medals for the biathlon and triathlon. These were Indians the town of Carlisle could own and honor, and a huge reception was organized for the returning heroes. Richard Kasetta's special role at the school allowed him to share vicariously in this glory. "I called Thorpe, Uncle Jim," he reminisced years later in an interview with a journalist. "He used to carry me around on his shoulders."[58] Perhaps his semicelebrity life-style influenced his behavior, because by the following year Jack Culbertson was growing impatient with the boy and wrote to tell the Carlisle school superintendent that Richard was "too mischievous" and required "better discipline." Martha Sharp, however, was clearly of a different opinion and, as her son-in-law explained, did "not want to give him up." For two years her feelings prevailed.

Then, when he was fourteen, Richard was removed from the white Carlisle High School. He was sent away to work for the Buchholz family in Philadelphia. Like his mother before him, he became part of the Indian School's Outing program. But this placement was not a success, and after a year Arthur E. Buchholz, an inspector for the Bureau of Health, recommended to the school superintendent that on his return, "The very best thing for him for two years would be strict military discipline in such a school as you have, and the less he visits his former surroundings the better it will be for him."[59]

It looked as if Richard Kasetta was going to spend several years training and drilling as an Indian student. But by this time Carlisle's mission to assimilate Indian children was facing fierce criticism nationwide, and the school itself had already been made the subject of a Senate investigation. Precipitously, in the summer of 1918, the Carlisle Indian Industrial School was closed. The Indian students were hurriedly sent home or dispersed to other schools. The auditor responsible for winding down the affairs of the Indian School wrote to the commissioner of Indian Affairs to explain the special situation of Richard Kasetta and to enquire what should become of him. Commissioner Cato Sells replied, "I consider it advisable to allow Mrs. Martha Sharp custody of the child."[60] So from the age of fifteen, young Dick Kasetta officially ceased to be a charge of both the Indian School and the federal government. Instead, he became the responsibility of a seventy-eight-year-old white woman and her family. It appeared that he had found a place for himself in this predominantly white, eastern colonial town. But that place would always be inseparable from his ascribed identity as "Indian."

Although the Carlisle Indian School no longer existed, former students and graduates still made return visits to the town and would drop in at Moses Blumenthal's store in the center of town, on North Hanover Street, where the Indian School teams had always bought their kit and equipment. When visiting Indians arrived, Blumenthal would send for Dick Kasetta to share stories and reminisce with them.[61] For the returnees, Kasetta provided a welcome, living link to their days at the Carlisle Indian School. For the local white population, his connection to the now-closed school and his dark skin continued to define his identity, and he was referred to locally as "the Indian." Living his whole life in Carlisle, he became the town's totemic Indian. In 1963, at a Civil War Centenary celebration, he was persuaded to play this role in all its stereotypical glory and wore a full, dress-up Indian costume for the parade through town. After the Carlisle Indian School's closure, Dick Kasetta was the only Indian living in town, apart from Montreville Yuda. Yuda's links to his tribe were as murky as Kasetta's. His father was probably an Oneida from New York State, but it seems that Montreville had grown up and attended public school in Los Angeles. Having left home and totally lost contact with his family, at the age of twenty-two he enrolled himself at Carlisle.[62] His son George, born in 1924, still lives in Carlisle and knew Dick Kasetta. Unprompted, he enquired of me which tribe Dick Kasetta had belonged to, and then he confirmed the confusion that always accompanied Kasetta's origins when he reflected that his father had always thought Kasetta to be a Crow Indian.[63]

After Kasetta's guardian, Mrs. Sharp, died in 1927, he continued to live with the Culbertsons at the house on West Pomfret Street, working on small jobs and helping manage the park at Bellaire. But by this time the pleasures of the park were in competition with other sources of entertainment made accessible by the newly acquired automobile. The popularity of its activities were declining, so slowly the Culbertsons sold off the holiday cabins they had built along the Conodoguinet Creek, but they never sold their own summer home in Bellaire Park. Jack and Mary Culbertson had no children, and when they died (Jack in 1929 and Mary in 1947), they left their cabin and the remaining grounds of Bellaire Park to Dick Kasetta.

One year after inheriting this substantial property, Kasetta married Helen Rice, whom he had known for many years. At this time he also, inexplicably, changed the spelling of his name to Kaseeta.[64] To what degree the sale of Kaseeta's childhood home on Pomfret Street, the loss of the last member of his adoptive family, and the acquisition of his own property prompted and enabled his decision to marry is unclear. Helen Rice was a local white woman, but from a social background far more modest than the one in which he had grown up. The degree to which his own racial marking impeded him from marrying within the social circles he frequented is hard to ascertain but warrants notice.

Helen Rice had earned her living as a domestic servant, like Kaseeta's mother. But her marriage and move into the house in Bellaire Park allowed her to re-create a lifestyle she had enjoyed before her family lost their farm in her childhood. The eldest of eleven children, Rice was sixteen when her mother died, and she brought up all her younger brothers and sisters. At Bellaire, Helen's siblings visited frequently with their children. When her sister Sarah died suddenly, Helen's niece, Tess, came to live with the

Kaseetas. Helen's marriage to Dick enabled her to re-create the home environment in which she grew up, and it also allowed Dick to become part of a new, ready-made white family.

But in Carlisle his Indian roots were not forgotten. Whenever Jim Thorpe was in the news, or when the Washington Redskins decided to locate their summer training camp at Dickinson College, Kaseeta was interviewed as Carlisle's "authentic Indian." He was willing to give personal details of Thorpe's sporting prowess in the days of the Indian School, but he was much vaguer when talking about his own background. He informed one journalist that he was a Chiricahua Apache orphan who had been brought to the Carlisle Indian School from Oklahoma. This version of events made some sense. Kaseeta was, after all, an orphan and an Apache, but it also glamorized and sanitized his story; it inaccurately linked Kaseeta to the famous Chiricahua Apaches and Geronimo, rather than the little-known Lipan Apaches, allowing him to embrace the romance of a known Apache past, and it left out the stigma of his illegitimacy. A vital component of Dick Kaseeta's life had been omitted: his mother.

It is unlikely that Dick Kaseeta ever knew who his mother was or had enough information to be able to piece together his own story. When he died of cancer in 1970, he was buried in Memorial Gardens cemetery on the western outskirts of Carlisle, the opposite side of town from where his uncle lay in the Indian School cemetery.[65] Twenty-nine years later, his wife was laid to rest beside him. Nothing about the Kaseeta plot gives any hint that one of its occupants was half Apache. Richard Kaseeta had lived his whole life with a white-inscribed "Indian identity." Although enjoying no tribal specificity or cultural contact, he was nevertheless racially marked and assumed the role of Carlisle's totemic Indian, unaware of his own parenthood and history. While his Indian identity was recognized by everyone, his gravestone gives no hint of this; it is engraved with just his name, using its most recent spelling, Richard Kaseeta, and dates. His Lipan Apache connection, which had shaped and defined his whole life, had been totally erased.

By this time, the Lipan Apache people had also lost much of their history and almost all their population. Reduced to a handful of individuals living on the Mescalero Reservation or dispersed around the Texas-Mexico border, they are mentioned most often in historical accounts focusing on the eighteenth or nineteenth century. When I started my research, no history of the Lipan Apaches had been published, and because they lacked the renown of the Chiricahuas, it was hard to find out about this once numerous group.[66] In an attempt to uncover more information about his mother's band as well as details of her capture, I decided to search the Internet. A short website history of the Lipan Apaches included the following paragraph: "In 1861 Ramon Castro and some followers were forced to settle at Fort Belknap, Texas, as a condition of their allegiance to the U.S. Government. It was also an attempt to exterminate the Lipan Apache. The U.S. Government moved the Lipan Apache people as prisoners of war and in 1867 they transferred the Lipan to Fort Griffin near Albany, Texas. By 1885 less than 20 Lipan Apache Band members were alive."[67]

This seemed to offer a possible link to Kesetta's people, so I emailed the author to tell him about the two Lipan children who had been captured by Colonel Mackenzie and taken to the Carlisle Indian School and to ask if he knew anything about them or their band. I received a reply the next day:

> It's my understanding that the children were never to be seen or heard from. I would be very interested in knowing the name and location of where they are buried, so that I, and our people, can visit them to give them a Lipan Apache blessing.
>
> Ramon Castro was my great-great-great uncle and it is said that the children taken were his children. They were taken from him to test his allegiance to the U.S. Government. One of main reasons why they continued to fight so hard was his sadness over the incident.
>
> Question, how did you find out about this?
>
> It's my understanding that only family members know about this story.[68]

Daniel Castro Romero Jr. had sent me evidence that 125 years after their capture by Mackenzie's cavalry, the Lipan children were still remembered by their own people. I learned too that their story had been told and retold through four generations. On the second Saturday in August every year, the Castro family holds a reunion where they recount their family history, hold a ceremony of remembrance for the Lost Ones, and pass round a sacred plate, on which everyone puts food for them. A chair is left empty.

The systematic photographic record that had been made at the Indian School meant that it was now possible for the Lipan Apaches to see their Lost Ones. Determined to send hard copies of photographs, not scans, I ordered the portrait of Kesetta and Jack together and a second photograph of Kesetta with three other Carlisle girls, packed them both up carefully, and mailed them to Daniel Castro Romero Jr. I received the following response:

> On the day I received the photographs, I was standing in line waiting to buy postage stamps when I opened your envelope. For a moment, I could see into my daughter's eyes, as my eyes watered at the picture of Kesetta. She looks exactly like my daughter. She has the same eyes, facial features, you name it she has it. I was very moved, I could only think of what her parents went through. My ancestors must have been at a loss not knowing where their daughter had gone, never to see her again.
>
> She will never again be forgotten, as she has made the journey back home.[69]

Ironically, Kesetta "made the journey back home" thanks to photographs created as part of the Carlisle Indian School's propaganda to publicize its program of cultural obliteration. Across the generations these pictures provided a link to confirm and bear witness to her story and substantiate the "landmark of memory" that had been laid down repeatedly for her by her people down the years.

In answer to Romero's request to know "the name and location of where they are buried," I was able to email a photograph of the Indian School cemetery with details of the location of Jack Mather's stone. But for Kesetta, the only information I had about her final resting place was encapsulated in a line added to her last Carlisle Student Record Card: "Died in Lahaska PA, December 24, 1906." For the Indian School this closed Kesetta's record and allowed her cards to be moved to the "dead" file.

But when I passed this information to Kesetta's great-niece, Tess Eichelberger, nearly a century later, it offered her the possibility of a different kind of closure. Knowing now that Kesetta had been cared for by Quakers and had died in Lahaska, Tess made contact with the Quaker community in the town and was told that their records confirmed that Kesetta had indeed been buried in the Quaker cemetery in a marked grave. The next day Tess made the hour-long drive from Philadelphia to Lahaska. There, under a sweet chestnut tree in the pretty, rustic Quaker cemetery, she found a plain grave with the simple inscription, "Kesetta Roosevelt, Died Dec. 24, 1906." To honor her great-aunt, Tess laid the wreath she had brought for her.

The Lost Ones' story is tragic. For them, Carlisle represented loss of all they held dear and exile, attended by a series of ruptures. Jack died young, and the Carlisle education Kesetta received equipped her to do no more than hold down a series of menial jobs. She worked hard all her life, but she joined white society at the very lowest level, as a live-in servant to a succession of white families. Totally alone in the world, without family or community, it seems likely that in her last Outing home she suffered sexual exploitation or abuse by a white man. After the birth of her son, she was banished from Carlisle Indian School in disgrace. She spent her final three years working and looking after him, but separated from everyone she had known in the white world in which she had been forced to live, before meeting an early death.

Yet, although despised and rejected by the school that had been her most consistent "home," in her real home in Texas Kesetta was never forgotten and always deeply mourned. As soon as Daniel Castro Romero Jr. learned where the Lost Ones had been taken, he was determined to travel to Carlisle, "to give them a Lipan Apache blessing." When he met with the leaders of the Ndé (Lipan Apaches) to tell them that the Lost Ones were found, "it was proclaimed by all that the spirits of the 'Lost Ones' will finally be allowed to make the journey home. What was forever changed, will now be one again, they say."[70]

So in May 2009, three Ndé elders, Daniel Castro Romero Jr., Lipan Apache Band of Texas chairman, Richard Gonzalez, its vice chairman, and Anita Anaya made the long drive from Texas to Pennsylvania to gather at Steve Brouwer and Susan Rose's home in Bellaire Park, just outside Carlisle. This was the same house that had been previously owned and lived in by Dick Kaseeta. With everyone seated on the porch, Daniel explained, "we have to tell their story from the 'other' side. Our people cannot move forward until our 'Lost Ones' are sent home." He reminded us of the significance of oral histories to Native peoples, explaining, "We put the same importance on our oral histories as the Bible." Smudging with white sage as he spoke words that had come down to him through three generations of

Ndé elders, Daniel told the story of an attack by American soldiers, killings, and the taking of two Lipan Apache children. At the end, he translated the Ndé into English. Those of us gathered to receive this gift of the Lost Ones' story had all played a part in locating fragments of information in order to piece together the Pennsylvania episode of their lives.[71] We had now been made privy to the details of their early years, an account previously known only to their family. The next morning we would reassemble in the Indian School cemetery for the spirit-releasing ceremony at the graveside of the Lipan Apache boy known at Carlisle Indian School as Jack Mather. It was a solemn occasion. Everyone was gifted with a shawl before the women were purified by being smudged with pollen and the men with ash from an oak that had survived a lightning strike. The elders had brought dried corn, pecan, pollen, tobacco, and white sage to leave at the grave, along with rocks and water from the last Texas river where he would have drunk, and a bag of earth from his Texas homeland, which we all helped sprinkle over the Pennsylvania soil. The Lipan Apache elders could not take their kinsman home, so they were bringing his home to him. These ceremonial items, the beat of the hand drum, and the singing of songs written for this occasion would release his spirit and enable it to return home. Walking from the cemetery, no one looked back, and each threw behind a living leaf or blade of grass as instructed, so that no spirits would be tempted to follow. We then all traveled to the other side of town to Cumberland Valley Memorial Gardens Cemetery for the ceremony at the grave of Dick Kaseeta. Afterward Daniel explained, "He's been alone all these years. By dawn he will be with his people." On Monday, May 18, 2009 (exactly 136 years after her capture at Remolino), the elders traveled to Lahaska, but before the spirit-releasing ceremony at Kesetta's grave, the Apache puberty ceremony had to be performed for her, because Kesetta had left her people as a girl and was returning to them as a woman. For Daniel and the Ndé elders, this final ceremony would start the healing the Lipan Apaches so desperately needed for their well-being. He explained that before he traveled to Pennsylvania, both his mother and his great-aunt had called him up to insist on the importance of what he was doing for both the living and the dead. "We can't move forward as a people until we pray for them and send them home. They're waiting for them. Let them come home." Daniel noted that May 18, the anniversary of Mackenzie's Remolino raid,

Fig. 23. Anita Anaya and Richard Gonzalez (Ndé/Lipan Apaches) performing a puberty ceremony and Lipan Apache Blessing ceremony for Kesetta, in Quaker cemetery, Lahaska, Pennsylvania, 2009. Photo by Tess Eichenberger.

was a fitting date for Kesetta to return to her people. For him, he assured us, when he woke up that morning it would be a day, not of sadness, but one of gladness. "Our lives become much richer with the knowledge that the Lost Ones have come home in our hearts and minds."[72] That August, when the family came together for their regular gathering, there would be no empty chair, and they would not pass around the sacred plate for everyone to place food for the missing children because there was no longer the need; the children had been sent home.

NOTES

1. Jacqueline Fear-Segal, *White Man's Club: Schools, Race, and the Struggle of Indian Acculturation* (Lincoln: University of Nebraska Press, 2007); Susan Rose and Manuel Saralegui, *The Lost Ones: The Long Journey Home*, in collaboration with Jacqueline Fear-Segal and Daniel Castro Romero, 2011, trailer at www.youtube.com/watch?v=_I4jF22bXeA. The full documentary (42 minutes, English and Spanish, with 20-minute "Piecing Together the Story" methodological reflection) is available from the Community Studies Center, Box 1173, Dickinson College, Carlisle PA 17013 or csc@dickinson.edu.

2. See chapter 12 by Margo Tamez in this collection for her Lipan Apache understanding of this story and its legacies.

3. National Archives and Records Administration (NARA), Record Group (RG) 75, Carlisle Indian School Student Files, Kesetta Roosevelt, file no. 1779.

4. Names, dates, and locations of her Outing homes are listed on her student cards.

5. Information provided by Daniel Castro Romero Jr., General Council chairman of the Lipan Apache Band of Texas, in an email sent to Jacqueline Fear-Segal, September, 25, 2002.

6. Helena Pohlandt-McCormick, "'I saw a nightmare . . .': Violence and the Construction of Memory (Soweto, June 16, 1976)," in *History and Theory* 39, no. 4 (December 2000): 23–44. She suggests too that silence can also disrupt an individual's ability to think historically.

7. Castro Romero to Fear-Segal, September 25, 2002.

8. The concept of "hidden transcripts" was developed and used by James C. Scott, *Domination and the Arts of Resistance: Hidden Transcripts* (New Haven CT: Yale University Press, 1999).

9. Glenn Welker and Daniel Castro Romero Jr., "The Castro Family History of the Lipan Apache Band of Texas," http://www.indians.org/welker/lipanap .htm. Ramon Castro was listed as a leader in the Tehuacama Creek Treaty Tribal Leadership List, dated January 16, 1845, at Tehuacama Creek, Texas.

Ramon was the only witness at the Treaty Council of Texas Tribes at Tehuac-ama Creek, Texas. This was an agreement with the Republic of Texas government and the U.S. government from August 27, 1845, to September 27, 1845, signed at Tehuacama Creek, Texas.

10. Remolino is also known as Rey Molino, Coahuila, Mexico.
11. Robert Wooster, *The Military and United States Indian Policy, 1865–1903* (New Haven CT: Yale University Press, 1988), 92.
12. John G. Keliher, "The History of the 4th U.S. Cavalry Regiment," 1960, rev. 2013, https://www.25thida.org/units/cavalry/4th-cavalry-regiment/.
13. In Carlisle Indian School, *Morning Star* 4, no. 14 (December 1884), an article titled "A Happy Carlisle Indian Boy" reports, "In the bushes near the camp, the soldiers found Jack and Kesetta."
14. Castro Romero to Fear-Segal, September 25, 2002.
15. Commissioner of Pensions Report for Charles Smith, November 17, 1919, NARA, RG 75, Carlisle Indian School Student Record Files, Richard Roosevelt file.
16. *Morning Star*, December 1884, 2.
17. Photograph in private collection of Celeste Sorgio, copy held at CCHS.
18. Carlisle's *Morning Star*, December 1884, names the army family who took an interest in them as that of Captain T. J. Wint, not Smith.
19. *Morning Star*, December 1884.
20. Carlisle Indian School, *Eadle Keatah Toh* 1, no. 2 (April 1880).
21. *Eadle Keatah Toh*, April 1880.
22. For good descriptions of the Apache puberty ceremony, see Ruth McDonald Boyer and Narcissus Duffy Gayton, *Apache Mothers and Daughters: Four Generations of a Family* (Norman: University of Oklahoma Press 1992).
23. *Morning Star* 4, no. 3 (October 1883); *Morning Star* 4, no. 4 (May 1884).
24. Jack Mather to Captain Pratt, November 29, 1884, in the *Morning Star*, December 1884.
25. Sarah Mather file, St. Augustine Historical Society FL.
26. Pratt, *Battlefield and Classroom*, 121, 218, 228.
27. Carlisle Indian School, *Indian Helper* 2, no. 24 (January 21, 1887).
28. Figures from "Castillo de San Marcos National Monument: Apache Indians (Imprisoned)," St. Augustine FL.
29. We learn that Miss Longstreth, a long-standing friend of the school, has presented to "the folks invalided in the hospital" a gift of story and picture books in *Indian Helper* 3, no. 25 (February 3, 1888).
30. Jack Mather was buried in the old cemetery in plot A33 as "Jack Martha." In the new cemetery, he is in plot C1. On the plot map of the old cemetery he is called Martha. There are two possibilities: either his name was correct on the original marker and mistranscribed when the new plot map was made, and

from there copied onto the new stone, or he was from the start buried under an inaccurate marker, which seems less likely.

31. A week later, Sibyl Marko, one of the Chiricahua girls transported to the school the previous April, was laid to rest beside Jack Mather. She was the seventeenth of the twenty-one Chiricahua children who would be buried in the school cemetery.

32. By this time the Lipan Apache Band residing in Texas at Fort Griffin had dwindled to fewer than twenty members. "Lipan Apache (Tindi)," http://www.indians.org/welker/lipanap.htm.

33. All information is from Kesetta Roosevelt's three Carlisle registration cards, NARA, RG 75, Carlisle Indian School Student Record Files.

34. *Indian Helper* 1, no. 15 (November 1885).

35. On all three of Kesetta Roosevelt's registration cards it is noted in the "Agency" box that she is a "prisoner."

36. Joseph P. Paxson to Superintendent of Carlisle Indian Industrial School, March 7, 1916, NARA, RG 75, Carlisle Indian School Student Files, Richard Roosevelt file.

37. Detailed descriptions of the weather are given in the papers. *Indian Helper* 40, no. 12 (December 20, 1896); *Indian Helper* 40, no. 11 (December 13, 1896).

38. Standard student cards were laid out with the following headings: English name; agency; nation; home address; whether parents were living or dead; age; weight, height; dates of arrival and departure (and reason for latter); number of years for which they were initially enrolled; details of each Outing.

39. *Indian Helper*, December 20, 1896.

40. Carlisle Indian School, *Red Man and Helper* 16, no. 7 (August 3, 1900).

41. "Application of Melosina H Diament for the Enrolment of Richard Roosevelt in the Indian School of Carlisle," August 15, 1907, NARA, RG 75, Carlisle Indian School Student Record Files, file no. 5196.

42. *Red Man and Helper* 18, no. 13 (October 10, 1902).

43. "Statement of Account of J. Titus Slotter," October 15, 1907, NARA, RG 75, Carlisle Indian School Student Record Files, Richard Kesetta, file no. 5196.

44. Carlisle Indian School, *Arrow*, December 1906.

45. "Statement of Account of J. Titus Slotter."

46. "Statement of Account of J. Titus Slotter."

47. "Application of Melosina H Diament."

48. "Student Record Card, Richard Kesetta," NARA, RG 75, Carlisle Indian School Student Record Files, file no. 5196.

49. *Arrow* 3, no. 49 (August 23, 1907); *Arrow* 3, no. 50 (August 30, 1907).

50. Reports for the years 1911, 1912, 1916, and 1918 in NARA, RG 75, Carlisle Indian School Student Record Files, file no. 5196.

51. She had been called Kesetta (sometimes Kasetta) since her capture. There

is no record of what her Lipan name was, but according to Daniel Castro Romero Jr., her name is very similar to a Lipan clan name and also to the Spanish *casita*, meaning "little house."

52. Genevieve Bell, "Telling Tales out of School: Remembering the Carlisle Indian Industrial School, 1879–1918" (PhD diss., Stanford University, 1998).

53. *Arrow*, December 2, 1898.

54. *Arrow*, January 3, 1913.

55. Snapshots in the family album assembled for Dick Kaseeta's wife, Helen Kaseeta (née Rice).

56. *Arrow*, September 30, 1910.

57. *Arrow*, September 30, 1910.

58. *Carlisle Sentinel*, October 30, 1968.

59. Arthur E Buchholz to John Francis, September 27, 1917, Carlisle Indian School Student Record Files, file no. 5196.

60. CIA Cato Sells to Claud V Peel, Travelling Auditor in charge, Carlisle School, July 27, 1918, Carlisle Indian School Student Record Files, file no. 5196.

61. Henry Flickinger, interviewed by Helen F. Norton, December 1, 1981, Carlisle PA; Cumberland County Historical Society. Flickinger lived locally, and his sister married Montreville Yuda.

62. Yuda became a strong personality on campus and a driving force behind the initiative for the Senate to investigate Carlisle.

63. George Yuda, interview by the author, November 26, 2002, Carlisle PA.

64. In a telephone conversation between Helen Kaseeta and Barbara Landis in June 1983, Helen said her husband chose to change the spelling of his name. We do not have an explanation.

65. Memorial Gardens Cemetery lies on Route 11, two miles south of Carlisle.

66. Enrique Meastas and Daniel Castro Romero Jr., "Culcajen-Ndé: Ancestry of the Lipan Apaches, Lipan Apache Band of Texas." This unpublished manuscript traces the history of the Lipan Apaches from the fifteenth to the eighteenth centuries. A more recent history of the Lipan Apaches is available online at "Lipan Apache (Tindi)," http://www.indians.org/welker/lipanap.htm.

67. "Lipan Apache (Tindi)."

68. Castro Romero to Fear-Segal, September 25, 2002.

69. Email from Daniel Castro Romero Jr. to Jacqueline Fear-Segal, December 11, 2002.

70. Lipan Apache Band of Texas, Inc., Daniel Castro Romero Jr., "Memorializing the Lost Ones," May 6, 2009, http://markerplans.blogspot.co.uk/2009/05/we-shall-remain.html.

71. Present were Susan Rose, Steve Brouwer, Jan Brouwer, Tess Eichelberger, Jacqueline Fear-Segal, Barbara Landis, Anne Geheb, and Manuel Saralegui.

72. Lipan Apache Band of Texas, Inc., "Memorializing the Lost Ones."

12

Necropolitics, Carlisle Indian School, and Ndé Memory

MARGO TAMEZ (NDÉ/LIPAN APACHE)

I bear witness to Ndé (Lipan Apache) experiences before our elders and traditional leaders, as well as the supportive academic community. In our collective effort to confront and address the history of Carlisle Indian School (CIS), we must also come to grips with a shared history of genocidal violence and the continuing impact of ignorance and denial in the United States, which obstructs indigenous peoples' access to truth and redress by marginalizing our voices, memories, and experiences. Indeed, the enduring policy of domination over indigenous peoples and indigenous property is still masked within U.S. domestic policies as social, political, and economic progress.

In 1873 two Lipan Apache (Ndé) children, who came to be known as the Lost Ones, were taken prisoner by the Fourth Calvary of the U.S. Army after a raid that killed their mother and other members of their village. After the massacre, another form of violence took place when these children were sent to the Carlisle Indian School, where they would undergo the cultural genocide imposed on students there, who for the most part lost their language, their culture, their Native names, and their identities.

The contemporary Ndé people, who have inherited both the trauma and the memory of these stolen children, are working to repair these losses imposed by the U.S. government and to challenge cultural amnesia. In this essay I explore the ways in which the 1873 abduction of these children (as well as others) and their incarceration in the CIS parallel the violence still experienced by the Ndé people; I also show how the contemporary Ndé are reclaiming their heritages and challenging white-dominated power structures. We must remember the past, but we must also pay attention to the struggles of contemporary indigenous peoples to restore and revitalize the land and the worldviews threatened by settler colonial usurpation and to achieve economic and social justice.

I am deeply appreciative of the Carlisle Indian School intergenerational survivors, scholars, artists, and poets, who embraced the Ndé delegation at the Carlisle Symposium at Dickinson College, October 5–6, 2012. With the host committee and delegates, indigenous peoples from the four directions came together and braided Ndé oral histories, testimonies, and memories into the collective voice, bearing witness to the ongoing ruptures of the U.S. boarding school experiment in indigenous peoples' lives. I hope that my contribution to this volume will open up new pathways of knowledge and understanding for indigenous and non-indigenous peoples to engage in conversation about this continuing legacy of violence, as well as, more immediately, help sustain pressure upon U.S. Army officials at the Carlisle Barracks to establish the CIS Farmhouse as a crucial site of indigenous crisis and memory.[1] CIS still remains an unresolved site of cultural genocide and state repression against indigenous peoples. CIS and its disturbing legacy, which produced and reproduces marginalization and violence in thousands of indigenous lives today, continues to fuel a rising consciousness among indigenous peoples and settler-descendants.

Indigenous peoples demand recognition and redress for the intergenerational violence that CIS and related institutions forced upon them. They will interrogate their histories in order to understand the responsibility of CIS and similar institutions in removing, separating, and isolating indigenous children from the influence of their parents, grandparents, uncles, aunties, cousins, and siblings. Furthermore, survivors demand recognition and redress for the loss of a sustained relationship with indigenous homelands, sacred landscapes, and landscapes of deep psychological, physical, and social significance upon which indigenous identity, culture, and nationality resides. These actions irreparably impaired indigenous children's emotional, physical, spiritual, and mental development. Intergenerational harms experienced by descendants of CIS survivors continue to reveal the enduring suffering inflicted on indigenous children, who were severed from their home territories and extended families. The alienation from their traditions and cultures and the effects of forced assimilation into the Euro-American dominant culture has had, and continues to have, negative consequences for indigenous peoples. The effects of assimilation, conflicted identity, and mental illness are some of the major themes in the scholarly literature.[2] However, more recently scholars and indigenous rights activists have emphasized the penetrating and damaging effects on indigeneity, indigenous epistemologies, ontologies, and cosmovisions, indigenous institutional governance systems based in the traditional extended family, and self-determination that is inherently bound up in indigenous collective relationships with lands and territories.[3] This is due in large part to hemispheric, transnational, transborder, and globally theorized and organized indigenous grass-roots activism partnered with indigenous-centered action-research initiatives emerging from indigenous land-based social movements whose social actors have elevated and framed the issue as a social justice movement focused on collective healing and reparations.[4]

This chapter is dedicated to the two Ndé prisoners of war of the Cúelcahén (Tall Grass) Clan, who, at the end of the nineteenth century were known as Kesetta and Jack, who lived and died while interned at the Carlisle Indian School in Pennsylvania, after being seized and taken from their occupied lands of Kónitsąąíí Gokíyaa—Ndé Big Water Country. Tragically these ancestral relatives were not the only Ndé taken as prisoners of war during invasions of our lands, a crucial component in the national and state formation of the United States as we know it today. I wish to honor our ancestor relatives' lives and experiences as sacred. I wish to acknowledge the fragmented evidence, painstakingly recovered from the state archives, and the critical partnerships between non-indigenous academics and Ndé Oral Knowledge authorities. As a result of a crucial research partnership between historian Jacqueline Fear-Segal and the documentary filmmaker Susan Rose, working in collaboration with the Cúelcahén, Goschich, and Kónitsąąíí Ndé Clans, we now have a more solid base to construct critical Ndé studies founded on critical engagement in officially sanctioned state memory and indigenous memory, epistemologies, and oral tradition.[5]

I want to address linkages and to narrow the perceived distance and spaces between the lives of the Ndé prisoners of war at CIS and those of their kin contemporaries in connected sites of crisis in Kónitsąąíí Gokíyaa, currently known to civil society as the Texas-Mexico region.[6] Narrowing the perceived gap between the violence inflicted on the Lost/Stolen Ones who were taken from their homeland to the Carlisle Indian School and the bifurcated region of present-day Texas-Mexico helps us begin to develop tools and new frameworks to deconstruct and understand the relationships between occupation, state-enforced violence, and cultural destruction.

Today we know that the destructive intent of the "educational" experiment directed at indigenous children was not limited to boarding schools in the United States. The state and powerful actors took a systematic approach to destroying indigeneity and indigenous peoples' core institutions and belief systems across Canada, Mexico, Australia, and other settler-nations. As a result of the Truth and Reconciliation Commission in Canada, concrete evidence has established that numerous religious, social, and political organizations are being implicated in acts of genocide.[7] The enforced separation of indigenous children from family, mother tongues, worldviews, and lineal inheritance systems severely impaired indigenous children's access to traditional knowledge systems and fractured their unique relationship to customary lands. One positive effect of truth commissions is they allow the victims to retrace memory, experience, and history across time, space, and place. For example, the TRC in Canada has enabled indigenous peoples to reconnect events that occurred long ago, across generations, and to narrate traumatic experiences in different places with great distances in between, in ways that cause a "shattering" effect on previous conceptions of historical processes.

Robbie Ethridge's theory of colonial "shatter zones," a systems framework, supports a nuanced approach to gain a clearer sense of the precarious physical, social, economic, and political situation of indigenous peoples already undergoing processes of violent colonization, and who in many ways were bi- or trisected by more than one colonizing group.[8] Furthermore, in the case of crimes against Ndé abductees, I believe we must analyze the colonial practices of forcibly taking indigenous women for profit and the widespread and catastrophic relationship between indigenous slave traffic, disease, and exploitation as crucial factors of settler-colonial domination.[9]

The framework of shatter zones helps make visible the multiple and intersectional forces affecting indigenous peoples' capacity to resist, and provide much needed dimensionality to the exploitation and predation exercised by colonizing groups across race, class, gender, vocation, and nationality. For example, in shatter zone theory, one can examine the introduction of biological pathogens and diseases promoting higher mortality and thereby weakening the subjugated group; introduction of capitalist relations and organized overtaking of indigenous economic systems; systematic replacements of indigenous kinship and ceremonial exchange systems based on reciprocity with ones based on commodification, profit, and hierarchy. Shatter zone theory allows us to conceptualize group-to-group relations in more specific, contextualized, and spatially dynamic ways, thereby animating the effects of the above factors as intersected by legal and cognitive imperialism, military colonization, and violent expropriation of land, resources, and the means of production. While Ethbridge anchors his analysis in the Mississippian region, I believe his framework could be extended to the Ndé in the late nineteenth century caught in entrenched shatter zone systems between competing settler-colonial societies who had occupied northeastern Mexico and southern Texas and could examine how Americans from the Northeast and Southeast naturalized these practices through the military Americanization of northeastern Mexico, southern Texas, and the Mississippi region. I argue that these interrelated histories and contexts intersected the lives of Kesetta and Jack, as well as many Ndé who stayed within the traditional territory after 1873, and these systems enjoined killing fields in Texas to the settler political economy in rural Pennsylvania's social systems.

In my analysis the cumulative losses and damage affecting the abducted and survivor generations were predicated upon shatter zones that underpinned the actions of numerous actors who participated in and those who benefited from the systematic dehumanization of indigenous peoples to mere objects of state abjection.

To address this disturbing reality in the United States, it is necessary for intergenerational survivors of CIS and other boarding schools to be heard and witnessed through a mechanism that structures truth telling, naming names, and accountability. Such a mechanism would serve the crucial purpose of healing on indigenous peoples' terms and providing crucial forums for meaningful dialogue between indigenous peoples and U.S. society. Official lies and negation of historical and cultural genocide against indigenous peoples persist in the United States (and Mexico) as a result of sanctioned censorship posing as official state history, ignorance, inefficient and inappropriate K–12 and postsecondary education, lack of access to justice for many unrecognized historic tribes still affected by U.S.

indigenous genocide history, and ongoing rejection across U.S. society of indigenous peoples' experiences, voices, memories, and, most importantly, indigenous inherent rights.

A general disregard for indigenous peoples' oral histories is most disturbing and is regarded by me as a sign of non-indigenous peoples' perception that our memory and knowledge systems are a threat to the government and to the settler-colonial status quo. Indigenous resilience despite intended destruction of our bodies, communities, nations, and worldviews still stands as a stark reminder of the ongoing dependency of Americans on the raw resources expropriated from indigenous peoples' unsurrendered homelands. On this note we must pay close attention to the state's excessive use of force as a domestic policy to manage indigenous peoples' resurgences in the current period, and we must assess whether state militarism used as a weapon of discipline and control is a form of disavowing accountability for historical state crimes.

Like many indigenous delegates who traveled to the Carlisle Symposium, Ndé were deeply troubled by the history of U.S violence that predated the founding of CIS as well as the societal-wide ignorance and denial of state-organized killing, forced separations, and dispossessions. We collectively recognized that these methods were integral to the settler-colonial nation's developing and extracting monetary profit through industrial economic development that has since supported generations of Americans at home and abroad. While indigenous peoples are struggling to address the intergenerational effects of the shatter zone of CIS—spatially, spiritually, psychologically, physically, economically, and politically—the settler society lags terribly behind in a collective exercise in addressing these interlocking and intersecting facets of the aggressive assimilative processes, past and present. The Ndé people, holders of numerous conventions ("treaties") with Spain, Mexico, Texas, and the United States, exist in a political "gray" zone with regard to American violence in Kónitsąąíí Gokíyaa. Ndé demands for truth and historical clarification have been repeatedly ignored by U.S. officials. As a consequence the Ndé people suffer collectively from the massive theft of knowledge and resources and the structured relationship of colonizer-colonized, which still pervades Americans' social and economic attitudes to indigenous peoples and to our unceded, customary homelands. The necessary step of engaging the shared histories between the settler society, the state, and indigenous peoples demands that we be mindful and attentive to indigenous peoples' ongoing struggles to reclaim, revitalize, and restore our knowledge systems. These are inherently and inextinguishably tied to customary lands, our elders, and the capacity to transmit knowledge to future generations. Indigenous peoples' perspectives and rights in international law must be taken seriously in order to be addressed meaningfully.

My reflections also link the Ndé memory-scape and social lives within the late nineteenth- and early twentieth-century armed conflict zone of southern Texas and northeast Mexico to Ndé scholars' and elders' current-day inquiries into the necropolitical actions of the U.S. government.[10] In 2003 Achilles Mbembe introduced the theory and concept of necropolitics, stating "the ultimate expression of sovereignty resides, to a large degree, in the power and the capacity to dictate who may live and who must die."[11] Furthermore, Mbembe argues, "To exercise sovereignty is to exercise control over mortality and to define life as the deployment and manifestation of power."[12] I argue that Kesetta and Jack were targets of American necropolitics at the moment of the killing field (the 1873 Remolino massacre), a landscape of significance well within Ndé customary homeland, though trisected politically by Mexico, Texas, and the United States. They were subjected to internment and identity changes between the killing field and U.S. military forts analyzed by Fear-Segal and the "Carlisle Indian Industrial School," which I would argue is an American euphemism for both the site of abjection and state exception, a legal gray zone where the state claims sovereign immunity and enacts impunity.[13] cis was a camp and site of reindoctrination, spatially distanced from sites of mass atrocity in many distinct indigenous homelands, and implicated as a space that, in the words of Hannah Arendt, "stands outside of life and death."[14] There is no question in my mind that any reclamation of cis must vocally and visibly articulate cis as a site of necropolitical crisis. Eurocentric linear history and Eurocentric consciousness must be disrupted in order to fully indigenize the spiritual, physical, and political consequences of Ndé dispossession of homelands, memory, and belonging along the lines of human dismemberment and political nonrecognition deployed against unceding indigenous nations—then and today.

I understand Ndé memory and oral history as a living embodiment of my people's ongoing resilience and our efforts to achieve social reconstruction and justice across our customary territories in Shimaa Isdzán Gokíyaa (our mother our home). I hope to tie "past-present-future" together from an indigenous temporal perspective. For indigenous peoples, place, memory, and oral histories are often more relevant and crucial than dates, so finding a balance between oral traditions and Western historical methods is complex.

A narrowing of this divide between two very different historical accounts of the Ndé prisoners of war first came about in 2002, when historian Jacqueline Fear-Segal and Lipan Apache elder Daniel Castro Romero Jr. began a productive collaborative relationship. Down the years, at the annual Ndé summer ceremonies conducted specifically for healing unresolved pain relating to loved ones, painful questions were always asked about the whereabouts of the Lost Ones. News that they had been taken to Pennsylvania initiated a visit of our elders to Carlisle for spirit-releasing ceremonies and the recording of this visit in Susan Rose's documentary, *The Lost Ones—Long Journey Home.*[15]

As a result of respectful dialogues between allied academics and the Ndé people, it was agreed that a deeper, sustained analysis of indigenous peoples' critical perspectives on CIS and the roles of indigenous memory and reclamation needed to be foregrounded. Discussions began at the Carlisle Symposium in 2012, but more needs to be done in the domestic legal sphere. Here mechanisms are virtually nonexistent for meaningfully redressing indigenous peoples' collective experiences with "soul wound." This is a term coined by Andrea Smith, one of the founders of the Boarding School Healing Project, to describe the embedded patterns of physical and sexual abuse suffered by indigenous children at boarding schools.[16] Transnational activism between indigenous peoples across borders has instilled a growing consciousness that the boarding schools and their legacy impinge on human rights. Sammy Toineeta (Lakota) insists: "Human rights activists must talk about the issue of boarding schools. It is one of the grossest human rights violations because it targeted children and was the tool for perpetrating cultural genocide. To ignore this issue would be to ignore the human rights of indigenous peoples, not only in the U.S., but around the world."[17]

Here I examine the function of CIS and related systems in the dispossessions of the Ndé nation from their legitimate claim to Kónitsą́ą́í Gokíyaa—

"Lipan country" in current-day Texas and northeast Mexico—as well as the theft of our children. Numerous indigenous peoples who are intergenerational survivors of CIS and related industrial-type schools modeled on this aggressive, assimilationist model have grown up with extremely low self-esteem manifesting in self-abuse, alcoholism, substance abuse, and suicide or suicidal thoughts. Self-inflicted injury is a high cause of death among indigenous peoples. Many have grown up feeling alone and not belonging either in an indigenous community or the dominant culture. Because of their past experiences, many express distrust of state-sponsored education. This leads to poverty and economic, social, cultural, and political divides between intergenerational survivors and the rest of society, which is unable or unwilling to comprehend or learn the truth.[18]

Accountability and redress are crucial steps in confronting indigenous peoples' awareness of the long-term impacts connected with intergenerational trauma, compromised family systems; loss of mother tongues and culture; loss of connections to ancestral sacred and religious beliefs; loss of crucial connections to ancestral cosmologies, legal philosophies, literacy and arts traditions, and ecological-economic social spheres; loss of crucial parenting skills; loss of the ability to trust, to nurture, to love, to accept love, and to make and maintain intimate relationships in a culturally relevant way.

Carlisle Indian School and Konitsaii Gokíyaa (Ndé Texas-Mexico Region)

For the Ndé people, boarding school histories predate the nation-state. They began after earlier religious, economic, and political invasions of Kónitsąąíí Gokíyaa under the Jesuits, Franciscans, Dominicans, Oblates, and Spanish monarchy, then Mexicans and Texans, and finally the United States. Traditional scholarly (mis)emphasis on U.S. boarding schools reflects how well the containment ideology of the elites has constrained an integrated analysis of these multiple colonial invasions. This long history of Indian boarding schools needs to be unpacked to reveal its links to other forms and expressions of both state- and church-imposed separations and destructions of families and communities. For the Ndé people, the link between violence and the taking of their children, Kesetta and Jack (as well as others), was undeniable and led to generations of suffering. They were not alone. Many indigenous victims of places like CIS suffer severe forms of posttraumatic stress disorder (PTSD), transmitting this syndrome intergenerationally. Until recently this has been deeply felt within indigenous communities but largely unacknowledged and unaddressed outside. The Cree/Métis scholar Kim Anderson writes:

> We live with the trauma that has plagued the previous generations. . . . I was crying for the losses experienced by my ancestors, but I was also crying for my own loss of identity. I have since seen many Native people cry in sharing circles for the same reasons. . . . [A]t some point we must begin to reclaim ourselves . . . and to see ourselves as grandchildren, members, and relations. In other words, we must disrupt allowing colonizers to infiltrate and penetrate our consciousness. We must take the courageous steps to the recognition of our inherent being as Indigenous peoples of our customary places that can never be extinguished from us or our future generations.[19]

Indigenous survivors have a right to know the truth and the right to the recognition of indigenous memory.[20] In the United States there is an urgent need for collective social justice practices with the capacity to engage, foreground, and integrate indigenous memory, knowledge, and testimony in order to achieve historical clarification and legal redress for state criminality.

The Ndé currently live with the knowledge that two ancestors were sent to CIS and never returned home. In 2008–9, when I learned about what had happened to our Lost Ones, I became aware of my lack of knowledge about CIS—past and ongoing. I attributed my lack of knowledge to the Eurocentric and denial approach that is mainstreamed in U.S. education systems and media. At the same time, I came to realize the extreme lack of awareness or comprehension about CIS, killing fields, and related systems of domination among the Ndé people. There are still critical gaps of knowledge among indigenous peoples about what took place at CIS and the U.S. and Mexican joint objective to exterminate the Ndé people. I sought to understand how the state and powerful interest groups normalized destructive processes, which involved the collaboration between church, state, citizens, and functionaries in micro-processes of destruction against indigenous polities, including the Ndé.

During a series of email and phone conversations with Chairman Daniel Castro Romero Jr. in 2008, as we prepared for the United Nations Permanent Forum on Indigenous Issues (UNPFII) 8th Session, I began to comprehend the psychological and emotional weight that he and a handful of traditional knowledge keepers had been carrying with regard to the taking of our children and its impact on Ndé political life—or bare existence, to be accurate. Specifically, he shared vivid accounts and images of the Cúelcahén (Tall Grass Peoples Clan) ritualized annual memorialization of the Remolino massacre (one of numerous), still kept alive by numerous clan members who are still haunted by these horrific events that occurred toward the end of the nineteenth century. The Ndé perseverance to remember and to recognize the absence of the Ndé children who were taken away from the killing fields as prisoners of war by the U.S. military in 1873, and the continuing reverberations of this in the present, forced me to dig deeper to explore the legacy of these events and their connections to what happened at CIS.

The reunion of Ndé chiefly leaders at the UN was a pivotal moment of reclamation at an international level. Ndé leaders began to participate collectively in international proceedings in a prominent way, and in a unified voice across clans, to articulate Ndé perspectives and principles of history, law, and self-determination. It was a key turning point to witness Ndé leaders thinking collectively and openly speaking about events at CIS in an international context, as they simultaneously prepared to travel to Carlisle to perform spirit-releasing ceremonies for the Lost Ones.

Indeed, an Ndé spiritual, intellectual, and political shift was occurring on a deeper, yet subtle level. As the Ndé leaders were building a quiet momentum to reclaim the disappeared Ndé chiefly abductees (aka the Lost Ones), so too they were beginning to make links between these traumatic Carlisle events and retraumatization from what was happening in Texas and the specter of a border wall being constructed on their lands. With Ndé women, who owned lands along the Texas border in the community of El Calaboz and who were starting to gain traction in their resistance to the U.S. border wall being constructed through their lands, the interrelated effects of two forms of detaining and separating Ndé from Ndé—the wall and CIS—were at the forefront of my mind.

Truth telling is difficult. There are scars that don't want to heal. The more painful the truth, the harder the story is to tell, and the deeper its wounding. But truth, knowledge, and shared stories brought home the Lost Ones and opened a new space for reunification between the severed, disbanded, broken Ndé family relations, which had been torn apart violently by the U.S. policies of persecution against Ndé people at the close of the nineteenth century and since then. Through truth, recollection, and mutual recognition of dangerous truths, Chief Romero and I made a commitment to reunify our clans. We committed to take the healing journey together as relatives. We committed to reclaim our Ndé ancestral ways, which had been targeted by CIS and the United States. We committed to the path of truth and justice. As history has been used as a weapon against us for so long, so too can indigenous historical clarification be an arrow of light and knowing.

As I came to learn more details about the life and death of the Ndé children who were categorized by the U.S. government and by CIS as "prisoners of war,"[21] I began to question the rhetoric about CIS maintained by mainstream sources and to interrogate the necropolitical function of CIS in Ndé decolonization. In other words, I came to recognize the inherent legal position of Ndé people as collective indigenous peoples with the legal right to self-determination through autonomy (not necessarily cession). This acknowledgment that CIS had been a key site of state-architected violence against the Ndé people contributed to my understanding of the multilayered processes of colonialism and thus of Ndé decolonizing.

Ndé people's lived experiences and empirical observations are the foundations for a complex and mostly underground oral history; it is one of inherent belonging, yet scarred by extreme marginalization. Ordinary Americans, even when well-meaning, lack the knowledge and information to see, feel, and comprehend this history and the horrendous injustices against the Ndé people in the nineteenth century and continuing to the present day. The struggle to voice actual realities, as understood from Ndé viewpoints, has always been seriously contested and threatened. In the following section the lived experiences of Kasita Castro raise important issues that compel us to construct new frameworks for shrinking the divide between Carlisle, Pennsylvania, and Konitsaii Gokíyaa (the Ndé Texas-Mexico region).

Kasita Castro

Ndé prisoners of war (aka Kesetta and Jack), held at CIS, were the direct lineal heirs and recipients of an oral tradition and oral history based on the Ndé knowledge system that predates Canada, the United States, and Mexico and that is embedded in the land and peoples of all three. These Ndé children of high status clans and chiefly peoples would have inherited specific knowledge of Ndé language, ceremonials, law, convenios (treaties), and mercedes (land grant) agreements conducted in the Ndé homeland with Europeans and with other indigenous nations as well.

According to the oral history recounted to me by hereditary Ndé Nanta'án Daniel Castro Romero Jr. of the Cúelcahén (Tall Grass Peoples),[22] Kasita was the daughter of a renowned and politically active line of chiefly Ndé peoples with a complex history of international conventions, mercedes, hidalgos, and international military alliances. Ndé lineal heirs of this rich political-economic background never ceded or surrendered their ancestral claims and struggles for autonomy in Kónitsą̄ą́íí Gokíyaa— Ndé Big Water Country. Castro Romero highlights Kasita's inherent rights to inherit chiefly rights to autonomous governance and to enact trade and commerce in the customary Ndé territory through her lineal relationships to both paternal and maternal Nanta'án and to Ndé yásitíń.[23] In a telephone conversation Castro Romero told me Kesetta's story:

> During Mackenzie's raid of 1873, her father, Ramon Castro, was hurt and injured. Her mother, Mariana Castro, who was killed, was a direct descendant of those from San Luis Potosi. He came from Cuelgas, and the [family] tree line passed to all the treaty signers of the 1844 treaty. They had served the Republic of Texas but were then betrayed by Texas and the U.S. It was very political. [After the attack], the Ndé came seeking out their chief, because they had not accounted for him as one of the dead at Mackenzie's raid. The other four hundred Ndé dispersed in all directions; the soldiers had only taken twenty prisoners. There were some who went to San Luis Potosi, to your people's places by the river, to Mexico City, to Raramuri country, and in many other directions in

the north, due to kinship lines that were already in place long before. Those lines run all across our traditional territory. This isn't just about trading relations, but deep family relations. We had [widespread] family ties too that were old, due to our food and water systems, our sacred places, our ceremonial and social places, and all the places we had made decisions amongst our allies.

We had agreed to go to San Luis Potosi to Mexican (state) authorities, to the furthest point we had traded with Mexican (Nahua-speaking) indigenous peoples. It was below Mexico City, and the Mexican government thought they'd be less of a threat. Those who came to San Luis Potosi, they didn't tell a lot of people. This was reflective of a state of armed conflict and political crisis. Our people were taken to our furthest southern point of commerce, trading, and kinship—the furthest south of our Ndé kinship tree . . . imagine the bigger map of the Ndé region, you have to redraw the whole map. When Mackenzie did the raid, they didn't kill all the people. They killed a significant number, but if they reported how many they didn't kill that would make them appear in a negative light to their superior officers. In other words, they cooked the books. Many Ndé survived Mackenzie's raid. So, Mackenzie went into Ndé Territory, now bounded up in Mexico, specifically to target the children. They learned that by taking children of chiefs or recognized leaders, whether head men, head women, clans, influential societies, medicine healers, etc., or the leaders of the indigenous confederacies, which were especially targeted in order to break the organized resistance, by taking the children they could control the political leaders. It's very intentional. Punishing, coercing, and manipulating the chiefs, such as Ramon Castro, did occur by taking his children from him.

Kasita means "little house" in Spanish. When Americans took her to Carlisle, they couldn't say it correctly; it means the little person/ mother who could take care of the wikiups/jacals (like the ones you have pictures of at your mom's ranchería). To take the little boy was to punish his mother's and father's peoples. This part, the taking of little boys, was new to the Ndé. In the past the Spanish and French mostly wanted the girls and women, because they were known for their excellent hide work and to break them into domestic work. They usually took girls and women, for reproduction and labor. The Americans had not taken the boys as much as girls and women. The old ones, they felt this was a new version of the slave runs (economies). This was one of the first times [in the oral history of the southern Ndé] that the Americans had taken the children with true intent to punish us and to control us and our movement in our territory. Kasita/Kesetta was being groomed to be a leader among the women, to marry into another family of leaders. This is crucial. The more I hear our people, the more I have learned how important she was politically to the alliances among our Ndé Nation. She honored us and her people by holding high stature among our indigenous peoples and the white people. She stepped into the role of Ndé woman but in a white world. She managed to do her best in the white world, although a radically different world, to the extent possible and where she could because she was trained and raised to survive, as this was key in our world. She knew her place was never to bow down and to be "regular." She knew she had to be a leader and role model. A lot of Natives were taught to be subdued due to their early childhood experiences under colonization, under rape, torture, imprisonment and by separation from their people. But she was not taught to ever surrender; rather, she was taught to hold her head up high. Just like Moctezuma, a warrior the Ndé had an oral history about long before the whites started writing about him, who held his head high even when he knew Cortez was going to kill him, he never let his authority down, never. That authority was never surrendered. She was able to lead other indigenous nations' children while she was incarcerated as a prisoner of war. Always remember she entered a prisoner of war and died a prisoner of war, something rarely talked about and never mentioned.

Our people are so proud of her. She left her mark for future generations, and now we have come back full circle, and that is because she did her people right. Her little brother . . . he too always represented his people, to the end, in dignity. He did not surrender.[24]

From Daniel Castro Romero Jr. I heard for the first time the Ndé oral history of our ancestors, who were taken away to Carlisle Indian School. Sometime later, at El Calaboz Rancheria, Texas, a screening of the documentary *The Lost Ones: The Long Journey Home* in June 2011 offered a way for some distanced Ndé to acknowledge their identities. Elder community members, who to this day still deny their indigenous identity and have accepted the imposed state identity of "Mexican American" as a result of decades of pervasive anti-indigenous policies in Texas systems, began asking questions about the deeper meanings. A female elder, who wishes not to be identified here, approached me shyly and gave me a hug. I noted tears welling up in her eyes. She is a direct descendant of Nahua-Tlaxcalteca and Comanche-Lipan indigenous peoples of the La Encantada Ranchería complex near El Calaboz. It was not an easy thing for her to speak these words through the decades of silence and institutionalized lies about her ancestors: "Thank you for telling us this story. I don't know why I'm crying. I knew that my mother was Indian, but she was ashamed to tell us we were too. I grew up believing it was bad to be Indio. Thank you for telling the truth. Will you come back and help us learn more about our ancestors?"

Another family with indigenous migrant Oaxaca ties, who attended the gathering and provided food to the feast sponsored by the clan of Eloisa Garcia Tamez, asked questions about the founders of the community they now call home—El Ranchito. This led the father of the family to say in a gentle and respectful manner: "We are honored to know this story in the film. This reminds me of things that have happened to us in Mexico. It is good to learn about the history and to know the history of this place we call our home. We have much to learn about what is being taught here, much to learn. Living here, no one teaches us about this reality that your families are the First Nations (Pueblos Indígenas) of this place. Thank you. We want to learn more."

At this gathering the Carlisle Indian Industrial School, internment camps, and other killing fields that are sites of memory in Ndé narratives intertwined with our collective sorrow, anger, and anxiety, and all were talked about in the shadow of the U.S. border wall, just yards away from where we were sitting. Ndé memory of the late nineteenth and early twentieth centuries and oral histories of the Lost Ones collided with the present-day psycho-social dimensions of experience in the shadow of the gulag wall.

Initially, when I learned about Kasita/Kesetta, I experienced shock. Yet listening to the oral accounts from those Ndé leaders who had direct knowledge, I was able to more deeply connect to and understand the Ndé people's complex responses to their difficult history. That year, in 2009, we were yet again facing severe despair over our increasing sense of loss of control over our lives. My recently gained knowledge of what had been done to Kasita/Kesetta in the nineteenth century was, I realized, inseparable from what was now happening close to home. Once more, the Ndé were experiencing loss of culture, militarization of the border, and the construction of our people as "the enemy" of the United States. Comparable events in the nineteenth century had forced the Ndé people to disperse, deny their identity, and lose their cultural ties and their coherence. In 1873 the Ndé had refused to acknowledge claims by the governments of Mexico, Texas, and the United States that the U.S.-Mexico border was either legal or legitimate. Rather, the Ndé sought peace agreements to find a negotiated path to share Kónitsąąíí Gokíyaa with the Euro-American nations and their citizens in an equitable manner that would ensure the sustainability of Ndé peoples for future generations. In the Ndé worldview Remolino and related attacks in their region were within Kónitsąąíí Gokíyaa—"Lipan country"—which we had every right to defend. Today, the Ndé (Lipan Apaches) once again are defending our Kónitsąąíí Gokíyaa and our rights to pass freely across our lands that span what has been made an international border. This is why, at the United Nations in New York City, Ndé chief Daniel Castro Romero Jr. publically linked these two intersecting issues: the history of what had been done to our Lost Ones and our present situation.

In May 2009, the same month that the recovery process for our Lost Ones was unfolding in Pennsylvania, the Nanta'án Daniel Castro Romero Jr. and a small delegation of Ndé traditional authorities, including myself, met at the Eighth Session of the United Nations Permanent Forum on Indigenous Issues in New York. At that session Castro Romero made reference to our oral history about the Ndé children prisoners of war taken to Pennsylvania and correlated these nineteenth-century abuses to current-day human rights violations occurring along the Texas-Mexico border.

Stolen and Lost Lives

Kesetta/Kasita and her brother's imprisonment and disappearance symbolize the legacy of individual stolen lives and of generations of lives lived inauthentically as forced replicas of white people.[25] We must imagine and grapple with the extent to which she herself might have remembered her childhood and kinship circles, her mother and father, and her grandparents and the extent to which she felt compelled to bury her memory of her true identity, just to survive in a marginalized existence. The mission of CIS to destroy Native cultures has not ended, and today Ndé people in Texas still suffer the stigma of indigenous peoples whose lives and identities have been stolen by the U.S. government. For this reason, CIS carries incredible weight in Ndé memory, and recently acquired knowledge of the violence experienced by the descendants of the Ndé prisoners of war who lived and died at Carlisle is still raw.

Yet Kasita's/Kesetta's life, abuse, physical death, and continued spiritual presence in the Ndé healing and justice road are especially notable. Her presence moves through us still, and especially after she received a going-home ceremony by the Ndé Clan authorities. Her significance reemerges today because it resonates so profoundly in the lives and situations of present-day Ndé people, whose political status is in limbo between "prisoner of war" and assimilated masses of unrecognized indigenous peoples in the United States. But I have certainty that many more Ndé experiences, besides those of the Lost Ones, are yet to be recovered and reclaimed in the ongoing truth-seeking process and will become the foundation for a major recovery project that Ndé peoples will direct. Significantly, during the time period of the discovery of Kesetta's life and death at CIS and in Pennsylvania, Ndé peoples were organizing to deploy Ndé memories as social reproduction in Texas "public spaces"—occupied Ndé sites of crisis and relevance.

Ndé Memory, Recovery, and Revitalization

Ndé council leaders, working alongside traditional oral history keepers and current-day Ndé researchers, collaborated to create and author their own history markers, reflecting an Ndé historical consciousness. At the 2009 collective Isanałesh Gotal Na'ii'ees feast, the community learned about other sites of crisis—beyond the Remolino massacre—which the peoples sought to reclaim. The right to know the truth and to articulate factual and balanced information about the Ndé memory in sites of significance was a collective social act of reunion with Kónitsąą́í Gokíyaa. Ndé peoples recognize that places in Kónitsąą́í Gokíyaa are alive—and can also be violated and traumatized, and can carry wounding that requires special healing practices that are distinct and unique only to the Ndé of Kónitsąąíí Gokíyaa. Ndé peoples recognize that the ancestors whose bodies and spirits were violated in those places must be acknowledged, respected, and given the correct ceremonies in order to bring harmony and peace to places. These collective actions, done in private ceremonies among the peoples, are acts of community healing and show the Ndé collectively seeking actively to combat the lethal consequences of violence, death, and desecration.

Increasingly, Ndé peoples have formulated and formalized their own relevant questions and research, and a strong desire to design and enforce Ndé protocols and principles on Ndé knowledge and intellectual property as measures to disrupt further distortion and appropriation of traditional and contemporary knowledge. Eduardo González Cueva, director of the International Center for Transitional Justice's Truth and Memory Program, posits, "New truth commissions that are formed will be entrusted with an ever-expanding list of conduct to investigate."[26] Since the United States has never been taken to task by indigenous peoples through a truth commission, this raises questions about collective capacity and an aligned focus. As truth commissions adapt to regional variations and the rise of indigenous social actors, Cueva argues, these "may go beyond a mere finding of facts to include the tasks of explaining the historical and structural roots of abuses, and the differentiated way in which vulnerable groups such as women, children, indigenous peoples and others have suffered them."[27] In 2012 Ndé peoples seeking a transitional justice pathways and historical clarification inquiry, sent me to an international training session on truth, memory, and truth commissions in order to gain skills and tools and to develop strategies with the support of international experts.[28]

Indeed, the common struggles of indigenous peoples—against forgetting, against further loss, against persistent dehumanization and increasingly technological forms of extermination—continue to inform new modes of revitalization. Memory, vivacious and active, is a crucial resource that also needs protection, in alignment with protection against the threat to indigenous languages, spiritual beliefs, cultural practices, and homelands. Indigenous memory demands refined and sophisticated approaches, especially in the contemporary U.S. society, whose history is based exclusively on written documents. If victims' rights to truth and justice with reparations are "a new continent in the international discussion about transitions from authoritarianism to democracy and from violence to peace,"[29] to what extent does critical indigenous memory serve to inform and mobilize the transformation of the current public imagination?

The Carlisle Symposium, at which indigenous memory was acknowledged, respected, and given credence, was a positive and crucial step toward pursuing an organized national collective framework that puts indigenous rights in the center of the frame. James Anaya, the UN special rapporteur on the rights of indigenous peoples, argues that indigenous peoples "find themselves engulfed by settler societies born of the forces of empire and conquest."[30] Decolonization of key sites of crisis, such as CIS, opens up a space whereby indigenous peoples and settler society can engage in meaningful learning and determine appropriate actions in order to engage a shared history and to address a present-day demand for redress. Indeed, major shifts in international law, such as the "United Nations Adoption of the Declaration on the Rights of Indigenous Peoples," and increasing movement internationally in favor of indigenous rights are direct outcomes of indigenous peoples' firm demands on decolonization and self-determination.[31]

In Canada, the Truth and Reconciliation Commission (TRC) has elevated and afforded legitimacy to indigenous peoples' memories, experiences, testimonies, and reparations. While neither perfect nor ideal, many indigenous people have utilized the Canadian TRC as a mechanism and tool to confront and challenge the state, church, and settler-colonial erasures and distorted accounts of the Indian residential schools.[32] The Canadian TRC puts primacy on indigenous peoples' testimonials to bear witness and to shift from "victims" to "survivors," and thus as social actors disrupting official cover-ups and lies; to document irreparable harms and human rights violations; to exercise the right to truth and to know; to enact indigenous ways of knowing; to preserve and document indigenous memory; and to expose the larger and organized patterns, systems, and necropolitical structures perpetrated against indigenous peoples, and the intimately intertwined character of a much-denied layer of indigenous and Canadian shared history. Getting to the root, historical processes are vitally crucial to reclaiming and recovering Ndé experiences—from the shatter zone, the killing field, and in between Texas and Pennsylvania rural settler societies.

Reclaiming the indigenous spiritual and religious beliefs, oral tradition, languages, social relations, and communal structures without addressing the intertwined roots of complicity between state, church, and society would make a mockery of indigenous self-determination struggles.

The Ndé people's involuntary entanglement with CIS has forced me to rethink the historical linkages between violence that pervades Ndé history and violence of the present day. Survivor generations raised well within the industrial settler-state complex carry the sad and bitter memory of our Lost Ones taken at Remolino, taken from many "Remolinos" across the Ndé sacred and social landscape. Now that we have learned so much more about the carceral experiences and deaths of our Ndé peoples in Pennsylvania, we are struck by the fact that this knowledge came to us at the very same moment we were fighting against the U.S. government, in 2009, to defend ourselves in El Calaboz and El Ranchito against the enclosure and containment of our lands by the Texas-Mexico border wall. The concurrence of these two events brought with it an eye-opening awareness of the uninterrupted onslaught of the United States on Ndé peoples. As one Ndé elder remarked, on hearing about Carlisle's mission to destroy Native cultures: "We are still here." This hauntingly echoes the "talking back" that Ndé isdzán Augustina Zuazua gave to American anthropologist Harry Hoijer in 1938, when she iterated the Lipan "remain," thereby contesting the anthropological narrative of the Lipan vanishing, disappearance, and extinction popularized by Americans and venture capitalists in Texas, northeastern Mexico, and the Southwest.[33] Ndé people have a pressing and continuing need to resist, to fight, to exercise self-determination, to be recognized, and to protect our language, our culture, our identity, and our lands for future generations.

NOTES

1. See Carolyn Tolman's essay on the Carlisle Farmhouse, chapter 14 in this collection.
2. Andrea Smith, "Soul Wound: The Legacy of Native American Schools," *Amnesty International Magazine* (2003): 14–17; Charles F. Wilkinson and Eric R. Biggs. "The Evolution of the Termination Policy," *American Indian Law Review* 5, no. 1 (1977): 139–84; David Wallace Adams, *Education for Extinction: American Indians and the Boarding School Experience, 1875–1928* (Lawrence: University Press of Kansas, 1995); Margaret Archuleta, Brenda J. Child, and K.

Tsianina Lomawaima, *Away from Home: American Indian Boarding School Experiences, 1879–2000* (Phoenix AZ: Heard Museum, 2000); Spero M. Manson, Janette Beals, Rhonda Wiegman Dick, and Christine Duclos, "Risk Factors for Suicide among Indian Adolescents at a Boarding School," *Public Health Reports* 104, no. 6 (1989).

3. Angela Cavender Wilson, "Introduction: Indigenous Knowledge Recovery Is Indigenous Empowerment," *American Indian Quarterly* 28, no. 3 (2004): 359–72; Margaret Elizabeth Kovach, *Indigenous Methodologies: Characteristics, Conversations, and Contexts* (Toronto: University of Toronto Press, 2010); Aileen Moreton-Robinson, "Whiteness, Epistemology and Indigenous Representation," in *Whitening Race: Essays in Social and Cultural Criticism* (Canberra: Aboriginal Studies Press, 2004), 1; Jodi A. Byrd, *The Transit of Empire: Indigenous Critiques of Colonialism* (Minneapolis: University of Minnesota Press, 2011); Carrie A. Martell and Sarah Deer, "Heeding the Voice of Native Women: Toward an Ethic of Decolonization," *North Dakota Law Review* 81 (2005); Walter D. Mignolo, "The Zapatistas's Theoretical Revolution: Its Historical, Ethical, and Political Consequences," *Review* (Fernand Braudel Center) 25, no. 3 (2002): 245–75; Alfred Taiaiake, "Colonialism and State Dependency," *Journal De La Santé Autochtone* 5, no. 2 (November 2009): 42–60; Alfred Taiaiake and Jeff Corntassel, "Being Indigenous: Resurgences against Contemporary Colonialism," *Government and Opposition* 40, no. 4 (2005): 597–614; Lester-Irabinna Rigney, "Internationalization of an Indigenous Anticolonial Cultural Critique of Research Methodologies: A Guide to Indigenist Research Methodology and Its Principles," *Wicazo Sa Review* 14, no. 2 (1999): 109–21; Andrew Woolford, "Ontological Destruction: Genocide and Canadian Aboriginal Peoples," *Genocide Studies and Prevention* 4, no. 1 (2009): 81–97; David Welchman Gegeo, "Cultural Rupture and Indigeneity: The Challenge of (Re)visioning 'Place' in the Pacific," special issue, *Contemporary Pacific* 13, no. 2 (2001): 491–507.

4. Andrea Smith, "Boarding School Abuses, Human Rights, and Reparations," *Social Justice* 31, no. 4 (2004): 89–102; Lindsay Glauner, "The Need for Accountability and Reparations: 1830–1976 the United States Government's Role in the Promotion, Implementation, and Execution of the Crime of Genocide against Native Americans," *DePaul Law Review* 51, no. 3 (2001): 911–61; Joseph P. Gone, "Redressing First Nations Historical Trauma: Theorizing Mechanisms for Indigenous Culture as Mental Health Treatment," *Transcultural Psychiatry* 50, no. 5 (2013): 683–706; Andrea Anne Curcio, "Civil Claims for Uncivilized Acts: Filing Suit against the Government for American Indian Boarding School Abuses," *Hastings Race & Poverty Law Journal* 4

(2006): 45; Lorie M. Graham, "Reparations, Self-Determination, and the Seventh Generation," *Harvard Human Rights Journal* 21 (2008): 47.

5. See Jacqueline Fear-Segal, *White Man's Club: Schools, Race, and the Struggle of Indian Acculturation* (Lincoln: University of Nebraska Press, 2007); Susan Rose and Manuel Saralegui, *The Lost Ones: Long Journey Home* (42 minutes; documentary film on Lipan Apache children sent to the Carlisle Indian School, 2009); Enrique Gilbert-Michael Maestas and Daniel Castro Romero Jr., *Anthropological Report on the Cúelcahén Ndé: Lipan Apache of Texas*, 2004, http://www.utexas.edu/law/centers/humanrights/borderwall/communities /indigenous-Anthropological-Report-on-the-Cuelcahen-Nde-Lipan-Apaches -of-Texas.pdf.

6. For more information on the Texas-Mexican border wall, see Margo Tamez, "The Texas-Mexico Border Wall and Ndé Memory," in *Beyond Walls and Cages: Prisons, Borders, and Global Crisis*, ed. Jenna M. Loyd, Matt Mitchelson, and Andrew Burridge (Athens: University of Georgia Press, 2012); "Plans for a Texas/Mexico Border Wall," Texas Law, The Texas-Mexico Border Wall, Rapoport Center, http://www.utexas.edu/law/centers/humanrights/border wall/; "Tamez Family," Texas Law, The Texas-Mexico Border Wall, Rapoport Center, http://www.utexas.edu/law/centers/humanrights/borderwall /communities/tamez-family.html.

7. Kevin Daniel Annett, *Hidden No Longer: Genocide in Canada, Past and Present* (International Tribunal into Crimes of Church and State and the Friends and Relatives of the Disappeared, 2010); Zia Akhtar, "Canadian Genocide and Official Culpability," *International Criminal Literature Review* 10, no. 1 (2010): 111–35; Alexander S. Dawson, "Histories and Memories of the Indian Boarding Schools in Mexico, Canada, and the United States," in *Latin American Perspectives* 39, no. 5 (September 2012): 80–99; Julie Cassidy, "Canadian Response to Aboriginal Residential Schools: Lessons for Australia and the United States," *eLaw Journal* 16, no. 2 (2009); Kim Stanton, "Canada's Truth and Reconciliation Commission: Settling the Past?," *International Indigenous Policy Journal* 2, no. 3 (2011); Matt James, "A Carnival of Truth? Knowledge, Ignorance and the Canadian Truth and Reconciliation Commission," *International Journal of Transitional Justice* 6, no. 2 (2012): 182–204.

8. Robbie Ethridge, "The Formation of a Colonial Shatter Zone," in *Routledge Handbook of World-Systems Analysis*, ed. Salvatore Babones and Christopher Chase-Dunn (London: Routledge, 2012); Robbie Franklyn Ethridge and Sheri Marie Shuck-Hall, eds. *Mapping the Mississippian Shatter Zone: The Colonial Indian Slave Trade and Regional Instability in the American South* (Lincoln: University of Nebraska Press, 2009).

9. Ned Blackhawk, *Violence over the Land: Indians and Empires in the Early American West* (Cambridge MA: Harvard University Press, 2009); Carl J. Ekberg, *Stealing Indian Women: Native Slavery in the Illinois Country* (Urbana: University of Illinois Press, 2007); Paul Kelton, *Epidemics and Enslavement: Biological Catastrophe in the Native Southeast, 1492–1715* (Lincoln: University of Nebraska Press, 2007).

10. Tamez, "Texas-Mexico Border Wall," 57–73; Margo Tamez, "Returning Lipan Apache Women's Laws, Lands, and Power in El Calaboz Rancheria, Texas-Mexico Border" (PhD diss., Washington State University, 2010).

11. J-A Mbembe and Libby Meintjes, "Necropolitics," *Public Culture* 15, no. 1 (2003): 11–40, 11.

12. Mbembe and Meintjes, "Necropolitics," 12.

13. Fear-Segal, *White Man's Club*, 255–82.

14. Hannah Arendt, *The Origins of Totalitarianism* (New York: Harvest, 1966), 444, as quoted in Mbembe and Meintjes, "Necropolitics," 12.

15. Rose and Saralegui, *Lost Ones*.

16. Smith, "Soul Wound."

17. Sammy Toineeta, as quoted in Smith, "Soul Wound."

18. Indigenous Foundations, "The Residential School System," University of British Columbia, http://indigenousfoundations.arts.ubc.ca/home/government -policy/the-residential-school-system.html.

19. Kim Anderson, *A Recognition of Being: Reconstructing Native Womanhood* (Toronto: Canadian Scholars' Press, 2000), 25.

20. Ann Florini, ed., *The Right to Know: Transparency for an Open World* (New York: Columbia University Press, 2007); Alexandra Barahona De Brito, Carmen González Enríquez, and Paloma Aguilar, eds., *The Politics of Memory and Democratization: Transitional Justice in Democratizing Societies* (Oxford: Oxford University Press, 2001).

21. See chapter 11 in this collection, "The Lost Ones: Piecing Together the Story," by Jacqueline Fear-Segal.

22. Translation of Nanta'án: "Head man; clan head; clan spokesperson; chief spokesperson; of a chiefly line; highly revered male person."

23. Translation of yásitíń: "Leader of the people."

24. Daniel Castro Romero Jr. telephonic oral history lesson, September 15, 2013.

25. For an account of these children's lives, see chapter 11, "The Lost Ones."

26. Eduardo González Cueva, "Where Are Truth Commissions Headed?," in *Transitional Justice: Handbook for Latin America*, ed. Félix Reátegui, Brazilian Ministry of Justice Amnesty Commission (Brasília: Brazilian Ministry of Justice Amnesty Commission, 2011), 328.

27. Cueva, "Where Are Truth Commissions Headed?," 328.

28. Margo Tamez, "Ndé Woman to Be Trained in Truth Commission," Lipan Apache Women Defense, http://lipancommunitydefense.wordpress .com/2012/09/07/nde-woman-to-be-trained-in-truth-commission/.

29. Félix Reátegui, "The Victims Remember: Notes on the Social Practice of Memory," in Reátegui, *Transitional Justice*, 333.

30. S. James Anaya, *Indigenous Peoples in International Law* (Oxford: Oxford University Press, 2004), 3.

31. United Nations, "United Nations Declaration on the Rights of Indigenous Peoples," resolution adopted September 13, 2007, http://www.un.org/esa /socdev/unpfii/documents/DRIPS_en.pdf. Self-determination is a fundamental right that indigenous peoples assert is inherent and inextinguishable; according to S. James Anaya, self-determination is applicable to all human beings, not just states or certain privileged groups, and is enshrined in international human rights legal principles. See S. James Anaya, "International Law and Indigenous Peoples: Historical Stands and Contemporary Developments," in "A Wave of Change: The United Nations and Indigenous Peoples," special issue, CSQ 18, no. 1 (Spring 1994), https://www.culturalsurvival.org /ourpublications/csq/article/international-law-and-indigenous-peoples -historical-stands-and-contempor. "Indigenous peoples are themselves largely responsible for the mobilization of the international human rights program in their favor. During the 1970s, indigenous groups organized and extended their efforts internationally to secure legal protection for their continued survival as distinct communities with historically based cultures, political institutions, and entitlements to land. In appeals to the international community, indigenous groups and supportive international non-governmental organizations (NGOs) linked their concerns with general human rights principles such as self-determination and nondiscrimination."

32. Truth and Reconciliation Commission of Canada, http://www.trc.ca/web sites/trcinstitution/index.php?p=3. See also Jeff Corntassel and Cindy Holder, "Who's Sorry Now? Government Apologies, Truth Commissions, and Indigenous Self-Determination in Australia, Canada, Guatemala, and Peru," *Human Rights Review* 9, no. 4 (2008): 465–89; Deena Rymhs, "Appropriating Guilt: Reconciliation in an Aboriginal Canadian Context," *English Studies in Canada* 32, no. 1 (2006): 105–23.

33. Harry Hoijer, "The History and Customs of the Lipan, as Told by Augustina Zuazua," *Linguistics* 13, no. 161 (1975): 28.

13

Sacred Journey

Restoring My Plains Indian Tipi

CAROLYN RITTENHOUSE (LAKOTA)

Editors' note: Carolyn Rittenhouse's story of being sent away as part of the Mormon Church's Indian Children Placement Program and the loss of her Lakota heritage evokes and repeats the experiences of children who attended the Carlisle Indian School a century earlier. Carolyn lives in the vicinity of Carlisle, Pennsylvania. Her connections to the Indian School, particularly her contributions to the memorial powwow held in 2000 to remember the students and the display and discussion of her tipi at the Carlisle Symposium in 2012, helped her chart her personal journey to reclaim her own heritage. Her story is one of strength, resilience, and repossession.

Although I was born in 1967 and my childhood years were lived in the final quarter of the twentieth century, I too was subjected to an educational program whose goals were in line with the Carlisle Indian School's and with Richard Henry Pratt's motto: "Kill the Indian and Save the Man." At the age of eight I was sent away from my home on the Cheyenne River Sioux Reservation in South Dakota to be fostered by a white Mormon family. I stayed with them until I graduated from the program in 1985. I spent my school years in Idaho and my summers on the reservation. My foster home experience was part of the Church of Jesus Christ of Latter-day Saints' (LDS) Indian Student Placement Program. This program, which operated from 1947 until about 2000, was designed to persuade me, and other Native students enrolled in it, not only to forget our Native languages and traditions but also to become assimilated into mainstream America. I grew up knowing I was Lakota, but because I was far from home, no one was there to teach me my own traditions.

The LDS program achieved a partial success. Upon graduation from high school I attended Brigham Young University, where I met my now Mormon husband. I moved to Pennsylvania, attended a local business school, and found a job in mainstream society. We later married and decided to

Fig. 24. Carolyn Rittenhouse's restored Lakota tipi at the Carlisle Symposium, 2012.
Photo by Waidner-Spahr Library staff, Dickinson College.

raise a family together in the East. Soon after settling into my new life, I
began to meet people who had never met a Native American before and
often asked me, "What is it like to be Indian?" Or they made statements
like, "You must be so proud of your culture and heritage." Comments such
as these conflicted with my experiences. Being an Indian was the very
reason why I had to leave my family and participate in the placement program, in order to become something I could be proud of. I had graduated
from the program and was considered a success, but at the same time I felt
empty and alone. I was aware of my loss, and this only intensified after I
had my own children. I wanted my children to know their Native culture
and heritage, so I began to research and learn more about my own Lakota
history. At the same time, my parents and relatives on the reservation
went to alcohol treatment and participated in the Red Road Approach, a
program developed and facilitated by a Lakota psychologist, Gene Thin

Elk.[1] This program reintroduced Lakota teachings and culture as a major part of the recovery process. My aunts and uncles from my mother's side had also participated in the LDS placement program and soon after had their own struggles with identity and life on the reservation. The temporary relief of alcohol from the all-too-real effects of poverty and oppression had taken its toll on my family. In 1987 this greatly affected my decision to leave the reservation and move to Pennsylvania. However, the Red Road Approach was integral to my family's healing and reclamation of a Native identity and culture. They included me by sending articles, books, and Lakota music and often called to share their experiences. I strongly felt that it was the regaining of identity and culture that contributed to their healing and ability to remain in recovery.

In 1991 my family and I traveled to the reservation for a Lakota naming ceremony planned by my parents. It was at this time that I experienced my first *inipi* (purification ceremony) and attended a *wi wayang wacipi* (Sun Dance ceremony). Christian religions as I had experienced them taught that traditional ceremonies and rituals were ways of the devil. I wanted to experience and decide for myself. My first experiences were overwhelming, and as I sat with the female Sun Dancers in the sweat lodge, I was immediately filled with peace and joy. Listening to their prayers and soft voices sing the *inipi* songs was calming and healing to my soul, and I cried. My emotions were many, and I wondered how something so beautiful and healing for me, these women, and the others could be misconstrued as evil? I had a lot to think about. I thanked God/Creator for these women including my mother and aunts. I was grateful for how they nurtured and showed me another way to connect with Wakan Tanka (Great Spirit). Shortly after the naming ceremony I had two very special experiences. First, my parents asked for a *hunkapi* (Making of a Relative) ceremony for me and my siblings. This ceremony is described by Black Elk: "In this rite we establish a relationship on earth, which is a reflection of that real relationship which always exists between man and *Wakan-Tanka* (Divine or Great Spirit). As we always love *Wakan-Takan* first, and before all else, so we should also love and establish closer relationships with our fellow men."[2] I received a new relative that day, my *Ina* (mother) Shelley, a *hunka* relative. She became a second mother to me and has supported and guided me over the years. After the *hunkapi*, an elder man approached and spoke to me in Lakota. I could not understand everything he was saying, but I understood "*takoja*" (grandchild) and "Hwo Waste Winyan" (Good Voice Woman). He then said in English, "Granddaughter, Good Voice Woman, you live a long ways from home now, tell the people who we are, tell them we are still here." These words have stayed with me and continue to resonate within. I was glad that my one-year-old daughter was there to experience the events with me. I hoped that one day she would recognize the feelings shared and want to know more too. She was happy being passed back and forth between relatives, who commented on her bright blue eyes.

We returned to Pennsylvania, and it took me several months to process my experiences. I felt renewed and strengthened and wanted to know more about my Lakota traditions. I looked forward to going home to the reservation every summer to experience these ceremonies. I read many books over the years on Native American history and Lakota culture. At times I had to stop reading because I was often overwhelmed with emotion; I was enraged at the treatment of Native Americans as a result of colonization, and I was saddened that I had been robbed of my language and culture. I was disenchanted that I had to leave my family at such a young age in order for me to get a "better education." I thought to myself, I could never send my children away. I took frequent breaks from my reading to pray. I prayed for the strength to forgive so that I could let go of the anger and frustration; it was something I learned how to do at an early age. I called home to the reservation many times to talk to family who cried with me. The light in all of this was discovering a beautiful culture that respected all living things and all creations. I was thankful that my Lakota ancestors were survivors who fought to preserve a cultural way of life. I knew I could go on because I was a part of them. Their strength and resilience flowed through my veins. I began to heal myself by learning more about the Lakota values and teachings. I found beauty and solace within the teachings, and I worked to incorporate them into my life and my children's lives. An elderly Lakota man was able to see into my future, when I could not. He knew that sharing my culture with others around me was an important work of healing that needed to be done. I now understand what he was saying because it has become a major part of my life's mission.

In 2000 I was invited to be on a planning committee for a first and one-time event: a Native American commemorative powwow to be held on the U.S. Army War College Barracks in Carlisle, Pennsylvania, the former grounds of the Carlisle Indian Industrial School (CIS), which operated from 1879 to 1918. I wanted to be a part of the event to ensure that these Native children were honored and remembered in a special and sacred way. I learned there were approximately 1,100 Sioux children who had attended the boarding school, and among them were many children from Cheyenne River. I recognized last names and a distant relative, Thomas Benjamin Hawk Eagle, who had played on the 1914 Carlisle football team. I wanted to learn more about the history of the Carlisle Sioux children and my connection to them and the Oyate (people).

I learned that "the proper name for the Sioux is Oceti Sakowin or Seven Council Fires."[3] Each of the council fires was made up of individual bands, based on kinship dialect and geographic proximity. Sharing a common fire is one thing that has always united the Sioux people. Keeping of the *peta wakan* (sacred fire) was important, and coals from a previous council fire were carefully preserved and used to rekindle the council fire at the new campsite. I learned that I am Mniconjou and Itazipco/Sans Arc. As I learned more about my cultural heritage, I shared it with my children, who often attended the CIS powwow planning meetings with me and often asked questions about Native American culture.

They also visited the school cemetery with me, and we found it difficult to walk among the graves. There were Sioux children who died while at the boarding school and never made it home. My children and I prayed for them. On the way home my daughter asked if she could jingle dress dance at the May 2000 powwow. The jingle dress comes from the Ojibwe Nation and is known as a healing dress.[4] My daughter wanted to dance and pray for all the Native children of Carlisle. Wearing her jingle dress, she was selected to be on the cover of the May 2000 edition of the *Central PA Magazine* that featured an article on the powwow. The powwow brought many descendants to Carlisle, and to witness my daughter embrace her Native culture as she proudly danced and prayed that day was incredible—a healing experience for me. A shadow had been cast over my cultural and traditional way of life. Over time I developed a strong desire to step outside this shadowy past in order to regain an identity and feel a sense of belonging to my people. My Plains Indian Tipi Project became both the expression and realization of this desire.

The project began when I was on a visit home to the Cheyenne River in 2010. That summer I asked my stepdad, "Why don't we have our own family tipi set up?" He often used to set up his tipi, but for ceremonial gatherings only. I was asking more questions about the tipi's origin and its connection to Lakota culture and history when he said, "Come here." I followed him to a rusted, broken-down car. He opened the trunk and revealed a haphazardly folded heap of canvas. When pulled onto the ground and unfolded, it slowly began to take the shape of a tipi; dirty and weather worn, but definitely a tipi. He said, "This is yours, my girl, if you want it. It's pretty big though. Take it and do what you want with it." He wasn't kidding when he said it was big. I didn't measure it then or quite yet fathom its size or weight. Instead, I focused on two small holes: evidence of country mice. He folded it up and put it into the luggage carrier fastened to the top of my minivan. I felt honored by this gift. I hadn't yet realized its significance, nor did I expect it to take me on the cultural odyssey that it did. The experiences of this project became a part of a sacred journey that had begun decades before, at my naming ceremony.

Back in Pennsylvania, I stored the tipi in my garage, where it stayed for a year. I wasn't sure what I was going to do with it, and I was totally overwhelmed at the thought of where to begin. It was a twenty-foot-high tipi. I had never raised a tipi nor even learned how, since I had lived a large part of my life off the reservation and out of contact with Lakota culture. I knew that traditionally women owned and cared for the family tipi or lodge, and it bothered me that I didn't know much about it, apart from it being a dwelling of the "nomadic" Plains Indians long ago. Very gradually, I arrived at the decision to restore and bring new life to my stepdad's tipi. I decided that for my anthropology senior project at Millersville University I would focus on the tipi. I knew it was going to be a huge endeavor, but I decided I was going to learn all I could about the tipi's cultural significance. And if I was going to do this research, then I was also going to paint the tipi and go all the way.

In the summer of 2011 I returned to Cheyenne River to find out as much information as I could about the tipi's place in Lakota culture and history. I wanted to research the stories and find my connections to them.

I planned to interview people on the reservation who were willing to share their knowledge. That summer marked the beginning of an experience that was integral to my spiritual journey "home." After the cultural dislocations of my childhood fostering, I was now ready to discover personal stories of familial and cultural history, so that these could provide the grounding for the tipi's artwork and design.

I arrived at Cheyenne River the same weekend that a local Isnati Awicalowanapi (Becoming a Woman) ceremony was held. It was perfect timing. Black Elk described this ceremony as "a rite performed after the first menstrual period of a young woman who must understand the meaning of this change and must be instructed in the duties that she is to fulfill. She is like Ina Maka (Mother Earth) and will be able to bear children, which should be brought up in a sacred manner."[5]

This ceremony prepares girls to take their place within the community as women and for bearing their own children some day. I was elated because part of the ceremony required the girls to learn how to set up and take down their own tipi, which is where they slept during the four-day ceremony. The ceremony leaders and young women participants agreed to let me interview them.

Prior to my interviews I learned from a book that "the nomadic dwelling structure of the American Indian is called different names by many different tribes. The Crow Nation calls the tipi *ashe* (home), the Blackfoot call it *niitoy-yiss* (the tipi), and the Lakota call it *tipestola* (tipis). In the last 175 years, the tipi has evolved in materials used, construction techniques, and usage. It has changed from buffalo and elk hides to synthetic materials of the twenty-first century."[6] My canvas tipi weighs nearly eighty pounds, and I could not imagine how heavy a hide cover with the same dimensions would be. In speaking with the leaders of the Isnati Awicalowanpi, my *hunka ina* (mom) and *unci* (grandma), I learned that they and the girls had painted four canvas tipis for the ceremony, which completed a *dream or vision* for one of the women's daughters.

Over the four-day ceremony, the girls were taught by older female relatives about their transition to their new roles as Lakota women and their responsibilities in relation to the Lakota spiritual values and motherhood. These values are *woc'ekiya* (praying), *wa o'hola* (respect), *wa on'sila* (caring), *wowijake* (honesty), *wacantognka* (generosity), *wah'wala* (humility), *woksape* (wisdom), *wowacintnka* (fortitude), and *woohitika* (bravery).[7] I interviewed three young women who had participated in the ceremony. They said it had been emphasized to them that in becoming a woman, they should act like one. They must treat themselves with respect and no longer sit cross-legged but instead sit with their legs to the side. Their dress should be modest, and they should always be aware of the messages they send to men and others by their dress. They learned that women are born with natural healing and nurturing ways. Women in America and in other countries are often oppressed and thought of as important for mainly reproductive purposes. We discussed how mainstream media sexualizes women, and how they are often thought of as incapable of making sound decisions. This idea was evident in early America, and "although Europeans first associated the Americas with the Indian women, they understood very little about Indian cultures and the importance of the women within these societies . . . their texts focused on Indian men in their public and formal roles—as chiefs, warriors, medicine men, and diplomats. But Indian women played equally important roles in the determination and survival of their people."[8] To hear that Lakota women are esteemed with respect and honor was very beautiful and intriguing to me. This concept relates to a sacredness special to women, which is why the Isnati Awicalowanpi is one of the seven sacred rites of the Lakota. I thought, this is how it should be for all women. These young women understood that they were sacred because of their role in the life-giving process. They were taught that motherhood and responsibility go hand in hand. One girl said, "Just as Ina Maka (Mother Earth) provides everything for us, we will provide everything for our children." They shared with me what they had learned about the tipi's origin. From Larry and Mark Belitz's book, *The Buffalo Hide Tipi of the Sioux*, I learned more about one of the tipi's origin stories: "a child took a cottonwood leaf and curled it to fashion a miniature wigwam. The shape of the leaf resembled a half circle, which led to the assembling of hides in a half circle that was placed around tipi poles."[9] Another story was from a Lakota male who said, "When children run to their *inas* or *uncis*, they are embraced and wrapped within the warmth of the women's shawl or blanket. The tipi is like the woman who lovingly embraces her children and family, providing warmth and shelter."[10] In all Plains Indian tribes, it is the women who owned and cared for the family lodge. The young women showed me how to set up and take down one of the sixteen-foot tipis they had painted and slept in days before. Upon completion of the Isnati Awicalowanpi ceremony, each girl became a "100 Horse Woman." They are now members of a women's society, the 100 Horses Society on Cheyenne River. It is important that they know their worth, which in our culture—where horses are seen as a measure of wealth—is seen as being the value of one hundred horses and more! I was grateful for that experience and for learning about the Isnati Awicalowanpi ceremony that prepares young girls for womanhood.

The Isnati women used fourteen poles; twelve were for the months in a year and two were for the smoke flaps. The number of poles may vary due to weather or the size of the tipi cover. Traditionally there was strict etiquette about how to behave inside a tipi. The door always faced east, toward the Wanagi (spirit world) and the rising sun, and

to enter, one had to be invited to come in. If the cover flap or door *tiyopa* was thrown aside, anyone was permitted to enter and even eat food from the fireplace. The Sioux said, "The chief's door is always open." Generosity was an important Lakota value. If smoke flaps were closed and door was closed, the owners were gone. If the smoke flaps were open and the door cover was closed, a visitor must let his presence be known by coughing by the door, scratch on the cover or shake the buffalo hoof rattle used by some tipi owners. If those inside didn't want to entertain, the request to enter was ignored. Women sat on the left side (south) because of the high sun, which is warm and nurturing and identified as feminine. The north side is associated with winter's challenges, demanding fortitude, and is identified as masculine.[11]

Today, the etiquette varies among different families and nations. The *tipestola* is no longer used for permanent housing but mainly for camping. They are often set up at *wacipis* (powwows) or different traditional ceremonial gatherings throughout Indian country.

My research consisted of interviews of several tribal members and cultural leaders on the Cheyenne River Reservation and a curator at the Smithsonian Institute Museum of the American Indian. I visited the Journey Museum and the Crazy Horse Monument in Rapid City, South Dakota, and the Cumberland Country Historical Society in Carlisle, Pennsylvania, to view ledger art and pictograph drawings from students of the Carlisle Indian Industrial School, and I read several books on tipis. Themes began to unfold that I wanted to represent in the artwork on the tipi that I had been given: historical, cultural, and familial themes. I wanted my tipi to give voice to and honor a forgotten people. I wanted the artwork to educate and reflect not only a historical tragedy but a victory of a people who fought to survive and preserve a cultural way of life. My ancestors' struggles were not in vain. I am here because of them. In some small way I wanted to honor my people and my family. I chose the following subjects: the Battle of Little Big Horn, 1876; the Buffalo Calf Woman Brings Sacred Pipe; and the Massacre at Wounded Knee, 1890.

Battle of Little Big Horn, 1876

On the wall of the airport in Rapid City, South Dakota, was a huge mural of photographs taken by photographer Bill Groethe during the September 2, 1948, Little Bighorn reunion. Pictured were the last eight surviving warrior chiefs of the 1876 Battle of Little Bighorn: Black Elk, Little Warrior, Pemmican, Little Soldier, Dewey Beard, John Sitting Bull, High Eagle, Iron Hawk, and Comes Again. The black-and-white photos portrayed aged men in full headdresses of eagle feathers, also called war bonnets. They wore fringed buckskins and moccasins. I was immediately filled with a sense of pride and wonderment. These men had been part of the greatest victory of the Plains tribes when they went head to head with the U.S. military in Montana. Then I noticed Chief Iron Hawk, who was one of the chiefs who fought in that great battle with Crazy Horse, Gall, Sitting Bull, and High Eagle (to name a few). I knew of an Iron Hawk *tiwahe* (family) on Cheyenne River. My niece, who had been living with my family and me since 2006, had Iron Hawk relatives. We contacted the Iron Hawk *tiwahe* and discovered that my niece is a direct descendant of Iron Hawk on her father's side of the family. We were thrilled to learn this. Suddenly the men in the photos were not so distant; my niece was happy with this newfound familial connection. We were intrigued and wanted to learn more, so we visited Sylvan Lake, the location where the 1948 Little Bighorn reunion had been held. It was beautiful, and we wondered if we were where these great leaders had once walked. While there, we purchased a book on Native American history, and my niece opened to a picture of Iron Hawk. With a big smile she said, "Look, that's my great-great grandfather!" At Crazy Horse Monument, we learned more about the great battle. And just like the sculptor, Korczak Ziolkowski, who dedicated his life to honoring Tasunka Witko (Crazy Horse), I too was enamored. These warrior men exemplified characteristics of intelligence, strength, bravery, fortitude, and a determination to fight to preserve a cultural way of life. I was proud to know that I come from a people of great men who strived to uphold traditional Lakota values of honesty, generosity, wisdom, and integrity in their everyday lives. Black Elk, a warrior and holy man of the Oglalas, was present at the Battle of Little Big Horn. He was a distant cousin of Crazy Horse and in *Black Elk Speaks* shared his experiences of the battle. These stories will not be forgotten—they are included in the ongoing design on the tipi liner.

The stars in the blue sky on the cover and smoke flaps of my tipi represent the *wanagi* (spirit world), specifically, remembering the spirits of Wakinyan Maza Tiospaye (Iron Lightning Clan) relatives who have passed on and impacted my life in a good way. We remember our ancestors and ask for their prayers and protection. An *unci* once told me, "Our ancestors are like our guardian angels," and I never forgot that. Because of that, I may have felt lonely, but I never truly felt alone. William K. Powers stated, "When a person loses *ni* (life or breath), his body dies but his *nagi* lingers on. It is believed that the *wanagi* after death grieves for its loved ones. *Wanagi Yuhapi* (ghost keeping) is accomplished by feeding the *wanagi* and after one year, they are fed for the last time, then depart to the south along the *wanagi tacanku* (ghost road), i.e., Milky Way."[12] In 2006, one year after my beloved sister passed away, my parents held a memorial dinner and giveaway. Traditionally, families mourned their loved ones for a year and went through a great sacrifice. They often cut off their hair and "gave all of their personal belongings to a needy person in memory of the deceased."[13] Today, usually held after burial services, although it is a hardship, a family will hold a giveaway in memory of the deceased by giving away material goods to close friends of the deceased as well as the community. It is also a way for families to say *pilamaya* (thank you) for mourning their loved one with them. The stars at the top of the tipi memorialize my deceased grandparents, aunts, uncles, cousins, and the largest star in the center has a twofold significance: it represents the morning star and honors my beloved sister, my niece's mother.

Buffalo Calf Woman Brings Sacred Pipe

Black Elk, a Lakota holy man, wanted to preserve the Siouan rites for his people. In "The Sacred Pipe" he tells how the sacred pipe came to the people. The Buffalo Calf Woman is included in the design of the tipi because she brought the *cannumpa* (sacred pipe), spiritual teachings, and sacred values to the Lakota Sioux people during a time of famine and hardship. She promised that if the people followed these teachings, Tunkasila (Creator) would bless them and replenish the earth with the buffalo. She brought spiritual and healing principles that were taught for the use of the *cannumpa*. When she left the people, she turned into a buffalo and changed into four colors, black, yellow, red, and finally white.[14] These colors are represented in the eyes of the four buffalo painted on the cover of the tipi. Buffalo Calf Woman is a symbol of hope and healing for the people, and in her hands she holds eagle feathers and the sacred *cannumpa*. However, as Rayna Green explains,

> after the government banned ceremonies, women's roles in the ritual life of their community were forever changed (as were men's roles too). Women who had once been central to their tribe's rituals experienced a diminution in social status. In Sioux society, women could no longer sponsor the Sun Dance or a vision quest. Female and male elders, once respected in traditional culture for their wisdom and guidance, found themselves held in low esteem by those of a European worldview. The medicines and ceremonial skills that women knew so well were reviled as quirks of savagery.[15]

The Buffalo Calf Woman on the tipi "reminds us of her sacred character that Lakota women are to emulate if they are to live a good and sacred life."[16] When I first read *Walking in a Sacred Manner* by Mark St. Pierre and Tilda Long Soldier, I immediately recalled memories of my *uncis* and how blessed I was to have known them. One time, when I was seven years old, my family and I visited my great-grandmother Wakinyan Maza (Iron Lightning) in a nursing home off the reservation. She sat in a wheelchair while I brushed and braided a purple ribbon into her long gray hair. She smiled and hummed a familiar melody. I sat close and leaned up against her, and in Lakota, she sang a lullaby in a soft high-pitched tone. I was quiet and listened and felt her unconditional love. It is for this reason that I honor Buffalo Calf Woman, for bringing hope to the people through her teachings and values. It is her goodness and sacred manner that the *uncis* and *winyans* (women) in my life strive to follow. I am grateful for their love and the good examples they are for me.

Massacre at Wounded Knee, 1890

My tipi's lower border shows silhouettes whose meaning is twofold: first, to honor all female ancestors for their roles in helping the culture and people survive, and second, to honor those who died on December 29, 1890, at Wounded Knee. I had visited the mass gravesite before. It was tragic to learn how my Minnecoujou ancestors died that day over one hundred years ago. It was difficult to read Dee Brown's account of the assassination of a great leader, Sitting Bull, and the Ghost Dance, a religious uprising with prophesies that scared local settlers and led to that fateful day in December—"In the Moon When the Deer Shed Their Horns."[17] It was difficult to look at the old black-and-white photos that captured the aftermath of the massacre of *Si Tanka* and his people. It was even more challenging to read Black Elk describe "the butchering at Wounded Knee."[18]

Prior to our trip to Wounded Knee, I picked up my family history from the tribal office and discovered that I am a direct descendant of Minnecoujou chief Si Tanka. Was it really true? Yes, we were related through my maternal grandmother's side of the family. We went to Wounded Knee, and this time the experience was different. Si Tanka was my great-great grandfather, so I had a kinship connection. His relatives were mine too, and I was deeply affected and mourned the tragic deaths of my Minnecoujou ancestors. Their names were no longer just names of people long ago. I envisioned familiar faces during a frightening time. Of the 333 of Si Tanka's band who died on December 1890, only 120 were men; the rest were women and children. In the back center of the tipi's border, I painted a silhouette of the monument that stands as a memorial next to the mass gravesite at Wounded Knee. This monument bears only some of the names of those who died. On the tipi border, I wrote by hand all the names of Chiefs Si Tanka and Bald Head Eagle and their tribal families. This was my way to honor and memorialize them. I have learned that the *oyate* (my people) are resilient and are survivors. I honor their courage and strength. At the request of my parents, I included the words *Tohe Ni Oniktu Ga Kteshi* ("You will not be forgotten, we will remember you").

After I chose the themes and stories to be displayed on the tipi, Dwayne Wilcox, a well-known Lakota ledger artist living in Rapid City, agreed to draw the designs. Dwayne works in the traditional ledger art style that was originally used on tipis and buffalo robes. When confined on reservations, Lakota and other Plains Indian men adapted their representational style of painting to paper, making drawings in account ledger books.[19] Dwayne used this style to draw the figures to represent themes in four- to six-inch illustrations. My challenge was to transfer his drawings onto the tipi and its border. I enlarged and traced the drawings to make them between four and eight feet in height, using an opaque machine. The tipi was laid out on a church gym floor that was available only three days in a week. I used exterior latex paint to color the figures, painting them one day and leaving them to dry for two days. This work took longer than expected, due to the humidity brought in by Hurricanes Irene and Lee. Seventeen poles were delivered to my house in the middle of Hurricane Lee. They are twenty-four feet long and all together weigh 340 pounds. When the storms passed and the cover had dried, the tipi was ready to be raised.

The Plains Indian Tipi project was a big part of my cultural and spiritual journey, but it was an educational endeavor as well. In November 2011, my tipi was displayed for the first time at Millersville University. In conjunction with this event the Deer Chaser Lakota Dance Troupe performed for students as part of the university events planned for American Indian Heritage month. In March 2012 I displayed and presented on the tipi at the Pennsylvania National Association for Multicultural Education Conference, hosted by Millersville University. In October 2012 I again displayed the tipi, this time at the Waidner Library of Dickinson College, where I told my story to delegates attending the Carlisle Symposium.

Having the opportunity to educate others on the lives, sacred sites, and traditions of Native peoples has been healing and a wonderful journey for me. On this journey I learned that I am a survivor, and I have embraced all of who I am. I embrace my Lakota culture so that my ancestors' struggles were not in vain. I do not intend to continue this journey alone. I embrace all people *mitakuye oyasin* (all my relations); all who want to learn and share in Native culture. This is necessary for healing. Black Elk cried to the Heavens recalling a vision sent from Wakan Tanka: "Today, I send a voice for a people in despair . . . at the center of this sacred hoop you have said that I should make the tree to bloom. I am old; it has withered . . . some little root of the sacred tree still lives. Nourish it that it may leaf and bloom and fill with singing birds. Hear me, not for myself, but for my people; hear me that they may once more go back into the sacred hoop and find the good red road, the shielding tree!"[20] I liken Black Elk's words to my own life. My experiences far from family and culture represent the withered tree under a shadow cast over a culture and way of life. I truly appreciate all the good things I learned while living off the reservation; however, it was the regaining of a Native identity and culture that has healed and nourished the little root of the sacred tree inside not only me but also my Lakota *tiwahe* as well. All of my experiences both on and off the reservation have fostered and guided me along a spiritual journey and have taken me "home" to the center of the sacred hoop.

NOTES

1. Gene Thin Elk, "Walking in Balance on the Red Road," *Journal of Emotional and Behavioral Problems* 2, no. 3 (Fall 1993): 54–57, https://reclaimingjournal .com/sites/default/files/journal-article-pdfs/02_3_Thin_Elk.pdf.
2. Joseph E. Brown, *The Sacred Pipe: Black Elk's Account of the Seven Rites of the Oglala Sioux* (Norman: University of Oklahoma, 1989), 101.
3. The Oceti Sakowin Seven Council Fires are Mdewakanton (Dwellers by the Sacred Lake), Wahpekute (Shooters among the Leaves), Sistonwan/Sisseton (People of the Marsh), Wahpetonwan (Dwellers among the Leaves), Ihank-town/Lower Yantonai (People of the End), Ihanktowana/Upper Yanktoni (People of the Little End), and Tetonwan, also spelled Titunwan (People of the Plains). I come from the Titunwan Council Fire. The seven bands of the Titunwan (People of the Plains) or Teton group are Hunkpapa (Camps at the Horn), Sicangu/Brule (Burnt Thigh; Rosebud and Lower Brule Reservations), Itazipco/Sans Arc (Without Bows; Cheyenne River Reservation), Sihasapa (Blackfeet; Cheyenne River and Standing Rock Reservations), Oglala (Scatters His Own; Pine Ridge Reservation), Oohenumpa (Two Kettles; Cheyenne River Reservation), Mniconjou (Planters by the River; Cheyenne River Reser-

vation). From Cheyenne River Sioux Tribe, "Our History," http://www.sioux
.org/index.php/main/inner/sioux/our_history.

4. "Origins of Women's Jingle Dress Dancing," January 28, 2011, http://indian
countrytodaymedianetwork.com/2011/01/28/origins-womens-jingle-dress
-dancing-13653.

5. Brown, *Sacred Pipe*, 116.

6. Linda A. Holley, *Tipis, Tepees, Teepees: History and Design of the Cloth Tipi*
(Layton UT: Gibbs Smith, 2007), 1, 4.

7. Cheyenne River Sioux Tribe, "Our History."

8. Rayna Green, *Women in American Indian Society* (New York: Chelsea House,
1992), 14.

9. Larry Belitz and Mark Belitz, *The Buffalo Hide Tipi of the Sioux* (Sioux Falls
SD: Pine Hill, 2006), 3.

10. Lakota spiritual leader, "Plains Indian Tipi," interview on this topic by the
author, June 2011.

11. Belitz and Belitz, *Buffalo Hide Tipi*, 76.

12. William K. Powers, *Oglala Religion* (Lincoln: University of Nebraska Press,
1977), 53.

13. Royal B. Hassrick, *The Sioux: Life and Customs of a Warrior Society* (Norman: University of Oklahoma Press, 1964), 37.

14. Mark St. Pierre and Tilda Long Soldier, *Walking in the Sacred Manner: Healers, Dreamers, and Pipe Carriers—Medicine Women of the Plains Indians*
(New York: Simon and Schuster, 1995), 38–41.

15. Green, *Women in American Indian Society*, 53–54.

16. St. Pierre and Long Soldier, *Walking in the Sacred Manner*, 42.

17. Dee Brown, *Bury My Heart at Wounded Knee: An Indian History of the
American West* (New York: Holt, Rinehart and Winston, 1989), 439–45, quote
on 439. The Lakota calendar has thirteen moons, and Wanicokan Wi ("Moon
When the Deer Shed Their Horns") is in the winter, usually during December.

18. Black Elk and John G. Neihardt, *Black Elk Speaks: Being the Life Story of a
Holy Man of the Oglala Sioux* (Lincoln: University of Nebraska Press, 1972),
259–68.

19. Ross Frank, "Ledger Art History," Plains Indian Ledger Art Project, University
of California, San Diego, https://plainsledgerart.org/history.

20. Black Elk and Neihardt, *Black Elk Speaks*, 279–80.

14

Carlisle Farmhouse

A Major Site of Memory

CAROLYN TOLMAN

On a forgotten corner of the grounds of the U.S. Army War College, in south central Pennsylvania, an old whitewashed brick farmhouse peeks through towering spruces. Although surrounded by the bustle of a modern army post, it sits peacefully secluded behind mature trees and lawn, overlooking a large spring. Vacant now as it awaits its coming renovation, this farmhouse has a rich and significant past.

The story is told that one day a young Jim Thorpe was walking to a softball game on the Carlisle Indian Industrial School campus, likely coming from his work on the school farm. As he approached the track and field, he noticed that the athletes could not clear the 5′9″ high jump bar. Unhindered by his farm overalls, Thorpe impulsively gave it a try and cleared it with ease. It was on this day that the legendary Pop Warner discovered Carlisle's most famous athlete and future Olympian.[1]

The school farm, from which Jim Thorpe was probably returning, played an integral role in the education and experiences of Carlisle's Indian students. At its heart was a stately brick farmhouse, spacious and inviting, which not only housed the head farmer and his family but also provided an agricultural classroom, sleeping quarters, and a dining room for the student farm laborers.

In 1918 the Indian School was closed, and eventually modern army garrison buildings were constructed on the farmlands. But the farmhouse remained and would later provide housing for officers and families from the War College, which has operated on the post since 1951. Until recently its significant connection to the Carlisle Indian School was largely forgotten, and having been allowed to fall into disrepair, the Carlisle Farmhouse was scheduled to be demolished to make room for modern family housing. However, thanks to the following research, and the last-minute

Fig. 25. The School Farmhouse at Carlisle Indian School, c. 1900. Photographer unknown. Cumberland County Historical Society, Carlisle PA. LS-D75.

efforts of many people, that decision was reversed at the Carlisle Symposium in 2012, and plans are now underway to convert the Farmhouse into the Carlisle Heritage Center as a lasting memorial to the Native American students of the Carlisle Indian Industrial School.

Early History

The Farmhouse predates most of the buildings at Carlisle Barracks and was originally a civilian home, outside of garrison boundaries. The original front portion of the house was built during 1853–56, most likely by Daniel B. Keiffer.[2] Its 109-acre farm encompassed all the land now occupied by the northeast quarter of Carlisle Barracks, including the area of the Commissary, the PX, the Chapel, Young Hall, Indian Field, the Strategic Studies Institute, and the Heritage Heights housing development.[3]

The Farmhouse was built in high style, according to the fashions of the time. The center gable with its decorative bargeboard and circular window, as well as the peaked attic windows, are fine examples of the Gothic Revival style, while the bracketed cornice adds an Italianate touch.[4]

Nine-foot ceilings and tall six-by-six windows throughout give it a spacious feel. Formal living and dining rooms, four large bedrooms, a generous basement, and an attic provide plenty of living and storage space. But the crowning feature of this home is the central entry passage, open to the attic, and the original staircase with its mahogany railing spiraling all the way up to the third story.[5]

On March 31, 1860, Daniel Keiffer sold the farm to Richard Parker, a descendant of "one of the first families of Pennsylvania."[6] Richard Parker also owned a house in Carlisle Borough on High Street directly behind the First Presbyterian Church, of which he was a prominent member, like his father before him.[7] With his brother-in-law, William M. Henderson, he owned the Henderson & Parker Milling & Distilling Company from 1837 to1848. They operated the old stone mill, which still stands on the Harrisburg Pike near the Wilson House, both now part of Carlisle Barracks property.[8] William Henderson's mother's first husband was the same Major James A. Wilson who lived in the Wilson House.[9]

Richard Parker had a wife, Hadassah Graham Parker, and three young children: Andrew Henderson Parker; Mary Parker (McKeehan); and Richard McCue Parker.[10] By 1862 he had built a frame tenant house and stables on the property, in addition to the Farmhouse and stone bank barn he had bought from Keiffer.[11] Many years later Mary P. McKeehan visited the Farmhouse and reminisced about her childhood there. She recalled that during the Civil War, when Lt. Gen. Richard S. Ewell's troops invaded Carlisle on June 27, 1863, a party of Confederate soldiers came to the Farmhouse and were fed and sheltered for the night by her mother.[12] The next morning they were called to Gettysburg.

Richard Parker died on March 4, 1864, and is buried at the Meeting House Springs Cemetery in Carlisle.[13] His widow and children moved back into their town house and rented out the farm, sixteen acres of which was used by the Cavalry School at Carlisle Barracks as a drill ground until April 1, 1871.[14] An 1872 map labels the property as "A. Parker, Big Spring" showing that son Andrew had inherited the farm.[15] By 1880,he and his wife, Mary Bishop Hammond Parker, and their infant son, David Hammond Parker, were living in the home with two servants.[16] Between 1880 and 1883 the gross value of the property jumped from $6,240 to $10,300, suggesting that it was during this time that the rear wing was added on to the house.[17]

The Indian School Era

In 1879 the War Department transferred the neighboring deserted army garrison to the Department of the Interior, and Capt. Richard H. Pratt established the Carlisle Indian Industrial School at Carlisle Barracks. His intent was to educate Native American children to be able to function in white society. Pratt wrote: "One of the most important branches of our industrial training at Carlisle is the agricultural. More than half of our boys will eventually find in agriculture their life work. It is healthful, profitable, and the most independent of all industries."[18] As soon as the school was organized, Pratt set out to acquire farmland for training his students. For the year 1880 he rented 10 acres of land adjoining the barracks property. From 1881 to 1883 he rented the entire 109 acres of the Parker farm; then in 1884 he purchased a 157-acre farm three miles away in Middlesex from Benjamin W. Hocker.[19]

By 1886 Pratt found the Hocker farm to be inadequate for the needs of his growing school and too far away to be truly effective in accomplishing his goals. He applied to Congress for funds to purchase the Parker farm:

> I am now able to buy the Parker farm, which bounds our property on the east, and is best adapted for our uses. It can be obtained for $18,000. It naturally drops in as a part of Government property and furnishes an outlet to the public road on two sides, an advantage never before possessed by the Government. It has one of the best and largest springs in the county, and running water along the whole west side. The buildings are a farm house of brick, commodious and well-built, a good stone barn, and a frame tenant house. The property contains 109.57 acres, and is worth the money asked.[20]

The money was granted, and on April 7, 1887, the Parker family sold their farm to the United States for $18,000 to be used by the Carlisle Indian Industrial School.[21] The school continued to use the Hocker farm as well, referring to it as the "lower farm" and the Parker farm as the "upper farm" or "near farm."

By 1892 the school, with the labor of the Indian students, had updated the Farmhouse, torn down the old stone barn, and built a spacious new yellow barn, which included a modern dairy and piggery.[22] In December 1896 a new telephone was installed in the Farmhouse connecting it to the school's administration building.[23] In 1918 the school farmer, James S. Giffen, wrote an article about the farm buildings:

One of the most attractive features of the farm to the pupils is the old-fashioned farm house, which was built some time before the Civil War and was occupied by one of the first families of Pennsylvania. . . .

To the rear of the house at the foot of a gentle slope is a bubbling spring, which rises in the old-fashioned stone spring house and forms a small lake, which does not freeze over in the coldest weather and is stocked with rainbow trout.

The house was planned for commodious hospitality and comfort. The rooms are large and of colonial style, having very high ceilings and a fireplace in nearly every room. A large colonial doorway opens from a wide porch into a hallway through the middle of the house, and from this hallway a winding stair with a mahogany railing extends to the attic. The house after being purchased by the school was slightly remodeled to meet the needs of its present use. It has been electrically lighted, has a steam heating plant, and running water. One room has been equipped as a school room and each day agricultural classes are held for the boys who work on the farm and dairy, covering the subjects of farming and stock raising, horticulture, farm machinery, types and breeds of farm animals, and dairying.

Overlooking the lake formed by the spring is a neat cottage for the dairyman. . . . The pride and joy of every Pennsylvania farmer is his barn, and very few in Cumberland County surpass in size the one at the first farm. The original barn had been made over a number of years ago, and is now of the prevailing style typical of this part of the country. . . . The boys who work on the dairy stay all night at the farm house and get their supper and breakfast, while the boys who work on the farm get their dinners only.[24]

The school's head farmer and his family lived in the Farmhouse and supervised the work of the students, as well as providing meals and beds for those who spent the night. In April 1914 the school newspaper reported that

Fig. 26. Small boys working on the school farm planting onions, c. 1902. Photo by Frances Benjamin Johnston. Cumberland County Historical Society, Carlisle PA. JO-01-14.

students Ed Bresette and Francis Obern were assigned to the first farm.[25] Besides the older boys who labored on the farm, many students loved to walk out to the farm as a fieldtrip or a Sunday afternoon excursion. One young boy wrote: "First we went and took a ride in the boat. It is big enough for us to take three at a time. Then we went down in the cellar and saw how they hatch eggs without a hen. They kept them in a box where it is warm. It is a dark place and they carry a lamp in the cellar, and we came out again to where they kept the little ones when they are hatched out."[26]

As Giffen's article pointed out, the school's head dairyman lived in a cottage overlooking the lake formed by the spring. It is likely that this cottage was the "frame tenant house" that was part of the property the Indian School bought from the Parkers. It is unknown exactly where this house stood, or when (after 1918) it was demolished. However, there does appear to be the roof of a small house down to the left of the Farmhouse in the earliest photos. This would fit with having an "outlook from the west balcony" over the spring pond (as described below).

In 1891 former Indian School student Richard Davis (Cheyenne) returned to the school to serve as its head dairyman. His wife Nannie Aspinall (Pawnee) had also attended the school, and the two had been married in the school chapel in 1888.[27] They now had two daughters, Richenda and Mary.[28] The dairyman's cottage was spruced up in preparation for their arrival. The school newspaper reported on October 9, 1891: "The balustrades on the front porch of Richard Davis' house at the near farm are the same that were built around the Captain's house in 1863"; and on October 23, 1891: "Richard Davis' house at the near farm is receiving its last touch of paint and will soon be ready for occupancy. Richard and Nannie will have a nice little home there. The outlook from the west balcony is beautiful."[29] A third daughter, Esther, was born on June 2, 1892, at their home on the school farm.[30] In November of that year, there was a near-disaster in the little home: "A small fire scare at Richard Davis' house at the near farm on Sunday morning last, created considerable excitement about inspection time. It was Richard's presence of mind that saved the house. The fire started near a lamp, but just how no one knows, for there were no lamps burning at the time. One of the little ones may have been playing with a match near the lamps."[31]

On January 12, 1901, the Indian School bought another farm of 175 acres from Christopher C. Kutz, which bordered the Parker farm on the north, extending out to the Harrisburg Pike and beyond.[32] The Kutz farm featured another farmhouse (no longer standing), a fine orchard, a large barn, and good stables.[33] The Hocker farm was no longer needed and was sold a few months later.[34] The Parker farm was now referred to as the "first farm" and the Kutz farm as the "second farm."[35] Together, the two farms provided enough food to the school to make it virtually self-sustainable.[36]

Post–Indian School Era

On September 1, 1918, with World War I drawing to a close, the War Department reclaimed Carlisle Barracks for use as a rehabilitation hospital for wounded soldiers returning from Europe. The Carlisle Indian Industrial School was closed, and General Hospital Number 31 was immediately opened in its place. The school farms, along with the farmers, were retained to serve the hospital by providing both food and rehabilitation for the soldiers: "The fresh milk and eggs from the farm, as well as fresh meat, did much to restore the convalescents to health. Many of the patients were assigned to duty on the farm and learned practical lessons in agriculture from the ex-instructors of the Indian School."[37]

By 1920 the number of patients had dwindled, so the hospital was closed and replaced by the Medical Field Service School. Again, the farms were maintained at their full capacity. As described by Thomas G. Tousey, "The two farms attached to the reservation grew great fields of wheat, hay and corn, requiring the full time of a detachment of colored soldiers. Proceeds from the sale of these products enriched the mess fund of the troops. The large 'yellow barn' located near the Spring housed a herd of pedigreed cattle, which supplied rich milk for officers' families and enlisted men, and a herd of pigs which furnished the garrison with fresh pork. Fortunate were those who served at the Medical Field Service School during the 'early days'!"[38]

Local tradition holds that during World War II the Farmhouse was used as a social club for segregated African American officers and enlisted soldiers.[39] The 1930 U.S. Census shows eleven "negro" soldiers living in a group on the army post.[40] It is unclear whether they lived in or near the Farmhouse, or even whether they were farmers; however, the 1920 and 1940 census data show no such group at Carlisle Barracks. This suggests that the eleven men were indeed the "detachment of colored soldiers" who worked on the farm full-time in the 1920s and 1930s (gone by World War II), probably socialized at the Farmhouse, and maybe even lived there.

Gradually the farms decreased in importance as the army's need for training space outweighed the demand for agricultural products. The dairy cows were "disposed of" in the early 1930s, and the big yellow barn was destroyed by fire on October 16, 1938. At the same time, the garrison was undergoing a major building program, and more of the farmland was occupied by the familiar buildings still standing on the post today.[41] It was about this time that the Farmhouse ceased to house farmers and became Officers Quarters for Carlisle Barracks.

A plaque that formerly stood near the house stated that it was remodeled in 1943, 1948, and 1981. However, no details are available of the changes it underwent at these times. A few interior elements remain that are likely original, such as the front door with its hardware, sidelights, and stained glass transom window, the staircase and banister, several other interior and exterior doors with hardware, most of the windows, and the stacked fieldstone foundation and hand-hewn floor beams visible in the basement. Although three chimneys remain, all the fireplaces but one have been covered over.

A Fading Memory

Over time the Farmhouse's significant connection to the Indian School was minimized and forgotten. In 1961 the remaining buildings of the Carlisle Indian School were designated a National Landmark. The Farmhouse, however, was overlooked and excluded due to its quarter-mile distance from the main campus. This was in spite of an evaluation declaring it to be "an important part" of the proposed landmark.[42]

In 1985 the Farmhouse was evaluated for placement on the National Historic Register but was rejected due to "unknown historical significance" and "average exterior and interior integrity" due to its several remodelings.[43] According to yet another evaluation in 1996: "The Building is not part of a potential historic district; it is isolated from other historic resources at the installation. As a potential individual property, the building does not convey its association with agriculture, since its barn and attendant agricultural outbuildings were demolished during the twentieth century. . . . The farmhouse does not possess architectural integrity for listing in the National Register of Historic Places."[44]

In 2004, as Carlisle Barracks saw the need to replace outdated family housing, a "Programmatic Agreement" was signed by the Pennsylvania State Historic Preservation Office, Carlisle Barracks, the Cumberland County Historical Society, and the Cheyenne-Arapaho Tribe of Oklahoma, agreeing that all buildings outside of the National Landmark designation were subject to removal if necessary.[45] Since the Farmhouse had been declared insignificant by the previous evaluations, none of these organizations saw any reason to preserve it.

In the fall of 2010 the official decision to raze the Farmhouse was made based on past evaluations and on the outdated condition of the house, which by this time was in sore need of renovation, particularly in its electrical, plumbing, heating, and cooling systems. New duplexes were replacing the 1950s housing in the adjacent College Arms neighborhood, and the large Farmhouse lot was needed for two new homes.[46] The only thing lacking was the necessary funding from Congress to move ahead with the project.

Significance Restored

In the meantime new residents had moved into the Farmhouse and experienced an overwhelming sense of its past importance. When inquiries of its history were met with insufficient answers, new research was conducted by this author and posted online in February 2011, revealing the Farmhouse's important connection to the Carlisle Indian School.[47] Thanks to a continued lack of funding, the demolition was postponed another year, during which time requests for reevaluation based on the new research were denied, citing the 2004 Programmatic Agreement.[48]

Funding was finally received in the summer of 2012, and the demolition of the Carlisle Barracks Farmhouse was officially announced and scheduled to take place in the coming fall. By this time, knowledge of the Farmhouse history had spread among descendants of Carlisle Indian School students, and Louellyn White (who is the author of chapter 5, "White Power and the Performance of Assimilation," and whose Mohawk grandfather attended the Carlisle Indian School) started an online petition that generated over nine hundred individually signed emails to the Public Affairs Office of Carlisle Barracks, each requesting that the Farmhouse be spared and giving their personal reasons why.[49]

This overwhelming social media campaign, combined with several news articles and the resulting concern expressed by a number of Native American tribes, finally prompted an official response from the garrison commander, Lt. Col. William G. McDonough, on August 24, 2012, citing the above justifications for razing the Farmhouse and insisting that due diligence had been done.[50] With generously donated legal advice, the newly formed "Coalition" of descendants, relatives, and friends of the Carlisle Indian School countered with precise arguments defending the preservation of the Farmhouse.[51]

The case for preservation was a strong one. Besides its historic and cultural connections to multiple eras and ethnic groups, the Farmhouse has distinctive attributes, making it unique among the historic buildings at Carlisle Barracks. Most importantly, with every other original Indian School building occupied by the U.S. Army War College, the Farmhouse is the only remaining building that has a direct link to the memories and experiences of Carlisle Indian School students. In fact, with the possible exception of Washington Hall, the Farmhouse is the only remaining building at Carlisle Barracks where Indian students slept, ate, and attended classes.[52] With the exception of the Hessian Guard House, the Farmhouse is the oldest Indian School–related building at Carlisle Barracks.[53] Furthermore, the argument that the Farmhouse had fallen into disrepair was invalid since it was the responsibility of Carlisle Barracks to maintain its historic buildings. Lastly, the criteria of the National Landmark status have changed since the 1960s, and new parameters of cultural relevance would most certainly bring the Farmhouse under Carlisle Indian School's National Landmark status.[54]

Aware of the upcoming symposium, "Carlisle PA: Site of Indigenous Histories, Memories, and Reclamations," hosted October 5–6, 2012, by neighboring Dickinson College, Carlisle Barracks officials knew the town of Carlisle and the garrison would soon be inundated by descendants, scholars, and friends of the Carlisle Indian School attending the symposium. As part of the symposium, a "Farmhouse Roundtable Discussion" was organized for the first day. Carlisle Barracks officials met with members of the Coalition of Carlisle Indian Industrial School Descendants and symposium delegates to discuss the cultural importance of the Farmhouse and possible future uses, such as a visitors' center dedicated to the Carlisle Indian School. This face-to-face meeting between representatives of the U.S. Army and Farmhouse supporters marked a turning point.

One coalition member stated that American Indians have been dispossessed of their land base, and historic preservation of these sites is all they have. The Carlisle Indian School is a land base, a visible landmark and site of memory. Another coalition member and Carlisle descendant expressed a desire to have the Farmhouse become a major destination where descendants and other Native Americans could learn of their ancestors' experiences in boarding schools and honor their memory.[55]

Iroquois singer Joanne Shenandoah had previously stated: "Our history gives us a sense of identity, understanding and [the opportunity to] apply this knowledge toward our future. Many Iroquois young people were brought to Carlisle and the influence of this era is still felt today. . . . Carlisle was the place where the Pan Indian Movement was born. It brought many Native nations together and this is where they began to defend their rights. . . . I feel that this important part of our history should be told and kept intact for future generations."[56]

The evening after the symposium roundtable discussion an official announcement was made at the Carlisle Barracks: the demolition of the Farmhouse had been put on hold indefinitely, pending an independent investigation into the history and significance of the house.[57] While only one tribe, the Cheyenne-Arapaho of Oklahoma, was specified in the 2004 Programmatic Agreement, the army officials now agreed that every tribe affected by the Carlisle Indian School, including those not federally recognized, would be consulted about the ultimate decision to keep or raze the Farmhouse.[58]

Less than one year after the army agreed to reevaluate the Farmhouse history, the U.S. Army Corps of Engineers completed their study and published an extensive report validating this research and recommending that the Farmhouse be nominated for inclusion in the existing National Historic Landmark designation of the main CIS campus.[59] The study clearly determined that "Building 839 is an important part of the historic context of the CIIS. Without this farmhouse, the whole physical history of the agricultural curriculum for the school is lost since housing has now replaced all the fields and barns."[60] The Farmhouse Project is now moving ahead, with a high degree of cooperation between U.S. Army officials and Farmhouse advocates.

N. Scott Momaday, who was present at the "Farmhouse Roundtable Discussion," told conference delegates that for him, the Carlisle Indian School is as important in American history as the battlefields of Gettysburg: it is a sacred place. General Joshua Lawrence Chamberlain once said of Gettysburg: "Forms change and pass; bodies disappear; but spirits linger, to consecrate ground for the vision-place of souls. And reverent men and women from afar, and generations that know us not and that we know not of, heart-drawn to see where and by whom great things were suffered and done for them, shall come to this deathless field to ponder and dream; and lo! the shadow of a mighty presence shall wrap them in its bosom, and the power of the vision pass into their souls."[61]

This "spirit of place" is strong within and surrounding the Carlisle Indian

School Farmhouse. Indeed, spirits linger, consecrating its ground. And reverent men and women from afar will be heart-drawn to see where and by whom great things were suffered and done for them. There is honor and healing in remembering our ancestors and in passing on their stories to future generations. May the Farmhouse long stand as a symbol of all that the Carlisle Indian School represents to Native America.

NOTES

1. Kate Buford, *Native American Son: The Life and Sporting Legend of Jim Thorpe* (New York: Random House, 2010), 42–43.
2. "Cumberland County, Pennsylvania Tax Rate Books," microfilm at Cumberland County Historical Society, Carlisle PA, shows the property owner in 1853 as Ulrich Strickler, with a two-story stone house. The year 1856 shows the property owner as Daniel B. Keiffer, with a brick house. Also see "Deed of Sale," from Ulrich Strickler to Daniel B. Keiffer, April 2, 1855, Cumberland County PA, Deed Book 2F, 342, at County Recorder's Office, Carlisle PA.
3. Christina Schmidlapp, *A Cultural Resource Overview and Management Plan for the United States Army, Carlisle Barracks* (Cumberland County PA: Archaeological and Historical Consultants, 1988), section 7, p. 10.
4. See Virginia McAlester and Lee McAlester, *A Field Guide to American Houses* (New York: Knopf, 1984).
5. James S. Giffen, "The Farm Buildings," *Carlisle Arrow and Red Man*, February 8, 1918, 18–19.
6. "Deed of Sale" from assignees of Daniel B. Keiffer to Richard Parker, March 31, 1860, Cumberland County PA, Deed Book 2L, 10, in County Recorder's Office, Carlisle PA; Giffen, "Farm Buildings," 18–19.
7. Map of Carlisle PA on wall of Hamilton Library, Cumberland County Historical Society, Carlisle PA, 1858.
8. Richard L. Tritt, *Here Lyes the Body: The Story of Meeting House Springs* (Carlisle PA: First Presbyterian Church, 2009), 85.
9. Jessica Sheets, "Wilson House," December 16, 2010 (Carlisle PA: U.S. Army Military History Institute, 2010).
10. Tritt, *Here Lyes the Body*, 82.
11. "Cumberland County, Pennsylvania Tax Rate Books," 1853 and 1856, Cumberland County Historical Society, Carlisle PA.
12. Giffen, "Farm Buildings," 18–19.
13. Tritt, *Here Lyes the Body*, 82.
14. Thomas G. Tousey, *Military History of Carlisle and Carlisle Barracks* (Richmond VA: Dietz Press, 1939), 264.

15. F. W. Beers, *Atlas of Cumberland County, Pennsylvania* (New York: F. W. Beers, 1872), 14.

16. 1880 U.S. Census, North Middleton, Cumberland PA, E.D. 73, p. 189D, dwelling 180, family 189; A. H. Parker, http://ancestry.com.

17. "Cumberland County, Pennsylvania Tax Rate Books," 1877, 1880, 1883, Cumberland County Historical Society, Carlisle PA. According to a Pennsylvania Historic Resource Survey Form in Schmidlapp, *Cultural Resource Overview*, section 7, 10, the rear ell is not original to the house. However, it exists in an 1895 photo. According to Giffen, "Farm Buildings," 18–19, the Indian School only "slightly remodeled" the home to meet the school's needs.

18. Richard H. Pratt, "Our Farm," *Morning Star/Eadle Keatah Toh*, May 1884, 1.

19. Pratt, "Our Farm," 1.

20. R. H. Pratt, quoted in Letter from the Acting Secretary of the Treasury, Transmitting Letter of Secretary of the Interior Relative to the Improvement of the Indian Industrial School at Carlisle PA, June 29, 1886, Box 9, Folder 13, Carlisle Barracks Collection, U.S. Army Military History Institute, Carlisle PA.

21. "Deed of Sale" from Hardarsah (*sic*) Parker, widow, Richard M. Parker and Mary P. McKeehan, April 7, 1887, Cumberland County PA, Deed Book 4C, 152, County Recorder's Office, Carlisle PA. The third Parker child, Andrew Parker, and his wife Mary had conveyed all their interest in the property to his mother on September 16, 1884 (Deed Book 3W, 374).

22. Based on several entries in Carlisle Indian School, *Indian Helper*, April 17, 1891; May 8, 1891; June 19, 1891; July 17, 1891.

23. *Indian Helper*, December 11, 1896.

24. Giffen, "Farm Buildings," 18–19.

25. Carlisle Indian School, *Carlisle Arrow*, April 17, 1914.

26. *Indian Helper*, May 15, 1891.

27. *Indian Helper*, March 23, 1888.

28. Barbara Landis, "Richard Davis and Paul Good Bear," http://home.epix.net/~landis/davis.html.

29. *Indian Helper*, October 9 and 23, 1892.

30. *Indian Helper*, June 17, 1892.

31. *Indian Helper*, November 4, 1892.

32. Thomas G. Tousey, *Military History of Carlisle and Carlisle Barracks* (Richmond VA: Dietz Press, 1939), 299.

33. Giffen, "Farm Buildings," 18–19.

34. Richard H. Pratt, "The Farms," *Red Man and Helper*, September 18, 1901.

35. However, in the 1960s, after the Parker farmland had been taken over by post buildings, the Kutz farm was referred to as "Farm No. 1" when it was sold off

to Dickinson College. See Box 22, Folder 14, Carlisle Barracks Collection, U.S. Army Heritage and Education Center, Carlisle PA.

36. *Carlisle Arrow*, September 10, 1909.

37. Tousey, *Military History of Carlisle*, 357–58.

38. Tousey, *Military History of Carlisle*, 364.

39. Based on a conversation by the author in January 2011 with a Farmhouse caretaker who was familiar with its history.

40. 1930 U.S. Census, North Middleton, Cumberland PA, E.D. 36, p. 6A, http://ancestry.com. Names of the negro soldiers: Arthur Booker, Arthur Cannon, James R. Carter, Charlie Felix, Earnest Harper, Theodore S. Hicks, Charlie Jackson, William Jefferson, Leslie Meadows, Robert E. Smith, Henry G. Weathers.

41. Tousey, *Military History of Carlisle*, 386.

42. Charles E. Shedd, "National Survey of Historic Sites and Buildings, Carlisle Barracks," Department of the Interior, National Park Service, September 6, 1960. Document at Reference Desk, U.S. Military History Institute, Army Heritage and Education Center, Carlisle PA.

43. Schmidlapp, *Cultural Resource Overview*, section 4, p. 14.

44. R. Christopher Goodwin and Associates, *Archaeological and Architectural Investigations at Carlisle Barracks, Cumberland County, Pennsylvania*, vol. 1 of 2, July 24, 1996, 111.

45. "Programmatic Agreement among Carlisle Barracks PA; Pennsylvania State Historic Preservation Officer for the privatization of family housing at Carlisle Barracks PA," August 31, 2004. Provided by Carlisle Barracks.

46. Ty McPhillips, on Farmhouse history, email to author, November 12, 2010.

47. Carolyn Tolman, "The Carlisle Indian School Farmhouse: A Major Site of Memory," The Farmhouse at Carlisle Barracks, https://sites.google.com/site/thefarmhouseatcarlislebarracks/.

48. Caroline D. Hall, "Advisory Council on Historic Preservation," letter to LTC William G. McDonough, Garrison Commander, Carlisle Barracks; and Jean Cutler, Pennsylvania Bureau for Historic Preservation, February 16, 2012. See "Farmhouse SHPO Demolition Agreement 2012," Facebook Group "Carlisle Farmhouse Friends," https://www.facebook.com/groups/CarlisleFarmHouse Friends/?fref=ts.

49. See Facebook Group "Carlisle Farmhouse Friends"; Louellyn White, "Carol Kerr: STOP the demolition of the historic CIIS Farmhouse," petition on Change.org (now closed but still accessible, https://www.change.org/p/u-s-army-war-college-public-affairs-officer-stop-the-demolition-of-the-historic-ciis-farmhouse).

50. The St. Regis Mohawk Tribe, the Potowatami Tribe, the Gun Lake Tribe, and the Saginaw Chippewa Tribe of Michigan expressed concern about destroy-

ing the Farmhouse; see "Roundtable minutes Oct 2012," document on Facebook Group "Carlisle Farmhouse Friends." For the response from Carlisle Barracks, see William G. McDonough, Garrison Commander, Carlisle Barracks, letter to Louellyn White, August 24, 2012. See "Letter from Carlisle Barracks Cmdr," document on Facebook Group "Carlisle Farmhouse Friends."

51. Legal service was provided by Walt Powell of Stone Fort Consulting, generously hired by Jeff Woods of the Whistlestop Bookshop, Carlisle PA. Louellyn White, letter to LTC William G. McDonough, Garrison Commander, Carlisle Barracks, August 27, 2012. See "Coalition_USAG-CB Letter," document on Facebook Group "Carlisle Farmhouse Friends."

52. Washington Hall, the former Indian School athletic dorm and hospital, is now a guesthouse for the U.S. Army War College.

53. The Hessian Guard House, built in 1777 by Hessian prisoners of war captured at Trenton during the Revolutionary War, was used as a guardhouse and detention center for the Indian School. It now houses a museum on the history of Carlisle Barracks, including a small exhibit on the Indian School. Almost every other building on post was built after the Confederate-started fires of 1863.

54. Louellyn White, "Roundtable minutes Oct 2012," document on Facebook Group "Carlisle Farmhouse Friends."

55. White, "Roundtable minutes Oct 2012."

56. Joanne Shenandoah, email to Louellyn White, August 27, 2012.

57. "Farmhouse Demolition on Hold: Army to Re-evaluate Building's History," *Army War College Community Banner*, October 5, 2012, http://www.carlisle .army.mil/banner/searchDisplay.cfm?id=2715&searchText=farmhouse. See also "Re-evaluation Letter from McDounough," document on Facebook Group "Carlisle Farmhouse Friends."

58. White, "Roundtable minutes Oct 2012."

59. Adam Smith et al., "Analysis of Building 839, Carlisle Barracks, Pennsylvania," Construction Engineering Research Laboratory, U.S. Army Corps of Engineers, ERDC/CERL SR-13-19, September 2013.

60. Smith et al., "Analysis of Building 839," 75.

61. Joshua Lawrence Chamberlain, "Dedication of Maine Monuments at Gettysburg," October 3, 1889, http://www.joshualawrencechamberlain.com /maineatgettysburg.php.

Part 5   Revisioning the Past

15

Research Note on the Carlisle Indian Industrial School Digital Humanities Project

MALINDA TRILLER DORAN

More than 10,500 students attended the Carlisle Indian School (CIS) between 1879 and 1918, and each one of them has a story. As has been made clear in this collection, most of these stories are yet to be told, and researching any one of them is a challenge. After the sudden closure of the school, materials documenting the school history and aspects of student lives, including photographs, letters, and the administrative files of the school, were dispersed. Some were lost, but others have been reassembled in various institutions. This scattered and incomplete historical record makes it difficult for descendants, scholars, teachers, and students to connect with the lives of the individuals who attended the school. For all these groups, there is much to be gained from reuniting the Carlisle Indian School sources that have survived. The Archives and Special Collections department of Dickinson College has partnered with the college's Community Studies Center, the Cumberland County Historical Society, Jacqueline Fear-Segal of the Department of American Studies at the University of East Anglia (UEA), and Dovie Thomason to create a website that will bring together and make freely available these widely dispersed materials.

The main archival records are held at the National Archives in Washington DC, but there is also a substantial collection at the Cumberland County Historical Society in Carlisle, Pennsylvania, and a smaller one in the Special Collections of Dickinson College. Much of the early Carlisle photographic record is housed by the Smithsonian Institution and can be viewed online.[1] Another more carefully annotated part is owned by the Cumberland County Historical Society and can be viewed there; an overlap of about one-third exists between these two collections.

To provide convenient access to all these resources, regardless of their geographic location, Jim Gerencser, college archivist at Dickinson, long dreamed of building an online resource. The heart-felt and enthusiastic response to the Carlisle Indian School Symposium, which drew an audience of more than 290 people to Dickinson College in 2012, provided the energy necessary to set a digitization project in motion. Gerencser collaborated with Susan Rose, professor of sociology and director of the Community Studies Center, and myself, special collections librarian, to develop a plan for an online Carlisle Indian School Digital Resource Center. In spring 2013 we received funding through an Andrew W. Mellon Foundation Digital Humanities grant and Dickinson's Research and Development Committee. Since that time we have sent several research teams to the National Archives in Washington DC to scan and photograph records located within the Bureau of Indian Affairs Record Group 75. These teams have scanned all the 6,300 individual student files held in the National Archives, totaling more than 150,000 pages of documents. Some files only contain a registration card. But others provide much more information and include photographs, correspondence, newspaper clippings, and administrative forms documenting the experience of these students while they were enrolled at the Indian School and after they returned to their homes. Twelve bound ledgers also provide an overview of the arrival and departure of students and their Outing assignments.

All the extant student files are now available online, as well as the contents of the ledger volumes as searchable and sortable text at the Carlisle Indian School Digital Resource Center: http://carlisleindian.dickinson. edu. We plan to continue adding resources to the CIS website through partnerships with other institutions that hold materials related to the CIS, such as the Beinecke Library at Yale University, which holds the papers of Richard Henry Pratt, and the U.S. Army Heritage and Education Center in Carlisle, which holds Indian School publications and photographs.

The ultimate goal is to provide a comprehensive searchable database that will facilitate research on the Indian School, whether an individual wishes to find information about a specific student or explore broader aspects of Carlisle's history. We are building interactive capabilities into the site to enable individuals who have ties to the school to contribute photographs, family documents, or oral histories. In addition, we plan to work with both Native and non-Native scholars, teachers, and community members to develop teaching and learning materials utilizing the resource center content. The Carlisle Indian School Resource Center will continue to grow as project staff add new content.

NOTES

1. John N. Choate Photographs of Carlisle School Students, circa 1879–1902, Smithsonian Institution Research Information System, http://siris-archives .si.edu/ipac20/ipac.jsp?uri=full=3100001~!2918!0.

16

Carlisle Indian Industrial School

Projects for Teaching

PAUL BRAWDY AND ANNE-CLAIRE FISHER

Public education in the United States, represented by schools across the country, stands as a paradox of public life. As a reminder of both the promise and shortcomings of the social, political, and economic forces shaping society, the American system of public education seems to at once prepare its citizens for an aspirational, self-governing, mobile society while at the same time reproducing the structural barriers associated with social inequity and social immobility.[1] As such, schools serve as places where children and families, as well as teachers, are exposed to subtle but persistent messages reflecting a set of social realities that not only insinuate the limits of student potential (based on class, race, or gender), but also define the contours of hegemonic relations, in part, shaping the school's "hidden" curriculum.

The nineteenth-century curriculum and program of the Carlisle Indian Industrial School offers a striking example of how education was used in the past as part of a deliberate, government-supported effort to assimilate and control a minority group. We believe that the historical example of Carlisle and its mission offers a fruitful way for current education majors to reflect on present-day educational issues. Dramatic demographic shifts in the ethnic makeup of today's student body are not matched in the teaching workforce, which remains largely white, middle class, and female.[2] This disparity will have an important impact on the experience and working lives of trainee teachers and is something for which they need to be prepared. Likewise, they need to be alerted to the power of the "hidden curriculum": the messages and lessons that students are taught at school, which may not be consciously intended or anticipated.[3]

In an effort to address these issues, we have summarized below a series of projects, relating to Carlisle, that all focus on making aspects of the hid-

Fig. 27. Student teachers looking at 1892 photograph of Carlisle Indian School students at Cumberland County Historical Society, 2011. Photo by Paul Brawdy.

den curriculum more clearly visible and raise issues vital for consideration by students who are preparing to become teachers. Visits to the Carlisle Indian School to see the physical environment of the Indian School were integral to each of these projects: the Carlisle Indian School was located on what is now the campus of the United States Army War College. Access to the library and archival documents of the Cumberland County Historical Society provided the teacher candidates with traditional archival materials. And the Carlisle Indian School Digital Resource Center also now offers a crucial online research resource. Together these sources provided student teachers with invaluable insights into a nineteenth-century public policy that (1) made use of education to target and systematically dismantle hundreds of Native cultures, (2) attempted to assimilate Native youth into the social and political economy of the day, and (3) used school curricula to reinforce the supremacy of the white elite, while at the same time enforcing the subordinate, servile status of Native nations.

We chose the Carlisle Indian School for our projects because of the many critical issues raised by its assimilation program, as well as the safe distance offered by a historical example, for our predominantly Caucasian, middle-class, and female teacher candidates. The example of the Carlisle Indian School provides a challenging, thought-provoking, but nonthreatening series of object lessons and moral dilemmas about the role of schools and teachers in a democratic, pluralistic society. This is not to say that this material does not stir up strong feelings, but that for many of our students these are less threatening than more contemporary conflicts relating to race and ethnicity, which touch their lives directly.

We followed a three-step approach in our pedagogy. First, we developed a capstone course to introduce core concepts associated with critical pedagogy that questioned the assumed "objective" role of education and educators. We then made visits to the Carlisle Indian School (CIS) campus and the Cumberland County Historical Society (CCHS) to experientially anchor these concepts to this historic place and educational experiment.[4] Teacher candidates were asked to personally interview Native and non-Native American high school students and their teachers who were included in the trip to CIS. Subsequently the teacher candidates transcribed, analyzed, and copresented their reflections at a conference.[5] We then explored the degree to which the capstone course and a greater understanding of the CIS experience helped inform teacher candidates about hegemony in schools, as well as guided their thinking toward strategies they might explore in their own teaching as forms of counter-hegemonic practice.

Core Concepts in Teaching

The projects discussed in this chapter were anchored in a theoretical framework that provided a guiding structure to our critical pedagogy. The core concepts we focused on were social reproduction, schooling, hegemony, conscientization, the transformative intellectual, sovereignty and self-determination, and dysconsciousness.

Social reproduction is the means by which an arbitrary authority, engaging in a power relationship with a subordinate individual or group, reproduces a system of cultural arbitraries characteristic of the prevailing social order, which not only conceals the full agency of subordinate groups or others but also reproduces and maintains the authority's position of dominance in the power relationship.[6] In other words, a system of arbitrary social values that ensures the perpetual stratification of the existing power structure is first regarded as the natural order of things and then communicated in ways that distract subordinate members of society from recognizing their inherent potential to make fully informed and free decisions about what is possible for themselves, their group, or the larger group as a whole. Once established as normative, the social order is then reproduced through time—all the while ensuring that those in power stay in power and those serving such arbitrary power continue to serve.

In education, the term "schooling" has come to represent, in part, the instruction of conduct, values, and modes of thinking that lead to the reproduction of the existing social order. For our purposes here, schooling is quite antithetical to the edification or personal liberation experienced through other forms of learning. In the service of schooling, teaching itself may be characterized as an act of symbolic violence. From our experience the concepts of social reproduction and schooling become particularly salient for teachers in training when they are immersed in the history and experience of the Carlisle Indian School. Specifically when students learn about the intentions behind the use of education to first assimilate Native peoples into nineteenth-century society and then to make use of an institution (schools) that not only targets Native youth but also has the capacity to target generations of youth in ways that systematically eradicated one set of cultural values and repeatedly replaced them with another. This belief is well coined in a quote attributed to Richard Henry Pratt, CIS's first superintendent: "Kill the Indian in him and save the man."[7] By learning about CIS, teacher candidates learn about past practices that prompt reflection on the ways various modes of social control play out and are reproduced in our modern schools.

Given that subordinate groups often represent a sizeable minority, how do such socially reproduced yet inequitable relations persist at the expense of so many? For instance, in the western New York district where much of our work takes place, Native American children make up nearly 40 percent of the school's total enrolment. With so many Native American students enrolled in school, why then are their interests not more completely represented in the curriculum, the school's culture, and the composition of the school's faculty and administration? One way that asymmetric power relations are reproduced is through forms of cultural or political hegemony.

According to Marxist scholar Antonio Gramsci, hegemony can be characterized by tacit forms of consent given by the masses to a dominant group related to control over the social order.[8] Though different from the use of direct force or the enforcement of the rule of law, hegemony evolves as a subtle form of coercion holding one group in power over another. Further, hegemony is shaped by a historic dimension. Gramsci believed that in many cases consent was shaped by the prestige that the dominant group historically possessed due to its ability to manage the conditions of work in society.[9] Among those prestige aspects associated with generating the consent of subordinate groups is the tacit assertion by the dominant class that it is inherently superior to other groups. Furthermore, such thinking is broadly considered to be "common sense" or the natural order of things, thus becoming enmeshed in what Gramsci referred to as notions of the civil society.[10]

In that schools become mechanisms for the institutionalization and transmission of that which constitutes, among other things, social norms and mores as well as all forms of socially constructed knowledge, we view schools as places where limiting power relations and access to social mobility are mediated and often reproduced through the work of teachers. The story of the Carlisle Indian School, because it primarily focuses on the many ways in which generations of Native children were systematically taught to prefer the values of another culture over their own, creates many opportunities for teacher candidates to consider and reflect upon their observations in public schools today, especially at a time when the ethnicity, racial identity, or class background of many teachers is quite different from that of the students they teach. Reflecting on the lessons of Carlisle, we simply ask our teacher candidates: "Are modern schools places where forms of cultural hegemony are reproduced by teachers today?"

To the extent that a pedagogy can liberate learners rather than oppress them, we value the work of Paulo Freire and the opportunity to promote and share in the experience of conscientization in our work. According to Freire, conscientization is defined by the awakening of a critical consciousness in ways that allow the individual to perceive social, political, and economic contradictions related to equity, mobility in society, and human freedom.[11] For Freire, conscientization evolves through dialogical learning experiences focused on problem-posing methods and encounters with the social realities of the other.[12] Rather than embracing the unproblematic "banking" practice of knowledge dissemination in our teaching, we problematize it in ways that call into question what is being learned and whose interests are being served by the curriculum.[13] In this way teaching can become a means by which a counter-hegemony develops. Learning about and visiting the Carlisle Indian school presented many opportunities to examine the ways in which the curriculum provided Indian children with access to another culture, but often only to the extent that this access, via education, prepared them to service the needs and aspirations of that culture. By bringing to light these early contradictions associated with Indian education, teacher candidates are able to fashion a critical lens through which similar contemporary contradictions in education may also be analyzed.

Such a pedagogy not only works against the interests of the dominant discourse embedded in the curriculum and in the practices of teachers, but it also requires a type of teacher otherwise known as a transformative intellectual. According to Stanley Aronowitz and Henri Giroux, teachers who are transformative intellectuals are those who make "the pedagogical more political and the political more pedagogical."[14] In our work associated with Carlisle, such a pedagogy first encourages teacher candidates to locate their practice and the work of teachers in a political and historical context that has largely worked against the interests of sovereign peoples in North America. Second, it then encourages teacher candidates to reconsider and then participate in educational experiences that treat Native American students as critical agents with ideas of their own about what it means to be respected and treated justly.

Sovereignty and self-determination figure prominently in the struggle against colonialism and global capitalism as principal sources of oppression for Native Americans in schools today. Unlike other marginalized minority groups in the United States, Native Americans seek less to have their voices heard in the democracy than to have their status as sovereign peoples recognized and their treaties upheld.[15] Consequently the work of teachers in public schools that seeks to be both edifying as well as emancipatory for Native American students needs to embrace a pedagogy that is sensitive to the importance of sovereignty and self-determination when preparing teacher candidates for the future. Because the Carlisle Indian

School offers a clear example of how education, as a means of "civilizing" Native people, was used to rationalize or justify a disregard for the sovereignty of Native peoples, it offers many unique opportunities to examine the impact of state educational standards as well as school curricula on the groups operating in society's margins in exchange for the education they are afforded.

Finally, educational field experiences linked with the Carlisle Indian School help make clear to teacher candidates forms of bias found within schools, otherwise referred to as "dysconsciousness."[16] Categorizing it as a form of hegemony, Joyce E. King described dysconsciousness as "an uncritical habit of mind (including perceptions, attitudes, assumptions and beliefs) that justifies inequity and exploitation by accepting the existing order of things as given."[17] For our part, the authors found that teacher candidates who took part in our projects, including visits to Carlisle with Native American students and their teachers, developed a sensitivity with which to frame the bias they observed in schools as well as the intellectual support and resolve to avoid participating in such biased discourse themselves, when placed as student-teachers in a minority American Indian public school as evidenced by their journals.

Step 1: Creating a Capstone Integrating an Experiential Encounter with Carlisle

The creation of the capstone seminar primarily focused on preparing our largely Caucasian, middle-class, and female teacher candidates to teach in schools of the twenty-first century where student cultural and linguistic demographics are projected to dramatically change. This class sought to introduce and develop content associated with critical multicultural education currently not taught in our teacher preparation program. Among these, special emphasis was placed on the role of the teacher, the curriculum, and the schools in a vibrant multicultural society where pluralism is valued as the life blood of democracy. In so doing, the authors hoped to encourage teacher candidates to reflect on the relevance of delivering existing standards-based curriculum (often reflective of a dominant paradigm) to student populations of culturally and linguistically diverse backgrounds (CLD) and to investigate the ways that accountability expectations by the state and federal government of student, teacher, and school performance reflect similar sets of values.[18] In this capstone course the authors aimed to equip students with the tools to process both discomfort and dissonance, when confronted by the inequitable realities present in many schools today. Many such inequities are often a result of the institutional failure to teach in a culturally responsive manner to the growing diversity present in the student body. For example, one of the areas investigated in depth was the growing body of scholarship chronicling the disproportionate enrollments of minority students and English language learners (ELLs) in special education (disproportionately high) and gifted education (disproportionately low) when compared to the enrollments of their Caucasian student counterparts.[19] Another was a more critical approach to multicultural education and white privilege.[20]

The capstone course met for ten weeks, and students focused on readings related to core concepts. The course was designed to be student-centered, with a focus on dialogue and problem posing, and was strategically placed in the semester prior to student teaching. Teacher candidates were directed to post weekly blogs on the readings (a minimum of five hundred words) using an e-learning platform. By the end of the course the teacher candidates were expected to revise their philosophy of education statement and submit a ten-page capstone paper. The initial pilot class was very small, composed of only three students, and usually took place around a meal, which allowed for a more intimate setting and relationship building. The second class was much larger with ten students and lacked the intimacy developed through breaking bread together.

In addition to readings focused on the core concepts of the course, students were also exposed to a number of guest speakers. Among these were local high school faculty members who, as indigenous persons, described the many challenges they faced as they "walked the two worlds." Representing three different generations of school workers, these indigenous women described the discomforts they faced as students and the challenges they encountered as professionals in the making. They talked eloquently about having to manage competing sets of cultural expectations and the trauma of being educated in the "white man's schools." As a result, the Caucasian teacher candidates seemed to develop a heightened sensitivity for how children of different cultural backgrounds might feel invisible or discounted in a classroom that relies on traditional curricula in our public schools.

The class also included a visit to the former site of the Carlisle Indian Industrial School. Accompanied by indigenous students from a local high school, their Native and non-Native teachers, and community elders, the teacher candidates were able to consider the historic legacy and the benefits weighed against the personal costs of acculturating generations of indigenous children into the white man's world via a Carlisle education. In visiting the physical space of the Carlisle Indian Industrial School with this diverse group, teacher candidates could directly encounter the alternative history of the other it represents. By witnessing the damage done to so many children and listening to accounts by community members of their experiences or their parents' experiences as children in Indian boarding schools, the teacher candidates were able to learn about some of the shadows of our national history as well as the high cost of colonialism.

Over the course of the day-long visit, teacher candidates, high school students, their teachers, university faculty, and community elders all visited the site of CIS together, walking through the main buildings, meeting on the bandstand, and visiting the Indian School cemetery, where some Native members of the group performed ceremonies with tobacco and burnt sage to honor the deceased. The physical visit was preceded and followed by visits to the Cumberland County Historical Society, where students and community members attended a lecture and hands-on exhibit about the history of the school and the time period. The evening consisted of college students helping Native students and adults research names of potential family members who might have attended the Carlisle school on lists provided by the CIS biographer, Barbara Landis. The experiences impacted teacher candidates in ways that allowed them to more fully grasp the importance of understanding the culture and history specific to the ethnicity of the students in their classroom and provided them with the experience of being a minority—some, for the first time.

Step 2: Learning from the Meanings of the Carlisle Indian School

Out of the capstone project a modest research agenda began to evolve. Building on our understanding of the theoretical framework that guided our efforts in the capstone as well as coming to an appreciation of the pedagogic value of being able to actually visit the historic site of the CIS, we wanted to move past the passive consumption of history toward more interactive learning opportunities. Specifically we wanted the teacher candidates to develop an intellectual relationship with the personal stories behind the school and a mature appreciation for concepts such as social reproduction, schooling, and hegemony, in ways that only the long view of history can safely provide. But more than this, we wanted to move the teacher candidates toward a place in their thoughts about teaching that located these concepts within the lives of students today, especially in relation to those who come from ethnic backgrounds different than their own. Toward that end we wanted the teacher candidates to share in the process of understanding how the CIS, as a historic institution that touched so many lives, is interpreted by Native American students and their teachers and also how a visit to the former site of the school and the CCHS offered a unique vantage point from which these same individuals could evaluate their own personal experiences, or perhaps even biases, related to Native American education in public schools today. Because we wanted the teacher candidates to engage with and understand the various meanings that teachers and students attached to the history of the CIS, we chose to include them first as interviewers and later as coresearchers in attempts to explore the phenomenology of a visit to the Carlisle Indian School.

Phenomenological inquiry is a type of qualitative research that uses an interpretive (hermeneutic) system of analysis to explore the essential meanings associated with a lived experience.[21] Our work focused on trying to understand the essential meanings of visiting the school's site as well as those meanings linked with the experience of Native American students and their teachers in schools today. During our trips to Carlisle, Pennsylvania, over the course of two days, faculty and teacher candidates interviewed individuals drawn from mixed groups of Native American high school students, their teachers, and community elders. The interviews often took place quietly over a meal, in an out-of-the-way corner in the hostel where we stayed, or maybe on the bus ride home. Some interviews could be finished quickly in a matter of minutes; others lasted an hour or more. In all, we included the thoughts and feelings of twenty-two respondents on our first trip in 2010 and similar types of responses from thirteen members representing the second group in 2011. The questions were open-ended in nature and encouraged a conversational interview process. For instance, at various points during the trip the basic questions that shaped our one-on-one interviews included the following:

1. Could you identify for me the most significant experience that you encountered on our trip to the Carlisle Indian School? What was this experience?
2. Can you explain to me why this particular experience was so meaningful to you, personally?
3. How has this experience, if at all, affected your view of schools with regard to serving the needs of Native Americans?
4. How has this experience, if at all, affected your view of curricula (what is taught) in schools serving the needs of Native American students?
5. How has this experience, if at all, affected your view of the role of the teacher in schools serving Native American students?
6. How has this experience, if at all, provided you with new insights into the experience of Native American students today?
7. What, if anything, do you plan to do (in your teaching, studying, parenting, etc.) as a result of this experience? What action would you like to take?

While answers varied from one person to the next on our 2010 trip to the CIS, an analysis of the interview transcripts allowed us to sift through our data to explore units of essential meaning among the respondents. Although it is beyond the scope of this chapter to report on these data or the process at length, we found that the experience of going to the CIS led to insights among the respondents that were consistent with Freire's notion of conscientization.[22] The experience of levering ourselves out of our respective routines and physically encountering the space of the CIS affected many in ways that led the group to reconsider a wide range of issues related to education. Concrete and metaphoric places appeared to be particularly important in prompting realizations that destabilized the consciousness of the status quo. Specific examples could be seen in the ways that the cemetery, Hessian Guard House, and "before-after" pictures captured the attention of so many as the most significant experiences associated with the trip. Such experiences of place seemed not only to prompt personal realizations among Native students such as "being in a place where my ancestors walked," but they also made history an accessible and stable vantage point from which to reflect upon their own personal set of circumstances, whether they be Native or non-Native, teacher or student. Through these reflections among Native students, many of whom named and reclaimed personal suffering, family dysfunction, personal alienation, and school-related problems, the present seemed to be better understood by placing it within the larger context of history.

Similarly, our student coresearchers in 2011 were able to help us identify generative themes linked with the respondents' visit to Carlisle, giving them further insight into the place that this history and the experience of attending or working in schools today occupies within the consciousness of Native students and their teachers. Sorting through the data, the researchers were able to identify essential themes linked with the meaning that respondents associated with this experience. In this follow-up study, our student coresearchers helped to identify examples of personal insights gained from the visit that made clear, but also made problematic, existing hegemonic relations in education that defined, in part, the experience of both teachers and Native students in schools today. Furthermore, this series of interviews also included a range of respondent comments associated with Carlisle's role in triggering thoughts about the politics of identity and education with special emphasis on Native sovereignty and the purpose of schools.

In addition to providing an opportunity to cultivate an awareness of the causal linkages associated with contemporary schooling practices, family dysfunction, and personal alienation from tradition, the Carlisle experience also engaged group members intellectually by presenting them with the contradictory realities associated with Carlisle (assimilation vs. eradication; forced enrollment vs. voluntary enrollment; educational tracking and child labor vs. Carlisle sport tradition, etc.). This in large part was due to the exceptional abilities of the CCHS staff, led by Barbara Landis, CIS biographer. Though for many the Carlisle Indian Industrial School is, by reputation, infamous, the students, teachers, administrators, and community members who participated in this experience were invited by these historians to decide for themselves, beyond the facts provided, how to evaluate the Carlisle Indian School experience and its legacy.

Step 3: Impact on Practice

So, what then were we to do with these lessons learned at Carlisle? While history helped us safely anchor abstractions such as social reproduction, schooling, and hegemony for our young teachers, the reflections shared by Native American students and their teachers gave these ideas currency, making them personal in ways that history alone could not. Thus, as we considered the future for our teacher candidates and ourselves, an important question arises: Now that we have become aware of specific accounts of asymmetric power relationships in schools and have some insight into their ability to reproduce social inequities in our communities, what, if anything, can be done about these issues through our work as teacher educators?

Because schools are considered by many to be politically neutral spaces, there are many school and university professionals who dismiss notions of schooling, social reproduction, and cultural hegemony as nothing more than intellectual distractions from the practice of teaching. According to Joyce King, when conditions of social inequity are accepted as being unproblematic, or the natural order of things, this thinking represents a form of "dysconsciousness."[23] She argues that one way to counter such dysconsciousness is to advocate for forms of pedagogy that challenge internalized ideologies and the subjective identities of white preservice teacher candidates; in other words, as Aroniowitz and Giroux suggest, to find ways to make the pedagogical more political.[24] Our work in the capstone and at CIS was essentially designed to question teacher candidates' internalized ideologies and subjective identities as white teachers. We became interested in ways that the capstone experience may have (a) helped the teacher candidates identify hegemonic discourse in schools, including dysconsciousness; or (b) influenced their teaching in ways that led them to clearly resist the status quo where social inequity was concerned.

Our research questions included the following:

1. Did the capstone experience affect the teacher candidates' level of sensitivity toward issues related to social equity/inequity in the school during their student teaching experience?
2. What specific barriers to an equitable education did the teacher candidates identify while working in the milieu of their student teaching placement?

3. What possibilities or strategies did the teacher candidates identify during their student teaching experience that could potentially lead to more equitable experiences in education for all students?

It was our intent to examine the extent to which the capstone, which included the visit to the CIS, helped develop a critical lens through which inequitable power relations within schools could be identified and analyzed. Furthermore, given the capstone's emancipatory bent—shaped by the work of Freire, Gramsci, Aronowitz and Giroux, and Grande[25]—we were also interested in the extent to which our students could imagine counter-hegemonic strategies for their own teaching that might neutralize or redress inequities found in their student teaching placements.

To learn more we launched a study where three teacher candidates were placed in a public school serving a significant minority population (+30 percent) of Native American students. All three teacher candidates had successfully completed the capstone course, and all three had been involved with the collection and analysis of interview data from one of the CIS studies. During student teaching, candidates were responsible for providing weekly journal entries related to their observations and insights focused on school culture, equity in education, and their experiences of working with a diverse population. Following the student teaching placement (placements were typically six and a half weeks) a post-placement interview was conducted with the candidates to collect their concluding reflections and insights related to their experiences. Excerpts from journal entries and interview transcriptions were then reviewed and analyzed for emergent themes by the investigators. Emergent themes were then assessed by the investigators for their fidelity to the study's theoretical framework.[26]

Although it is beyond the scope of this chapter to present the narrative data associated with student teacher accounts of their experience, the results of the study, presented elsewhere, suggested that focused coursework prior to student teaching may enhance a teacher candidate's ability to name and frame inequity in schools.[27] Further, such coursework may also help our students imagine alternative strategies toward more culturally responsive forms of pedagogy. Moreover, the results suggested that being able to anchor such experiences in interpersonal relationships (whether in a direct sense or via association) may be equally important for student teachers when attempting to imagine transformative, culturally responsive forms of teaching for their students. In other words, while structured learning opportunities at the university may be helpful to student teachers when interpreting and seeking solutions to problems of social inequity, an appreciation for the other's cultural narrative, via personal relationships, may be just as helpful when attempting to stretch and extend one's pedagogy across the often problematic interpersonal space where differences make cultures distinct.

Concluding Thoughts

There are a number of aspects to our multiple visits to Carlisle that made them particularly valuable as experiential learning opportunities in teacher education. First, we place a high value on those activities that "disrupt" prescribed routine and curricula when attempting to stimulate critical thinking and problem posing. Second, while Carlisle helped us open meaningful conversations with our students about contemporary issues in education that were at cross-purposes with democratic forms of social participation, history helped provide a less threatening vantage point from which schools were safely made the object of critique. Third and finally, in weighing the "successes" of the school's assimilationist agenda against the grim realities that define its infamous and costly legacy, Carlisle offers young teachers an opportunity to critically consider the future "successes" of contemporary curricula and methods that are promoted as a means of liberating the marginalized, yet all the while continue to maintain hegemonic relations in society through education.

NOTES

1. Stanley Aronowitz and Henry Giroux, *Education under Siege: The Conservative, Liberal, and Radical Debate over Schooling* (London: Routledge, 1985).
2. William Hussar and Tabitha Bailey, "Projections of Education Statistics to 2022" (Washington DC: U.S. Department of Education, National Center for Education Statistics, 2014), 194.
3. The "hidden curriculum" is a term that dates from the 1980s. It is the unplanned side effects of an education, "[lessons] which are learned but not openly intended," as first presented by Henry Giroux and David Purpel, eds., *The Hidden Curriculum and Moral Education: Deception or Discovery?* (Berkeley CA: McCutchan, 1983).

4. Paul Brawdy, Anne-Claire Fisher, Claudette Thompson, Melissa DiBattista, Lauren Peterson, and Ashleigh Schroeder, "Considering Culturally-Responsive Praxis in Student Teaching: The Development of a Pilot Capstone Course," paper presented at the International Conference of the National Association for Multicultural Education (NAME): Empowering Children & Youth: Equity, Multiculturally Responsive Teaching & Achievement Gaps, Las Vegas NV, 2010.

5. Paul Brawdy and Anne-Claire Fisher, "The Experiential Impact of History: Grounding Our Pedagogy in the Landscape of Carlisle," paper presented at the Annual Meeting of the American Education Research Association (AERA), New Orleans LA, 2011.

6. Pierre Bourdieu and Jean-Claude Passeron, *Reproduction in Education, Society, and Culture*, 2nd ed. (Thousand Oaks CA: Sage, 1990).

7. David Wallace Adams, *Education for Extinction: American Indians and the Boarding School Experience, 1875–1928* (Lawrence: University Press of Kansas, 1995), 52.

8. Quintin Hoare and Geoffrey Smith, eds., *Selections from the Prison Notebooks of Antonio Gramsci* (New York: International, 1971).

9. Hoare and Smith, *Selections from the Prison Notebooks*.

10. Hoare and Smith, *Selections from the Prison Notebooks*.

11. Paulo Freire, *Education for Critical Consciousness* (New York: Continuum, 1973).

12. Paulo Freire, *Pedagogy of the Oppressed* (New York: Continuum, 1994).

13. Freire, *Pedagogy of the Oppressed*.

14. Aronowitz and Giroux, *Education under Siege*, 36.

15. Sandy Grande, *Red Pedagogy: Native American Social and Political Thought* (Lanham MD: Rowan & Littlefield, 2004).

16. Joyce E. King, "Dysconscious Racism: Ideology, Identity, and the Miseducation of Teachers," *Journal of Negro Education* 60, no. 2 (1991): 133–46, quote on 135.

17. King, "Dysconscious Racism," 135.

18. Paul Brawdy and Rena Egan, "The Ersatz Teacher: Seeking Authenticity in the Mirrored Halls of Accountability," *Educational Studies* (Winter 2001): 438–52; Paul Brawdy, Anne-Claire Fisher, Faith Bain-Lucey, Kim Hlavaty, Suzanne Kush, Abigail Schaaf, and Karen Vester, "Borderland Praxis and Teacher Education," paper presented at the International Conference of the National Association for Multicultural Education (NAME), "Reworking Intersections, Reframing Debates, and Restoring Hope Conference," Chicago, 2011.

19. Jacob Hibel, Susan Faircloth, and George Farkas, "Unpacking the Placement of American Indian and Alaska Native Students in Special Education Programs and Services in the Early Grades: School Readiness as a Predictive

Variable," *Harvard Educational Review* 78, no. 3 (2008): 498–528; Federico Waitoller, Alfredo Artiles, and Douglas Cheney, "The Miner's Canary: A Review of Overrepresentation Research and Explanations," *Journal of Special Education* 44, no. 1 (2010): 29–49.

20. Wanda Blanchett, "Disproportionate Representation of African American Students in Special Education: Acknowledging the Role of White Privilege and Racism," *Educational Researcher* 35, no. 6 (2006): 24–28; Christine Sleeter, "Preparing White Teachers for Diverse Students," in *Handbook of Research on Teacher Education: Enduring Questions in Changing Contexts*, 3rd ed., ed. Marilyn Cochran-Smith, Sharon Feiman-Nemser, and John McIntyre (New York: Routledge and Association of Teacher Education, 2008), 559–82.

21. Amedo Giorgi, ed., *Phenomenology and Psychological Research* (Pittsburgh: Duquesne University Press, 1985); Max Van Mannen, *Researching Lived Experience: Human Science for an Action Sensitive Pedagogy* (London ON: University of Western Ontario–Althouse Press, 1990).

22. Freire, *Education for Critical Consciousness*.

23. King, "Dysconscious Racism."

24. Aronowitz and Giroux, *Education under Siege*.

25. Freire, *Education for Critical Consciousness*; Aronowitz and Giroux, *Education under Siege*; Hoare and Smith, *Selections from the Prison Notebooks*; Grande, *Red Pedagogy*.

26. Grande, *Red Pedagogy*.

27. Paul Brawdy and Anne-Claire Fisher, "Putting Critical Pedagogy into Practice: The Challenges and Opportunities of a Racially-Diverse Student Teaching Placement," paper presented at the Annual Meeting of the American Educational Research Association, Vancouver BC, 2012.

Part 6   Reflections and Responses

17

The Spirit Survives

DOVIE THOMASON (LAKOTA AND KIOWA APACHE)

Can you remember the times
That you have held your head high
And told all your friends of your Indian claim
Proud good lady and proud good man
Your great, great grandfather from Indian blood came
And you feel in your heart for these ones
Oh it's written in books and in song
That we've been mistreated and wronged
Well over and over I hear those same words
From you good lady and you good man
Well listen to me if you care where we stand
And you feel you're a part of these ones
When a war between nations is lost
The loser we know pays the cost
But even when Germany fell to your hands
Consider dear lady, consider dear man
You left them their pride and you left them their land
And what have you done to these ones?

From "Now That the Buffalo's Gone," Buffy Sainte-Marie, as performed at
the symposium by Dovie Thomason

They tell me it was cold that late August day, now almost ten years ago.
They tell me it was cold; but that's not what I remember about the day. I
remember my daughter, because we were standing in a cemetery.

It was the last weekend of her summer vacation. She could not quite
understand why her mother had decided to take her to a cemetery
for the last weekend of her summer vacation. She was standing there
fidgeting, going from foot to foot in her very pricey high-tech shoes;

Fig. 28. Dovie Thomason (Lakota/Kiowa-Apache) in the Indian School cemetery, 2012. Photo by Chip Fox.

you know the ones, they've changed in ten years and gotten more expensive. She was fidgeting, but she wasn't asking any questions. She's learned, as I have learned, that you learn more by watching than by asking what you think you need to ask. And her eyes were looking out at the headstones.

So many headstones, identical headstones, and they march on and on, uniform and laid out in military precision. We weren't alone; there were other people—some of you now in this room—walking through that cemetery searching for names, touching stones, finding names, leaving gifts. Soft voices, many not speaking English, moved through that cemetery. My daughter was trying to figure out the story that would explain why we were there. She was reading the names.

At last, her face turned to me as she said, "There are a lot of Lakota graves here."

And I said, "I know . . . I know, honey."

Puzzled, she said, "But they call them Sioux."

And I said, "Well, they didn't know what to call us back then; this was around 1879."

She kept looking at the graves and then she said, "There's Apache graves here, even more Apache graves. That's you; you're Lakota and Apache."

And I said, "I know . . . I know, honey, but none of my family is here." I could see her next question on her face, troubling her.

There are some stories you don't want to tell your children.

There are some stories you need to tell your children.

I said, "None of your relatives are here, sweetheart. Lots of your family went to these kinds of schools. Some of your family went to school here; I've shown you old-time photos of some of them, remember? But no graves of your relatives are here.

"Grandpa went to government school, but not this school. Grandpa wasn't even born when this school was starting. Grandpa went to a school in Canada that was even older than this school."

Before I could answer the questions I knew were filling her, we were interrupted by other voices. Louder, questioning voices.

You see, all these graves, they're on a military base. Now, it's not a big military base, as some of you know. It's the Barracks, a residential community for military families; but this is post-9/11 and there's checkpoints. The soldiers were at a checkpoint behind us, and they were nervous. I could hear it in their voices; they were on edge. For some reason, they made me uneasy. I felt strongly that I needed to pull my daughter close to me.

There's always been soldiers. During the American Revolution, there were soldiers here, and even before that time. It was a base during the Civil War, deploying soldiers recalled from the Indian Wars, then burned on the day the Battle of Gettysburg began. The Seventh Cavalry trained here before they rode West with Custer. There's always been soldiers . . .

Now there were too many cars going through the checkpoint for a normal Labor Day weekend, too many cars from too many states, even from Canada. Honestly, once again, there were too many Indians for sleepy Carlisle, Pennsylvania.

I started to braid my daughter's hair as I stood there. It's a thing mothers do; we think it comforts you, but we know it comforts us both. I stood there, without words, braiding her hair as she kept looking around. And I thought, how am I going to tell her, how am I going to tell her about this? She doesn't know why we're here; she's not prepared for this. Why should a mother have to tell a daughter these things?

There's some stories you don't want to tell your children.
There's some stories you don't want to tell at all.
There's some stories you have to tell your children.

So, I was standing in the graveyard when I began to tell my daughter about the Carlisle Indian Industrial School. "You know, it was eighty-two Lakota children, they were the first to come here. Children of chiefs, Spotted Tail, American Horse, Red Cloud. They were brought here as 'hostages for the good behavior of their parents,' that's a quote from a man named Ezra Ayres Hayt, commissioner of Indian Affairs, then under the Department of War.

"The Apache children? Well, they came a bit later, around the time my Grandma Dovie was born. That's when the Apache children came, in the early 1890s. They'd been in a prison called Fort Marion, in Florida."

So many children taken. So many never made it home. How was I going to tell my daughter this story?

There's some stories you have to tell.

I looked up and said, "You know, the old entrance to the school was about two miles from here; they had to walk two miles from the train station. You know, the people in the town, they were a little uneasy about these Indian children coming here. These were the children of the men who had killed Custer and the Seventh Cavalry. We say, when we defeated Custer at the Greasy Grass; others hold onto the idea of the 'massacre at the Little Big Horn.' It was just three years after that, 1879, when these children were arriving in the night, walking in the cold. The townspeople were a big crowd at the train station. The older Indian boys sang songs aloud in order to keep their spirits up and remain courageous, even though they must have been frightened."

I turned to my daughter and said, "You know, I've got a newspaper clipping from that day; I'll show it to you sometime if you want."

She shook her head and asked, "How do *you* know all this stuff? I don't know this stuff. Is this stuff I'll get in high school?"

And I thought to myself, she's not going to get it in high school. I didn't get it in high school. I visit schools every week, every year, and most of the young people I meet in high schools, they don't know this "stuff." My own Grandma, who told me stories from before I was old enough to listen, until the last days of her life, she never told me this stuff. My Grandma had gone to Mission School. Her own children had gone to government school. Taken? Did she let them go? I don't know. My Grandma never told me this story.

There are some stories you don't want to tell your children.

And so, I looked at my daughter and said, "We're here so maybe more people will know these things. We all need to know these things. We're here to honor the lives of all the Indian children who went to this school. We're here because, after over a hundred years, we're going to put up a marker, a historical marker, so that people who drive past this cemetery will know that these are not the graves of soldiers. These are the graves of a battle, a war that came and took our children.

"You see, at the end of the Plains Indian Wars of 1860 to 1890, about the time my Grandma was born, the indigenous population of this continent which had been twenty to fifty million, some say even more, was reduced to 250,000. Two hundred fifty thousand Indians left and half of them were children. And then the soldiers came for the children."

My daughter knew some of this story, though not from me. She heard this story from her grandfather. Her grandfather went to government school in Ontario, and he talked to me about it when I married Samm's father. He would talk about residential school to me because, well, my Grandma taught me to listen. He'd start telling his stories, and Grandma would reach over, put her hand on his knee, and she'd say, "Don't be talking about that, don't be talking about that." And she'd look at me and she'd say, "It's not good to be talking about these things; it upsets him. We're not going to be talking about that; that was long ago, it does no good." So, Grandpa began talking to me privately, except for those stories my daughter overheard.

But she didn't know how I came to know about the government schools. It was nothing I overheard my family talking about. You see, my parents got divorced when I was two years old. My father was Kiowa Apache and Scot Gypsy and my Mom was Lakota; they met in a bar in Chicago after World War II. After their divorce, I left Chicago with my Dad and went down to Texas to live with his people. Grandma didn't talk about the past, other than to tell me the old stories. She taught me the first stories I ever heard or learned, but she never spoke about these things. My dad, an Air Force veteran who loved stories about the stars, never mentioned these things.

I knew nothing about my mother's family; they weren't even a memory. When I was fifteen, once again my family was broken by divorce. I became emancipated and went looking for my mother. I found her in Chicago, but I didn't find the answers to my questions. She didn't have them, or she had learned not to talk about them, too. I learned the rules of my mother's silent house very quickly: "Don't mention your father. . . . Quit quoting his mother. . . . And don't talk about Indian things. It was long ago, there's no point."

She only told me one story about Indians in the few years I knew her. She said that she was in her late teens right around the time of World War II. A lot of jobs were opening up, a lot of men going overseas, and she thought she would get herself a job. At the first job where she went to apply there was a sign on the door that said, "No Indians or dogs need apply." She went home without applying and dyed her hair red.

Don't talk about it, it was long ago, it does no good.

There's some stories you don't want to tell.

So I went away to college, questions unanswered. I got myself a minority academic scholarship. There were only two scholarship students at the posh private school that recruited me. I was one, and the other was a Black girl from a sharecropper's family in Mississippi. Everybody else from that school was privileged, the sons of ambassadors and captains of industry. Ironically, I had gotten my scholarship through the generosity of the heir to a railroad dynasty—the same railroad that broke the Fort Laramie Treaty to come across Lakota lands. It paid my way through college.

The college had plans for me: I was going to enter government service. The CIA was interested in me (for different reasons than they are today). Back then all they found interesting about me was that I was trilingual; I spoke three foreign languages fluently. I spoke French, I spoke Spanish, and I spoke English. Three foreign languages, and I didn't know a word of either of my ancestral tongues.

Well, I was clear about not going to work for the CIA. Did I mention this was in 1966? You young students may have to Google it. I decided I was going to major in American Indian studies. Now, many of you in this room know that in 1966 there was no such thing as a degree in American Indian studies. And I was the only Indian on the campus. They had no faculty or even a single course about anything "American Indian" beyond "Primitive Art."

So I proposed that it could be an independent study. There was a lot of that going on in the Sixties. *Come on, a lot of Independent Study going on in the Sixties . . .*

My college adviser just didn't quite know what to do with me; I was a "minority" student on an academic "free ride." The final decision was I would need to complete a double major with a "legitimate" field, and then they set me loose in their library. It was a massive library, but the American Indian section was smaller than the inadequate section in bookstores today. You know that pitiful section on Indian studies that's in your average bookstore? This university's library was smaller and older and dustier, with more books "about" Indians than "by" Indians.

I just looked at that solitary shelf and thought, "How am I going to make that few books last for four years?" I haunted that library wondering how to start, wishing for a sympathetic adviser to guide my research. I remember standing in the library when I saw a slim volume that didn't look to be a hundred years old—a slim volume that was called *American Indian Stories,* and I thought "catchy title." As I reached for it, it almost fell off the shelf into my hand, and when it hit my hand, it opened to a chapter called "School Days of an Indian Girl." I remember thinking, "This is weird. Here I am eighteen years old, the only Indian at this school, and this book opens to this page, "School Days of an Indian Girl." I closed the cover to see who wrote it and saw that it was written by this woman with two names. Her name was Gertrude Bonnin / Zitkala-Ša. I now know I pronounced it wrong in my mind; remember, I had very little of my maternal Lakota language: Zitkala-Ša. Ša is "red," but I had no idea of the meaning of the unpronounceable Z-word. I now know it's "bird," so Red Bird; we Plains folks have a wonderful story about a red bird who saves two lonely, abused children.

I read the cover notes that were written by (forgive me, I know I went to college, but I always get them confused, you know?) an anthropologist or ethnographer. And one of those guys wrote the blurb on the book that said: "One of the most important women ever to live in U.S. history." And I thought, "What? An Indian woman, one of the most important women ever to live in U.S. history . . . an *Indian woman*, and I don't know about her?" I started reading. That was the day that the library started haunting me.

I read about this girl, eight years old, little Gertie Simmons. She was a child of the Prairies, growing up in a buffalo-hide lodge on the Yankton Reservation with her mother, Ellen Simmons, Taté Iyòhiwin (Every Wind or Reaches for the Wind). Her Euro-American father had abandoned the family before Gertie was born.

One day she ran to her mother and told her about the big-hearted men with the big hats; that's how she described the Quaker missionaries—big-hearted men with big hats—and they told her that she could go to school. She wasn't sure what school was. Her brother had been taken to school, but Gertie didn't know her mother had been threatened with losing her rations if she didn't make her mark on a paper she could not read. Young Gertie had a child's curiosity and loved to learn. She loved to listen. She loved when people would come to visit and, after everybody had eaten, the long nights of stories; she loved to just sit quietly and take them all in. Gertie decided she wanted to go to school.

What surely helped make up her mind was when that big-hearted man with the big hat told her about apples. Gertie had only had a few apples in her life. He told her that if she would come with him and go to this place called school, there were apples hanging just above your head like clouds, so many that you could reach up and just take apple after apple. So Gertie ran home and told her mother that she wanted to go to the Land of Red Apples. She begged her mother to consent, but her mother shook her head and said nothing. Her son had returned a near-stranger from the school; she wasn't going to lose her baby girl.

But Gertie could be a willful child, and in the pages of that book I held in my hands when I was not much older than my own daughter, I read as she described her stubborn behavior, stamping her foot and refusing to listen to her mother. So that little Dakota girl did what girls did then and what they will still do now; when you can't get something from your mother, you go to your aunt. She went to her mother's sister and told her she wanted to go to the land of red apples, and her aunt talked to her sister, and her mother again reluctantly put her X on the papers she couldn't read.

Gertie was only eight years old, and yet she was the oldest of the children they took that day. She had three- and four-year-olds, holding them by the hands as they got on the train wrapped in the blankets their mothers had decorated so carefully. When she got on the train she didn't know how many days she would be traveling, she didn't know how far she was going, she didn't know she wouldn't see her mother for three years. When she got to the school, it was snowing. There were no apples. There were no beds. So little Gertie took her mother's blanket, wrapped up in it, curled up with the other children on the floor. There she spent her first night away from home. In her words, "My tears were left to dry themselves in streaks, because neither my aunt nor my mother was near to wipe them away."

The next day a girl who had a few words of English brought Gertie a warning of something she had overheard. "They're going to cut our hair today." Gertie knew why people cut their hair: you cut your hair if you're grieving, you cut your hair because you're mourning a relative, or your enemies would cut your hair in a ragged, shingled cut to show they think you're a coward. Gertie refused to be a coward. She could not allow even the thought that she could have lost a relative in the time she was on the train. "I will not submit," she told her friend, "I will struggle first!"

The next day, when they came to get little Gertie Simmons, they couldn't find her. After a long search, they found her hiding in a dark corner of a storeroom. Little Gertie was underneath the stored furniture, and as they dragged her out, she was fighting. She was kicking, scratching, and screaming. They tied her into a chair; she felt the cold steel of the scissors on her neck. She heard the heavy thud of her braids hitting the floor. She cried herself to sleep that night. "Then I lost my spirit," she wrote years later in "School Days of an Indian Girl." Again she cried alone and far from home until one of the older girls in the dorm came over and curled up beside her and started to comfort her and calm her and soothe her in gentle words, in our language—those words you use with a fussy baby. Gertie finally calmed beside her, and once Gertie had stopped sobbing, the girl said, "Don't ever let them hear you use our language. Don't ever let them hear you speak these words. They're strong, and they'll hurt you."

That's part of the boarding school story my daughter knew, but she didn't know that because of little Gertie, and she didn't know it because of me. She knew it because of Grandpa. Grandpa was only four years old when they came for him. He lived alone with his Grandpa and his "Grandma."

She was his Grandpa's sister, his great-aunt some folks would say today. But the government said they weren't "immediate family" and they took a four-year-old child away, off his reserve and across the river to the school. Though he tried to escape and go home, he never saw his Grandpa again. All he spoke was his Grandpa's language.

At the school they worked those children hard, even the little ones. He remembers working in the potato fields there, digging the potatoes that they'd planted. Every now and then the boys would sneak off into the barn, where they would talk their language. They'd scratch it on the boards of the barn. They'd talk their language, they'd remember Oneida words and make their marks, and then they'd go back to work. They usually worked more hours than they went to classes.

Sometimes they'd take a few potatoes from the field and stuff them inside their shirts and when they got back to the dormitory they'd sneak downstairs to the boiler room when they were supposed to be doing something else. They'd take those potatoes out of their clothes and put them behind the boiler. Later that night, when they were supposed to be sleeping, they'd sneak back downstairs and they'd get those roasted potatoes out and eat. He told me that he was given a "strapping" for that once. He was beaten for eating potatoes he had grown and harvested; they called it stealing. "And how can I be stealing something I planted, something I grew, something I dug from the earth? How could that be stealing?" He was a child. They were all children, and they were hungry. The children ate the scraps that the staff threw out the windows for the birds.

"The Mush Hole would have closed without our work in their fields and with their livestock." He says those words in his eighties with the same defiance that got him a strapping as a boy, and he says it with the same anger and bitterness. "The Mush Hole. I raised their chickens, I raised their eggs—gathered them everyday. Did I ever eat an egg? No. Did I ever eat chicken? No. Chicken and eggs, that was for the government visitors and the missionaries and the good people to see how the Indian children were progressing. The Mush Hole, that's what I ate every day of my life here. Twelve years at that school. All I ever ate was mush!" Grandma's right, talking about the schools does upset him.

There are some stories you don't want to tell.
There are some stories you need to tell.

So now I was taking my daughter walking on the journey, the journey that was begun for me in the story of an eight-year-old girl. A story that, forty years later, brought me to Carlisle, Pennsylvania, and the Indian School. Gertrude Bonnin's writings gave me a glimpse of the stories that nobody had told me, that nobody could speak of—the stories that have been silenced.

The children were hungry in Gertie's time, too, and sick. So much sickness, and so much of it was avoidable. Trachoma, a disease of the eyes that is caused by malnutrition and poor hygiene, resulted in a generation wearing glasses that never would have needed them had they been fed properly and cared for as children. Measles, small pox, tuberculosis, chronic stomach problems, diseases that were never diagnosed but kept the children sick and weakened. They fell asleep to nightmares and bedwetting. They woke up, sometimes sleepwalking. They'd wake up in corridors, far from their beds, and they'd wake up ready to fight. They were plagued with conditions that often stayed with them throughout their lives.

After a time they figured no one was coming for them, and they weren't going home, though many tried. So they did what their relatives had taught them to do; they watched, they observed, they figured it out. Many of the children wanted to learn. Like Gertie, many of the children had asked to go to school. Many of the children wanted a chance to hear more, learn more, understand more, experience more, and so that's what they started doing. They started watching. They started figuring it out. They started to understand how they were meant to behave, understand how to be in this new situation. They learned how to adapt, to survive.

Gertie wanted to learn. She had a gift for language and a musical gift. Her voice was meant for recitation and for song. One of her Quaker sponsors recognized her gifts, put a violin in her hand, and found she had a musical skill. She became a concert violinist, and she took up debating under the tutelage of her Quaker instructors. She learned about abolition. She learned about suffragists. She learned about emancipation. Her mind was engaged and questioning. As a competitive and thoughtful debater, she argued whether Indian people should have the vote and citizenship in this country. She took first prize in her school and received praise and a bouquet of violets. Later she was chosen to represent her school in a statewide competition, and was well prepared to present this argument she had crafted so carefully. Just as she began to speak, she looked up.

Students from the other school had dropped a banner from the balcony with some rude caricature of an Indian woman, making fun of her school for allowing their team to be represented by a "squaw." She wasn't able to finish her presentation that day. She walked off the stage in tears.

Following this disrespect and humiliation, she was struck by the stomach sickness that had bothered her when she was first a student at the school. After a short time of worsening health, she was asked to leave the school. You see, they were afraid that she might die, and if she died on their property, she would count as a statistic. As was the custom at many government and mission schools, she was taken off campus, so her death would just be in the civilian population instead of the mortality figures of the Indian experiment.

She went home to visit her mother at that time, and when she got there she wrote another chapter of her book. "How could my mother be of any help to me? My mother, a woman who could not read or write. How could she understand her daughter, this woman who thought that anything I had learned was not worth the freedom and health I had lost in the learning of it? I no longer belonged there. I was neither a wild Indian nor a tame one. I looked around at this place that was my home and saw that even the land didn't recognize me."

So she turned her back on South Dakota. She turned her back on her family, and once again she faced East. She came to Carlisle. She became a teacher at the Carlisle Indian School; and though she didn't teach here for long, she was beloved by her students. Her debate team was unrivaled. She performed for presidents. Pratt borrowed a dress from the Smithsonian, making a note that "I brought them several already, surely they will loan me one for this occasion." It was buckskin dress like the one that had been taken from her the day that she started school. Pratt let her wear this dress so that she could be "our Minnehaha" as she recited Longfellow's *Hiawatha* for the poet's niece and President McKinley. Soon she was supported by another wealthy sponsor.

After a brief return to South Dakota, actually recruiting students for Pratt and the Carlisle Indian Industrial School, Simmons began to take issue with the assimilationist philosophies of the schools and the complete absence of students' tribal cultures in their studies. She began challenging Pratt and wrote articles for the popular press about her opposition, with topics like: How is it that Indians are a problem? What do you mean the Indian Problem? How can a people be a problem? How can you experiment on a race of people? How can you involve people in an experiment that will mean the end of their existence? Surely these Indian children should have connections to their cultures?

Soon it became clear that Pratt could not tolerate keeping her on staff at Carlisle. With the support of a new sponsor, she went to the New England Conservatory of Music and studied violin. She was supposed to go to Paris for the Paris Exposition. She summered in Long Island. She was a guest of the famous photographer Gertrude Käsebier, whose photographs of Simmons are extraordinary. She was an Indian success story. The newspapers called her a "person who interests us." And she continued to write about her experiences and the status of Indian people. She was living in Boston, preparing for the Paris tour, when she got the news that her fiancé, Thomas Marshall, had died. He went to Dickinson and was a house parent for the little boys in the Carlisle dormitories, where he caught the "malignant" measles that ended his life.

As I told my daughter this story, I led her through the cemetery to a central stone, different from the others. It's a larger, dark gray stone, surrounded by the identical white markers of the children's graves. A weeping cherry hangs over that stone. We walked silently to it and laid sweet grass on the stone. I wanted my daughter to know that history is the lives of people. Gertie didn't return from Boston for his funeral, but I know that she sent white roses.

My daughter was just on the cusp of her teen years. When she heard about the white roses, she looked at me and asked, "White roses? For pure love?" How could we know what she was thinking? I answered, "I don't know, I don't know what she was thinking."

Was she just grieving the death of Thomas Marshall or was she feeling all the deaths? All the loss? All that seemed to be ending around her? I don't know. What I do know is she took off the flowing Victorian dresses she was wearing for polite, literary society and began wearing buckskin. I do know that her hair that had been held in twists and braids with tortoise shell combs in the manner of fine Victorian ladies changed. She pulled those combs out of her hair and started braiding her hair in long heavy braids. She changed her name from Gertrude Simmons to Zitkala-Ša.

As Zitkala-Ša, her writing and publishing intensified: "An Indian Teacher among Indians," "The Soft-Hearted Sioux," "Why I Am a Pagan," "A Warrior's Daughter," and others. The reviews of her writing in the Carlisle *Indian Helper* (Zitkala-Ša liked to call the *Indian Helper* the "Indian Kicker") were bitter and offended: "All that Zitkala Sa has in the way of literary ability and culture she owes to the good people, who, from time to time, have taken her into their homes and hearts and given her aid. Yet not a word of gratitude or allusion to such kindness has ever escaped her in any line of anything she has written for the public. By this course she injures herself and harms the educational work in progress for the race from which she sprung." These writings became *American Indian Stories*, published in 1901, and the book that introduced me to her during my own school days as an Indian girl. Then she turned her back on the East and returned to living on a reservation in Utah. She saw that the old people were getting older and fewer and that they had in their minds ideas and stories that would not survive if someone didn't listen. She wrote them down and put them in another slim volume called *Old Indian Legends* that sits above my desk today, as it has for over forty years.

Now, I can't tell you everything I know about Zitkala-Ša/Gertrude Bonnin. I know she has become a part of my own story; that somewhere her narrative and my narrative have been braided together. I learn new things from and about her still. I never knew this until I began working on this story; but I know now that, when I tell stories, I couldn't tell you for certain sometimes whether it's a story that my own Grandma told me or whether it's a story I read of Gertrude Bonnin's. In a strange way, in that long ago library, it's like I found my lost Lakota grandmother in this woman who used the language of one culture to translate the threatened values of another.

I was lost in these thoughts, when my daughter, patient, if puzzled beside me in the cemetery, brought me back. She tapped me gently on the elbow, "Grandpa's trying to get your attention."

We had a ceremony waiting for us. I'd been pulled into the project by Barb Landis. Many of you know her. That's her over there, front row. A good-hearted woman, as we all know. A good-hearted woman who pulled me into a project that was one she'd been pulled into because of her mailing list of transcribed *Indian Helpers* and her dedication to get the names of all the children buried at Carlisle back to their nations.

Carlisle Descendants, many who had found their family stories in old *Indian Helpers* and tribal listings of every student posted on Barb's Carlisle Indian School website, decided that they were going to try to get permission from the state to put up a historical marker at this cemetery. They wanted to honor their ancestors' and relatives' experiences at Carlisle and end the confusion once and for all with a sign telling part of the story of these graves of Indian children. The Viola White Water Foundation, which I chair, helped sponsor the project, as we help sponsor Barb's website. The descendants worked together to come up with the language for the marker; and now we gathered, all these people, at the edge of this cemetery to unveil this marker, and to tell our stories.

I made my way over to where a podium had been set up outside the cemetery there on that little clear area outside the fence. Chairs were set up, and everyone was sitting there, speaking in soft voices. My daughter's Grandpa came up to me and said, "I decided I want to talk."

I said, "You want to talk? In front of all these people? Dad, you'll have to use the microphone, but I think you should, if that's what you want. You should just get up there and tell your story."

And he said, "I'm not telling no story, you tell the story. I just need to talk."

His granddaughter stood there, not knowing what I knew. Her Grandpa had already spent a lot of time talking with lawyers up in Canada. He'd even had to go talk to a psychologist up in Toronto. He called me when he went to see the psychologist. He said, "I don't know if I can talk to him. I'm afraid if I start talking about this, I'll never be able to stop. I'm afraid that if I start talking about this, if I start feeling this, I'll never be able to stop again."

I said, "Yes, Dad, it will stop. It won't be the same. We're going to be there. We're going to be listening. You've got your family around you and all these people, they've had their own experiences, some same as you."

I knew that what he wanted to talk about was something he hadn't told his own boys. I was married to one of them at the time, and I thought he should tell this story to his sons. I thought he should let them know that he talked to lawyers, that he talked to psychologists, and that he was part of the Truth and Reconciliation case up in Canada, the class action suit against the provincial governments, the Canadian government, and a number of churches about the abuse of children in the schools. I thought that his sons should know their father's story. A man who grew up without parents to comfort him or anyone to protect him, other than other boys, maybe relatives, at the residential school. A man who, for twelve years, went to sleep without the comfort of knowing his parents would be looking in on him.

If they listened to what he needed to tell them, maybe they would understand what a good father he had become, and an even better grandfather. But he wouldn't tell the story to his boys, now all fathers themselves. I did. And now he wanted to talk, this man who'd found the courage to talk to lawyers and psychologists, wanted to talk in front of a group of strangers, but I guess I didn't know what he knew.

He knew he wasn't talking to strangers. He got up there and he talked. He told his story. He told an angry story. He told a sad story. He told a heart-wrenching story. He wept in front of all these people, people who were strangers no longer because they'd heard his story, and other people talked and there were all kinds of stories. There were stories of the president of his class, fine careers in service to their communities, military reputations and careers, families and friendships made at the Carlisle School that lasted a lifetime, marriages that came out of there with generations of descendants sitting there in that space. Some joyful stories, some nostalgic stories, some wounded stories, wounds that will not heal until we clean them, until we gently remove the scab and tend the wound. Many people talked that day. There was laughter, there were tears, and then there was a feast and a picnic, and we ate as the Indian children did when they got to leave the school and go play in the parks, a century before. A lot of stories were told that day; it changed everyone who was there.

There are stories we need to tell.

Now when we hear stories like these, what do we do? I've heard people talking already this morning about what do we do with all of this? What can we do with the hurt, the pain? How can we help the wounds to heal?

Well, let me tell you a final story.

When I was an undergraduate during those turbulent years of war and peace and the Indian Renaissance of the Sixties, I found another hero. Zitkala-Ša/Gertrude Bonnin was the first, but there was another. Her name is Buffy Sainte-Marie, and it's her that I have given you at the beginning of my story, with her permission and kind support. When I came to the end of this story and didn't know what to do, I found the answer on Buffy's website, www.cradleboard.org; you can find it easily. She started a foundation in the Sixties called the Nihewan Foundation, and it was about changing the way we educate our children. It's about bringing a joyful spirit to do a thing, as Barb Landis always says, "in a good way," to do a hard thing in a good way. To find a soft path for a hard journey. And Buffy wrote about this; it's in a monograph that she has on her website that is there free for teachers to use and that she gave me permission to use in this story. She calls it "Guilt and Bitterness." In it she asks what do we do when we hear these horrible stories? These stories that were shared again and again during this symposium. What do we do when we hear this information? When these stories are of lives we, or our relatives, have lived, on either side of the experience?

Well, I'll tell you what we do sometimes, we hurt ourselves. We take it in, and we hold it in, and sometimes we hurt ourselves. We hurt our families. We abandon our children. We try to stop the hurt. We get angry. We go on the offensive. We get sad. We die, sometimes at our own hands—too often at our own hands.

What do white people do? They feel bad. They feel guilt. Sometimes they deny it. Sometimes they're ashamed of it. Sometimes they defend it. Sometimes they just get defensive. This is a story I've shared with many Quakers in many Quaker schools. They meant well. True, there were two schools of thought about how to resolve the Indian Problem. One said educate them, and the other said kill them all. They meant well; no one imagined the conflicted legacy it would leave behind, or that we would be talking as we have at this symposium.

Well, what do we do with it? I know that when we carry that anger, when we carry that pain, it's all that you can see of us when we keep it in front of us like a mask or a shield, it's confusing. All you see is—I'm mad, I'm so mad. And someone else's shield is—I'm sorry, I'm so sorry. Those feelings are real; but they can't be your identity.

Maybe Buffy's story can give us an idea of what to do.

Imagine Indian women. Isn't that easy to do? Just look around this room.

Imagine those old-style Plains women, Indian women in buckskin. Imagine them on open prairie, not this green land of Carlisle. Imagine open prairie; some of you know open prairie.

And their eyes are scanning the far distance, and suddenly they see something and they start moving toward it. They've got sacks over their shoulders, and when they get to what they saw, they bend over and pick it up and put it in the sacks, and they keep looking. They scour the prairie, picking up these gifts off the prairie and putting them in the sacks. What were they gathering?

They were gathering the droppings of buffalo. In the open country, in that rolling prairie, the buffalo droppings bake under the sun. You don't want to pick them up when they're fresh. You've got to let the sun work on them. You've got to let the wind work on it. You've got to let the earth work on it. You've got to let time work on it and, when you do, this amazing thing happens. It becomes fuel.

You can gather them, these dried buffalo droppings, and you can use them to do that magic humans can do—to make fire. Then you can extend the light of day. You could cook a hot meal. You could read a book. You could write a book. You can see a beloved face. You can crumble it and scatter it in your garden and make food that builds strong bodies. You can crumble it really fine and diaper a baby, so she never gets a rash. You can build a community around a fire.

What happens if you pick it up too soon? It's all anybody will remember about you.

So what are we going to do with all this shit I just told you?

We're here, we're gathered here in Carlisle, Pennsylvania, almost a hundred years after they closed the Indian School down. The sun has worked on it, the earth has worked on it, the wind has worked on it, time has worked on it; now it's all fuel. Now it can help us see clearly, instead of the guilt, and the shame, and the anger, and the blame.

Well, I know we've survived a lot. We survived Columbus. We survived Custer. We survived Carlisle. We even survived Costner. But I need you to know I'm a mother myself now. And like my mother, I have my simple rules:

If our children need to hear these stories.

Then everyone needs to hear these stories.

And I want something better than survival for my daughter.

Pilamaye . . . Thank you.

Mitakuye Oyasin . . . All My Relations.

18

Response to Visiting Carlisle

Experiencing Intergenerational Trauma

WARREN PETOSKEY (ODAWA AND LAKOTA)

In October 2012 my wife and I accompanied a group to the Carlisle School Symposium at Dickinson College in Carlisle, Pennsylvania. The subject matter of the symposium centered on the infamous Carlisle Indian School, which opened in 1879 and closed in 1918.

I have mulled over what I might write and pass on regarding what we saw, experienced, and understood during our visit. At the Carlisle Symposium, we heard powerful Native and non-Native speakers talk about the history of Carlisle and its impact on Native children. Over 10,500 children passed through that school in the nearly forty years it was open. The two tribes with the largest number of children were the Sioux and the Chippewa, both nations with around a thousand of their children attending. From my immediate family my grandfather, his sister, and my great-aunt were among the many other children from tribes across the United States who also attended.

My grandfather graduated in 1902. It is our belief that when my grandfather's dad walked on, his two children were taken to Carlisle. Our lives as a family would never be ordinary or normal due to the psychological effects my grandfather displayed. Not only was he dealing with all the conditions brought on our people by the foreign occupation and takeover; in addition he had to try to process what he was forced to go through at a military-style boarding school and the abuse he experienced while at Carlisle.

Due to the behaviors of my grandfather, he and my father had no relationship at all. When Carlisle came into the picture and after hearing all the stories from the elders who experienced Carlisle, I knew why my grandfather was the way he was.

My grandfather walked on when I was three. They tell me he would come to visit when I was born and wanted to hold me and be a grand-

Fig. 29. Warren Petoskey (Odawa) at the entrance to the Indian School cemetery playing his flute, 2012. Photo by Chip Fox.

father to me, as much as he knew how, but that was limited because he was raised in an institution with no parents or elders around him to teach him or be examples. He appeared suspended between two worlds, one his Native origin, and the other the false world that was taught him.

The residual effects of the boarding school experience is evident in every Native family. We continue to perish at a mortality rate 400 percent higher than any other ethnic population in the United States. Disease, suicide, sudden infant death syndrome, crime, and spousal and child abuse are higher than for any other ethnic population in the United States.

My wife's great-grandmother and great-grandfather were survivors of the Trail of Tears. She did not even know she was Indian until we met, and her father revealed it to her. She is Choctaw and Cherokee.

My wife and I met in April 1967 and were married at the end of June that same year. We just celebrated our forty-fifth anniversary. Through those forty-five years the demons we battled and the baggage we carried and had to get rid of were evident. The presence of this baggage in our lives was also evident. We passed residuals on to our children, and they have struggled, and some continue to struggle. My wife, Barb, and I established a better home environment than we grew up in, but we still passed some of the baggage on because we were unable to identify it for what it was.

At the time of writing I am sixty-seven years of age, and my wife is sixty-one. We have worked together to attempt to address historical trauma as it relates to us and identify the dysfunctional conditions we harbored and exampled, feeling we needed to give back. As we were doing this, we shared information with some of our family and saw the improvements in their life perspective and behaviors.

Fifteen years ago we began Dawnland Native Ministries in our effort to address these residual issues and present as much of history from Native perspectives as we knew.

What to do with our experience at the Carlisle Symposium?

We knew we had to go to the site of the Carlisle Barracks and visit the small graveyard that in no way represents the number of deaths that actually occurred during Carlisle Indian School's tenure. Many children were sent home when it became clear they were seriously ill. Others died when on "Outing" and were buried in cemeteries in Pennsylvania, New Jersey, and New York. Some of those buried in the Indian School cemetery were later lost when the cemetery was relocated to make way for other army buildings. There would be no way anyone could go onto the grounds now and by the new seismographic process discover unmarked graves. Carlisle Barracks is currently a military base with a "war" college onsite.

I prayed the night we went to the graveyard at Carlisle Barracks and asked the Creator what I should do in honor of my grandfather, great-aunt, and all my relatives that perished in this hellhole. I do not have the training of a pipe carrier, but I saw myself doing a pipe ceremony and a flute song sending our prayers up with so many others over the years to assure the spirits of all these children, those who experienced Carlisle and survived, but have walked on since, and those first-generation children who have suffered from the residuals the Carlisle experience deposited in their moms' and dads' and grandfathers' and grandmothers' lives.

I did not know how I would react to what I would feel and see once we arrived. I do not want to return to the feelings of anger, grief, and revenge I used to know, but I wanted to let all my relatives know that I have finally made the journey to them to honor them and connect with them in that infamous place where the unforgiveable happened. I assured them of my desire to be a better advocate and activist representing them in an age where a government and foreign nations want us just to forget what happened and join them as "Americans." My grandfather was made a United States citizen in 1924 at forty years of age, but he was not given permission to vote until 1941. He walked on in 1948.

So, what is to be done? I believe the First Nations and Métis of Canada have already laid the groundwork for the work that needs to be advanced in the United States. Healing, reparation, and reconciliation need to take place. Crimes committed need to be made public. The actual number of children who died in the boarding schools needs to be published. Apologies need to be made, and religious and political institutions need to be held morally and legally accountable.

We are doing a little better according to the recent census. Our original populations were estimated to be between 18 and 122 million; within two hundred years, from 1700 to 1900, our populations were reduced through genocide, germ warfare, medical experiments, sterilizations, and the conditions in which we were incarcerated to less than 250,000. We now number 6.5 million, but it has been and remains a struggle to get healthier spiritually, physically, and mentally.

19

The Presence of Ghosts

MAURICE KENNY (MOHAWK)

Editors' note: Maurice Kenny was unaware that the house in Bellaire Park where he chose to stay so happily during the symposium was already part of the wider story. It was once the home of Dick Kaseeta, son of Kesetta Roosevelt, the Lipan Apache Carlisle student whose story was the inspiration for the symposium. Now the home of Susan Rose and her family, in 2009 the house had been named "an Apache house" by the Lipan Apache elders who stayed there during their visit to Carlisle to give blessing ceremonies for their ancestors.

I saw the light from the street. The window was white. I shuddered, but I was bound to enter this historic old house in Carlisle, the Guest House at Dickinson College where I was meant to stay. But I sensed the presence of ghosts. So we left the old Guest House. Shortly we entered a house of furry dogs, young smiles, and a large cup of hot tea with lemon and honey that awaited my fierce cold in a charm of a house outside the city in the woods. I felt at home immediately. I would stay here. No strange lights, no thin hallway, no ghosts, and where I knew the furry dogs would keep me warm and safe during the nights. It was a house of books: on the table, in the bathroom, on the kitchen sink, wherever an open place: books. Where poems were discussed and read, and a hot ham dinner had been waiting our arrival.

Carlisle, Pennsylvania, is an important place in Native history in America. The Carlisle Indian Boarding School had been cold and bloody as genocide always seems to be. A school determined by the American Army to cut the braids, tighten lips not to speak, to forget their beautiful languages, and to wear uniforms that choked the neck and broke tears to wet the grounds of this prison. Babies in the arm, young frightened little girls wrapped in blankets, ten-year-old boys frightened nearly to comatose and who would never dance a traditional war dance, a sun dance, a moccasin dance again, blow their breath into a flute, a flute singing of love and bright futures as hunter/warriors . . . man/womanhood proud to live for the community of their Native peoples, their individual families, to govern their Nation. Babes, children! Unbelievable in America where all are born free, free to speak, to pray, to love, to live in harmony with all around and especially nature itself . . . not to worry that in the dark of night soldiers of whatever kind would descend and pull you from the arms of your natural mother and force you off to a new style of life without sibling, parent, or teaching uncle; a holy place to pray and receive life guidance from a vision given to you from the spirit world. Life as they had known was totally denied! No gruel might replace a plate of meat soup, no quilt could replace a mother's arm nor father's protection, nor elder's guidance. A cold, most unfriendly world was there offering a cold welcome to reality with no mother smiling or father approaching the home with a line of fish or wild duck, nor an aging grandparent's smile.

Stripped of all a child's knowledge of the culture that had spawned its people for centuries untold and that here at the Boarding School would then end . . . forever more.

It was without a shred of doubt a pleasure to be invited to this symposium.

To partake as a Mohawk person, a poet, an amateur historian in such an array of Native elders and their younger legitimate academic historians, speakers of varying persuasions, and an audience compiled of many Native Americans, many of whom were descendants of the children brought to the Boarding School those many years ago—1879–1918 . . . a long time of pain, misery, loneliness, let alone great loss of family and fireside, coupled with indifference and punishment.

Throughout the sun's movement we heard the notes of a flute float across the auditorium, notes soft, low, sad, nay tragic, notes blown by a young Native musician (Brian Frejo, Pawnee and Seminole) whose music reminded us, as if we could forget, of the hollow lives of those imprisoned children who suffered at this school. Poetry read by a gravel-voiced Mohawk poet (myself) followed a deeply moving opening Thanksgiving Prayer by J. Peter Jemison (Seneca). The day was now set; ribbons of expectation gently moved through the audience as speech after speech was offered to the assembled, speeches dealing with the harsh past history of the school as well as its future. Dovie Thomason offered a story to which all attending sat in surprise and pleasure. There were important times when the audience took the opportunity of openly speaking their thoughts of memory or of the history or suggesting new routes to understanding the plight of the Carlisle Indian School's history and survival.

The impression of the days was of great import . . . that the memory, the history of such a phenomenon as Indian boarding schools, or any other of such nature, might be abolished for the sake of the children involved and their future lives and the future of America itself. As the country suffered war camps during the Second World War by placing Japanese citizens in camps, an abomination, no American citizen of whatever stripe or color should be thusly punished. And we should never forget the horrors of black slavery allowed those hundreds of years in this "free land." The informed speeches of the various voices were for the most part short, pithy, and often thrilling to hear, yet at times anger rose in the emotions upon hearing details of ruthless administrating of the lives of the children committed to relocation and deduction of Native lifestyle and world philosophy. Jennifer Denetdale (Navajo) offered a greatly moving assessment of a blood relation's children here at the school—the two sons of Navajo chief Manuelito, one of whom died at the school and the other who died shortly after being brought home. Heartbreaking, unforgettable. There were times when tears rose and fell at various speeches and audience participation in the programs.

Yet with all the reliving of the sadness and tragedy, there loomed a comradeship and unburdening of the remembered sorrow at the unforgettable history of the often infamous story of these thousands of small children and their trek to adulthood through the auspices of the U.S. Army. And if one could not forget the hate and burning by Washington of Iroquois villages he set afire in the early wars in the eastern United States, or the massacres at Sand Creek, or Wounded Knee, to name only a tenth of outrageous plunder and killings of individuals and Native nations, the plunder of the culture, the death of the human being, the individual who long had first rights, and last, one might add. There was sadness and anger in the audience, but more importantly there were words spoken and truly believed by most of resurrection, resiliency, the future in all aspects, utter belief in the individual rights and successes to come mainly through the efforts of their young, a solid belief in time and what time may mend.

A highlight of the event was a film, *The Lost Ones: Long Journey Home*, a documentary film by Susan Rose and Manuel Saralegui, a film dealing with two Lipan Apache siblings brought to the Boarding School and the consequence of that action. Moving, hypnotic in the sense of disbelief that such horrors might befall two absolutely innocent children guilty of nothing but to be Native Americans. Powerful! Unforgettable! It might well be used in every classroom of the country, beautifully filmed with economy of waste without disrespecting punctured truth. One other delight of import was again taking the warm hand of N. Scott Momaday, a Pulitzer Prize–winning author of fiction, *House Made of Dawn*.

It was a great honor and pleasure to work with and listen to the voices of the creators of this symposium, mainly Jacqueline Fear-Segal, Susan Rose, Barbara Landis, and others with the mammoth aid of Dickinson College and its staff.

One comes away from the prayers, speeches, the flute, the poem, the audience responses, and the robust enthusiasm with a feeling of a job very well done, and it accomplished wonders without sword, without blood, but ended on a positive beat that more meetings and symposiums should be encouraged and arranged with perhaps more college students and teachers of whatever persuasion not only being participants of the audience but participating in the event itself.

It can only be hoped those people responsible for this venture will be rewarded with the knowledge that not only was a great and needed gathering successful, but that their hard labor will be respected and admired for many years to come. It was accomplished brilliantly.

It is hoped that those in the woods, in the house of dogs and kids and books and hot tea and hot ham and much, much pleasure and joy, will be free of ghosts for many years to come, and that the white lights of the college Guest House will warm and remain welcoming to other visitors who have no fear.

20

A Sacred Space

SHARON O'BRIEN

This was the most extraordinary symposium I've ever attended. Because of the non-academic, Native structure and sessions, mingling stories with poems with videos with papers with the most heartfelt audience response I've ever seen, this symposium engaged us all as whole people—mind, heart, and spirit. Several attendees and participants spoke of "healing" as a process that took place during it, and I think that process was connected with the creation of a safe and Native "space" that was both physical (the Anita Tuven Schlecter [ATS] auditorium, the Dickinson campus, and the Carlisle Barracks) and emotional. Given that we were dealing with the traumas inflicted by another school and another space in Carlisle—the Indian School—the fact that healing could be linked with Carlisle and an academic institution had a kind of circular karma to it that itself could be part of Native storytelling. The conference felt like a return, but also like a new beginning.

One kind of miracle happened: the bunker-like ATS, everyone's least favorite building on the Dickinson campus, became a kind of sacred space right from the beginning when Pete Jemison delivered the blessing and the opening plenary. The blessing itself linked visible and invisible worlds and brought nature into our somewhat sterile surroundings. Jemison's poem-like blessing had the repeated line "And now we are as one," and that hypnotic repetition had the effect of us feeling that in this time and space Native and non-Native separations could be bridged—while still making clear that we were in Native space. The ways in which the conference enacted the erasure of the boundary between Native and non-Native continued with the first presentation, "Coming to Carlisle," a panel featuring two non-Native speakers (Barbara Landis and Jacqueline Fear-Segal) and one Native (Dovie Thomason). Barbara was the first to speak, and she was so overcome with emotion—with tears she tried to hold back but could not—that it was clear right away that this would be a space for emotion, for the heart. What was also clear is that the separation between Native and non-Native could be bridged when a white woman was weeping for the stories of the Carlisle children—and that of their descendants. The space was safe for expressing anger as well as sadness. As this session was coming to a close, a Native woman expressed great anger as she asked the politically pressing question: "*When* are we going to stop calling it Columbus Day?" The question prompted powerful and intense responses. The audience realized that there must be activism in dealing with the repercussions of indigenous and U.S. history. Where do we go from here?

The question for me was: How could there be an "ending" to this extraordinary conference? Would there be conflict? Separation? Decisions on future activism? Unity? And given all that had gone on, how could we feel that we had come to a resting place so that we could leave with a sense of completion? We were fortunate beyond words in having N. Scott Momaday end the conference with his spiritually grounded gravity and wisdom. What he did was both extraordinary and right. He reminded us that those who suffered were *children* and so brought us back to the reality of the Indian school, and to Native American history and loss. He then described the important day he had had, visiting the battlefield at Gettysburg and thinking about Lincoln's Gettysburg Address. He illuminated for me the importance of the Carlisle Indian School to Native American history by saying that its name and history should be as prominent as Wounded Knee and Little Big Horn. And by juxtaposing the Indian School to Gettysburg, he placed what happened at Carlisle in American history more broadly: this is a story about all of us. And it should be told. Lincoln was honoring the dead in his Gettysburg Address, and so should we honor these children, and their descendants, as we make the Carlisle Indian School part of our history. *Every Dickinson student needs to know about the Indian School,* I thought; somehow, somewhere, this needs to be part of a common curriculum. My own understanding of the Indian School's importance had been illuminated and deepened by the words I was hearing; I would want to pass the wisdom I had received from Momaday on to my students.

When Momaday finished his remarks and the applause died down, everyone was silent and still. You could have heard a pin drop in ats. No one was going anywhere. Momaday had returned us to the sacred space that Jemison had created at the beginning and had elevated and deepened our symposium by giving us a mission: *make the story of this school part of American history*, let its name be known. Given that the Indian children lost their Native names as part of the socialization process, being able to name the school, and name what happened there, could also be a kind of circular process that can lead to healing and reconciliation. But only if the truth is told and listened to, as it was that weekend.

I felt changed by that weekend; I now feel attached to this symposium and its future in a profound way. I have joined something. I was part of something for two days, and I want to stay connected to what happened since the conference released living energies that are going to lead somewhere. And I will teach my Dickinson students about Carlisle.

21

Carlisle

My Hometown

CHARLES FOX

From 1996 through 1998 I used to bring my family back to Carlisle to escape from our urban setting of Philadelphia and allow my own sons to revel in the outdoor pleasures I had known as a child. On an evening of one such trip, the hour of midnight had passed, and a frigid December night had produced a particularly clear sky. The stars above looked down, burning bright with a fierce intensity, making their presence known. I sat beside the banks of the Letort Spring Run. The moonlight danced upon the rippled surface of the water. It was neither a dance filled with emotions of joy or sorrow, but rather an unwavering, seamless maneuver. Its dance was not new to me. Its waters had been a constant in my life. I grew up along its banks experiencing endless summer adventures filled with lightning bugs and grasshoppers, bonfires and campouts. It was the fabled limestone fly-fishing water that was the passion of my father's life and too often a competitor for his attention. It was where I chose to propose to my wife, on an equally cold December night. A child of the mountains knows the language of the wind, but I was a child of the water's edge. Never envious of fish or desiring to be a natator, I was comfortably land-locked with the trees I grew up climbing on as companions. But I knew the language of the water. The womb-like sound of the Letort's lapping waters against rocks and earth was always a comfort, a lullaby for the soul, and that is what brought me there on this night. My soul was disturbed, my mind uneasy.

Like many children, as a young boy I had a fascination with Indians, and I too "played Indian." Through the woods I tiptoed, with an imitation bear hide on my back, my war bonnet on my head, and a tomahawk in my hand. A collection of totem poles, which my father had brought back from annual salmon fishing trips to Canada, lined the top of my dresser, casting shadows on the wall. And though that interest had continued off and on over the decades that followed, I began to feel led in a different direction, pulled by a new gravitational force. That night, voices too ineffable to be heard, but felt all the same, called me. The drone of nearby Interstate 81 filled the air, interrupting the tranquility of the setting. I was sure that if I could silence that roadway, I might be able to hear these voices whose presence I felt so strongly.

Yet when I read about Native American history, it always took me someplace else. From the Dakota Plains to the forced removal of the Cherokee Nation in North Carolina and Georgia, to the Nez Perce in the Northwest, to atrocities such as the massacres at Sand Creek and Wounded Knee. I never thought about my hometown.

But I remember reading a collection of Native American writings and coming across an excerpt from Luther Standing Bear's book *My People the Sioux.* There was a chapter titled "First Days at Carlisle." I started reading, expecting little more than tales of Jim Thorpe and the football team, but out of nowhere, like a cold winter wind, it slapped me across the face. His words did not speak of happy schoolchildren and great athletes, but told the tale of forced assimilation and the destruction of Native culture. I felt like a dark family secret had been exposed, and my feelings about my hometown were never going to be the same. I knew about the Indian School, but in only the most superficial of ways. We all knew of Jim Thorpe, the great Indian School athlete, who had starred in the 1912 Olympics and later as a professional football and baseball player, and Glen "Pop" Warner, the famous football coach, but I knew little else about the Indian School, despite having lived a mile and a half from the site for over twenty years. No one ever thinks of something notable happening in their sleepy hometown, but the reality and the darkness of Carlisle's significance was there in Luther Standing Bear's words:

One day when we came to school there was a lot of writing on one of the blackboards. We did not know what it meant, but our interpreter came into the room and said, "Do you see all these marks on the blackboard? Well, each word is a white man's name. They are going to give each one of you one of these names by which you will hereafter be known." None of the names were read or explained to us, so of course we did not know the sound or meaning of any of them. . . . Soon we all had the names of white men sewed on our backs.

Now, after having my hair cut, a new thought came into my head. I felt I was no more an Indian, but would be an imitation of a white man.[1]

I felt naive. I felt stupid. Growing up, I can't remember one minute of any history class in school ever being devoted to the Indian School. Though I had a Geronimo action figure, no one ever told me that the conquered warrior rode horseback through the streets of the town while visiting students from his Chiricahau Apache tribe. The only "Redskins" discussed in conversation were the NFL team that used to hold its training camp in Carlisle at Dickinson College.

So I made one of my first ever searches of the Internet and came across Barb Landis's website on the Indian School. I started the virtual tour of the school grounds, and on the first stop, at the main gate, a shiver went up my spine as I learned about students flooding the Letort in winter to create an ice-skating area. I have never seen a ghost in my life, but I felt that the water that flowed between the banks of the Letort had opened up a connection between us, and I needed to know more.

Over the years I have tried to find ways to deal with the dark shadow that hangs over my hometown. Through books such as *Education for Extinction* (David Wallace Adams), *Killing the White Man's Indian* (Fergus M. Bordewich), *The Wolf at Twilight* (Kent Nerburn), *White Man's Club* (Jacqueline Fear-Segal), *Indian School Days* (Basil H. Johnston), *Carlisle vs. Army* (Lars Anderson), I have tried to add to my knowledge.[2] I tried (and failed) to learn Lakota to make up for the students who weren't allowed to speak their Native languages. Each of my three sons did projects on the Carlisle School during their elementary school years. It was the one school project on which I insisted. I would go into their classrooms to tell Native American folktales. I would always start out with some humorous tales about animals and tricksters and then end up with tales based around Luther Standing Bear and that first group of students at Carlisle. It wasn't my heritage, maybe it wasn't my story to tell, but I was determined to tell the classmates of my sons a story that was never told to me in school. I would end the Carlisle story with the following scene, which I had adapted from Adams's *Education for Extinction* and Pratt's *Battlefield and Classroom*.[3]

The boys were told their long hair must be cut. They were confused. In their traditions, the cutting of hair had always been associated with the death of a family member, a way to show their grief. Robert American Horse exclaimed, "If I am to learn the ways of the white people, I can do it just as well with my hair on."

One day, the boys saw large chairs arrive at the school. One-by-one, they were taken out of class, returning with nearly shaven heads till one of the older boys remained steadfast in his refusal to have his hair cut. Since her husband, Captain Pratt, who ran the school was away, Mrs. Pratt chose not to make an issue of the matter till her husband returned. That night, she was awoken by a strange sound. It was a human sound, filled with sorrow and unlike anything she had ever heard.

The young man who had refused to have his hair cut had gone to the school parade grounds. Knife in hand, he sang a traditional song of mourning, while he cut off his long locks. The other children woke and joined their voices to his song. Their voices rose into the night sky as if all at once, they realized that they were indeed mourning a death, the death of their traditional Indian ways, the death of the lives they had known.

I know it's a small victory. I can't change history and heal the wounds it caused, but I felt the need to tell the story. As I would tell the students, "Some stories just refuse to be silent . . . I tell it to you because it wasn't told to me."

I hadn't been to Carlisle much in recent years, and a significant amount of time had passed since I last sat on the banks of the Letort. But on my return this time it would be the living rather than the ghosts of the past that would speak to me. I traveled to Carlisle in the fall of 2012 for the symposium Dickinson College was holding on the Carlisle Indian School. While there, a Native American group from Michigan agreed to let me visit the cemetery at the Carlisle Barracks with them. Warren Petoskey would perform a pipe ceremony to help bring peace and healing to himself and his family. We walked through the gates of the cemetery on October 6, the anniversary of the first class arriving at Carlisle in 1879. The cemetery is lined with 192 bleached white gravestones of students who died while attending school there, most victims of disease. Though I have been there many times, I was not prepared for the intensity of the emotions experienced by the Michigan visitors. As they walked past the identical graves, the sobs began and the tears flowed. It was clear that 133 years had not healed the scars or reversed the damage done by the Carlisle School and the numerous other boarding schools that were modeled after it throughout the United States and Canada. "It's not ancient history. It's current in the way it affected our community. It's intergenerational trauma," said Faye Gibbon, executive director of American Indian Services, whose great-grandmother attended Carlisle. Her twin sister, Kay McGowan, added, "There are many, many problems in Native American communities as a result of boarding schools. We have a suicide rate three times the national average. We have problems with domestic abuse and sexual abuse. All problems directly related to the kind of abuse Native children suffered at the boarding schools." Warren Petoskey, whose grandfather and great-aunt also attended Carlisle, explained the school's program: "Boarding schools forbid the languages, forbid the culture, did a lot of character assassination, denigrated the people for their tribal origins, disenfranchised them emotionally, and tried to give them a false identity." Daisy Three Irons, a retired schoolteacher from Montana whose grandfather had attended Carlisle around the turn of the century, explained, "When I was a child I had an uncle who would always threaten us, 'If you don't behave yourself, they'll put you in a bag and ship you off to Carlisle.'" It is sobering to one day discover your hometown has a negative connotation to a whole race of people. No one thinks of his or her hometown as the "Bogey Man."

The responses of these Carlisle descendants had made me see that this school, and the numerous boarding schools that would be modeled after it, had severed Native American cultures in a way that could never be repaired. The school was a misguided attempt to give these students a future, to assimilate them into white civilization, but by taking away their past it doomed their future as well. "Sometimes they didn't see their families for eight or ten or twelve years, and when they went home they were strangers. They couldn't speak their languages. They looked different and they acted different. . . . It created a group of people who didn't feel like they belonged anywhere and had this high level of dysfunction in our society," says Dr. Kay McGowan, whose great-grandmother attended the school.

The following morning I stopped by the cemetery before leaving town.

I waited for a quiet moment between tours where I could have a few minutes of reflection alone. I walked through the white gravestones that stood in perfect rows like a formation of soldiers. They had been denied the opportunity as students to express their respective cultures, to speak their languages. Yet again, under these identical gravestones, they were again denied the opportunity to express themselves, to tell their stories. The white gravestones were simply another version of the military-style uniforms they were forced to wear as students. I paused at the grave of Rebecca Little Wolf and left a small offering, because her death date was the same as my birthday. Was it Rebecca who had called out to me so many years ago along the banks of the Letort? Or was it Amos LaFromboise, the thirteen-year-old Sioux boy who was the first student to die at Carlisle? He was initially buried at nearby Ashland Cemetery until it was determined nonwhites could not be buried there; his body was exhumed, and a cemetery was created on the school grounds. In a strange coincidence, Ashland was where my parents lay buried, a site they had innocently chosen for its bucolic atmosphere and historical ties to the Civil War.

As I stood there on the former school grounds among the bleached gravestones, the words of humanitarian and physician Dr. Paul Farmer, who is best known for work providing health care for "third world" people and cofounding Partners In Health, came to mind: "The idea that some lives matter less is the root of all evil in the world." It didn't really matter whether it was an individual voice or the collective voices that had called out to me so many years ago. They had made themselves known and pulled me along like the current that flowed downstream from where I sat along the Letort. As I stood on this plot of land I had so often passed by in ignorance earlier in my life, any response I could offer seemed inadequate.

Epilogue

I thought I had typed the final sentence for this essay. So with the essay done and 150 miles to drive that day, I had time to think. I had a great-uncle, Dr. L. Webster Fox, a well-known Philadelphia ophthalmic surgeon. I knew of Uncle Webster, but I had never met him because he had died in 1931. When relatives spoke about him, they mainly talked about the final years of his life when he traveled to the Blackfeet Indian Reservation in Browning, Montana, to perform free eye operations. His "Fox Technique," or tarsectomy, would become significant, in both positive and negative ways, in the battle against trachoma among Native peoples. So appreciative were the Blackfeet for the more than three hundred operations he performed that they made him an honorary tribal member. That was the extent of the story I knew. I even had a photograph that my Uncle George had given me of Webster proudly wearing the regalia that the Blackfeet had presented him with. It hangs in our home looking over my shoulder by my desk.

It crossed my mind that if Uncle Webster had been willing to travel repeatedly to northern Montana, maybe there was a chance he had traveled to the Carlisle School. Upon returning home, I did a quick Internet search. I soon found myself looking at a reprint of the *Carlisle Arrow and Red Man* from June 7, 1918, and staring at an image that looked like a middle-aged version of my father. I discovered that Webster's relationship with the Carlisle school had extended over twenty years, treating hundreds of students for free. My breath grew short. I went to rise from my chair, only to have my knees buckle. Why hadn't I known this obvious connection before? If my Uncle George knew about this, why didn't he mention this to me when he presented me with Webster's photograph? My father had been a history buff, blessed with a great memory, who could expound upon family and personal history as easily as he could describe the events of the Battle of Gettysburg. Yet, he never mentioned this. Both were now gone from this world, so those questions would go unanswered.

Where would my new knowledge of Uncle Webster lead? I trusted that in time the future would reveal the past. I had learned to believe these things had their own time schedule, much like the Letort, which moved cautiously and unhurried but still managed to erode and reveal. In places the water flowed shallow and transparent and in other locations dark pools hid revelations below the surface. I knew the water's dance. Its current had brought me here, and its current would send me forth to learn more.

NOTES

1. Luther Standing Bear, *My People the Sioux* (Lincoln: University of Nebraska Press, 1975), 136–37, 141.
2. David Wallace Adams, *Education for Extinction: American Indians and the Boarding School Experience, 1875–1928* (Lawrence: University of Kansas Press,

1995); Fergus M. Bordewich, *Killing the White Man's Indian: Reinventing of Native Americans at the End of the Twentieth Century* (New York: Double-day, 1996); Kent Nerburn, *The Wolf at Twilight: An Indian Elder's Journey through a Land of Ghosts and Shadows* (Novato CA: New World Library, 2009); Jacqueline Fear-Segal, *White Man's Club: Schools, Race, and the Struggle of Indian Acculturation* (Lincoln: University of Nebraska Press, 2007); Basil H. Johnston, *Indian School Days* (Norman: University of Oklahoma Press, 1988); Lars Anderson, *Carlisle vs. Army: Jim Thorpe, Dwight Eisenhower, Pop Warner, and the Forgotten Story of Football's Greatest Battle* (New York: Random House, 2007).

3. Richard Henry Pratt, *Battlefield and Classroom: Four Decades with the American Indian, 1867–1904*, ed. Robert Utley (New Haven CT: Yale University Press, 1964).

22

The Ndé and Carlisle

Reflections on the Symposium

DANIEL CASTRO ROMERO JR. (NDÉ/LIPAN APACHE)

"We are here and we are ready to tell our story."

The Carlisle Symposium opened up a space for us to tell our story, to say we are not extinct—we are still here. It was a healing time—we faced the past, integrated it—we had to do that in order to move forward as a people. It was important to share the stories of our people . . .

We, Ndé, we carry our traditions orally. The memory of the Lost Ones was carried down in our oral history, across the generations. For over 130 years, we didn't know what happened to the two children who disappeared after the massacre of our village known as "The Day of Screams." Their father, Ramon Castro, who returned after a hunting trip to find the village decimated and his wife and others killed, could not find his children. He died of a broken heart not knowing what happened to them. Then a connection was made by Jacqueline Fear-Segal—and we found out they had been taken to Carlisle. We made the trip there to do the Blessing ceremonies so the Lost Ones could be sent home. And a powerful film (*The Lost Ones: Long Journey Home*) was made that documents their story, our story. We showed it at our family reunion with Spanish subtitles, since many of our people do not speak English, and it has helped our community heal. People cried as we recognized our story, as we again felt the pain and the loss, but also the healing. And now we can share our story.

From the very earliest period in my life that I can remember, there was always a family reunion in August and we always had empty chairs. I remember as a I child I tried to sit in one of the chairs, and my aunts would scold me. "Don't sit in the chair please, there is someone there." And I would ask, "Mom, there's no one there?" and my mum would say, "But there is, you just can't see them, we have them in our heart, we have them in our memory, and until the day we find them and we find out where they're at, and we come to help them and bring them home, we'll put out a chair for them." We're talking about children, the Lost Ones, who never completed their cycles of life—about Kesetta, who never had a puberty ceremony. The young man, Jack, who was never taught his traditional oral histories and rites of passage.

In being able to discover what happened to them and to be able to tell our story, our sense of space and our sense of spirituality have now been rebalanced; they're back in balance now. The symposium brought all that together. And I was really, really astounded because I thought that the conference was only going to produce a handful of people, but when I looked up, there were hundreds.

So, the first day everybody's looking, they're probing and they're talking, they're asking questions—it's like everyone had sent their scouts out. And they discovered the importance of what we were doing, that this was not just an academic conference, this was a conference for people to vent. This was a conference for people to express what they feel, and in essence the symposium brought that plate and that setting and that table to life. They gave it a sense of "You now made it home. You're here. You're welcome to say what you want to say." And it gave people the opportunity to let out what's been inside their and the community's hearts for hundreds of years for some of them. And for some of them, people who had lost grandparents who were part of the school—people who were directly affected with their experience of the Indian boarding system.

They came here to see how they can express themselves, and whether or not it's okay. And the symposium pretty much opened the door and said it is okay for you to express your feelings. It's okay for you to have anger. It's okay for you to let go of that spirit, that spiritual part that is clinging on to you that has so much hate and remorse. You can let it go now. You can benefit from this so that your people can move forward, so you don't dwell on it, live your whole life making fry bread, thinking, "God Almighty. You know, every time I make fry bread, I'm so mad. You know, they taught us, this is all they taught us how to do, is bake. I wish I would have had a normal childhood." Like maybe now they can say, "You know, come over here, grandson, granddaughter, I have a story to tell you. I want to share this history with you so that you can pass it on." As elders we need to tell our children, our people, about our history—both the positive and the negative so that there is a sense of balance. That's another thing that the conference did; it allowed people the opportunity to ask those kinds of questions. It made a lot of people feel uncomfortable, but it was not about scolding people. It was just about allowing the people to express themselves, to talk about that internal pain, because for a lot of these people, they're the main elders for their tribes that were coming to this event. There were a few elders who even I know by name, and in their communities they are known as being famous elders. And they went back to their communities and they spread the news that it's okay. They gave them the template to understand what had happened to them, and also how to express what had happened to them, but to move beyond that. Okay, now that we've thrown the baggage away, we can move forward, and that's what your conference did, but we're not going to forget about that baggage that's lying down on the ground. We're going talk about it, we're going to preserve it, it's part of our history—and that was the biggest hurdle my people need to get over.

It was funny because after the conference, we went back home, and it wasn't too much later that we had our family reunion. When everybody came, they're asking, are we blessing the plates yet? And I go, "No," and they're like, "Why not, Uncle?" And I go, "That time has passed, we've gone beyond that. We no longer need to do this. We don't forget it, it's part of our history, but we've now moved forward." And some of them say, "Why, you know, it's part of our history?" "Yes, but it's also part of our history that we've matured now, we've crossed our hurdle, we're now in a different phase, we've grown out of that cocoon and we're now flying around, and you know what, we're ready to take on new challenges for our people." It was a day of healing.

Epilogue

N. SCOTT MOMADAY (KIOWA)

The Carlisle Indian Industrial School is a landmark in the cultural history of the United States. In the years of its existence, 1879–1918, the nation was in an ambiguous state of being. The Civil War left a festering wound on the moral and patriotic intelligence of most Americans.

In the West expansion was ongoing. The so-called Indian Wars were winding down, and the once formidable horse culture of the Great Plains was ended. Even in absolute defeat the Indian was in the way of "Manifest Destiny." Methods of removal included massacres at such places as Sand Creek, Wounded Knee, the Washita—and atrocities more nearly genocidal in California.

More subtle, if no less effective, was the founding of the school at Carlisle by Richard Henry Pratt, who was driven by a determination to "kill the Indian and save the man," an equation that by definition negated the cultural existence of the Indian. Pratt's experiment was performed on helpless children, and it was performed many times over in numerous boarding schools modeled on the Carlisle prototype.

The story of Carlisle is told on the conscience of America. We must hope and believe that there is compassion in the telling.

Chronology

Recent historical, anthropological, and archaeological studies of the Native peoples of northeastern North America suggest a six-stage periodization:[1]

1. From perhaps 12,000 BC to approximately AD 1550: Gradual development of the many Native groups living in the "Pennsylvania" region.[2]
2. From approximately 1550 to 1625: Indirect contacts with European cultures.
3. From approximately 1625 to 1675: Responses to the European invasions.
4. From approximately 1675 to 1754: Economic dependency and tenuous cultural autonomy. Main groups around Carlisle: Susquehannocks; Lenapes; Piscataways; Delawares; Munsees; Shawnees.
5. From the beginning of the Seven Years' War in 1754 to the last major Pennsylvania Indian land cession in 1794: Indian wars fought for independence.
6. From 1794 to the present: Invisibility to the dominant culture of the United States.

1875–78: Capt. Richard Henry Pratt accompanied Cheyenne (thirty-three), Kiowa (twenty-seven), Comanche (eleven), Arapaho (two), and Caddo (one) leaders and warriors from Fort Sill, Oklahoma, to Fort Marion, St. Augustine, Florida, for an indefinite period of imprisonment. He set up a fortress school for the younger men, which gave him the idea to found the Carlisle Indian School. All the prisoners were released in 1878.

1878–79: Pratt took twenty-two of the young ex-prisoners to the Hampton Institute, Virginia. They formed the basis for a separate Indian Program at this institution, which had been founded in 1868 to educate the freedmen. Pratt stayed at Hampton for a year.

1879: Pratt gained the support of Secretary of the Interior Carl Schurz and Secretary of War Andrew McCrary to convert the disused barracks at Carlisle into an Indian school. He was the founder and the first and longest-serving superintendent of the Indian School. Eleven of the ex–Fort Marion prisoners came to Carlisle to help Pratt set up the school.

October 5—Close to midnight, the first group of students arrived from the Rosebud and Pine Ridge Agencies, Dakota. From the start, students were drilled daily. Enrollment for the first year was 131.

November 26—First student died (Amos LaFromboise, Sisseton Sioux) and was buried in local Ashland Cemetery.

1879–1902: John Nicholas Choate worked as unofficial school photographer.

1880: Student-run "court-martial" system set up by Pratt to enforce school rules. "Outing" organized during first summer for twenty-four students, matching the system Pratt had initiated at Hampton. School rented ten acres of farmland adjoining the Carlisle Barracks.

January 17—Second student died (Abe Lincoln, Cheyenne), and an Indian cemetery was opened at the Indian School.

June—Spotted Tail, Red Cloud, and nearly forty other Sioux leaders visited the Indian School.

1881: Summer Outing for sixty-six students (twenty-two boys, forty-four girls).

1881–83: School rented the Parker Farm (109 acres).

1883: First male student ran away (Josiah Wolf, Odawa/Otawa/Ottawa).

1884: Hospital built, Washington Hall. Hocker Farm purchased, 157 acres (Middlesex County).

1887: Dawes General Allotment Act was adopted by Congress.

1887: Gymnasium built by students. Farm #1 (Parker) deeded to Indian School.

1888: Highest death rate for a single year (twenty-one).

1889: First graduating class of fourteen students. First student expelled from school.

1890: December 29—Wounded Knee Massacre; more than two hundred Lakota men, women, and children killed by the U.S Seventh Cavalry Regiment.

1891: Plenty Horses released from prison with murder charge dropped.

1891–92: Administration building built by students.

1893: Carlisle Indian football team played their first season recognized by the National Collegiate Athletic Association. School had Columbian Exposition exhibit and students marched.

1893–96: Carlos Montezuma (Yavapai), school physician.

1895: Front section added to gymnasium (later called Thorpe Hall). Laundry built.

1898: First female student ran away (Crow).

1899–1900: Charles Eastman worked as Carlisle Outing agent and recruiter (not physician).

1899–1901: Zitkala-Ša (Gertrude Simmons) taught at school and was also sent west to recruit students.

1899–1903: Glenn "Pop" Warner, head football coach (first time).

1901: Farm #2 (Kutz) deeded to Indian School—175 acres bordering Farm #1.

1902: Grandstand built on Indian Field. Replaced by larger structure in 1940.

1903: Glenn "Pop" Warner returned to school. Largest graduating class of forty-seven students.

1904: Pratt forcibly retired as superintendent. Jim Thorpe (Sac and Fox) arrived at school, aged fifteen.

1904–8: Capt. William A. Mercer, superintendent.

1905: Carlisle band and students marched at Theodore Roosevelt's Inaugural Parade behind six famous Indian leaders in full regalia.

1906–15: Angel de Cora (Winnebago/Ho-Chunk) appointed by Commissioner of Indian Affairs Francis Leupp to teach Native arts at school.

1907: Leupp Indian Art Studio designed and built by Indians. Jim Thorpe (Sac and Fox) began his serious athletic career at Carlisle. Lewis Tewanima arrived at Carlisle.

1907–14: Glenn "Pop" Warner back at school.

1908–14: Moses Friedman, superintendent.

1908: Washington Hall converted into housing for the athletic teams. Doctor's quarters built (Pratt Hall). New hospital built (Ashburn Hall)

1909: Print shop built. Gateposts at west entrance on Pratt Avenue built.

1911: Carlisle football team beat Harvard.

1911–15: Marianne Moore taught at school.

1912: Carlisle football team beat West Point Military Academy, 27–6.

Jim Thorpe won gold in the pentathlon and decathlon, and Lewis Tewanima silver in the 10,000 meters at the Olympics. Model home built on campus.

1913: Highest number of runaways in a year—140 (on average one a week during Friedman years). Petition signed by 276 students requesting an investigation of conditions at the school. Colonial-style portico added to superintendent's quarters.

1914: Senate investigation into the Carlisle Indian School and its sports program published. Football coach "Pop" Warner, Superintendent Moses Friedman, and Bandmaster C. M. Stauffer were dismissed. Highest number of expulsions in a single year (twenty-seven).

1914–17: Oscar Lipps, superintendent.

1917–18: John Francis Jr., superintendent

1918: August—School closed, and Carlisle Barracks immediately became the U.S. Army Base Hospital Number 31, to treat soldiers wounded in World War I.

1927: Indian School cemetery removed to smaller plot on the outer edge of grounds of Carlisle Barracks. All those buried (except Thomas Marshall) given new headstones.

1934: War Department made responsible for cemetery; U.S. Army renovates cemetery and reports it could hold 229 bodies.

1935: First non-Indian buried in Indian School cemetery.

1961: Surviving buildings of the Carlisle Indian School on the campus of the U.S. Army War College designated a National Historic Landmark (Farmhouse not included).

1983: Master Sergeant Clarence F. Barr buried in Indian School cemetery. Cemetery declared closed.

1985: Carlisle Farmhouse's first evaluation for placement on the National Historic Register: rejected.

1996: Carlisle Farmhouse's second evaluation for placement on the National Historic Register: rejected.

2000: "Powwow 2000: Remembering the Carlisle Indian School" held at Carlisle Barracks, attended by descendants from across the United States.

2003: "Carlisle Indian Industrial School" marker erected beside the cemetery by descendants and friends, to give it public visibility.[3]

2004: Pennsylvania State Historic Preservation Office signed Programmatic Agreement stating that all buildings of Carlisle Barracks outside the National Landmark were subject to removal if necessary.

2005: Last burial in cemetery—June Wagner Barr buried with her husband.

2010: Official decision taken to raze the Carlisle Farmhouse to build two new homes for army personnel.

2011: Research indicating the building's importance to the Carlisle Indian School's history posted online.

2012: June—Funding for demolition of Farmhouse and for new housing in its place approved.

July—Farmhouse Coalition (Carlisle descendants and friends) created to save the Carlisle Farmhouse.

September—Petition with nine hundred signatures delivered to Public Affairs Office at Carlisle Barracks.

October 5–6—Carlisle Symposium, Dickinson College, Carlisle, Pennsylvania.

October 6—Representatives of the U.S. Army met with representatives of the Farmhouse Coalition at a Carlisle Symposium Roundtable. Plans for demolition immediately suspended.

2013: Carlisle Farmhouse is recommended for inclusion in the National Historic Landmark of the main Carlisle campus by Carlisle Barracks. Demolition of Farmhouse permanently cancelled.

2014: October 10–11—*Carlisle Journeys* conference 1, "American Indians in Show Business," Cumberland County Historical Society. Plan drafted for renovation of the Farmhouse and creation of Carlisle Indian School Heritage Center.

2015: Farmhouse Coalition Committee holds regular meetings to execute plans for Carlisle Indian School Heritage Center (ongoing).

2016: May 10—U.S. Army representatives meet with representatives of Plains tribes in South Dakota and agree to allow students' remains in the cemetery to be repatriated.

2016: October 7–9—*Carlisle Journeys* conference 2, "Celebrating the American Indian Sports Legacy," Cumberland County Historical Society.

1. As presented in an excellent article by Daniel K. Richter, "A Framework for Pennsylvania Indian History," *Pennsylvania History* 57, no, 3 (July 1990): 236–61, https://journals.psu.edu/phj/article/download/24825/24594.

2. This thirteen-and-a-half-millennia-long period, of course, actually comprises dozens of epochs; far from being "people without history," the Natives of what would become Pennsylvania were the products of long indigenous processes of cultural development.

3. Wording on the marker agreed by descendants: "This school was the model for a nation-wide system of boarding schools intended to assimilate American Indians into mainstream culture. Over 10,000 indigenous children attended the school between 1879 and 1918. Despite idealistic beginnings, the school left a mixed and lasting legacy, creating opportunity for some students and conflicted identities for others. In this cemetery are 186 graves of students who died while at Carlisle."

Selected Bibliography

ARCHIVAL SOURCES

Beinecke Rare Book and Manuscript Library, Yale University
  Pratt (Richard Henry) Papers
Cumberland County Historical Society, Carlisle PA
  Manuscripts: http://www.historicalsociety.com/CIIS_Manuscripts.html)
  Photograph Collection:
    Choate Photos of Carlisle Indian School Students/Visitors—By Nation:
      Photos by J. N. Choate (named students and visitors by nation): http://
      www.historicalsociety.com/uploads/CHOATE_PHOTOS.pdf
    Jim Thorpe Photo Collection (descriptions): http://www.historicalsociety
      .com/uploads/Jim_Thorpe_Photo_Collection.pdf
Dickinson College Archives and Special Collections, Dickinson College, Carlisle PA
  Carlisle Indian School papers: http://archives.dickinson.edu/collection-
  descriptions/carlisle-indian-school-papers
Smithsonian Institution, National Anthropological Archives, Suitland MD
  John N. Choate Photographs of Carlisle School Students, 1879–1902: http://
  siris-archives.si.edu/ipac20/ipac.jsp?uri=full=3100001~!2918!0
U.S. Army War College Library and Archives, Carlisle PA
  Carlisle Barracks: http://cdm16635.contentdm.oclc.org/cdm/ref/collection/
  p16635coll9/id/1081
  Carlisle Indian Industrial School Photograph Collection Boxes: http://
  cdm16635.contentdm.oclc.org/cdm/ref/collection/p16635coll15/id/1628

PUBLISHED SOURCES

Adams, David Wallace. *Education for Extinction: American Indians and the
  Boarding School Experience, 1875–1928*. Lawrence: University of Kansas Press,
  1995.
Anderson, Lars. *Carlisle vs. Army: Jim Thorpe, Dwight Eisenhower, Pop War-
  ner, and the Forgotten Story of Football's Greatest Battle*. New York: Random
  House, 2007.

Archuleta, Margaret L., Brenda J. Child, and K. Tsianina Lomawaima. *Away from Home: American Indian Boarding School Experiences, 1879–2000*. Phoenix AZ: Heard Museum, 2000.

Bass, Jennifer. "Casting a Spell: Acts of Cultural Continuity in Carlisle Indian School's *The Red Man and Helper*." *Wicazo Sa Review* 26, no. 2 (Fall 2011): 13–38.

Batemen, Fiona, and Lionel Pilkington, eds. *Studies in Settler Colonialism*. London: Palgrave Macmillan, 2011.

Bell, Genevieve. "Telling Stories out of School: Remembering the Carlisle Indian Industrial School, 1879–1918." PhD diss., Stanford University, 1998. UMI #9908713.

Bentley, Matthew. "Playing White Men: American Football and Manhood at the Carlisle Indian School, 1893–1904." *Journal of the History of Childhood and Youth* 3, no. 2 (Spring 2010): 187–209.

———. "The Rise of Athletic Masculinity at Carlisle Indian School, 1904–1913." *International Journal of the History of Sport* 29, no. 10 (July 2012): 1466–89.

Bloom, John. *To Show What an Indian Can Do: Sports at Native American Boarding Schools*. Minneapolis: University of Minnesota Press, 2000.

Brasfield, Charles R. "Residential School Syndrome." *BC Medical Journal* 43, no. 2 (2001): 78–81.

Buford, Kate. *Native American Son: The Life and Sporting Legend of Jim Thorpe*. Lincoln: University of Nebraska Press, 2012.

Bull, Linda R. "Indian Residential Schooling: The Native Perspective." *Canadian Journal of Native Education* 18, suppl. (1991): 1–63.

Burgess, Marianna (Embe). *Stiya: A Carlisle Indian Girl at Home*. Cambridge MA: Riverside Press, 1891. http://babel.hathitrust.org/cgi/pt?id=wu.89098873425 ;view=1up;seq=11.

Carlisle Indian School. *Arrow*. August 25, 1904–June 19, 1908. Name changed to *Carlisle Arrow* in 1908. Name changed to *Carlisle Arrow and Red Man* in 1918. Published weekly until 1918.

———. *Eadle Keatah Toh*. April 1880–March 1882. Name changed to the *Morning Star* in April 1882. Name changed to *Red Man* in January 1888. Name changed to *Red Man and Helper* in 1900. Published monthly until 1904.

———. *Indian Craftsman*. February 1909–January 1910. Name changed to *Red Man* in 1910. Published monthly. Merged with *Carlisle Arrow* in 1917; name changed to *Carlisle Arrow and Red Man*. Published weekly through June 7, 1918.

———. *Indian Helper*. 1885–1900. Published weekly.

———. *Morning Star*. April 1882–December 1887. Published monthly.

———. *Red Man*. January 1888–June 1900. Published monthly.

———. *Red Man*. February 1910–June 1917. Published monthly.

———. *School News*. June 1880–May 1883. Published monthly.

Carlisle Indian School Digital Resource Center, Dickinson College. http://carlisle indian.dickinson.edu.

Carlisle Indian School Symposium: Site of Indigenous Histories, Memories, and Reclamations. http://blogs.dickinson.edu/carlisleindianschoolsymposium/.

Child, Brenda J. *Boarding School Seasons: American Indian Families, 1900–1940*. Lincoln: University of Nebraska Press, 1999.

———. "Runaway Boys, Resistant Girls: Rebellion at Flandreau and Haskell, 1900–1940." *Journal of American Indian Education* 35, no. 3 (Spring 1996): 49–57.

Cobb, Amanda J. *Listening to Our Grandmothers' Stories: The Bloomfield Academy for Chickasaw Females, 1852–1949*. Lincoln: University of Nebraska Press, 2000.

Coleman, Michael. *American Indian Children at School, 1850–1930*. Jackson: University Press of Mississippi, 2007.

———. *American Indians, the Irish and Government Schooling: A Comparative Study*. Lincoln: University of Nebraska Press, 2009.

Davis, Julie. "American Indian Boarding School Experiences: Recent Studies from Native Perspectives." OAH *Magazine of History* 15, no. 2 (2001): 20–22.

Deloria, Philip J. *Indians in Unexpected Places*. Lawrence: University of Kansas Press, 2004.

Denetdale, Jennifer Nez. *Reclaiming Diné History: The Legacies of Navajo Chief Manuelito and Juanita*. Tucson: University of Arizona Press, 2007.

Dunbar-Ortiz, Roxanne. *An Indigenous Peoples' History of the United States*. Boston: Beacon Press, 2014.

Eastman, Elaine Goodale. *Pratt, the Red Man's Moses*. Norman: University of Oklahoma Press, 1935.

Ellis, Clyde. *To Change Them Forever: Indian Education at the Rainy Mountain Boarding School, 1893–1920*. Norman: University of Oklahoma Press, 1996.

Fear-Segal, Jacqueline. "Historic Maps of the Carlisle Indian School." Carlisle PA: Dickinson College, 2000.

———. "The Man-on-the-Bandstand at the Carlisle Indian School: What He Reveals about the Children's Experiences." In *Boarding School Blues: Revisiting American Indian Educational Experiences*, edited by Cliff E. Trafzer, Jean A. Keller, and Lorene Sisquoc, 99–122. Lincoln: University of Nebraska Press, 2006.

———. "Nineteenth-Century Indian Education: Universalism versus Evolutionism." *Journal of American Studies* 33, no. 2 (1999): 323–41.

———. *White Man's Club: Schools, Race, and the Struggle of Indian Acculturation*. Lincoln: University of Nebraska Press, 2007.

Fontaine, Theodore. *Broken Circle: The Dark Legacy of Indian Residential School; A Memoir,* Victoria BC: Heritage House, 2010.

Gere, Anne Ruggles. "Indian Heart/White Man's Head: Native-American Teachers in Indian Schools, 1880–1930." *History of Education Quarterly* 45, no. 1 (March 2005): 38–65.

Gilbert, Matthew Sakiestewa. *Education beyond the Mesas: Hopi Students at Sherman Institute, 1902–1929.* Lincoln: University of Nebraska Press, 2010.

Hixson, Walter L. *American Settler Colonialism: A History.* London: Palgrave Macmillan, 2013.

Hoxie, Frederick. *The Final Promise: The Campaign to Assimilate the Indian, 1880–1920.* Lincoln: University of Nebraska Press, 1983.

Hultgren, Mary Lou, and Paulette Fairbanks Molin. *To Lead and to Serve: American Indian Education at Hampton Institute, 1878–1923.* Charlottesville: Virginia Foundation for the Humanities with Hampton University, 1989.

Hyer, Sally. *One House, One Voice, One Heart: Native American Education at the Santa Fe Indian School, 1890–1990.* Santa Fe: Museum of New Mexico Press, 1990.

Indian Rights Association. *Annual Reports of the Executive Committee of the Indian Rights Association.* Philadelphia: Indian Rights Association, 1883–1910.

———. *Proceedings of the Annual Meeting of the Lake Mohonk Conferences.* Philadelphia: Sherman, 1883–1916.

Jacobs, Margaret D. "The Habit of Elimination: Indigenous Child Removal in Settler Colonial Nations in the Twentieth Century." In *Colonial Genocide in Indigenous North America,* edited by Andres Wooford, Jeff Benvenuto, and Alexander Laban Hinton, 189–207. Durham NC: Duke University Press, 2014.

———. "Indian Boarding Schools in Comparative Perspective: The Removal of Indigenous Children in the United States and Australia, 1880–1940." University of Nebraska–Lincoln, Faculty Publications, Department of History. Paper 20. 2006. http://digitalcommons.unl.edu/historyfacpub/20.

———. *White Mother to a Dark Race: Settler Colonialism, Maternalism, and the Removal of Indigenous Children in the American West and Australia, 1880–1940.* Lincoln: University of Nebraska, 2009.

Jenkins, Sally. *The Real All Americans: The Team That Changed a Game, a People, a Nation.* New York: Doubleday, 2007.

Johnston, Basil. *Indian School Days.* Norman: University of Oklahoma Press, 1988.

Keller, Jean A. *Empty Beds: Indian Student Health at Sherman Institute.* East Lansing: Michigan State University Press, 2002.

Lawrence, Adrea. *Lessons from an Indian Day School: Negotiating Colonization in Northern New Mexico, 1902–1907.* Lawrence: University Press of Kansas, 2011.

Lindsey, Donal F. *Indians at Hampton Institute, 1877–1923.* Urbana: University of Illinois Press, 1995.

Lomawaima, K. Tsianina. *They Called It Prairie Light: The Story of Chilocco Indian School.* Lincoln: University of Nebraska Press, 1995.

Ludlow, Helen W. *Are Eastern Industrial Schools a Failure?* Philadelphia: Indian Rights Association, 1886.

———. "Indian Education at Carlisle and Hampton." *Harper's New Monthly Magazine* 62 (April 1881): 659–75.

MacDonald, David. "First Nations, Residential Schools, and the Americanization of the Holocaust: Rewriting Indigenous History in the United States and Canada." *Canadian Journal of Political Science* 45, no. 2 (2012): 427–49.

Malmsheimer, Lonna. "'Imitation White Man': Images of Transformation at the Carlisle Indian School." *Studies in Visual Communication* 2, no. 4 (Fall 1985): 54–74.

Mann, Henrietta. *Cheyenne-Arapaho Education, 1871–1982: A Drama of Human Dimensions about Individuals, Families, Tribes, and the Federal Government.* Niwot: University Press of Colorado, 1997.

Margolis, Eric. "Looking at Discipline, Looking at Labour: Photographic Representations of Indian Boarding Schools." *Visual Studies* 19, no. 1 (2004): 72–96.

Matthews, Jessica Ruggieri. "Killing a Culture to Save a Race: Writing and Resisting the Discourse of the Carlisle Indian School." PhD diss., George Washington University, 2005.

Mauro, Hayes Peter. *The Art of Americanization at the Carlisle Indian School.* Albuquerque: University of New Mexico Press, 2010.

McBeth, Sally. *Ethnic Identity and the Boarding School Experience of West-Central Oklahoma American Indians.* Washington DC: University Press of America, 1983.

Mihesuah, Devon A. *Cultivating the Rosebuds: The Education of Women at the Cherokee Female Seminary, 1851–1909.* Lincoln: University of Nebraska Press, 1993.

Miller, J. R. *Shingwauk's Vision: A History of Native Residential Schools.* Toronto: University of Toronto Press, 1996.

Nabokov, Peter, ed. *Native American Testimony: A Chronicle of Indian-White Relations from Prophecy to the Present, 1492–1992.* Foreword by Vine Deloria Jr. New York: Penguin Books, 1992. (This collection of testimony includes some former Carlisle Indian School staff, students, and visiting tribal headmen.)

Nagy, Rosemary, and Robinger Karu Sehdev. "Introduction: Residential Schools and Decolonization." *Canadian Journal for Law and Society* 27, no. 1 (2012): 67–73.

National Indian Defense Association. *Preamble, Platform and Constitution of the National Indian Defense Association.* Washington DC: R. H. Darby, 1885.

Navarro-Rivera, Pablo. "Acculturation under Duress: The Puerto Rican Experience at the Carlisle Indian Industrial School, 1898–1918." *Centro Journal* 18, no. 1 (2006): 222–59. http://www.redalyc.org/articulo.oa?id=37718113.

Noriega, Jorge. "American Indian Education in the United States: Indoctrination for Subordination to Colonialism." In *The State of Native America: Genocide, Colonization, and Resistance,* edited by M. Annette Jaimes, 371–402. Boston: South End Press, 1992.

Parker, Dorothy R. *Phoenix Indian School: The Second Half-Century.* Tucson: University of Arizona Press, 1996.

Paulet, Anne. "To Change the World: The Use of American Indian Education in the Philippines." *History of Education Quarterly* 47, no. 2 (May 2007): 173–202.

Pfister, Joel. *Individuality Incorporated: Indians and the Multi-cultural Modern.* Durham NC: Duke University Press, 1946.

Pratt, Richard Henry. "Address before the National Educational Association," Ocean Grove, August 11, 1883, in *Indian Industrial School Carlisle.* Printed by Indian School, 1901. Dickinson College rare books collection.

———. "Address to the Lake Mohonk Conference." *Red Man* 12 (January 1896).

———. "American Indians Chained and Unchained, being an address before the Pennsylvania Commandery," October 23, 1912.

———. *Battlefield and Classroom: Four Decades with the American Indian, 1867–1904,* edited by Robert Utley. New Haven CT: Yale University Press, 1964.

———. "The Indian Industrial School, Carlisle, Pennsylvania: Its Origins, Purposes, Progress and the Difficulties Surmounted." 1908. Reprint, *Cumberland County Historical Society Publications* 10, no. 3 (1979).

———. "The Indian No Problem." *Red Man and Helper,* June 24 and July 1, 1904.

———. "Negroes and Indians: Address of Brigadier General Richard H. Pratt, U.S.A. Retired, Made before the Pennsylvania Commandery, Military Order of Foreign Wars of the United States." Bellevue Stratford Hotel, Philadelphia. January 14, 1913.

Proceedings of the Annual Meeting of the Lake Mohonk Conference. Lake Mohonk NY: Lake Mohonk Conference, 1883–1916.

Prucha, Francis Paul, ed. *Americanizing the Indians: Writings by "Friends of the Indians," 1880–1900.* Lincoln: University of Nebraska Press, 1973.

Regan, Paulette. *Unsettling the Settler Within: Indian Residential Schools, Truth Telling, and Reconciliation in Canada.* Vancouver: UBC Press, 2010.

Reyhner, Jon, and Jeanne Eder. *American Indian Education: A History.* Norman: University of Oklahoma Press, 2006.

Riney, Scott. *The Rapid City Indian School, 1898–1933.* Norman: University of Oklahoma Press, 1999.

Simonsen, Jane E. *Domesticity and Native American Assimilation in the American West, 1860–1919*. Chapel Hill: University of North Carolina Press, 2006.

Slivka, Kevin. "Art, Craft, and Assimilation: Curriculum for Native Students during the Boarding School Era." *Studies in Art Education* 52, no. 3 (Spring 2011): 225–42.

Smith, Andrea. *Conquest: Sexual Violence and American Indian Genocide*. Boston: South End Press, 2005.

———. "Soul Wound: The Legacy of Native American Schools." *Amnesty International Magazine*, March 26, 2007. http://www.amnestyusa.org/node/87342.

Smith, Linda Tuhiwai. *Decolonizing Methodologies: Research and Indigenous Peoples*. London: Zed Books, 1999.

Spack, Ruth. *America's Second Tongue: American Indian Education and the Ownership of English, 1860–1900*. Lincoln: University of Nebraska Press, 2002.

———. "Zitkala-Sa, *The Song of Hiawatha*, and the Carlisle Indian School Band: A Captivity Tale." *Legacy: A Journal of American Women Writers* 25, no. 2 (June 2008): 211–24.

Standing Bear, Luther (Ota Kte). *Land of the Spotted Eagle*. Cambridge MA: Riverside Press, 1933. Reprint, Lincoln: University of Nebraska Press, 1978, 2006.

———. *My People the Sioux*. Cambridge MA: Riverside Press, 1928. Reprint, Lincoln: University of Nebraska Press, 1975, 2006.

Steckbeck, John S. *Fabulous Redmen: The Carlisle Indians and Their Famous Football Teams*. Harrisburg PA: J. Horace McFarland, 1951.

Szasz, Margaret Connell. *Education and the American Indian: The Road to Self-Determination since 1928*. Albuquerque: University of New Mexico Press, 1999.

———. "'I knew how to be moderate. And I knew how to obey': The Commonality of American Indian Boarding School Experiences, 1750s–1920s." *American Indian Culture and Research Journal* 29, no. 4 (2005): 75–94.

———. *Indian Education in the American Colonies: 1607–1783*. Albuquerque: University of New Mexico Press, 1980.

Trafzer, Clifford E., Jean A. Keller, and Lorene Sisquoc, eds. *Boarding School Blues: Revisiting American Indian Educational Experiences*. Lincoln: University of Nebraska Press, 2006.

Trafzer, Clifford E., Matthew Sakiestewa Gilbert, and Lorene Sisquoc, eds. *The Indian School on Magnolia Avenue: Voices and Images from Sherman Institute*. Corvallis: Oregon State University Press, 2012.

Trennert, Robert A. "Educating Indian Girls at Nonreservation Boarding Schools, 1878–1920." *Western Historical Quarterly* 13, no. 3 (July 1982): 271–90.

———. *The Phoenix Indian School: Forced Acculturation in Arizona, 1891–1935*. Norman: University of Oklahoma Press, 1988.

———. "Selling Indian Education at World's Fairs and Expositions, 1893–1904." *American Indian Quarterly* 11, no. 3 (Summer 1987): 203–20.

Trouillot, Michel-Rolph. *Silencing the Past: Power and Production of History*. Boston: Beacon Press, 1995.

Trout Gallery. *Visualizing a Mission: Artifacts and Imagery of the Carlisle Indian School, 1879–1918*. Carlisle PA: Trout Gallery, Dickinson College, 2004.

Troutman, John W. *Indian Blues: American Indians and the Politics of Music*. Norman: University of Oklahoma Press, 2009.

Truth and Reconciliation Commission of Canada. http://www.trc.ca/websites/trc institution/index.php?p=7.

U.S. Bureau of American Ethnology: Charles C. Royce. "Indian Land Cessions in the United States." In *18th Annual Report of the Bureau of American Ethnology*. Washington DC: Government Printing Office, 1899.

U.S. Bureau of Education: Alice C. Fletcher. *Indian Education and Civilization: A Report Prepared in Answer to Senate Resolution of February 23, 1885*. 48th Cong., 2nd Sess, Senate Exec. Doc. no. 45. Washington DC: Government Printing Office, 1888.

U.S. Bureau of Education: Estelle Reel. *Course of Study for Indian Schools of the United States: Industrial and Literary*. Washington DC: Government Printing Office, 1901. https://archive.org/stream/cu31924013973650#page/n5 /mode/2up.

U.S. Bureau of Indian Affairs. *Annual Reports of the Superintendent of Indian Schools*. Washington DC: Government Printing Office, 1883–1918.

———. "Annual Reports of the U.S. Indian School at Carlisle." In *Annual Reports of the Commissioner of Indian Affairs*. Washington DC: Government Printing Office, 1879–1918.

———. *Rules for Indian Schools with Course of Study*. Washington DC: Government Printing Office, 1890.

———. *Teaching Indian Students to Speak English*. Washington DC: Government Printing Office, 1904.

———. *Vernacular Teaching in Indian Schools*. Washington DC: Government Printing Office, 1888.

U.S. Department of the Interior. *Annual Reports of the Board of Indian Commissioners*. Washington DC: Government Printing Office, 1869–1918.

U.S. Senate. *Hearings before the Joint Commission of the Congress of the United States*. "Investigation of the Carlisle Indian School, 1913/14." Joint Commission to Investigate Indian Affairs, 63rd Cong., 2nd sess., 1914. https://archive .org/details/hearingsbeforejo01unit.

Utley, Robert M. "The Ordeal of Plenty Horses." *American Heritage* 26, no. 1

(December 1974). http://www.americanheritage.com/content/ordeal-plenty
-horses?page=2.

Vučkovic, Myriam. *Voices from Haskell: Indian Students between Two Worlds,
1884–1927.* Lawrence: University Press of Kansas, 2008.

Waggoner, Linda M. *The Life of Angel de Cora, Winnebago Artist.* Norman: University of Oklahoma Press, 2008.

Warrior, Robert Allen. *The People and the Word: Reading Native Non-fiction.*
Minneapolis: University of Minnesota Press, 2005.

Wharton, Donald R., and Brett Lee Shelton. "Let All That Is Indian within You
Die!" *Native American Rights Fund's Legal Review* (Summer/Fall 2013). http://
www.narf.org/cases/boarding-school-healing/.

Witmer, Linda F. *The Indian Industrial School, Carlisle, Pennsylvania, 1879–1918.*
Carlisle PA: Cumberland County Historical Society, 1993.

Wolfe, Patrick. *Settler Colonialism and the Transformation of Anthropology: The
Politics and Poetics of an Ethnographic Event.* London: Bloomsbury, 1999.

Women's National Indian Association. *Annual Reports of the Women's National
Indian Association.* Philadelphia: 1883–1890.

Woolford, Andrew. *This Benevolent Experiment: Indigenous Boarding Schools,
Genocide, and Redress in Canada and the United States.* Lincoln: University
of Nebraska Press, 2015.

Zitkala-Ša, "The School Days of an Indian Girl." In *American Indian Stories, Legends, and Other Writings.* 1900. Reprint, New York: Penguin Books, 2003.

Published Resources for Researching the Carlisle Indian Industrial School

This is by no means an exhaustive list. The works included here are secondary sources that will be of value to anyone conducting research on this institution; most make significant reference to Carlisle. This list shares some titles with the Selected Bibliography.

Adams, David Wallace. *Education for Extinction: American Indians and the Boarding School Experience, 1875–1928*. Lawrence: University of Kansas Press, 1995.

———. "More Than a Game: The Carlisle Indians Take to the Gridiron, 1893–1917." *Western Historical Quarterly* 32, no. 1 (Spring 2001): 25–53.

Anderson, Lars. *Carlisle vs. Army: Jim Thorpe, Dwight Eisenhower, Pop Warner, and the Forgotten Story of Football's Greatest Battle*. New York: Random House, 2007.

Archuleta, Margaret L, Brenda J. Child, and K. Tsianina Lomawaima. *Away from Home: American Indian Boarding School Experiences, 1879–2000*. Phoenix AZ: Heard Museum, 2000.

Bass, Jennifer, "Casting a Spell: Acts of Cultural Continuity in Carlisle Indian School's *The Red Man and Helper*." *Wicazo Sa Review* 26, no. 2 (Fall 2011): 13–38.

Bell, Genevieve. "Telling Stories out of School: Remembering the Carlisle Indian Industrial School, 1879–1918." PhD diss., Stanford University, 1998. UMI #9908713.

Bentley, Matthew. "Playing White Men: American Football and Manhood at the Carlisle Indian School, 1893–1904." *Journal of the History of Childhood and Youth* 3, no. 2 (Spring 2010): 187–209.

———. "The Rise of Athletic Masculinity at Carlisle Indian School, 1904–1913." *International Journal of the History of Sport* 29, no. 10 (July 2012): 1466–89.

Bloom, John. *To Show What an Indian Can Do: Sports at Native American Boarding Schools*. Minneapolis: University of Minnesota Press, 2000.

Buford, Kate. *Native American Son: The Life and Sporting Legend of Jim Thorpe*. Lincoln: University of Nebraska Press, 2012.

Burgess, Marianna (Embe). *Stiya: A Carlisle Indian Girl at Home*. Cambridge MA:

Riverside Press, 1891. http://babel.hathitrust.org/cgi/pt?id=wu.89098873425 ;view=1up;seq=11.

Carlisle Indian School Digital Resource Center, Dickinson College. http://carlisle indian.dickinson.edu. Primary documents.

Carlisle Indian School Symposium: Site of Indigenous Histories, Memories, and Reclamations. http://blogs.dickinson.edu/carlisleindianschoolsymposium/.

Coleman, Michael. *American Indian Children at School, 1850–1930.* Jackson: University Press of Mississippi, 2007.

Deloria, Philip J. *Indians in Unexpected Places.* Lawrence: University of Kansas Press, 2004.

Denetdale. Jennifer Nez. *Reclaiming Diné History: The Legacies of Navajo chief Manuelito and Juanita.* Tucson: University of Arizona Press, 2007.

Eastman, Elaine Goodale. *Pratt, the Red Man's Moses.* Norman: University of Oklahoma Press, 1935.

Enoch, Jessica. "Resisting the Script of Indian Education: Zitkala Ša and the Carlisle Indian School." *College English* 65, no. 2 (November 2002): 117–41.

Fear-Segal, Jacqueline. "Historic Maps of the Carlisle Indian School." Carlisle PA: Dickinson College, 2000.

———. "The Man-on-the-Bandstand at the Carlisle Indian School: What He Reveals about the Children's Experiences." In *Boarding School Blues: Revisiting American Indian Educational Experiences*, edited by Cliff E. Trafzer, Jean A. Keller, and Lorene Sisquoc, 99–122. Lincoln: University of Nebraska Press, 2006.

———. "Nineteenth-Century Indian Education: Universalism versus Evolutionism." *Journal of American Studies* 33, no. 2 (1999): 323–41.

———. *White Man's Club: Schools, Race, and the Struggle of Indian Acculturation.* Lincoln: University of Nebraska Press, 2007.

Gamache, Ray. "Sport as Cultural Assimilation: Representations of American Indian Athletes in the Carlisle School Newspaper." *American Journalism* 26, no. 2 (April 2009): 7–37.

Haller, Beth A. "Cultural Voices or Pure Propaganda: Publications of the Carlisle Indian School, 1879–1918." *American Journalism* 19, no. 2 (April 2002): 65–86.

Jenkins, Sally. *The Real All Americans: The Team That Changed a Game, a People, a Nation.* New York: Doubleday, 2007.

Leahy, Todd, and Nathan Wilson. "'My First Days at the Carlisle Indian School,' by Howard Gansworth, an Annotated Manuscript." *Pennsylvania History: A Journal of Mid-Atlantic Studies* 71, no. 4 (Autumn 2004): 479–93.

Malmsheimer, Lonna. "'Imitation White Man': Images of Transformation at the Carlisle Indian School." *Studies in Visual Communication* 2, no. 4 (Fall 1985): 54–57.

Mauro, Hayes Peter. *The Art of Americanization at the Carlisle Indian School.* Albuquerque: University of New Mexico Press, 2010.

Nabokov, Peter, ed. *Native American Testimony: A Chronicle of Indian-White Relations from Prophecy to the Present, 1492–1992.* Foreword by Vine Deloria Jr. New York: Penguin Books, 1992. (This collection of testimony includes some former Carlisle Indian School staff, students, and visiting tribal headmen.)

Navarro-Rivera, Pablo. "Acculturation under Duress: The Puerto Rican Experience at the Carlisle Indian Industrial School, 1898–1918." *Centro Journal* 18, no. 1 (2006): 222–59. http://www.redalyc.org/articulo.oa?id=37718113.

Pfister, Joel. *Individuality Incorporated: Indians and the Multi-cultural Modern.* Durham NC: Duke University Press, 1946.

Pratt, Richard Henry. *Battlefield and Classroom: Four Decades with the American Indian, 1867–1904.* Edited by Robert Utley. New Haven CT: Yale University Press, 1964.

Prucha, Francis Paul, ed. *Americanizing the Indians: Writings by "Friends of the Indians," 1880–1900.* Lincoln: University of Nebraska Press, 1973.

Rosa, Sonia M. "The Puerto Ricans at Carlisle Indian School." *Kacike: Journal of Caribbean Amerindian History and Anthropology* (January 2003). https://archive.org/stream/KacikeJournal_34/soniarosa_djvu.txt.

Slivka, Kevin. "Art, Craft, and Assimilation: Curriculum for Native Students during the Boarding School Era." *Studies in Art Education* 52, no. 3 (Spring 2011): 255–42.

Spack, Ruth. *America's Second Tongue: American Indian Education and the Ownership of English, 1860–1900.* Lincoln: University of Nebraska Press, 2002.

———. "Zitkala-Sa, *The Song of Hiawatha*, and the Carlisle Indian School Band: A Captivity Tale." *Legacy: A Journal of American Women Writers* 25, no. 2 (June 2008).

Stanciu, Cristina. "'That Is Why I Sent You to Carlisle': Indian Poetry and the Demands of Americanization Poetics and Politics." *American Indian Quarterly* 37, no. 2 (Spring 2013): 34–76.

Standing Bear, Luther (Ota Kte). *Land of the Spotted Eagle.* Cambridge MA: Riverside Press, 1933. Reprint, Lincoln: University of Nebraska Press, 1978, 2006.

———. *My People the Sioux.* Cambridge MA: Riverside Press, 1928. Reprint: Lincoln: University of Nebraska Press, 1975, 2006.

Steckbeck, John S. *Fabulous Redmen: The Carlisle Indians and Their Famous Football Teams.* Harrisburg PA: J. Horace McFarland, 1951.

Trennert, Robert A. "Educating Indian Girls at Nonreservation Boarding Schools, 1878–1920." *Western Historical Quarterly* 13, no. 3 (July 1982): 271–90.

———. "From Carlisle to Phoenix: The Rise and Fall of the Indian Outing System, 1878–1930." *Pacific Historical Review* 52, no. 3 (August 1983): 267–91.

Trout Gallery. *Visualizing a Mission: Artifacts and Imagery of the Carlisle Indian School, 1879–1918.* Carlisle PA: Trout Gallery, Dickinson College, 2004.

Troutman, John W. *Indian Blues: American Indians and the Politics of Music.* Norman: University of Oklahoma Press, 2009.

U.S. Senate. *Hearings before the Joint Commission of the Congress of the United States.* "Investigation of the Carlisle Indian School, 1913/14." Joint Commission to Investigate Indian Affairs, 63rd Cong., 2nd sess., 1914. https://archive.org/details/hearingsbeforejo01unit.

Utley, Robert M. "The Ordeal of Plenty Horses." *American Heritage* 26, no. 1 (December 1974). http://www.americanheritage.com/content/ordeal-plenty-horses?page=2.

Waggoner, Linda M. *The Life of Angel de Cora, Winnebago Artist.* Norman: University of Oklahoma Press, 2008.

Warrior, Robert Allen. *The People and the Word: Reading Native Non-fiction.* Minneapolis: University of Minnesota Press, 2005. (See esp. chap. 3, "The Work of Indian Pupils.")

Wharton, Donald R., and Brett Lee Shelton. *Let All That Is Indian within You Die! Native American Rights Fund's Legal Review* (Summer/Fall 2013). http://www.narf.org/cases/boarding-school-healing/.

Wheeler, Lesley, and Chris Gavaler. "Impostors and Chameleons: Marianne Moore and the Carlisle Indian School." *Paideuma: Studies in American and British Modernist Poetry* 33, nos. 2–3 (2004): 53–82.

Witmer, Linda F. *The Indian Industrial School, Carlisle, Pennsylvania, 1879–1918.* Carlisle PA: Cumberland County Historical Society, 1993.

Woolford, Andrew. *The Benevolent Experiment: Indigenous Boarding Schools, Genocide, and Redress in Canada and the United States.* Lincoln: University of Nebraska Press, 2015.

Contributors

MARK C. ALDRICH is an associate professor of Spanish at Dickinson College. His research focuses on contemporary Spanish prose and poetry, with a critical study on the poet Rafael Pérez Estrada forthcoming. He has translated numerous contemporary poets into English, including Jordá, Pérez Estrada, Juvenal Soto, and Pablo García Baena, among many others.

CHRISTOPHER J. BILODEAU, associate professor of history at Dickinson College, focuses his research on the history of French, English, and Indian interaction during the colonial period, paying particular attention to the roles of religion and structural violence in the borderlands of the Northeast. He has published essays in *American Indian Quarterly, Maine History, French Colonial History,* and *Early American Studies.* He teaches courses on American Indian history, colonial America, the American Revolution, and the roles that violence played in colonial contexts.

JOHN BLOOM is an associate professor of history and philosophy at Shippensburg University of Pennsylvania. He is the author of several articles and book chapters on sports at federally operated boarding schools for Native Americans, as well as the book *To Show What an Indian Can Do: Sports at Native American Boarding Schools* (University of Minnesota Press, 2000). He has also published sports biographies of Barry Bonds and Howard Cosell and edited an anthology of critical work on sports and race, *Sports Matters: Race, Recreation, and Leisure* (New York University Press, 2002).

PAUL BRAWDY has an EdD from the University of Northern Colorado. He teaches physical education in the Teacher Education program at St. Bonaventure University. His research and teaching interests include an emphasis on social justice, critical pedagogy, and work with indigenous communities. Since arriving in western New York in 1998 he has maintained a strong relationship with local indigenous communities and professionals in the schools that service these populations. With his research partner and teaching colleague, Dr. Anne-Claire Fisher, he has coauthored numerous papers and made scholarly presentations focused on the experience of teachers, teacher candidates, and students in U.S. public schools that service a large ethnic minority population of American Indians.

DANIEL CASTRO ROMERO JR. (Ndé/Lipan Apache) has an MSW and MA in history from the University of Texas. He is the General Council chairman of the Lipan Apache Band of Texas, an oral historian, and a representative for indigenous peoples at the UN. He is coeditor of the "Anthropological Report on the Cúelcahén Ndé: Lipan Apache of Texas" (2004) and author of "Cúelcahén Ndé: The Castro's of the Lipan Apache Band of Texas" (2004).

JACQUELINE FEAR-SEGAL is a professor of American history and culture at the University of East Anglia, UK, and was co-organizer of the October 2012 Carlisle Symposium. She lived in Carlisle, Pennsylvania, for two separate years and taught at Dickinson College. She is a partner in the Carlisle Indian School Digital Resource Center. Her research interests and writing focus on Native America. Author of *White Man's Club: Schools, Race, and the Struggle of Indian Acculturation* (University of Nebraska Press, 2007), winner of the American Studies Network Best Book in 2008, and editor of *Indigenous Bodies: Reviewing, Relocation, Reclaiming* (SUNY Press, 2013), she is currently completing a monograph on the Carlisle Indian School photographs: *Re-viewing and Re-framing the Colonial Bequest of Indian School Photographs*. In 2006 she cofounded and continues to codirect the Native Studies Research Network UK.

ANNE-CLAIRE FISHER has an EdD from the University of Arizona. She teaches in the Differentiated Instruction master's program at St. Bonaventure University. Her research and interests address issues of social justice in education, particularly in special education, and working with parents "on the margins" usually absent from schools. In New York since 2007, Fisher has collaborated with Dr. Paul Brawdy on numerous papers and scholarly presentations, mostly dealing with how predominantly Caucasian preservice teachers address the shifting demographics of the United States.

CHARLES FOX has been a staff photographer at the *Philadelphia Inquirer* for twenty-six years. Previously, he worked at the *Pittsburgh Press* and the *Journal Tribune* in Biddeford, Maine. A graduate of Syracuse University, he grew up in Carlisle, Pennsylvania, along the banks of the Letort, just one and a half miles upstream from the former grounds of the Carlisle Indian Industrial School. He has photographed recent events at the Indian School, including Powwow 2000 and the Carlisle Symposium in 2012.

PETER JEMISON is a Heron clan Seneca from Cattaraugus. He is manager of the Ganondagan State Historic Site, a re-creation of a seventeenth-century Seneca village, located in Victor, New York. He represents the Seneca Nation of Indians on repatriation issues, serves on the Advisory Council on Historic Preservation, and formerly served on the board of directors of the American Association of Museums. He is the faithkeeper to the Cattaragus and the Seneca Nation chairman of the Haudenosaunee Standing Committee on the

Burial Rules and Regulations. A renowned artist and cultural specialist, he is consulted on various Haudenosaunee issues. He has also served as a consultant to the Smithsonian Institute's Native American Museum Training Program and to the National Endowment for the Arts. His paintings and drawings have been shown in solo exhibitions at the Albright-Knox Art Gallery in Buffalo and at the Fenimore Art Museum in Cooperstown, New York. He was the founding director of the American Indian Community House Gallery in New York City. He received a BS in art education and an honorary doctorate in fine arts from Buffalo State College in Buffalo, New York. He is a direct descendant of Mary Jemison, the famous adoptee from the eighteenth century.

EDUARDO JORDá is a Spanish poet and novelist. He has published two novels, three volumes of short stories, four travelogues, and several books of poetry. Since 2005 he has taught a creative writing workshop in Seville, the city where he currently lives.

MAURICE KENNY (Mohawk) was born in Watertown, New York, in 1929. He was educated at Butler University, St. Lawrence University, and New York University, where he studied with the eminent American poet Louise Bogan, who helped direct his growing sense of voice and craft. Kenny was a leading figure in the Renaissance of Native American poetry from the 1970s. His work has been published in almost one hundred journals, including *Trends, Calaloo, World Literature Today, American Indian Quarterly, Blue Cloud Quarterly, Wicazo, Saturday Review, New York Times,* and *Studies in American Indian Literature.* His book *Tekonwatonti: Molly Brant, Poems of War,* first published in 1992, is now in its sixth edition. He won the National Public Radio Award for Public Broadcasting in 1984 and the Signal Poetry Cup Award in 1990, and served on many literary and art panels. He walked on, Saranac Lake, New York, April 16, 2016, while this collection was in press.

BARBARA LANDIS is the library and archives specialist for the Carlisle Indian School Collections of the Cumberland County Historical Society in Carlisle, Pennsylvania. She assists library patrons with information about the first off-reservation government boarding school for Native American Indian children. She maintains a blog at http://www.ciis.blogspot.com/ with the purpose of getting the names of Carlisle Indian School students to their respective nations. Through her pages a group of descendants of Carlisle Indian School students proposed and organized the installation of a historic marker at the site of the school in the Indian cemetery at Carlisle. The marker was installed by the Pennsylvania Historical and Museum Commission on August 31, 2003. In the summer of 2000 she was one of the principle organizers of Powwow 2000: Remembering Carlisle Indian School. Her tour of the CIS was produced and filmed as an hour-long televised event for the popular PCN Tours featured on cable TV. She is author of a number of essays, among them "Putting Lucy Pretty Eagle to Rest," published in *Boarding School Blues* (University of Nebraska Press, 2006), and "To the Height of Civilization," published in *The Oneida Indians in the Age of Allotment, 1860–1920* (University of Oklahoma Press, 2006).

N. SCOTT MOMADAY (Kiowa) is a novelist, scholar, painter, printmaker, and poet, with a PhD from Stanford University. Through his novels, poems, plays, books of folktales and memoirs, essays, and speeches, he has won international respect. He won the Pulitzer Prize for Fiction in 1969 for his first novel, *House Made of Dawn*. In 1979 he was awarded Italy's highest literary award, the Premio Letterario Internationale "Mondello," and in 1992 he received the first Lifetime Achievement Award from the Native Writers' Circle of the Americas. In 2007 he was awarded the National Medal of Arts by President George W. Bush. He holds twenty honorary degrees from colleges and universities and is a fellow of the American Academy of Arts and Sciences. One of the most distinguished Native American authors writing today, he is chiefly known for novels and poetry collections that communicate the oral legends of his Kiowa heritage. He is featured in a number of award-winning documentary films, including *Remembered Earth: New Mexico's High Desert* and Ken Burns and Stephen Ives's documentary *The West*. He lives in Santa Fe and teaches at the University of New Mexico.

SHARON O'BRIEN is the James Hope Caldwell Professor of American Cultures at Dickinson College. She is the author of two biographies of Willa Cather and of a family memoir, *The Family Silver* (University of Chicago Press, 2004). Her research interests include sites of memory, medical humanities, and lifewriting. She facilitates lifewriting workshops in the community, working with non-academic writers to help them find their stories.

WARREN PETOSKEY is an Odawa and Lakota elder, teacher, writer, and musician. Author of a memoir, *Dancing My Dream* (2009), for the past fifty years he has been an activist and advocate for indigenous rights. His father and grandfather were both boarding school survivors, and he has developed a program to educate audiences about the history and legacy of these schools.

CAROLYN RITTENHOUSE (Lakota) has a BA in cultural anthropology from Millersville University (2012), where she is currently a graduate student. She is an administrative assistant and Cultural Exchange program co-ordinator at Millersville University and also works as a presenter on Native culture, holistic health, and wellness. She has worked extensively on the Cheyenne River and Pine Ridge Reservations of South Dakota, in Pennsylvania, and at Millersville University to educate others on the lives, sacred sites, and traditions of Native peoples.

SUSAN D. ROSE is Charles A. Dana Professor and Chair of Sociology, director of the Community Studies Center, and codirector of the Carlisle Indian School Digital Resource Center at Dickinson College. She was co-organizer of the October 2012 Carlisle Symposium and director of *The Lost Ones: Long Journey Home* (Honorable Mention CINE Film Festival). In her book *Challenging Global Gender Violence* (2013) and in an article in *Te Awatea Journal*, "Using Culture as a Resource in the Process of Decolonization: Fighting Gender Violence in the U.S. and New Zealand" (2012), she examines the ways in which colonization led to a transformation in gender norms that contributed to an increase in gender and family violence that was not traditional among indigenous people in the United States and New Zealand.

MARGO TAMEZ (Kónitsąąíí Cúelcahén Ndé/Big Water and Tall Grass Peoples), MFA, PhD, is an enrolled member of the Lipan Apache Band of Texas and an assistant professor in the Indigenous Studies program at the University of British Columbia. Born and raised in the Ndé Kónitsąąíí Gokíyaa (Big Water Peoples' Country/Texas), she is the author of *Naked Wanting* (2003) and *Raven Eye* (2007). She is currently writing two books: "We Remained! Being, Belonging, and Dispossession in Ndé Kónitsąąíígokíyaa, Big Water Country, 1546-2015," a historical memory and recovery project culminating ten years of community-based, participatory research with and alongside indigenous peoples from the Lower Rio Grande; and "Nizhoni Shitaa, Nizhoni Gokiyaa (In beauty my father, In beauty my country)," a new volume of poetry that explores intergenerational loss and violence in the Ndé social topographies and storied landscapes after the Remolino massacre (1873), and the destruction of Ndé families and males' roles as nurturers. She grapples with consequences of genocide denial and introduces new indigenous poetic forms in confrontation of destruction, hate, shame, and guilt surrounding violence against Ndé peoples.

DOVIE THOMASON (Lakota and Kiowa Apache) is an award-winning storyteller, recording artist, and author. As a child she learned old Indian stories from her Kiowa Apache and Lakota relatives. She began telling stories "publicly" while teaching literature and writing at an urban high school in Cleveland. In the twenty years since then, she has shared stories throughout North America and overseas, with NASA and Indian education programs on reservations, at Shakespeare's Globe Theatre and the National Geographic Society, on NPR's *Living on Earth* and the BBC's *My Century*, and at cross-community programs in Northern Ireland, powwows, conferences, schools, and libraries from Belgium to California. A winner of the Parents' Choice Gold Award, the Storytelling World Honors Award, the Audiofile Award, and the American Library Association/Booklist Editor's Choice Award for her recordings of traditional

Native stories, she has been described as a "valuable resource for multicultural education." In winter 2015 she was the storyteller-writer-in-residence at the University of Manitoba in Winnipeg, where she recorded "The Spirit Survives" for the archives of the Truth and Reconciliation Commission.

CAROLYN TOLMAN graduated from Brigham Young University in 1993 with a BA in family and community history studies. Since then, while raising five children near Salt Lake City, Utah, she has nurtured her keen interest in genealogy by researching for clients as well as her own family. She also carries on a family tradition of choral singing with the Mormon Tabernacle Choir. While her husband, Col. Derek J. Tolman, was attending the U.S. Army War College at Carlisle Barracks, Pennsylvania, in 2010–11, she was delighted to be assigned to the old Farmhouse, not realizing the impact it would have on her life. Feeling privileged to have contributed to the Native American effort to reclaim this aspect of their cultural past, she is now an active participant in the Farmhouse Coalition and committed to realizing the best possible future for the Farmhouse and the people it represents.

MALINDA TRILLER DORAN is a Special Collections librarian at Dickinson College in Carlisle, Pennsylvania. She also serves as library liaison to Africana studies, American studies, and women's and gender studies. She has contributed to a number of digitization projects, including the James Buchanan Resource Center and the Slavery and Abolition in the U.S. sites; both were Library Services and Technology Act–funded projects involving the digitization of nineteenth-century documents. She holds an MLIS from the University of Pittsburgh and an MA in applied history from Shippensburg University.

LOUELLYN WHITE (Mohawk) is from Akwesasne and grew up in the Mohawk Valley of central New York. She is currently an assistant professor in First Peoples studies at Concordia University in Montreal. She completed her PhD in American Indian studies at the University of Arizona (2009) with a dissertation that focused on indigenous education and language revitalization. She was a postdoctoral fellow at the University of Illinois at Urbana–Champaign (2009–10). Her current research interests focus on residential schooling, particularly the Carlisle Indian Industrial School, which her grandfather and other family members attended. She is the author of *Free to Be Mohawk: Indigenous Education at the Akwesasne Freedom School* (2015).

Index

waves of, 91, 93; entrance to, *39*; federal support for, 6; first group sent to, 1, 71, 90–91, *92–93*, 96, 188, 358; founding of, 7–8, 357–58; Gettysburg parallel to, 23, 44–45, 285, 342; graduation from, 2, *97*, 100–101, 104n7, 118, 358, 359; history of, 5–15, 343; indigenous students interpreting, 305; investigation into, 10, 130, 164, 221, 232n62, 360; as landmark, 15, 282, 284, 285, 355; motto of, 18, 45, 107, 116, 355; music at, *97*, as National Landmark, 282; necropolitical function of, 244; number of students sent to, 5; official record of, 3–4, 19, 89–90, 94, 103n1, 187, 293; Pan Indian Movement born at, 285; as part of American history, 342–43; positive experiences of, 3, 106, 178; propaganda for, 19; reclamation of, by War Department, 10–11, 164, 171; reindoctrination at, 239; research on, 17–18, 294–95; silence surrounding, 20–21, 242–43; student life at, 131–36; timeline of, 357–61; tours of, 8, 16; website of, 88–90, 329, 346. *See also* cemetery at Carlisle; Farmhouse; Outing program; sports at Carlisle

Carlisle Indian School Digital Resource Center, 294, 297

Carlisle Journeys conferences, 361

Carlisle PA: British troops in, 69; cemetery politics in, 157–59, 180n9; history of, 8, 64–65, 66–72; as hometown, 29, 344–50; insularity of, 71; racial segregation of, 133–34, 180n9; racism in, 70; white refugees moving to, 69

Carlisle Symposium, 4–5, 17–30, 234, 240, 338–40, 361; and cemetery, 17, 335, 347–48; emotion at, 342, 353; healing at, 5, 341, 352, 353–54; and memory, 252; Rittenhouse tipi at, *259*; as sacred space, 341–43

Carr, Lena, 182n47

Casey, Edward W., 3, 100

Castro, Mariana, 245

Castro, Ramon, 206, 224, 229n9, 245, 352

Castro Romero, Daniel, Jr., 21–22, 29–30, 35, 231n51, 232n66; on Carlisle Symposium, 352–54; correspondence of, 21, 203–4, 224–25, 240; on Kesetta, 225, 245–47, and "Lost Ones," 226–29, 243; pride of, in Kesetta and Jack, 247, and reunifying clans, 244; at United Nations Permanent Forum on Indigenous Issues, 249

Cave, Wayne, 175

cemeteries, landscaped, 156–57

cemetery at Carlisle, 26–27, 29, 43–53, 143–97, 306, *316*; after school's closure, 164–65; appearance of graves in, 160–61; babies buried in, *191*, 192–93, 196; ceremonies at, *53*, 174–79, 183n66, 195, 227–29, 304, 335, 347–48; closure of, 172; in disrepair, 164, 170, 183n56; Dovie Thomason's visit to, 315–19, *316*; gifts left in, 51, 176; history of, 159–61, 164–65; ignored in official information, 15–16, 153; as "Indian Burial Ground," 164; lack of photographs of, 153, 179n3; location of, current, 152, 185; location of, original, 153, *154*, 179n4; marker for, 32n24, 152, 177–79, 319, 328–30,

Haskell Institute, 30n4, 101, 183n72
Haudanosaunees, 22–23
Hawk Eagle, Thomas Benjamin, 262
Hayes (son of Friday), 150
Hayes, Ira, 134
Hayt, Ezra Ayres, 318
headstones: babies not receiving, 192–93; lack of individuality of, 163, *166*, 167, 349; lack of information on, 185, *186*; original, 160, 167, 182n47
healing: at Carlisle Symposium, 5, 341, 353–54; ceremony and, 227, 240, 347; cultural sharing as, 261, 271–72; on indigenous peoples' terms, 237, 251, 253, 331–32, 335; Lakota practices and, 262, 269; Ndé practices and, 244, 250, 251; Red Road Approach and, 260; truth and, 176, 237, 336, 343
Henderson, William M., 276
Her Pipe, Dora, 188, 189
Hessian Guard House, 284, 289n53, 306
Hessian Powder Magazine, 15
Hiawatha, 116–18, 122n48
hidden transcripts, 206, 229n8
High Eagle, 267
Hill, Robert, 101
history: appropriation of, 171–73; contested, 20, 22, 111–19, 251–52; and emotion, 347–48; interrogating, 19; memorials and, 152–53, 166–67; oral and written, 251–52; production of, 21; shared, 238–39; and silence, 229n6, 346; telling of, to children, 317–19, 332, 353–54; use of, in understanding the present, 307, 310
Hocker Farm, 277, 280, 358
Hodge, William, 101

Hogee, Ernest, *86*, *87*
Hoijer, Harry, 253
Hollow Horn Bear, 91, 189
Honey Sweet, 119n3
Hospital Number 31, 280–81, 360
House Made of Dawn (Momaday), 12
Hudson, Frank, 134
hunger, 188, 324, 325
hunting, 56–57, 58, 61–62, 75n11

identity: loss of, 107, 207–8, 242, 248, 334; racial, 160, 216, 220, 221–22, 223; regaining, 260, 262–63, 272; and shame, 247–48, 250, 259; and trauma, 331
Indian boarding school program, 1, 236; abuse in, 11, 13, 135, 324; backlash to, 45–46; cultural rupture caused by, 2, 6, 176, 234; impact of, 11, 12–13, 18; letters from students in, 30n4, 120n7, 149; shame instilled by, 12, 13
Indian Helper, 53n2, 90, 94, 96, 192–93, 212, 328
The Indian Industrial School (Witmer), 104n2, 119n3
"Indian Problem," 1–2, 327
Indian Student Placement Program (Latter-day Saints), 27–28, 258
Indian Time, 119n2
Indian Wars, 7, 319, 355
indigenous people(s): conflict between, 75n11; diaspora of, 2, 4, 160; educational experiences of, 303; as exotic, 67, 71; hatred of, 69–70; health of, 325, 336, 350; and indigenous identity, 248; "inferiority" of, 45, 115, 116, 119; in international proceedings, 243, 257n31; and loss of control, 249; monolithic

indigenous people(s) (*continued*)
understanding of, by whites, 160;
mortality rate of, 334; in Pennsylvania after Seven Years' War,
71, 79n59; populations of, 319,
336; prehistory of, 54, 357, 361n2;
redress for, 234, 240, 241, 242, 252;
as savage, 67, 114–15, 202–3; and
savage/civilized binary, 202–3;
shame instilled in, 12, 247–48,
250, 259; sites of white atrocities
against, 45, 53n1; as social actors,
252–53; sovereignty of, 301–2; stereotypes of, 112, 114, 116, 117–18,
172–73, 221; stories important to,
21; subjugation of, as "natural," 115;
visual representation of, 25, 83–87,
140; well-being of, 2, 234; white-
authored narratives about, 116, 117
*An Indigenous Peoples' History of the
United States* (Dunbar-Ortiz), 12
International Center for Transitional
Justice, 251
Internet: activism using, 177, 283; Carlisle resources on, 88–90, 103n1,
187, 293–94, 346; networking via,
21, 88, 89, 90, 104n4, 178, 203
Ireland, Merritte W., 164, 165
Iron Hawk, 267–68
Iron Lightning Clan, 268, 269–70
Iroquois Confederacy, 22–23, 56,
57, 58–59, 60–61, 64; burning of
towns of, 339; dependent relations
with, 63, 64; land appropriation by,
62, 65; selling of land by, 65, 67–68

Jack (Lipan Apache boy), 21–22, 177,
201–2, *208, 209*, 249–50; abduction of, 201, 202, 206, 230n13; and
Apache prisoners of war, 211–12;

blessing of, 227; at Carlisle, 207–8;
death of, 202, 203, 212, 226; grave
of, *53*, 168, 212, 225, 230n30; life of,
before Carlisle, 206–7; move of,
to Florida, 210–12; name of, misspelled, 168; names for, 204, 206,
207, 208; and Ranald Mackenzie,
210. *See also* "Lost Ones"
Jacobs, Genevieve, 106, 118, 119n3
Jemison, Peter, 22–23, 338, 341
Jenkins, Sally, 128, 130–31, 135
jingle dress dance, 262
Johnson, Jimmy, 131
Jones, Mary, 102–3, 195
Jones, Willard, 102–3, 175, 195
Jordá, Eduardo, 26

Käsebier, Gertrude, 327
Kaseeta, Helen Rice, 222–23, 232n64
Kaseeta, Richard, 203, 216–23, *218*;
Bellaire Park left to, 222; birth of,
215; blessing of, 227; burial of, in
Memorial Gardens Cemetery, 223;
at Carlisle, 216–21; changing name
of, from Kasetta, 222, 232n64;
house of, 337–40; marriage of, to
Helen Rice, 222–23; as mascot, 220,
221–22, 223; Outings of, 220–21;
with white family, 219–20, 222
Keiffer, Daniel B., 275, 276, 286n2
Kelcusay, Isabel, 150
Kenny, Maurice, 25, 29
Kesetta (Lipan Apache girl), 21–
22, *208, 209*, 212–16, 223, 244–
47; abduction of, 201, 202, 206,
230n13; at Carlisle, 207–8, 212–13,
214, 215–16; ceremonies for, 210,
227, *228*, 250, 353; chiefly rights of,
245, 247; death and burial of, 202,
215, 216, 225–26; estate of, 215–16,

Roosevelt, Kesetta. *See* Kesetta (Lipan Apache girl)
Roosevelt, Richard. *See* Kaseeta, Richard
Roosevelt, Theodore, 129, 359
Rose (daughter of Long Face), 188, 189
Rose, Henry, 193, 196
Rose, Susan D., 21–22, 35, 226, 232n71, 235, 240, 337–40
Rosebud Agency, students from, 1, 71, 90–91, *92*, 96, 168, 188–89
Rosenthal, Joe, 134
Rosine Home, 215, 216
Rosskidwits, Kate, 150

Sainte-Marie, Buffy, 330–31
Sand Creek Massacre, 339, 355
"The School Days of an Indian Girl" (Zitkala-Ša), 19
Schurz, Carl, 7, 8, 211, 357
Scots-Irish settlers, 64–65, 66, 67, 70
Seanilzay, Clement, *86, 87*
Seattle, Chief, 85
segregation, 113–14, 133–34, 157–60, 164–65, 180n9, 281, 288n40
self-determination, 235, 243, 244, 252–53, 257n31, 301–2
Sells, Cato, 221
Senate investigation, 10, 130, 164, 221, 232n62, 360
Senoche, Fred, 182n47
Serracino, Mrs. George, 133
Seven Council Fires, 262, 272n3
Seven Years' War, 67, 357
Sharp, Martha, 219–20, 221, 222
Shawnees, 24, 34n40, 63–64, 65, 70, 357
Shenandoah, Joanne, 284–85
Shenk's Ferry People, 55
Sickles family, 184n73
silence, 20–21, 320; and historical thinking, 229n6; judgment and,

216; need to break, 248, 317–19, 329–30, 353–54; and violence, 205; white, 346–47
Silencing the Past (Trouillot), 19, 20
Simmons, Ellen, 322
Simmons, Gertrude. *See* Zitkala-Ša
Sioux students, 187–90, 262. *See also* Lakota(s)
Si Tanka (Spotted Elk), 270, 271
Sitting Bull, 270
Sitting Bull, John, 267
slavery, 246–47, 339
Slotter, Elizabeth, 215, 216
Smith, Andrea, 240
Smith, Charles, 207, 230n18
Smith, Jack. *See* Jack (Lipan Apache boy)
Smith, Kesetta. *See* Kesetta (Lipan Apache girl)
Smith, Mollie, 207
Smithsonian Institution, 293
Song of Hiawatha (Longfellow), 116–18, 122n48, 326
Sorgio, Celeste, 207
soul wounds, 240
sovereignty, 239, 301–2
Spanish-American War, 101
spirits (ghosts), 29, 155, 173, 268, 285–86, 337–40
sports at Carlisle, 25–26, 101–2, 124–36, 358–59; and Carlisle's reputation, 124, 130–31; "civilizing" function of, 126; criticism of, 130–31; and defeating white opponents, 132; dichotomous nature of, 124–25, 131–34, 135–36; exploitation and, 133; and football team (1912), *129*, 359–60; held to double standard, 130; as public memory for students, 132; and Senate investigation, 130; as temptation, 134–35

CPSIA information can be obtained
at www.ICGtesting.com
Printed in the USA
LVHW022137070922
727802LV00001B/28